Urban Politics
and Public Policy

The City in Crisis

Urban Politics and Public Policy

The City in Crisis

EDITED BY

Stephen M. David AND Paul E. Peterson

PRAEGER PUBLISHERS
New York · Washington · London

PRAEGER PUBLISHERS
111 Fourth Avenue, New York, N.Y. 10003, U.S.A.
5, Cromwell Place, London SW7 2JL, England

Published in the United States of America in 1973
by Praeger Publishers, Inc.

© 1973 by Praeger Publishers, Inc.

Library of Congress Catalog Card Number: 72-75693

Printed in the United States of America

Contents

Acknowledgments

This type of reader owes its greatest debt to the numerous scholars who have begun to probe the relations between urban politics and public policy. Our own interest in such matters was stimulated by the late Wallace Sayre and by Grant McConnell; those familiar with the works of these men will notice the many ways in which their ideas influenced the construction of these essays. We owe a more particular debt to J. David Greenstone, who generously permitted us to use material that he and one of the editors worked out for their study *Race and Authority in Urban Politics*.

The necessary permissions to reprint previously published articles would not have been obtained without the faithful, efficient assistance of Lorraine Dwelle. Finally, we are especially grateful that Janet and Carol are as patient and indulgent—even in the most unlikely places—as they are.

Introduction: Urban Policy and the Study of Power

This collection of essays focuses on the relation between the processes of urban politics and the substance of public policy. In so doing, it seeks to build upon the major studies of urban politics that have, in the last two decades, transformed the study of local government into a heated but fascinating series of debates over the nature of urban political systems. At one time, the study of local government was confined to examination of variations in formal and legal structures. In more recent years, debate has raged over broad questions concerning the less formal but more important power relationships that "really" affect what happens in a community. A variety of approaches have been developed by sociologists and political scientists to provide answers to these questions. Some researchers have identified the individuals holding major formal positions of responsibility, others have tried to determine which persons have the greatest reputation for influence, and still others have tried to locate the people making decisions. Although all these approaches have their value, this reader argues that the distribution of power in cities cannot be known without focusing—at least in part—on the policy consequences of urban politics. A review of the "power structure" debate, as the controversy over community power has come to be known, helps to illuminate the importance of the study of urban public policy.

Floyd Hunter and a number of other sociologists advanced what has become known as the *elitist* interpretation of the structure of power in American cities.[1] These "elitists" have claimed that a small number of individuals, consisting primarily of high-ranking business executives, have enormous influence in local communities. They determine the issues that will receive public attention, and their informal connections with local governments give them an inordinate degree of influence over a broad range of urban policies. It is further argued that this influence is used to protect business interests.

The data supporting this elitist interpretation have been typically obtained by asking reasonably well-informed local community activists for the names of the individuals who seemed to have a great deal of influence in their community. One of Floyd Hunter's questions, for example, ran as follows: "If a project were before the community that required *decision* by a group of leaders —leaders that nearly everyone would accept—which [leaders] . . . would you choose?"[2] Even though the question did not directly ask, "Who's got clout around here?" the answer would seem to give a pretty good estimate of who people *thought* had a good deal of influence. And, when it comes to influence, what people *think* becomes crucial—as anyone can discover if he tries to promote an idea in a setting where he is little known or poorly regarded. Thus, Hunter and other sociologists believed they had quite good evidence for their elitist interpretation when those with the greatest reputation for influence usually turned out to be businessmen.

Their approach to the study of power was seriously criticized, however, by a number of political scientists, who have become known as *pluralists*.[3] These pluralists argued that elitists like Floyd Hunter had only studied people's reputation for power, not the actual exercise of power. Even those with great resources for influencing governmental action often do not have much impact on public policy—simply because they do not care enough about particular issues to mobilize their resources and coordinate their efforts with like-minded leaders. According to pluralists, the study of power, therefore, needs to focus not on reputations but on the actual decisions taken in the course of governing a city. Thus, in their analyses, they have attributed power to an individual only when he successfully initiates or vetoes a proposal.[4]

When pluralists applied this approach to the study of community power, they discovered a far more elusive set of power relationships than the elitists had found. As Robert Dahl argues in his seminal study of New Haven, no single group of individuals dominates decision-making in all areas of public policy.[5] A person who has influence in one area may be totally without influence in any other; and the influence that any group or individual wields fluctuates rapidly over time. Dahl admits that elected officials have considerably more influence over policy than other citizens have, but he stresses that politicians cannot hold office without the support of a majority of the voters. In fact, Dahl suggests that it hardly makes sense to talk about a power "structure," for that word implies something permanent, enduring, persisting over some substantial period of time. Instead, pluralists speak of political "processes," political activities that change so rapidly that it is hard to find any "structure" to them. Businessmen have influence in local politics, particularly on those matters of concern to them. But so do labor unions, ethnic groups, homeowners, taxpayers, PTA members, and almost every other group of individuals who care deeply enough about some aspect of public affairs to do something about it.

The pluralist argument is a powerful rebuttal to the elitist position. Although the reputational method probably does identify people of considerable political influence, any interpretation of urban politics that sees policy as merely the product of the decisions of a small elite overlooks the complexity of urban politics. The pluralists are also certainly correct in stressing the variation in power relations from issue to issue, the host of groups, organizations, and individual participants involved in the process, the conflicts *within* the business community, and the critical role that elections can play in shaping power relationships. Above all, the pluralists are able to show that power is fragmented into separate, functionally specific policy areas, such as housing, education, and transportation, each of which usually activates a distinct set of political groups.

If the pluralists rightly see complexity and multiplicity of forces in urban politics, serious questions about power relations in American cities still remain. Although it is unlikely that any one small group controls all policy decisions, the over-all pattern of power relationships can still be biased in favor of the rich, the well organized, and a host of specialized business and commercial interests. The elected politician may make many of the policy decisions; but as he makes these decisions, he may more carefully consider the interests of those who can finance his campaign, have good access to the news media, and can mount effective propaganda campaigns, than the interests of a poorly informed voter majority. The influence of specific individuals may vary from issue to issue, but in almost every specific functional policy arena, biases may be found that advantage the better-off at the expense of the less well-off or some special interests at the expense of consumers or the public at large. A variety of groups may be involved in the policy-making process, but the policies that are the result of these decisions may not benefit all groups in any roughly equal manner.

One of the major problems with the pluralists' analyses is that, in studying who was making the decisions, they paid no attention to *what* decisions were being made. Dahl's study of New Haven, for example, discusses the politics of urban renewal without ever focusing on the groups that benefited and the groups that lost as a result of urban-renewal policy. This ignores one of the very best ways of obtaining information about power relations in a city, for it is not unreasonable to conclude that groups that gain a good deal from governmental policies probably had something to say about their enactment. Looking at public policy in order to reach conclusions about political power is looking at who controls the field at the end of the battle. Although it cannot tell you all the factors that affected the outcome of the struggle, it gives you a fairly good idea of who in the end mustered the greatest force behind their position. On the other hand, if one looks at only the ongoing struggle without keeping in mind the eventual outcome, one may find such a wide variety of competing forces and ephemeral, changing power relationships that one concludes that power was widely shared—even when in the end one side was decisively defeated.

The study of urban public policy can thus make an important contribution to our understanding of power relations in American cities. By looking at how specific urban policies are made and the consequences these policies have for the lives of different groups living in a metropolitan area, we can see whether government responds to the needs and aspirations of unorganized and poorer groups in our society, or whether it listens primarily to the demands of the affluent and/or narrowly focused special interests. In the selections that follow, the reader will not find any simple or uniform answer to this question. Indeed, he will have to draw his own conclusions from the array of viewpoints and evidence that is presented. But, in our introductory essays, we shall not disguise our own conclusion that policy analysis reveals a far less open political process, a policy-making structure far more in the service of specialized and already advantaged interests, than is desirable in a society committed to democratic traditions and ideals. Indeed, the biases in our urban political structures are so great that American cities, even in a period of great national wealth and prosperity, are undergoing severe crises. Government seems incapable of responding to widely recognized problems, and citizens feel they are unable to influence its direction. These dual but interrelated problems of urban governance and citizen participation lie at the political heart of the urban crisis. They cannot be understood without an examination of the close relations between political power and public policy.

In order to develop this argument, we have divided this reader into three parts. Part I sets forth the two major political problems —urban governance and citizen participation—facing our cities. The crisis of urban governance is twofold, for metropolitan areas are fragmented along both geographical and functional lines, creating politically autonomous spheres of influence for special elites both in specific community areas and policy-specific arenas of power. At the same time, opportunities for participation in the urban political process are severely circumscribed. Not all readings in Part I agree with this assessment of the urban situation; rather, we have tried to present both sides of the argument on each of these topics so that the reader can draw his own conclusions.

Part II examines the crises of governance and participation in the context of four specific policy areas—housing, transportation, education, and police. In a sense, this part provides data that can be used to evaluate the opposing contentions developed in the first section of the reader. The evidence is not always unequivocal, and once again the reader may wish to draw his own interpretation on the basis of the material presented. But the editors have concluded that the preponderance of information concerning each of these four policy areas suggests that power is concentrated in the hands of professionals and specialized, narrowly focused group interests within each functional power arena. To be sure, the groups exercising power vary from area to area. In that sense, there is no single power elite that dominates American politics. On the other hand, if commercial and bureaucratic interests dominate policy-making in each policy area, producing policies that work to the disadvantage of consumers, minorities, and the poor, this hardly adds up to a pluralistic structure of power where the whole range of interests in the community are fairly represented.

From this perspective, the concluding part of the study examines the possibilities for change in power relationships and public policy. It considers the viability of a broad alliance of middle-class reformers, organized labor, and minority groups. In the end, however, we are unable to reach an optimistic conclusion about the prospect for major political change in urban America.

NOTES

1. Floyd Hunter, *Community Power Structure* (Garden City, New York: Doubleday, 1963). For other essays, see Willis D. Hawley and Frederick M. Wirt (eds.), *The Search for Community Power* (Englewood Cliffs, New Jersey: Prentice Hall, 1968).
2. Hunter, *op. cit.*, p. 63.

3. Robert Dahl, *Who Governs?* (New Haven: Yale University Press, 1961); Aaron Wildavsky, *Leadership in a Small Town* (Totawa, New Jersey: Bedminster Press, 1964); Edward Banfield, *Political Influence* (New York: Free Press, 1961); and Nelson Polsby, *Community Power and Political Theory* (New Haven: Yale University Press, 1963).
4. Dahl, *op. cit.*, pp. 332–33.
5. *Ibid., passim.* Dahl's generalizations about power in America more generally, which are largely based on his New Haven study, are presented in the selection by Dahl reprinted in this reader.

I
Governments Without Purposes;
Citizens Without Power

The Urban Crisis and Its Historical Roots

THE URBAN CRISIS

American cities face two equally fundamental, though apparently contradictory, political problems. One has to do with governance; the other, with citizen representation. According to some perspectives, the first problem is paramount. Governments in urban areas are so fragmented, power is so dispersed, authority is so decentralized among a host of competing agencies and jurisdictions that political institutions lack the capability to solve the common problems of the community.[1] A second perspective sees citizen representation as the critical issue. Ordinary citizens, particularly the less financially able and the more dependent upon governmental services, are unable to influence public policy. Power is concentrated in the hands of political, bureaucratic, and business elites to such an extent that it makes a mockery of the democratic formalities that legitimize local government.[2]

At first glance, urban governance and citizen representation may appear to be mutually exclusive objectives. If power is centralized so that decisions can be made and executed with efficiency and dispatch, most people would seem to have little opportunity to influence the outcome. On the other hand, if power is widely dispersed so that many individuals and groups can influence decisions, government's capacity to resolve common problems would seem to be sharply limited. Accordingly, one goal could be achieved only at considerable cost to the other. In the case of American urban politics, however, the problem is not that these are two horns of a political dilemma. The problem in American cities is *not* that power is so centralized in the hands of a small, controlling elite that citizens cannot participate in policy formation. Nor is the failure to resolve the mutual problems of metropolitan areas due to the fact that opportunities to participate in decision-making are so widespread.

What is distinctive about the political crisis of American cities is that neither effective government nor citizen participation is being achieved. Instead, the structure of government is so fragmented that those in authority seem incapable of effectively governing the metropolitan community. And, at the same time, many citizens seem—and certainly feel—powerless to influence the positions that governments take.

GOVERNMENTAL FRAGMENTATION

First, let us consider the question of governance. Urban areas are faced with both geographical and functional fragmentation, making it almost impossible for systematic, coordinated policies to be developed for the metropolitan areas. Indeed, the very word "metropolitan" was coined because older words like cities, communities, and towns made no sense in this totally new, highly fragmented political order. In the past, the political jurisdictions of cities expanded as they grew in size. But in twentieth-century America, and particularly during the postwar period, urban areas growing at an exponential rate were not annexed to the central city responsible for their development in the first place. Ironically, as urban areas have grown rapidly, the large central cities around which this growth has been occurring have been actually losing population. Metropolitan areas have become divided into cities and suburbs, and only the most haphazard arrangements link them together for the resolution of common metropolitan problems. As a result, no one has assumed responsibility for directing the development of the metropolitan community as a whole. Instead, bankers are concerned with banking, suburban politicians are concerned with their own small community, big-city politicians seek to keep control of the central city, and bureaucrats are worried about the future of their agencies. Only a few planners, some altruistic citizen groups like the League of Women Voters, and perhaps a newspaper editor or two are concerned about the larger community. In short, although decisions are made in metropolitan areas, Norton Long can convincingly argue (in the article reprinted below) that no one makes decisions for metropolitan areas.[3]

Not everyone sees the fragmentation of the metropolitan area as a problem, of course, and we have included in this reader Banfield and Grodzins's analysis of some of the advantages of diverse governmental jurisdictions within one highly interdependent socio-economic community. As they point out, a large number of distinctive suburbs do give people opportunities to live in communities that suit their particular life style. Jews, Catholics, and Episcopalians each tend to group together, older people look for a low-tax suburb, young families want good schools, some people prefer zoning laws that require large lots and huge lawns, and others prefer to live close to the metropolitan center. Clearly, one should not equate the metropolitan problem with a variety of distinctive communities within a metropolitan area.

Banfield and Grodzins overstate their case, however. Fragmentation does create problems for public policies that do require coordinated planning throughout the metropolitan area. Some general planning is necessary to build a transportation system that connects workers with their jobs, links homes and recreation areas, and does not quickly clog with even moderate increases in usage. But, as Doig points out in his extensive analysis of the New York transportation system, governmental fragmentation has inhibited such planning. Moreover, geographical fragmentation rigidifies inequalities in urban areas. An educational system that has lavish facilities in one community and inadequate schools in another close by does provide citizens with a choice. But since the cost of land in the two communities is likely to vary accordingly, this choice may be open only to the well-to-do. Housing opportunities for low income groups can also become severely restricted when no agency has the metropolitan-wide authority necessary to build the facilities. Each local community is likely to oppose low income housing within its jurisdiction, fearing that such housing would generate a variety of social problems for the community. As a result, either the housing is concentrated in central cities that are already suffering a decline in their tax bases and job opportunities, or it is not built at all. In sum, the multiplicity of governmental jurisdictions in metropolitan areas makes coordinated, equitable public policies almost impossible to obtain.

Functional fragmentation within the central city itself is no less an impediment to effective government. As Lowi points out in his analysis of "Machine Politics—Old and New," public bureaucracies have developed a base of power in big-city politics that almost forecloses any close centralized supervision. Bureaucracies have a number of techniques by which they sustain their autonomy. First of all, the professionals directing the bureaucracy have an advantage in terms of experience, expertise, and control over information. They quietly carry out their business—in the manner that best suits them—while public attention is diverted elsewhere. Adaptations may be necessary when a storm of public concern is immediately threatening, but, with patience, such turbulences can be weathered by hardy bureaucrats. Secondly, bureaucracies develop a coterie of producer and employee organizations to which they turn for advice and information, backing for their plans of expansion, and general political support. To shield the bureaucrats themselves from public controversies, these interest groups often carry on the battle for them. As Sayre and Kaufman note, policemen's associations thus can become informal spokesmen for police departments, especially when the latter prefer to remain nominally neutral. In the concluding selection of this reader, Lipsky points out that long-standing groups in the housing policy arena play a key policy-formation role when protest groups focus attention on housing problems. As a result, only unusually strong mayors can develop the resources to do much more than "disturb," to say nothing of directly control, the workings of these islands of functional power.[4]

It is, of course, too simplistic to blame everything on bureaucracies. As James Wilson points out, people often criticize bureaucracies for decisions that are mandated by the law. In other cases, the bureaucrat, caught in the middle, is forced to choose between competing demands from groups with directly opposite preferences. If he compromises the issue, both sides condemn his equivocation. In still other cases, bureaucracies lack the resources to provide the services that they are expected to provide.

Although bureaucracies should not be blamed for every problem, the autonomy of urban bureaucracies has had three significant policy consequences. First, bureaucracies have often been able to forestall, undermine, and sabotage reform proposals—whenever they disturb the organizational routines of the bureaucracy. For example, police have successfully resisted civilian review boards, fearing they would lessen the discretion of policemen. Highway departments have resisted systematic consideration of aesthetic or environmental values that are too far removed from their overriding concern with traffic flow to be easily included within the departments' routine mechanisms for defining problems and developing solutions. Secondly, the needs and preferences of the providers of government services typically take precedence over the needs of the consumers of these agencies. For example, Francis Piven has shown that expenditures on city services have dramatically increased in recent years, substantially fattening bureaucratic budgets and creating an urban fiscal crisis.[5] The primary beneficiaries of these substantial increases seem to have been employees of city agencies, who have enjoyed significant salary increments. Thirdly, administrators, if left to their own devices, attend to the needs of their most organized clients. This, in fact, is what has given rise to the great influence that *producer groups* have achieved over many public policies.

Producer groups represent the interests of industries or professionals engaged in the production and distribution of goods and services. In effect, they represent people in their occupational roles. Thus, specific producer groups represent such interests as those of truckers, policemen, teachers, bankers, and other comparable occupational groups. Because highway policies have a major consequence for truckers, educational policies a major impact on teachers, and so forth, producer groups pay a great deal of attention to the specific policy area in which they have a major stake. They usually support stable organizations with sophisticated leaders, who develop close associations with elected or appointed officials responsible for the policies affecting them. Oftentimes, they are consulted before officials are selected to serve in the agencies that most directly affect the group's livelihood. In this way, close, enduring relationships are built between certain producer groups and specific governmental agencies. The agency watches out for the group interest, and the producer group supports agency plans for institutional survival and expansion.

The concern that producer groups have for policies affecting them is quite understandable. The problem arises when their interests compete with consumer interests, which are not represented by any comparably sophisticated organizations. Consumer organizations find it far more difficult to build a stable, enduring relationship with public bureaucracies, because they tend to represent diffuse interests—those widely shared "public" interests that everyone has to some extent but that no one in particular has to any considerable extent. An illustration may help to clarify the point. The billboard industry has a great stake in obtaining permission to place signs along the highway; each traveler has a small but widely diffused stake in being able to see the countryside instead of a continuous parade of huge signs. Yet, countryside lovers have no organization comparable to that of the billboard industry, which has struggled to keep roads free of any government ban on signs. The fragmentation of policy-making into functional arenas, where organized interests and bureaucratic elites join to make policy, makes the representation of diffuse, consumer interests far more difficult. When the consumers are the poor, their particular lack of political resources accentuates the problem. For example, as we shall see in our discussion of housing policy, housing agencies consider more carefully the problems of the construction industry and financial institutions than the needs of low-income potential homeowners.

CITIZEN PARTICIPATION

While the fragmentation of the urban political structure has limited the "governing" capacities of urban authorities, this has in no way been offset by an increase in citizen participation. If the price paid in terms of coordination, efficiency, and equity throughout the metropolitan area were redeemed by a concomitant increment in the level of citizen participation in public affairs, the trade-off in goals might possibly be acceptable. But, for all the fragmentation of urban areas, citizens still seem to have limited chances to shape governmental action.

One should, of course, avoid unrealistic expectations as to the level of citizen participation that is in any way feasible. Participation clearly cannot consist of direct involvement by every adult in each of the various decisions made in the metropolitan area. In a modern, industrial, highly specialized society, people neither have the time, nor the financial resources, nor the inclination to participate in most policy decisions. On the other hand, people would like government to be responsive to their problems and complaints when they do become interested and involved. And they do expect that their interests will be represented by their officeholders even when citizens themselves do not become directly involved.

In his analysis of political leadership reprinted in this volume, Dahl makes the argument that governments do in fact respond to the pressure activities of groups of ordinary citizens, particularly when these groups feel strongly about a matter. He argues further that politicians cannot in general depart too significantly from what most people expect of their government; to do so would lead to imminent political defeat. From this perspective, the "problem" of participation, if indeed it is a problem, involves the apathy of citizens concerning the processes of government rather than any unresponsiveness on the part of the political order.

Although Dahl's argument carries considerable weight, too exclusive a dependence on this interpretation, we believe, overlooks the way in which the structural arrangements of our urban governments positively discourage citizens from participation. The fragmentation of governmental authority into sanitation boards, pollution-control boards, metropolitan water districts, school districts, counties, villages, housing authorities, and so forth, leaves the citizen baffled as to which jurisdiction he is living in, to say nothing of the way in which he can go about influencing its operations. Moreover, so many officials are elected for such obscure offices that the voters, unaware of their activities, can hardly instill in these officeholders any fear that their policies could lead to political defeat. And those few elected officials with some public visibility, such as the mayor of the central city, may not have enough control over most public agencies to be able to substantially alter their policies. Given the low probability of success, why should the citizen even try to influence government activity?

The problem runs even deeper. Most citizens simply do not receive quickly and conveniently the information that is necessary to induce them to take action on a policy question. Agencies develop their longer-range plans quietly, holding off public meetings until the plans are on the verge of being implemented. Press, radio, and television, by focusing on immediate, newsworthy topics, too often fail to arouse the public until it is too late to alter a policy. In their constant search for *new* news, they constantly move to fresh issues before the old ones are resolved, leaving the latter in the hands, once again, of the full-time paid professionals specializing in the policy area.

Given the high costs of acquiring the information needed to influence policy and the low probability of having any impact if one does participate, what is surprising is not citizen apathy but the frequency with which citizen groups do in fact try to shape local policy. If only sporadically, groups of consumers, community organizations, and representatives of the poor sometimes engage in almost "heroic" efforts to influence policy. Michael Lipsky's study of protest in the concluding article to this volume analyzes one such attempt. Yet, the typical pattern is for public policy-making to be dominated by a few entrenched, specialized, usually producer interests.

The limited nature of citizen representation and the fragmentation of urban governments are not opposed but complementary problems. Each feeds upon and perpetuates the other. Power is fragmented in part because of the high costs of influencing decisions. Because most citizens are not willing to pay these costs, decisions are taken by the professionals and producers who have great stakes in the matter. More-diffuse, less-organized interests are squeezed out of the decision-making process. If fragmentation occurs because few people participate, fragmentation in turn retards participation. Once established relationships have developed among powerful interests in particular policy areas, they make it difficult for new groups to penetrate the policy-making process. Producer-bureaucratic control of policy further increases the cost of participation to outsiders, thereby further reducing the incentives to participate in urban politics. As a result, adequate representation of diffuse, unorganized interests, and particularly the interests of minority groups and the poor, whose political resources are even more limited, is not often achieved within the framework of a highly fragmented, decentralized urban political order.

A HISTORICAL PERSPECTIVE ON THE URBAN CRISIS

The roots of these interrelated urban problems are deeply embedded in American history and culture, which created two distinctive political forces and sets of institutions in American cities: the political machine and the reform movement. Both developed because America has always been a liberal society that knew neither a feudal aristocracy nor a class-conscious socialist movement.[6] Without an aristocratic legacy, the American rich had little sense of civic responsibility. Whereas, in Britain, distinguished public service was the mark of a gentleman, well-to-do Americans, after the first days of the Republic, avoided dirtying their hands in politics. As an astute English observer of nineteenth-century American politics commented, "[America has] no class with a hereditary prescription to public office, no great families whose names are known to the people, and who, bound together by class sympathy and ties of relationship, help one another by keeping offices in the hands of their own numbers."[7] At the same time, the working masses in America were quite confident of their own ability to govern and did not "defer" to their "betters" in the same way that European workers at one time did. Thus, uneducated, rough-tongued, tobacco-spitting politicians could grab political office. Or, as Max Weber, another European analyst of this period in American politics, reported, Americans claimed to "prefer having people in office whom we can spit upon, rather than a caste of officials who spit upon us as is the case with you [Europeans]."[8]

If American workers did not defer to their wealthier neighbors, neither did they hate them with the passion that inspired a great socialist movement in Europe. Indeed, the capitalist values which encouraged individual initiatives were accepted as legitimate by the workers themselves. Realistically or not, the great majority of nineteenth-century white Americans hoped that they or their children would achieve material success either in urban trade or in farming on the frontier. Any version of class politics which sought collective rather than individual betterment accordingly had limited and sporadic allure at best. However, Americans responded quickly to the prospect of engaging in politics in order to secure direct, personal economic gain. Because Americans seemed to believe in salvation through material success, public life became simply another arena where financial rewards could be secured, and the public treasury offered still another opportunity for the individual to better himself.

In this context, machine politics grew and flourished. If the rich had little sense of civic responsibility, and the poor had little common identity as members of one class, politics could be organized by the economically ambitious, who used public goods to their private advantage. And the rapidly expanding number of urban immigrants who spoke strange tongues, knew little about American political institutions, and were usually unfamiliar with democratic procedures provided the votes that the machine politicians could so efficiently organize.

This seamy side of machine politics should not hide a signal contribution that political organizations made to the functioning of the urban community: They provided some semblance of order in otherwise chaotic urban conditions. As Mandelbaum points out in his account of *Boss Tweed's New York*, the communication and transportation problems in the nineteenth century were enormous.[9] The post office was incredibly inefficient; some twenty-five newspapers each had their own parochial audience; many residents were entirely illiterate; and streets were clogged with traffic, jammed with market stalls, and filled with dangerous potholes. Unable to provide for all the city's children, the schools ignored compulsory attendance laws despite absenteeism which regularly ran above 50 per cent. Welfare services were left to small private agencies, and private entrepreneurs provided such essential services as shipping docks, mass transit, and even fire control. One of the few major but seemingly simple public services the government did undertake, garbage collection, was notoriously bad. But, as Mandelbaum persuasively argues, "the failure to clear the streets properly could not entirely be laid at the door of the politicians." Rather, "precisely because street cleaning under the conditions of that time was doomed to failure . . . the cleaners . . . took their prestige from an outside organization, the political party."[10]

By privatizing politics, by appealing to the narrower interests of ethnic neighborhoods or even the individual and his family, the machine politicians, in effect, made up some of the deficit of political support for the government which administrative laxity created. They distributed administrative positions according to partisan criteria and bought support directly from voters through corruption, graft, and patronage, rather than acquiring it through popular public policies. In pursuit of this goal, they shaped urban institutions in a congenial fashion. The civil-service merit system was opposed, except to "blanket in" party supporters when the leadership feared an imminent defeat. Aldermen were selected from small wards so that men who knew their neighborhoods could assign patronage most advantageously. Many public officials were elected on partisan ballots, increasing direct party control over a large number of governmental positions. And the machine appealed to neighborhood and ethnic loyalties through careful balancing of the lengthy electoral ticket.

As Greenstone and Peterson argue in *Race and Authority in Urban Politics: A Study of Community Participation in the War on Poverty*, this appeal to particularistic interests did help secure public order by diffusing and privatizing conflict.[11] Business and labor, blacks and whites, Italians and Germans, Catholics and Jews were all successfully appealed to in ways that minimized the potential conflicts among them. Indeed, political conflict was so well controlled that in many American cities a one-party system emerged. Once in office, the dominant party used available patronage and contracts to solidify its base of power. In certain "inner city" wards, whose low-income residents were especially receptive to the precinct captain's favors, the opposition became co-opted. In exchange for cooperation on vital matters, including only token opposition in general elections, the ruling party distributed some of its patronage to the minority party, whose leaders used these resources to insure control over their own primaries.[12] Thus, as James Bryce noted seventy years ago at the height of the machine's power: "In many cities the party majority inclines so decidedly one way or the other (e.g., New York City is steadily Democratic, Philadelphia, Republican) that nomination is in the case of the dominant party equivalent to election."[13]

If the machine relied on individual corruptibility to organize urban politics, the reformers, outraged at the inefficiencies and manipulative activities of these politicians, developed a contrasting theory that was based on a belief in the potential honesty and decency of the urban American. The reformers believed both in widespread citizen participation in politics and in efficient, honest, even scientific management of public affairs by technically trained experts. They could link these two goals, because they believed, with John Stuart Mill, that the workers' participation in politics would enhance the quality of the workers' own lives and make them better citizens. In order to secure such participation, however, the reformers had to rid the community of the vested interests, the corrupt politicians, and the vote buying and vote stealing of the political machine. With the elimination of these pernicious influences and the spread of universal education, it was expected that citizens would vote freely and rationally in choosing their leaders.

The reformers consequently promoted numerous devices to increase what they regarded as free, open, and public-spirited voting. They suggested nonpartisan elections, where the partisan affiliations of candidates would be deleted from the ballot, weakening the influence of the corrupt parties. They sought at-large rather than ward elections to the city council, so that candidates would have to campaign in terms of what was best for the city as a whole rather than for what was best for any particular ward. They advocated the initiative, which allowed voters to place on the ballot proposed laws that could not be passed in the state legislature; the referendum, which allowed the voters to repeal legislative action; and the recall, which allowed voters to petition for a special election to remove from office men who blatantly defied the public will. In all these proposals, reformers expressed their faith in free, unfettered, direct voter participation in political life.

But, if rational voters were expected to choose wise leaders, these leaders were expected to rely on the advice of experts in the science of government to implement their policies. Reformers advocated the city-manager form of government, in which an expert was hired to coordinate and administer local services. Police superintendents, highway engineers, urban planners, housing experts, and school superintendents were all to be selected for the specialized training and technical skill they could bring to their administrative tasks. With such professional competence in key positions, the efficiency of public services would rise, rewarding the citizens for their wise choice of leaders. With a civil-service system, there would no longer be a corrupt patronage system to tempt the voters. The perfectibility of government and citizens would replace the corruptibility of both under the urban machine. In this way, majority rule and good government could become not mutually exclusive but highly interdependent goals.

Future developments at best gave such reform optimists only sporadic encouragement, however. American voters did not always recognize the talents of the reformers who claimed to be sacrificing their private lives to serve the city. In part, this was due to the lack of deference working men and women had for their betters. As Ostrogorski observed, "The men of higher rank who come down as it were from the moon to exhort the people to vote for honest candidates opposed to the Machine, are strangers to them, and the people have no confidence in them because they belong to another social sphere."[14] Unless there was an especially earth-shaking scandal, the reformers had difficulty in sustaining political support. In the words of that Tammany Hall machine politician, George Washington Plunkitt, reformers tended to be "mornin' glories." They "looked lovely in the mornin' and withered up in a short time, while the regular machines went on flourishin' forever, like fine old oaks."[15] Consequently, in order to win elections, reformers at times had to stoop to such machine-style devices as slating ethnic candidates. In 1933, for example, New York reformers reluctantly nominated Fiorello La Guardia, the one reformer likely to capture the Italian vote.[16]

Yet, the reformers used their mornings of triumph, including La Guardia's administration, to eliminate much of the patronage and graft upon which the machine had depended. Meanwhile, certain secular trends (increasing income, more formal education, the advent of radio and television) made many citizens unwilling to sell their votes at a price the machine could afford to pay, or to rely for political information entirely on the friendly precinct captain. And the increased bureaucratization of welfare programs, especially since the 1930's, reduced the importance of the machine politicians' informal assistance to their neighbors.

As the machine weakened, the reform movement could no longer avoid explicit recognition of the tension between its dual commitment to both expertise and democratic participation. On one side, citizens did not always fulfill the reformers' hopes concerning rational voting behavior. Denied partisan cues, voters chose candidates on racial, religious, and ethnic criteria rather than for reasons having to do with their fitness for office. In the face of such behavior, some reform groups became increasingly suspicious of the voting public and sought less democratic mechanisms for protecting the city from corruption. For example, in order to satisfy reform demands in such cities as New York, Philadelphia, and Chicago, blue-ribbon panels of experts and prestigious citizens were given the power to prepare lists of school board nominees from which the mayors were expected to make their selection.

In the end, the reformers did little to increase participation in urban politics. In fact, many of their schemes had exactly the opposite effect. Fewer citizens, and particularly fewer working-class citizens, voted in nonpartisan elections than in partisan ones.[17] The initiative and the referendum were used by special interests who could at times pass more self-serving legislation by securing the backing of small groups of supporters among an apathetic public than they could through the state legislature. At-large elections created a much greater distance between the citizen and his representative than that provided by the old ward elections favored by the machine. The destruction of the machine did not necessarily pave the way for participatory democracy.

The fundamental problem was rooted in the reformers' own political theory. They believed that the destruction of the corrupt politicians would eliminate the hidden power of special interests. They thought the voter, freed from the enticements of patronage and special favors, would actively pursue goals that were in the public interest. But voters, even after the decline of the machine, have proven to be more concerned about their ethnic, class, racial, or other group interests than with some vague formulation of the public interest. Moreover, even if citizens were more concerned with the welfare of the community as a whole, it is not clear whether their individual efforts would have much effect. Because political participation is a costly activity, citizens need simplifying mechanisms that help them to influence policies without spending days and weeks in political action. If, instead of trying to reform the electoral process, the reformers had developed strong political organizations that would have assisted the voters in this way, their impact on citizen participation might have been much greater.

The reformers also came to discover that the increasing influence of experts in city government did not necessarily produce rationalized policies in the public interest. For one thing, administrative expertise and a theory of scientific management proved of little use in choosing among general policy alternatives. Rather than faithfully executing policy, officials in administrative bureaus and agencies developed specific organizational interests of their own, which they vigorously defended in bargaining with other administrators. Ironically, the reformers' own innovations encouraged such developments. In order to preclude the influence of machine politics, civil-service reforms often protected the job of every member of a bureau except its chief. But this arrangement made it virtually impossible to reshuffle key personnel in order to change policies. In some cases, the mayor did not even choose the heads of important bureaus. In other cases, reform rules forced him to make his selection from among officials who had already served for many years in the agency they were supposed to change. And, no matter how the administrator was chosen, the mayor risked accusations of political interference if he then tried to control his subordinates' activities. Urban bureaucracies had become free to operate in their spheres with little regard for either outside pressures or the conflicting goals of other agencies with overlapping jurisdictions.

The twin legacies of reform efforts are the crises of participation and fragmentation. The problem is, to be sure, deeply embedded in the structure of American government and politics, and it would be unfair and inaccurate to attribute all of our present discontent to the mistakes of reformers. For one thing, they have not had enough power to achieve all their goals. Reform efforts to achieve metropolitan government, for example, have had little success, because many other interests, created and protected by existing governmental institutions (not the least of which being suburban and central city officeholders), have been potent defenders of the *status quo*. Nonetheless, after a half-century of reform attempts to democratize and rationalize our cities' governing structures, these goals seem as far from reality as they ever have been. Political and social equality in urban America is still a distant goal. If the urban crisis is to be resolved, more is needed than simply the good will that many reformers undoubtedly had. Needed as well is an understanding of the social and political forces whose influence affects the actual operations of our political institutions and, eventually, the shape of urban public policy. The readings included below hopefully provide at least a beginning in this direction.

Notes

1. For this argument, see Wallace Sayre and Herbert Kaufman, *Governing New York City* (New York: W. W. Norton, 1965); David Riesman, *The Lonely Crowd* (Garden City, New York: Doubleday, 1953).
2. This view is expressed by Floyd Hunter, *Community Power Structure* (Garden City, New York: Doubleday, 1963).
3. All references in the text to works that are not footnoted refer to articles reprinted in this reader.
4. The point is well documented in Sayre and Kaufman, *op. cit.*, Chs. 8 and 9.
5. Frances Fox Piven, "The Urban Crisis: Who Got What, and Why," in Robert Paul Wolff (ed.), *1948 Revisited* (New York: Random House, forthcoming.)
6. Louis Hartz, *The Liberal Tradition in America* (New York: Harcourt, Brace and World, 1955).
7. James Bryce, *The American Commonwealth* II (New York: MacMillan, 1895), p. 54.
8. H. H. Gerth and C. Wright Mills (eds.), *From Max Weber: Essays in Sociology* (New York: Oxford University Press, 1946), p. 110.
9. Seymour J. Mandelbaum, *Boss Tweed's New York* (New York: John Wiley and Sons, 1965).
10. *Ibid.*, p. 168.
11. Some passages in this section closely follow material in J. David Greenstone and Paul E. Peterson, *Race and Authority in Urban Politics: A Study of the War on Poverty* (New York: Russell Sage Foundation, 1973). We thank David Greenstone for granting us permission to draw upon this material.
12. Harold Gosnell, *Machine Politics: Chicago Model* (Chicago: University of Chicago Press, 1968), p. 44; Leo Snowiss, "The Metropolitan Congressman," (unpublished Ph.D. dissertation, Department of Political Science, University of Chicago, 1965), p. 92.
13. Bryce, *op. cit.*, p. 97.
14. M. Ostrogorski, *Democracy and the Organization of Political Parties:*

The United States (Garden City, New York: Doubleday, 1964), p. 221.
15. William Riordan, *Plunkitt of Tammany Hall* (New York: E. P. Dutton, 1963), p. 17.
16. Arthur Mann, *La Guardia Comes to Power, 1933* (Philadelphia: J. B. Lippincott Co., 1965), Ch. 3.
17. Oliver P. Williams and Charles Adrian, "The Insulation of Local Politics under the Non-Partisan Ballet," *American Political Science Review* LIII (December, 1959), 1058–61; and Robert Salisbury and Gordon Black, "Class and Party in Partisan and Nonpartisan Elections: The Case of Des Moines," *American Political Science Review* LVIII (September, 1963), 589–90.

Bibliography

Agger, Robert, et al. *The Ruler and the Ruled.* New York: John Wiley and Sons, 1964.
Banfield, Edward. *Political Influence.* New York: Free Press, 1961.
———. *The Unheavenly City.* Boston: Little, Brown, 1968.
Banfield, Edward, and Wilson, James. *City Politics.* Cambridge, Mass.: Harvard University Press, 1963.
Bellush, Jewel, and David, Stephen, eds. *Race and Politics in New York City.* New York: Praeger, 1971.
Dahl, Robert. *Who Governs?* New Haven: Yale University Press, 1961.
Greenstone, J. Davis, and Peterson, Paul E. *Race and Authority in Urban Politics: A Study of the War on Poverty.* New York: Russell Sage Foundation, 1973.
Hunter, Floyd. *Community Power Structure.* Garden City, New York: Doubleday, 1963.
Lowi, Theodore. *At the Pleasure of the Mayor.* New York: Free Press, 1964.
Marris, Peter, and Rein, Martin. *Dilemmas of Social Reform.* New York: Atherton, 1967.
Sayre, Wallace, and Kaufman, Herbert. *Governing New York City.* New York: W. W. Norton, 1965.
Wood, Robert. *Suburbia.* Boston: Houghton Mifflin, 1968.

Can Cities Be Governed?

GOSNELL'S CHICAGO REVISITED
VIA LINDSAY'S NEW YORK

THEODORE J. LOWI

We can begin to introduce perspective by immediately setting aside Gosnell's opening claim . . . to the representativeness of the Chicago experience. It is the very uniqueness of Chicago's experience with the machine that gives the study value. New York is the representative big city, not Chicago. In 1967, political power in Chicago has an extremely strong machine base; political power in New York has an entirely new and different base. As New York was being revolutionized by the New Deal and its successors, Chicago politics was being reaffirmed. When New York was losing its last machine and entering into the new era of permanent Reform, Chicago's machine politics was just beginning to consolidate. New York became a loose, multiparty system with wide-open processes of nomination, election, and participation; Chicago became a tight, one-party system. New York sought to strengthen a weak mayor already operating under a strong-mayor government; Chicago has had the opposite problem of an already strong mayor in a weak-mayor government.

To evaluate the machine we must ask whether, by surviving, machine politics, Chicago model, in any way distorted Chicago's

From Theodore J. Lowi, "Gosnell's Chicago Revisited Via Lindsay's New York: Foreword to the Second Edition," in Harold F. Gosnell, *Machine Politics: Chicago Model*, pp. 7–16. Reprinted by permission of the author and The University of Chicago Press. Introduction © 1968 by The University of Chicago Press.

growth and development. How much change would there have been in Chicago's history if the nationalization of politics had made possible in Chicago, as it did in virtually every other big American city, ways of "licking the ward boss" and altering precinct organization, means of loosening the hold of the county organization on city hall, power for freeing the personnel and policies of the professional agencies of government? We cannot answer these questions for Chicago because the basis of machine strength still exists, and the conditions for its continuity, as Gosnell so accurately captures them, may continue through the remainder of the century. We might be able to answer them, however, at least better than before, by looking at Gosnell's Chicago through the contemporary experience of New York.

New York city government, like government in almost all large American cities except Chicago, is a product of Reform. It is difficult to understand these cities without understanding the two strains of ideology that guided local Reform movements throughout the past three-quarters of a century. *Populism* and *efficiency*, once the foundations of most local insurgency, are now, except in rare holdout cases like Chicago, triumphant. These two tenets are now the orthodoxy in local practice.

Populism was originally a statement of the evils of every form of bigness and scale in the city, including big business, big churches, and big labor as well as big political organizations. Decentralization was an ultimate goal. In modern form it has tended to come down to the charge to eliminate political parties, partisanship, and, if possible, politics itself.

Efficiency provided the positive program to replace what populist surgery excised. The doctrine calls essentially for a new form of centralization; that is, centralization and rationalization of government activities and services to accompany the decentralization of power. Some assumed that services do not constitute power. Others assumed the problem away altogether by defining a neutral civil servant who would not abuse centralized government but could use it professionally to reap the economies of scale and specialization. That was the secret of the business system; and, after all, the city is rather like a business. ("There is no Republican or Democratic way to clean a street.")

While there are many inconsistent assumptions and goals between these two doctrines, they lived well together. Their coexistence was supported by the fact that different wings of this large, progressive movement were responsible for each. Populism was largely the province of the working-class, "progressive" wing.

Doctrines of efficiency were very much the responsibility of the upper-class wing. Populism resided with the politician-activists. Efficiency was developed by the intellectuals, including several distinguished university presidents, such as Seth Low, Andrew Dickson White, Harold Dodd, and, preeminently, Woodrow Wilson, who wrote a classic essay while still a professor of political science proclaiming the virtues of applying Prussian principles of administration in the United States.

These two great ideas were, by a strange and wonderful chemistry, combined into a movement whose influence is a major chapter of American history. Charters and laws have consistently insulated government from politics (meaning party politics). It became increasingly necessary with each passing decade to grant each bureaucratic agency autonomy to do the job as its professional commissioner saw fit.

On into the 1960's the merit system extends itself "upward, outward and downward," to use the Reformers' own dialectic. Recruitment to the top posts comes more and more often from the ranks of lifetime careerists in the agencies, party backgrounds increasingly signifying automatic disqualification. Reform has succeeded in raising the level of public morality and in making politics a dirty word. "Good press" for mayors consists of a determination to avoid intervening in the affairs of one department after another. The typical modern mayor is probably eager to cooperate, because this is a release from responsibility. Absolution-before-the-fact has become part of the swearing-in ceremony.

Reform has triumphed, and the cities are better run than ever before. But that, unfortunately, is not the end of the story, nor would it have been even without a Negro revolution. The triumph of Reform really ends in paradox: Cities like New York are now *well run but ungoverned*.

Politics under Reform is not abolished. Only its form is altered. *The legacy of Reform is the bureaucratic state*. Destruction of the party foundation of the mayoralty cleaned up many cities but also destroyed the basis for sustained, central, popularly based action. This capacity, with all its faults, was replaced by professionalized agencies. But this has meant creation of new bases of power. Bureaucratic agencies are not neutral, they are only independent. The bureaucrat may be more efficient and rational and honest than the old amateur. But he is no less political. If anything, he is more political because of the enormously important decisions so willingly entrusted to his making.

Modernization in New York and other modern cities has

meant replacement of Old Machines with New Machines. The bureaucracies—that is, the professionally organized, autonomous career agencies—are the New Machines.

Sociologically, the Old Machine was a combination of rational goals and fraternal loyalty. The cement of the organization was trust and discipline created out of long years of service, probation and testing, slow promotion through the ranks, and centralized control over the means of reward. Its power in the community was based upon services rendered.

Sociologically, the New Machine is almost exactly the same sort of organization. There are more New Machines in any given city. They are functional rather than geographic in their scope. They rely on formal authority rather than upon majority acquiescence. And they probably work with a minimum of graft and corruption. But these differences do not alter their definition; they only help to explain why the New Machine is such a successful form of organization.

The New Machines are machines because they are relatively irresponsible structures of power. That is, each agency shapes important public policies, yet the leadership of each is relatively self-perpetuating and not readily subject to the controls of any higher authority.

The New Machines are machines in that the power of each, while resting ultimately upon services rendered to the community, depends upon its cohesiveness as a small minority in the midst of the vast dispersion of the multitude.

The modern city is now well run but ungoverned because it now comprises islands of functional power before which the modern mayor stands impoverished.[1] No mayor of a modern city has predictable means of determining whether the bosses of the New Machines—the bureau chiefs and the career commissioners—will be loyal to anything but their agency, its work, and related professional norms. Our modern mayor has been turned into the likeness of a French Fourth Republic premier facing an array of intransigent parties in the National Assembly. The plight of the mayor, however, is worse: at least the premier could resign. These modern machines, more monolithic by far than their ancient brethren, are entrenched by law and are supported by tradition, the slavish loyalty of the newspapers, the educated masses, the dedicated civic groups, and, most of all, by the organized clientele groups enjoying access under existing arrangements.

The Reform response to the possibility of an inconsistency between running a city and governing it would be based upon the assumption of the Neutral Specialist, the bureaucratic equivalent to law's Rational Man. The assumption is that if men know their own specialties well enough they are capable of reasoning out solutions to problems they share with men of equal but different technical competencies. That is a very shaky assumption indeed. Charles Frankel's analysis of such an assumption in Europe provides an appropriate setting for a closer look at it in modern New York: "[D]ifferent [technical] elites disagree with each other; the questions with which specialists deal spill over into areas where they are *not* specialists, and they must either hazard amateur opinions or ignore such larger issues, which is no better. . . ."[2]

During the 1950's government experts began to recognize that, despite vast increases in efficiency flowing from defeat of the machine, New York City government was somehow lacking. These concerns culminated in the 1961 Charter, in which the Office of Mayor was strengthened in many impressive ways. But it was quickly discovered that no amount of formal centralization could definitively overcome the real decentralization around the mayor. It was an organized decentralization, and it was making a mockery of the new Charter. The following examples, although drawn from New York, are virtually universal in their applicability:

(1) Welfare problems always involve several of any city's largest agencies, including Health, Welfare, Hospitals, etc. Yet, for more than forty years, successive mayors of New York failed to reorient the Department of Health away from a regulative toward more of a service concept of organization.[3] And many new aspects of welfare must be set up in new agencies if they are to be set up at all. The new poverty programs were very slowly organized in all the big cities—except Chicago.[4]

(2) Water pollution control has been "shared" by such city agencies as the Departments of Health, Parks, Public Works, Sanitation, Water Supply, and so on. No large city, least of all New York, has an effective program to combat even the local contributions to pollution. The same is true of air pollution control, although for some years New York has had a separate department for such purposes.

(3) Land-use patterns are influenced in one way or another by a large variety of highly professional agencies. It has proved virtually impossible in any city for any one of these agencies to impose its criteria on the others. In New York the opening of Staten Island by the Narrows Bridge, in what may be the last large urban frontier, found the city with no plan for the revolution of property values and land uses in that Borough.

(4) Transportation is also the province of agencies too numerous to list. Strong mayors throughout the country have been unable to prevent each agency from going its separate way. For just one example, New York pursued a vast off-street parking program, at a cost of nearly $4,000 per parking space, at the very moment when local rail lines were going bankrupt.

(5) Enforcement of civil rights is imposed upon almost all city agencies by virtue of federal, state, and local legislation. Efforts to set up public, then City Council review of police processes in New York have been successfully opposed by professional police officials. Efforts to try pairing and busing of school children on a very marginal, experimental basis have failed. The police commissioner resigned at the very suggestion that values other than professional police values be imposed upon the Department, even when the imposition came via the respected tradition of "legislative oversight." The superintendent of education, an outsider, was forced out. He was replaced by a career administrator. One education journalist at that time said: "Often . . . a policy proclaimed by the Board [of Education], without the advice and consent of the professionals, is quickly turned into mere paper policy. . . . The veto power through passive resistance by professional administrators is virtually unbeatable. . . ."

The decentralization of city government toward its career bureaucracies has resulted in great efficiency for the activities around which each bureaucracy was organized. The city is indeed well run. But what of those activities around which bureaucracies are not organized, or those which fall between or among agencies' jurisdictions? For these, as suggested by the cases above, the cities are suffering either stalemate or elephantitis—an affliction whereby a particular activity, say urban renewal or parkways, gets pushed to its ultimate success totally without regard to its balance against the missions of other agencies. In these as well as in other senses, the cities are ungoverned.

Mayors have tried a variety of strategies to cope with these situations. But the 1961 mayoral election in New York is the ultimate dramatization of their plight. This election was confirmation of the New York system in the same way the 1936 election was confirmation of Gosnell's Chicago. The 1961 New York election will some day be seen as one of the most significant elections in American urban history. For New York it was the culmination of many long-run developments. For the country it may be the first of many to usher in the bureaucratic state.

The primary significance of the election can be found in the spectacle of a mayor attempting to establish a base of power for himself in the bureaucracies. The mayor's "organization" included the following persons: his running mate for president of the City Council had been commissioner of sanitation, a position which culminated virtually a lifetime career in the Department of Sanitation. He had an impressive following among the sanitation workers, who, it should be added, are organized along precinct lines. The mayor's running mate for comptroller had been for many years the city budget director. As a budget official he had survived several administrations and two vicious primaries pitting factions of the Democratic Party against one another. Before becoming director he had served a number of years as a professional employee in the Bureau. The leaders of the campaign organization included a former, very popular fire commissioner who retired from his commissionership to accept campaign leadership and later to serve as deputy mayor; it also included a former police commissioner who had enjoyed a strong following among professional cops as well as in the local Reform movement. Added to this was a new and vigorous party, the Brotherhood Party, which was composed in large part of unions with broad bases of membership among city employees. Before the end of the election most of the larger city bureaucracies had political representation in the inner core of the new Administration.

For the 1961 election Mayor Wagner had put his ticket and his organization together just as the bosses of old had put theirs together. In the old days the problem was to mobilize all the clubhouses, districts, and counties in the city by putting together a balanced ticket about which all adherents could be enthusiastic. The same seems true for 1961, except that by then the clubhouses and districts had been replaced almost altogether by new types of units.

The main point is that destruction of the machine did not, in New York or elsewhere, elevate the city into some sort of political heaven. Reform did not eliminate the need for political power. It simply altered what one had to do to get it. In the aftermath of twenty or more years of modern government it is beginning to appear that the lack of power can corrupt city hall almost as much as the possession of power. Bureaucracy is, in the United States, a relatively new basis of collective action. As yet none of us knows quite what to do about it.

These observations and cases are not supposed to indict Reform cities and acquit Chicago. They are intended only to put Chicago in a proper light and to provide some experimental means of assessing the functions of the machine form of collective action. Review of Reform government shows simply and unfortunately that the problems of cities, and the irrational and ineffectual ways city fathers go about their business, seem to be universally distributed without regard to form of government or type of power base.

All cities have traffic congestion, crime, juvenile delinquency, galloping pollution, ghettoes, ugliness, deterioration, and degeneracy. All cities seem to be suffering about equally with the quite recent problems of the weakening legitimacy of public objects, resulting in collective violence and pressures for direct solution to problems. All cities seem equally hemmed in by their suburbs and equally prevented from getting at the roots of many of their most fundamental problems. Nonpartisan approaches, even approaches of New York's Republican mayor to Republican suburbs and a Republican governor, have failed to prevent rail bankruptcy in the vast Eastern megalopolis, to abate air or water pollution, to reduce automobile pressure, or to ease the pain of the middle-class Negro in search of escape.

The problems of the city seem to go beyond any of the known arrangements for self-government. However, low morality and lack of what Banfield and Wilson call "public-regardingness" may be a function simply of mass pressure, poor education, and ethnic maladjustment. The old machine and its abuses may have been just another reflection of the same phenomena. If that is so, then the passage of more time and the mounting of one sociocultural improvement after another might have reformed the machines into public-regarding organs, if they had not been first too much weakened to be repaired.

NOTES

1. Compare Wallace Sayre and Herbert Kaufman, *Governing New York City* (New York: Russell Sage, 1960), pp. 710 ff.
2. Charles Frankel, "Bureaucracy and Democracy in the New Europe," *Daedalus* (Winter, 1964), p. 487.
3. Sayre and Kaufman, *op. cit.*, p. 274.
4. Compare Paul Peterson, unpublished doctoral dissertation, University of Chicago, 1967.

THE BUREAUCRACY PROBLEM

JAMES Q. WILSON

The federal bureaucracy, whose growth and problems were once only the concern of the Right, has now become a major concern of the Left, the Center, and almost all points in between. Conservatives once feared that a powerful bureaucracy would work a social revolution. The Left now fears that this same bureaucracy is working a conservative reaction. And the Center fears that the bureaucracy isn't working at all.

Increasing federal power has always been seen by conservatives in terms of increasing *bureaucratic* power. If greater federal power merely meant, say, greater uniformity in government regulations—standardized trucking regulations, for example, or uniform professional licensing practices—a substantial segment of American businessmen would probably be pleased. But growing federal power means increased discretion vested in appointive officials whose behavior can neither be anticipated nor controlled. The behavior of state and local bureaucrats, by contrast, can often be anticipated *because* it can be controlled by businessmen and others.

Knowing this, liberals have always resolved most questions in favor of enhancing federal power. The "hacks" running local administrative agencies were too often, in liberal eyes, the agents of local political and economic forces—businessmen, party bosses, organized professions, and the like. A federal bureaucrat, because he was responsible to a national power center and to a single President elected by a nationwide constituency, could not so easily be bought off by local vested interests; in addition, he would take his policy guidance from a President elected by a process that gave heavy weight to the votes of urban, labor, and minority groups. The New Deal bureaucrats, especially those appointed to the new, "emergency" agencies, were expected by

From James Wilson, "The Bureaucracy Problem," *The Public Interest*, No. 6 (Winter, 1967), pp. 3–9. Copyright © National Affairs Inc., 1967. Reprinted with permission of author and publisher.

liberals to be free to chart a radically new program and to be competent to direct its implementation.

It was an understandable illusion. It frequently appears in history in the hopes of otherwise intelligent and far-sighted men. Henry II thought his clerks and scribes would help him subdue England's feudal barons; how was he to know that in time they would become the agents of Parliamentary authority directed at stripping the king of his prerogatives? And how were Parliament and its Cabinet ministers, in turn, to know that eventually these permanent undersecretaries would become an almost self-governing class whose day-to-day behavior would become virtually immune to scrutiny or control? Marxists thought that Soviet bureaucrats would work for the people, despite the fact that Max Weber had pointed out why one could be almost certain they would work mostly for themselves. It is ironic that among today's members of the "New Left," the "Leninist problem"—i.e., the problem of over-organization and of self-perpetuating administrative power—should become a major preoccupation.

This apparent agreement among polemicists of the Right and Left that there is a bureaucracy problem accounts, one suspects, for the fact that non-bureaucratic solutions to contemporary problems seem to command support from both groups. The negative income tax as a strategy for dealing with poverty is endorsed by economists of such different persuasions as Milton Friedman and James Tobin, and has received favorable consideration among members of both the Goldwater brain trust and the Students for Democratic Society. Though the interests of the two groups are somewhat divergent, one common element is a desire to scuttle the social workers and the public welfare bureaucracy, who are usually portrayed as prying busybodies with pursed lips and steel-rimmed glasses ordering midnight bedchecks in public housing projects. (Police officers who complain that television makes them look like fools in the eyes of their children will know just what the social workers are going through.)

Now that everybody seems to agree that we ought to do something about the problem of bureaucracy, one might suppose that something would get done. Perhaps a grand reorganization, accompanied by lots of "systems analysis," "citizen participation," "creative federalism," and "interdepartmental co-ordination." Merely to state this prospect is to deny it.

There is not one bureaucracy problem, there are several, and the solution to each is in some degree incompatible with the solution to every other. First, there is the problem of accountability or control—getting the bureaucracy to serve agreed-on national goals. Second is the problem of equity—getting bureaucrats to treat like cases alike and on the basis of clear rules, known in advance. Third is the problem of efficiency—maximizing output for a given expenditure, or minimizing expenditures for a given output. Fourth is the problem of responsiveness—inducing bureaucrats to meet, with alacrity and compassion, those cases which can never be brought under a single national rule and which, by common human standards of justice or benevolence, seem to require that an exception be made or a rule stretched. Fifth is the problem of fiscal integrity—properly spending and accounting for public money.

Each of these problems mobilizes a somewhat different segment of the public. The problem of power is the unending preoccupation of the President and his staff, especially during the first years of an administration. Equity concerns the lawyers and the courts, though increasingly the Supreme Court seems to act as if it thinks its job is to help set national goals as a kind of auxiliary White House. Efficiency has traditionally been the concern of businessmen who thought, mistakenly, that an efficient government was one that didn't spend very much money. (Of late, efficiency has come to have a broader and more accurate meaning as an optimal relationship between objectives and resources. Robert McNamara has shown that an "efficient" Department of Defense costs a lot more money than an "inefficient" one; his disciples are now carrying the message to all parts of a skeptical federal establishment.) Responsiveness has been the concern of individual citizens and of their political representatives, usually out of wholly proper motives, but sometimes out of corrupt ones. Congress, especially, has tried to retain some power over the bureaucracy by intervening on behalf of tens of thousands of immigrants, widows, businessmen, and mothers-of-soldiers, hoping that the collective effect of many individual interventions would be a bureaucracy that, on large matters as well as small, would do Congress's will. (Since Congress only occasionally has a clear will, this strategy only works occasionally.) Finally, fiscal integrity—especially its absence—is the concern of the political "outs" who want to get in and thus it becomes the concern of "ins" who want to keep them out.

Obviously the more a bureaucracy is responsive to its clients—

whether those clients are organized by radicals into Mothers for Adequate Welfare or represented by Congressmen anxious to please constituents—the less it can be accountable to presidential directives. Similarly, the more equity, the less responsiveness. And a preoccupation with fiscal integrity can make the kind of program budgeting required by enthusiasts of efficiency difficult, if not impossible.

Indeed, of all the groups interested in bureaucracy, those concerned with fiscal integrity usually play the winning hand. To be efficient, one must have clearly stated goals, but goals are often hard to state at all, much less clearly. To be responsive, one must be willing to run risks, and the career civil service is not ordinarily attractive to people with a taste for risk. Equity is an abstraction, of concern for the most part only to people who haven't been given any. Accountability is "politics," and the bureaucracy itself is the first to resist that (unless, of course, it is the kind of politics that produces pay raises and greater job security.) But an absence of fiscal integrity is welfare chiseling, sweetheart deals, windfall profits, conflict of interest, malfeasance in high places— in short, corruption. Everybody recognizes *that* when he sees it, and none but a few misguided academics have anything good to say about it. As a result, fiscal scandal typically becomes the standard by which a bureaucracy is judged (the FBI is good because it hasn't had any, the Internal Revenue Service is bad because it has) and thus the all-consuming fear of responsible executives.

If it is hard to make up one's mind about how one wants the bureaucracy to behave, one might be forgiven if one threw up one's hands and let nature take its course. Though it may come to that in the end, it is possible—and important—to begin with a resolution to face the issue squarely and try to think through the choices. Facing the issue means admitting what, in our zeal for new programs, we usually ignore: *There are inherent limits to what can be accomplished by large hierarchical organizations.*

The opposite view is more often in vogue. If enough people don't like something, it becomes a problem; if the intellectuals agree with them, it becomes a crisis; any crisis must be solved; if it must be solved, then it can be solved—and creating a new organization is the way to do it. If the organization fails to solve the problem (and when the problem is a fundamental one, it will almost surely fail), then the reason is "politics," or "mismanagement," or "incompetent people," or "meddling," or "socialism," or "inertia."

Some problems cannot be solved and some government functions cannot, in principle, be done well. Notwithstanding, the effort must often be made. The rule of reason should be to try to do as few undoable things as possible. It is regrettable, for example, that any country must have a foreign office, since none can have a good one. The reason is simple: it is literally impossible to have a "policy" with respect to *all* relevant matters concerning *all* foreign countries, much less a consistent and reasonable policy. And the difficulty increases with the square of the number of countries, and probably with the cube of the speed of communications. The problem long ago became insoluble and any sensible Secretary of State will cease trying to solve it. He will divide his time instead between *ad hoc* responses to the crisis of the moment and appearances on Meet the Press.

The answer is not, it must be emphasized, one of simply finding good people, though it is at least that. Most professors don't think much of the State Department, but it is by no means clear that a department made up only of professors would be any better, and some reason to believe that it would be worse. One reason is that bringing in "good outsiders," especially good outsiders from universities, means bringing in men with little experience in dealing with the substantive problem but many large ideas about how to approach problems "in general." General ideas, no matter how soundly based in history or social science, rarely tell one what to do tomorrow about the visit from the foreign trade mission from Ruritania or the questions from the Congressional appropriations subcommittee.

Another reason is that good people are in very short supply, even assuming we knew how to recognize them. Some things literally cannot be done—or cannot be done well—because there is no one available to do them who knows how. *The supply of able, experienced executives is not increasing nearly as fast as the number of problems being addressed by public policy.* All the fellowships, internships, and "mid-career training programs" in the world aren't likely to increase that supply very much, simply because the essential qualities for an executive—judgment about men and events, a facility for making good guesses, a sensitivity to political realities, and an ability to motivate others—are things which, if they can be taught at all, cannot be taught systematically or to more than a handful of apprentices at one time.

This constraint deserves emphasis, for it is rarely recognized as a constraint at all. Anyone who opposed a bold new program on the grounds that there was nobody around able to run it would be accused of being a pettifogger at best and a reactionary do-nothing at worst. Everywhere except in government, it seems, the scarcity of talent is accepted as a fact of life. Nobody (or almost nobody) thinks seriously of setting up a great new university over-night, because anybody familiar with the university business knows that, for almost any professorship one would want to fill, there are rarely more than five (if that) really top-flight people in the country, and they are all quite happy—and certainly well-paid—right where they are. Lots of new business ideas don't be-come profit-making realities because good business executives are both hard to find and expensive to hire. The government—at least publicly—seems to act as if the supply of able political executives were infinitely elastic, though people setting up new agencies will often admit privately that they are so frustrated and appalled by the shortage of talent that the only wonder is why disaster is so long in coming. Much would be gained if this constraint were mentioned to Congress *before* the bill is passed and the hopes aroused, instead of being mentioned afterward as an excuse for failure or as a reason why higher pay scales for public servants are an urgent necessity. "Talent is Scarcer Than Money" should be the motto of the Budget Bureau.

If administrative feasibility is such a critical issue, what can be done about it? Not a great deal. If the bureaucracy problem is a major reason why so many programs are in trouble, it is also a reason why the problem itself cannot be "solved." But it can be mitigated—though not usually through the kinds of expedients we are fond of trying: Hoover Commissions, management studies, expensive consultants, co-ordinating committees, "czars," and the like. The only point at which very much leverage can be gained on the problem *is when we decide what it is we are trying to accomplish.* When we define our goals, we are implicitly deciding how much, or how little, of a bureaucracy problem we are going to have. A program with clear objectives, clearly stated, is a pro-gram with a fighting chance of coping with each of the many aspects of the bureaucracy problem. Controlling an agency is easier when you know what you want. Equity is more likely to be assured when over-all objectives can be stated, at least in part, in general rules to which people in and out of the agency are asked to conform. Efficiency is made possible when you know what you are buying with your money. Responsiveness is never easy or wholly desirable; if every person were treated in accordance with his special needs, there would be no program at all. (The only system that meets the responsiveness problem squarely is the free market.) But at least with clear objectives we would know what we are giving up in those cases when responsiveness seems necessary, and thus we would be able to decide how much we are willing to tolerate. And fiscal integrity is just as easy to insure in a system with clear objectives as in one with fuzzy ones; in the former case, moreover, we are less likely to judge success simply in terms of avoiding scandal. We might even be willing to accept a little looseness if we knew what we were getting for it.

The rejoinder to this argument is that there are many government functions which, by their nature, can never have clear objectives. I hope I have made it obvious by now that I am aware of that. We can't stop dealing with foreign nations just because we don't know what we want; after all, they may know what *they* want, and we had better find out. My argument is advanced, not as a panacea—there is no way to avoid the problem of administration—but as a guide to choice in those cases where choice is open to us, and as a criterion by which to evaluate proposals for coping with the bureaucracy problem.

Dealing with poverty—at least in part—by giving people money seems like an obvious strategy. Governments are very good at taking money from one person and giving it to another; the goals are not particularly difficult to state; measures are available to evaluate how well we are doing in achieving a predetermined income distribution. There may be many things wrong with this approach, but administrative difficulty is not one of them. And yet, paradoxically, it is the last approach we will probably try. We will try everything else first—case work, counseling, remedial education, community action, federally-financed mass protests to end "alienation," etc. And whatever else might be said in their favor, the likelihood of smooth administration and ample talent can hardly be included.

Both the White House and the Congress seem eager to do something about the bureaucracy problem. All too often, however, the problem is described in terms of "digesting" the "glut" of new federal programs—as if solving administrative difficulties had something in common with treating heartburn. Perhaps those seriously concerned with this issue will put themselves on notice that they ought not to begin with the pain and reach for some administrative bicarbonate of soda; they ought instead to begin with what was swallowed and ask whether an emetic is necessary. *Coping with the bureaucracy problem is inseparable from rethinking the objectives of the programs in question.* Administrative reshuffling, budgetary cuts (or budgetary increases), and congressional investigation of lower-level boondoggling will not suffice and are likely, unless there are some happy accidents, to make matters worse. Thinking clearly about goals is a tough assignment for a political system that has been held together in great part by compromise, ambiguity, and contradiction. And if a choice must be made, any reasonable person would, I think, prefer the system to the clarity. But now that we have decided to intervene in such a wide range of human affairs, perhaps we ought to reassess that particular trade-off.

WHO MAKES DECISIONS IN METROPOLITAN AREAS?

NORTON E. LONG

The peculiarity of "the metropolitan problem" is that it is characteristically felt to be a problem requiring a governmental solution
for which there is no readily available appropriate governmental
machinery. This means that there is no structured decision-making
process that has been developed for dealing with this order of
problem. The lack of such a structured process means further
that there is little institutional support for decision-makers en-
visioning their primary role as representing a "metropolitan public
interest" rather than the interest of their particular group, organization or local government. The most likely role to be called
into play in a territory without common political loyalty and institutions is that of the special interest ambassador.

The term, metropolitan problem, almost seems to assume that
there is a metropolitan common interest, and the assumption that
there is a metropolitan common interest leads easily to the notion
that there is a metropolitan community. Many earnest souls have
thought that the European problems should follow this same
logic, to say nothing of the even more ambitious World Federal-
ists. Common problems may create a community among those
who share them. However, much history, especially where people
have become accustomed to living under different governments,
with different values and resources, underscores the painful fact
that common problems may do little more than produce common
quarrels.

What this adds up to is that the term decision in our title may
be optimistic. One makes a decision in a business, a government,
a conference of ambassadors, maybe even sometimes at the sum-
mit, but these are structured decision-making institutions. What
is characteristic of metropolitan areas is the lack of overall decision-

From Norton E. Long, *The Polity*, © 1962 by Rand McNally & Company,
Chicago, pp. 156–64.

making institutions. This does not mean that there are not institutions with power in metropolitan areas. It does mean that there are not institutions with sufficient power and overall responsibility to make decisions settling metropolitan issues and solving metropolitan problems. As a consequence, it is rare that we can speak of who makes metropolitan decisions. What we can speak about is who make decisions that have a significant effect on metropolitan problems.

Characteristically, metropolitan issues do not relate to problems that are solved by decisions in the sense we would use that term in a business or governmental organization, and naturally so, since the metropolitan area is not organized so as to be capable of making decisions. What does happen is that issues and problems have a career and over time processes of interaction develop through which interested and powerful parties exercise influence over the outcome.

We might then concern ourselves with who make decisions that influence the processes by which metropolitan problems and issues get handled. As in a business, one hates to admit that the concern just drifts along by guess and by god, so we are reluctant to admit that this is the way that a metropolitan area runs. This is especially true if one has little faith in an unseen hand guiding the selfish interests of the particular groups and local governments to an unintended but beneficent metropolitan result. Yet in large measure, the metropolitan area is a kind of natural governmental ecology in which institutions, groups and governments have developed a system of largely unintended cooperation through which things get done and the area considered as a system functions. The owls and the field mice, the oaks and the acorns, the flora and fauna of the woodlot have worked out over time a most effective system of unintended cooperation that, barring catastrophe, preserves and maintains a systemic balance, though one that evolves over time.

By and large, we accept a similar system of unintended cooperation for running our economy. The complex task of supplying the city of Philadelphia occurs without any central planning machinery. The fact is we are used to a largely unplanned economy producing functional results. It's a little difficult for us to accept this of an unplanned polity, but to a considerable degree this is just what happens in a metropolitan area. To be sure, the analogy to the economy may be closer to oligopoly than free market competition. What we have is a number of institutions, public and private, sharing a common territory, making demands on each other, cooperating, hindering, damaging and helping in an inter-dependent set of relations with no overall government exercising control.

The relationships among the governments, government depart-ments, Federal, State and Local, businesses, associations, news-papers, and the myriad groups whose activities intersect and interact have grown up over time. They have a history, they have cre-ated habits and customs, use and want, ways that are accepted for handling problems that arise. The metropolitan area as a sys-tem for handling common problems is a going concern. The rather considerable problems of very large populations living under great diversity of governments have been managed.

If we look at the who, who make decisions in the metropolitan areas, we will be most interested in the actors, individual and institutional, that play the major roles in the process by which the metropolitan system handles the issues that confront it. We can best appreciate these actors if we see them as dealing with metropolitan problems from the limited point of view of a par-ticular institutional base. This particular institutional base de-termines the point of view of the actor and how he scores his own success or failure. Much of the blame that is heaped on the heads of actors in the metropolitan scene for their lack of a sense of overall responsibility stems from the failure to recognize the con-straints of their institutional reality. It is idle to blame a down-town store for behaving like a downtown store or the Port of New York Authority for behaving like the rubber based, toll fed, revenue bond undertaking that it is. There are very few actors whose particular institutionalized interests parallel in any com-plete way the metropolitan area. Just as there are almost no insti-tutions, private or public, whose interests and organization cover the metropolitan territory, so there are few, if any, whose interests extend to any considerable number of the problems of the metro-politan area.

By and large, actors and institutions in the metropolitan area, civic ritual apart, are confined in their interests to particular areas and particular problems. Highways, schools, sewer and water, housing, parks and recreation, these problems have their peculiar clientele just as the diseases that afflict the human body have their special funds. Thus, in the highway area you may have a Port of New York Authority, a Bob Moses and the Triborough Bridge Authority, a New York City Transit Authority, Commuter Railways and Buses, two or more state governments and their assorted departments, a variety of political communities, businesses, trade associations, civic organizations, newspapers, all involved. Quite probably, the issues in the transportation field will be agitated with little effective concern for overall problems of coordination and none whatever for the implication of highway resource allocation for other claimants in the metropolitan area.

If we were to make a typology of the key actors in the typical metropolitan area, it might run as follows. First, we would have the metropolitan dailies. In almost all cases, they would exhibit a commitment to the preservation of downtown real estate, a consequent concern for mass transit, extending frequently to the advocacy of subsidy, a belief in planning and a disposition to favor some form of metropolitan integration. These newspapers are in a position to agitate the issues they favor, reward with publicity the politicians and civic leaders who agree with them and by appropriate news selection determine to a large extent what most people will be thinking are the hot issues. Rarely, except in a place like Miami, can the metropolitan press carry a general proposal for governmental change. On piecemeal bond issues and administrative matters, however, it can do much. Beginning to enter the field as a competitor in some areas are television and radio. Just how the structure of their interests will differ from that of the metropolitan press is not clear.

Frequently opposing the metropolitan dailies and following a particularist line is the community press. Usually, they support the interests of small business threatened by planning and the parochialism of suburban city governments.

Of equal importance with the media are, of course, the public officials concerned with the production of public services that cut across political boundaries or require resources that must be allocated among a number of claimants. These officials run the gamut from village to state and nation. They embrace such disparate undertakings as schools, watersheds, airports and a host of other things. Quite often it is the service departments of the governments badgered by their clientele that press the metropolitan issues with still other government officials in their budgetary capacity playing the role of reluctant Solomons.

Downtown stores, real estate interests concerned with central city property values, commuter railways, central city banks, central city and even other politicians concerned with the implications of the worsening of the central city tax base frequently make common cause with the press, university professors, the foundations and the civic leaders in a crusade to save downtown. A subsidy at the expense of the highway user for mass transit, a massive urban renewal program, a new layer of metropolitan government, at the very least, a metropolitan planning agency, all or some combination of these, comprise a set of symbolic and frequently more than symbolic acts by which a multitude of parties with the most varied concerns express their feeling about the dynamic changes that are transforming urban America.

However, these overall actions have all too often bogged down in the quagmire of divisive local interests and electoral conservatism. Given the circumstances of local public life it is usually easy to mount a campaign of metropolitan reform. The electoral consultation which our home rule tradition insists on forces such proposals to run the gauntlet of the antagonism of suburban voters to the central city, vested interests of all kinds in the status quo, central city ethnic and minority groups who fear any dilution of their achieved central city power and a host of public officials and employees who may fear the unsettling of their empires and jobs. Certainly, high among the list of the who that make metropolitan decisions, if no more than negatively, are the varied active electorates called into play by referenda and the officials who have a stake in the existing system.

The revolutionaries who wish to overturn the status quo are most often university professors, foundations, Leagues of Women Voters, Chambers of Commerce, civic leader businessmen especially those with a stake in downtown, those with a concern in the planning of major metropolitan highways and utilities, suburban residents, officials and real estate promoters needing sewer and water facilities, the media people seeking a cause and the intellectuals of local government who follow the thinking of *Fortune*, The National Municipal League and "the authorities."

The attempts at revolution have mobilized financial support from elements of the business community such as Civic Progress, Inc., in St. Louis, and the Cleveland Development Foundation. They have usually enjoyed the support of the metropolitan dailies, the League of Women Voters, the professors and most of the do-gooders. The opposition the campaigns have mobilized, especially where general metropolitan integration has been sought, has been sufficient to insure defeat at the polls. These defeats have usually been as much due to the political ineptitude and lack of energy of the proponents of change as to the power of the opposition.

It must be remembered that the existing metropolitan areas are going concerns—going systems—as systems we can expect them to react vigorously to attempts to seriously alter them. If the existing system of local government could be easily changed it would be intolerably unstable. If no powerful interests were vested in the status quo, the existing order would have so little allegiance it could scarcely run, much less endure. Some such situation obtained in Miami, the one successful case of metropolitan integration and a case where change won by an eyelash and the decision could have gone either way.

If we turn from overall decisions such as those that are embodied in researching county charters, studying metropolitan regions, writing new local constitutions and campaigning to the piecemeal decisions that are by their sheer cumulative weight determining the future of the metropolitan areas, a different order of actions emerged. Clearly among the most significant decisions affecting our metropolitan areas are those which determine the importation of cheap rural labor from the South, Puerto Rico and Mexico, without any provision for adequately housing it in standard housing. The demand for labor insures no equivalent demand for standard housing; it is in fact a demand for slums. Given the desire of the average low income rural immigrant to the city for television, the automobile and the other gadgets of the affluent society, plus his habitation to a very low housing standard in his place of origin, it is not surprising that expensive standard housing should be low on his list of priorities.[1] Doubtless, we could force urban immigrants to buy housing rather than other consumer goods by outlawing substandard housing. We probably won't and this is a key decision in metropolitan areas. The central city has a vested interest in slums as do those employers of cheap labor and those sellers of consumer goods which compete with housing for the slum dwellers' dollar.

Another key decision made by real estate people, bankers, building and loans, suburban neighborhoods and the rest, is whether the new minorities, Negroes, Puerto Ricans and Mexicans, but especially Negroes, will be able to follow the earlier ethnics into the melting pot of middle-class America or whether the color bar will prevent assimilation. This decision which will be made by a myriad of individual decisions will determine whether or not we create our own version of Algeria in our larger cities with an alienated group of second-class citizens led by an unassimilated, rejected but educated elite.

The decisions by our businesses on the location of industry, of manufacturing, retail trade and office buildings will over time critically determine the fate of downtown, the relation of residence and place of work and the future of our system of metropolitan transportation. While we may talk bravely of a pattern of land use control and a massive rehabilitation of the central city, the odds are probably with Professor Raymond Vernon of Harvard that our public expenditures and our controls are unlikely to be sufficiently massive or powerful to offset the natural locational forces. This seems the more likely if dozens of communities scramble to beef up their tax base in a competition for industry to meet mounting municipal costs. With the property tax still a major reliance of central city and suburbs, the struggle for tax base will conflict with and in all probability override efforts at a general plan of metropolitan land use.

While it is unpopular to say it, one of the crucial decisions in the metropolitan area will relate to the preservation of the middle-class values of American culture. Despite all its clumsiness the separate but not watertight compartments of the suburban communities prevent the flooding of schools and neighborhoods by an undigestable mass of immigrants of a different culture. In all probability, despite an uneasy conscience, there will be efforts by middle-class neighborhoods to preserve the political dikes that protect their values. However unsatisfactory, and it is clearly unsatisfactory, the present system of social absenteeism in the massive change in the central city has probably rendered impossible a desirable balance between the social classes. The recolonization of the central city by disenchanted suburbanites is probably little more than the utopia of the builders of luxury high rise apartments.

We can confidently expect that as the incomes of the mass of central city residents rise they will make the same key metropolitan decisions that the earlier middle-class ethnics made—to cross the tracks into suburbia.

Since the positions of power in our society can be expected to fight for survival, it can be expected that the vested interests in downtown should fight as hard for the preservation of outmoded central city land values as the embattled farmers have to preserve an outgrown pattern of agriculture. When one looks at the vested stake in central city real estate it is hard to imagine that the fight to achieve public subsidies to resist its obsolescence will be less than that put up by agriculture. Certainly, there might seem to be a greater appeal for spending the massive sums that now go into subsidizing an unproductive agriculture on the maintenance of our obsolescing central city plant. The sentimental appeal that persuades us to save the family farm can and has been raised to save "downtown." As yet the appeal goes no further than the appeal for urban renewal, and the subsidization of commuter railways and mass transit. If this does not work, we can expect the ante will be raised rather than the end abandoned.

An older generation accustomed to what Mumford has called the eotechnic city, the city of steam and mass transit can be frightened by a specter, the specter of the city of the automobile, Los Angeles. Lord Marple, the British Minister of Transport, said recently, "I saw Los Angeles, the city of the future, a fate we must avoid." Perhaps one day we will cease to regard Los Angeles as a monstrosity and accept the technological obsolescence of the older city. Our agricultural experience indicates the old will die hard.

One last decision, the greatest, I think, in our lifetime and the one nobody made but that has changed everything. In 1929 the shape of the American income was a pyramid with a broad base of the bulk of society close to the means of subsistence living at a family income of below $2,000. In the twenty-five years that *Business Week* once said remade America, 1929 to 1954, the income structure changed from a pyramid to a diamond—America had become a middle-class country. Even in 1929, the middle-class values led to a family centered suburban standard of life. This has been the dynamic. As the lower half of the present diamond of our income structure shrinks with the growth in its income we can expect the new middle classes to continue the trek and the pressure of their movement to continue to tax the public sector of our local economies.

Beyond the dynamic of the growth of the new middle class is the growing market orientation of industry and the new pattern of settlement of business in the metropolitan areas. How the community earns its living will, as always, be a vital determinant of the structure of metropolitan areas.

Ours, however, is an affluent society and the increasing desire to consume public goods will press constantly on our governments. Thus, the rush to the week-end especially with the four-day work week may mean that the peak loads for play will outweigh the peak loads for work on our highways.

The decisions then that may be most important in our metropolitan areas are economic, piecemeal, harmonized if at all by market forces. This is not to say we could not generate enough political power to make effective public metropolitan decision-making possible; it is to express a doubt that we will, in more than a piecemeal way, substitute government action for the forces of the economy. I suspect that as long as the existing system functions even tolerably well, we will tinker with it getting rid of the worst annoyances but putting up with what we know rather than venturing on untried seas. Should Miami and other areas provide an attractive imitable lesson, however, we can expect new civic fashions to spread. The unresolved problem of local government remains the desire for sharply increased amounts of public goods but at the same time stable or decreased taxes, the desire for the fruits of planning and control and the desire for the energy and enterprise of unregimented economic individualism.

Perhaps it is our successful capacity to live with and entertain these contradictory desires that is the genius of our tradition. As an Englishman once told an exasperated French colleague, "England is governed by parliament, not logic."

NOTE

1. I wish to credit Anthony Downs of the University of Chicago with the forceful development of this point.

THE LOGIC OF
METROPOLITAN REORGANIZATION

EDWARD BANFIELD AND MORTON GRODZINS

In much of the discussion of metropolitan reorganization it is difficult to tell precisely what the nature of the problem really is. Frequently it is not clear on what grounds reorganization is thought necessary. Usually no convincing reasons are given for fixing the bounds of the metropolitan area in one way rather than in another. And there is seldom much critical examination of the assumptions, arguments, and conclusions with respect to various schemes for reorganization. This chapter attempts to clarify some of these matters.

Often the assumption is implicit, if not explicit, that it must be extremely wasteful to have many—perhaps several hundred—independent governing bodies within a single metropolitan area. Recently, for example, an insurance company president told a national conference on metropolitan problems:

> The businessman finds himself in a crazy quilt of communities of all sizes, shapes and systems. These are growing without planning—without reasonable relationship one to the other. These illogical governmental boundaries in many respects are like tariff walls, and the effect has been to increase immeasurably the cost of doing business. Such a wonderland of waste, paid for by tax dollars, is offensive to the tax-paying businessman.[1]

It is not likely that the speaker considers the insurance business a "wonderland of waste" because it is carried on by hundreds of companies of all sizes, operating within boundaries which are, from any general standpoint, illogical. If such a charge were made against the insurance business, he would be quick to point out the advantages which arise from the specialization of certain companies in one or another type of highly technical business, the encouragement to enterprise and risk-taking that results from the independent operation of small companies, and the gain to the consumer from being able to choose from a wide variety of offerings. He might even add that the lack of cooperation within the insurance business is not as great as it may appear to the outsider: there are many informal devices—trade associations, for example— through which the companies regulate their relations when it is in their mutual interest to do so.

Not uncommonly, of course, genuine savings may be made by consolidation of enterprises, whether they be local governments or insurance companies, or by formal arrangements to bring about greater coordination. And it is certainly true that wasteful governments can proliferate in a way denied to insurance companies. Many factors may perpetuate an ineffective business; yet a business does have a balance sheet as a relatively harsh criterion of effectiveness. No similar yardstick exists for governments. Furthermore, large organizations—in both industry and government—may make possible through economies of scale new functions (including research) that would otherwise be impossible. In industry, consolidations also diffuse risk-bearing; the analogous consideration in governmental consolidation is the widening of the tax base, which frees the local community from dependence upon the decision of the few owners of industrial property who, by controlling a large tax source, may thereby control the community itself.

Despite these qualifications, the simple number of government units in a given locality, or their lack of uniformity, simplicity, and symmetry, is at best only a rough indicator of the need for reorganization.

Sometimes the necessary distinction is not made between "problems which exist in metropolitan areas" and "problems which exist by virtue of the inadequacies of governmental structures in the metropolitan areas." Recently, for example, the Conference on Metropolitan Area Problems sponsored by the governors of Massachusetts, Connecticut, New York, New Jersey, and Pennsylvania and the mayor of New York City listed a number of "problems confronted by the metropolitan areas." Along with recommendations on mass transit, air pollution, waste disposal, and water pollution was the following: "It is essential that some playgrounds and other facilities be located within easy reach of the mother with the baby-carriage and the child on roller-skates."[2] Lack of playgrounds within easy reach of mothers and children may indeed be a problem in metropolitan areas; it is not, however, a problem which requires for its solution any reorganization of governments.

Some writers have sought to find the optimum scale for the organization of each public function in the nature of its technology and to infer from this an optimum size for the city government as a whole. Aside from the fact that technology is always changing, the main difficulty of this approach is that it does not take into account the nonmonetary advantages and disadvantages which are associated with a given scale of organization. Suppose, for example, that without any loss of services a suburb could reduce its tax rate by $1 per $100 of assessed valuation by becoming part of the central city. Presumably this would be a measure of the economies of scale that would result from consolidation. The suburbanites, however, might judge that the satisfaction of remaining apart from the city and controlling their own affairs in their own way was worth all it cost and more. If they made this judgment, consolidation would represent less rather than more efficiency, for in judging efficiency *all* valued outputs, not merely those measured in the market, must be taken into account.

The discussion of these matters by some advocates of metropolitan consolidation seems to assume that the suburbanite is wrong in valuing nonmonetary satisfactions as highly as he often does; that the pleasure of being identified with an autonomous suburb is illusory or socially irresponsible. Actually, the concern of the ordinary citizen for social status, and for housing and community surroundings as a symbol of status, is one of the driving forces of American life. If the upward mobile masses—the "new immigrants" in Samuel Lubell's term—want to buy the status advantages that go with residence in a town which has a name and an identity apart from the central city, and if they are willing to pay the added costs that this entails, it is hard to see why they should be discouraged. From a policy standpoint, only two questions are relevant: are they actually bearing all of the extra costs and are they aware of them? If the answer to these questions is "yes," there is little basis for public concern.

Even if intangibles like status are left out of account, and the calculation is made solely in terms of quantities which can be measured and priced, it is not clear that widespread consolidation of local governments would yield much of a saving. Posed in this oversimplified way, the problem of discovering the optimum scale of a single function, to say nothing of all functions together,

would still be very difficult. Police protection may best be organized on one scale, sewage disposal on another, and recreation on
still another. What, then, is the optimum size for a city which
performs all three functions and many more besides?

Increases in the volume of work, in government as in industry,
decrease the unit cost of work output. But in both cases there is
a point of diminishing returns. The situation for government is
complicated because the larger the population aggregate, the more
extensive and more expensive the services required and demanded.
Per capita expenditures for governmental services in cities generally increase with size of city. If costs, not services, were the criterion, this fact would argue for smaller, not larger, governments.
Per capita expenditures, of course, must be distinguished from
costs of a given service at a given standard. And here there seems
to be little doubt that the latter grow less expensive with increases
in size of city, up to a population of about 50,000. Costs per unit
of service do not seem to decrease much in still larger cities.[3]

Moreover, even if it could be proved that larger work units lead
to lower costs, it would not follow that consolidation of local
governments would be desirable from an economic standpoint:
the city which is too small to provide certain services efficiently
may arrange to buy them from a nearby city which can produce
them efficiently. In other words, absorption of one government
by another is not the only way of securing adequate scale.

It is often assumed that if sentimental and political obstacles
("irrationalities," they are often called) did not stand in the
way, it would be possible to delineate a metropolitan area which
would form the "logical" basis for an all-purpose local governmental jurisdiction.

Sometimes it is taken for granted that political boundaries
ought to correspond to some features of the natural environment.[4] This thinking has led many geographers to delineate
"natural regions" (e.g., drainage basins) and to recommend them
as the "logical" units on which to base political and administrative jurisdictions. In the case of the metropolitan area, however,
the physical feature usually fixed upon is not "natural" at all: it is
the perimeter of contiguous urban settlement. This standard is
usually highly ambiguous in application, since one hardly ever
finds a sharp, sudden break in the continuity of settlement; usually the urban and rural places run together on the fringes of the
cities in such a way that even a rather broad line must be arbitrary. One might, by taking one view of contiguity, regard the

area from Portland, Maine, to Richmond, Virginia, as a single metropolitan area, although surely no governmental problem requires this particular jurisdiction for its solution.

If it were possible to delineate clear-cut population areas, it would not necessarily follow that these would be appropriate bases for local governmental jurisdictions. A large population occupying a single contiguous area might very well comprise two or more virtually distinct economic, social, or political communities. The difficulties in defining a "community" are as great as those in defining a "natural population block,"[5] and a single "community," even if defined, would not necessarily provide an appropriate base on which to organize all, or even any, local governmental services. If the community were large enough for one function (according to criteria of economy), it might be too large—or not large enough—for others.

It is often argued that as a matter of justice the level of services —education, police, fire, public health, and so on—should be equal throughout the metropolitan area, or at least the uniformity of service levels cannot be attained unless there is an authority with jurisdiction over the whole area.

There are, obviously, certain minimum standards—especially those connected with health and education—below which it is intolerable that any community should fall. If these minima are met, there is no good reason to demand that all service levels be everywhere precisely, or even approximately, the same. Moreover, even if uniformity is desired, it is hard to see why it should be uniformity within the metropolitan area rather than within some larger area. If, for example, uniformity is desirable within the New York–New Jersey area, why is it not also desirable within the Richmond–Boston area, of which the former is a part? And if it is desirable within the Richmond–Boston area, why not throughout the United States? The argument leads to the conclusion that standards of local service should be defined and enforced for the whole country by the Federal government.

Provided minimum standards are everywhere met, there is much to be said for encouraging differentials in service levels. Many people do not wish to buy more of the services supplied by local government than absolutely necessary. Some are able to enjoy the satisfactions of homeownership because they are willing to forego—and because the market allows them to forego—other satisfactions, including those which would come from higher levels of local governmental service. Certainly freedom to make choices of this kind should be encouraged, not discouraged.

Apart from this, differentials in service levels may serve the useful function of discouraging settlement in places where it is not desirable. Herbert A. Simon has observed:

> To the extent that the higher cost of service, or the poorer quality of service provided to such an area, acts as a deterrent to its development until the more central portions of the city have been completely settled, differentials stemming from this particular cause must be considered beneficial—they are a penalty, so to speak, which reflect the higher cost of servicing the urban population when scattered over a large area, than when compactly distributed.[6]

Inequality of service levels does not constitute a problem of metropolitan area organization. Failure to maintain minimum service levels is a problem, although, as the later discussion will show, not one that requires drastic metropolitan reorganization.

The metropolitan-area problem is sometimes said to arise from the lack of an all-purpose (or at least multipurpose) government able to plan and carry on functions which are best conducted on an area-wide basis. When these functions are listed, they often include most of what local government does.[7] Housing is one of the very few matters which is not usually thought to require metropolitan administration.

The claim that a certain function should be administered on a metropolitan basis may rest on one or the other of two grounds: that it is more economical to perform it on an area-wide basis, or that there are important needs which cannot adequately be met except by area-wide organization.

The issue of economy has already been discussed (pages 30 to 34). The issue of adequacy must be distinguished from it. "Economical" action is action that minimizes waste; "adequate" action results in the attainment of purpose. Some functions can be performed on a less-than-metropolitan basis in an "economical" fashion (without waste), and others can be performed on this basis even though they are "uneconomical," i.e., involve waste. But the claim now under examination goes beyond the issue of economy. It holds that some governmental needs cannot be adequately fulfilled at all, whatever the cost or waste, on anything less than an entire metropolitan basis.

What are the needs that demand metropolitan organization to be "adequately" fulfilled?

What is a "need," as well as what is an "adequate" performance in meeting the need, is in the last analysis a matter of opinion. Air-pollution control, for example, is a need only as someone—a professional group or the whole public—defines it as one. And it is a need which requires area-wide action only if the definition is such that nothing less than area-wide action will meet it.

If the "needs" and levels of "adequacy" as defined by the professional groups are accepted at face value, a few functions seem generally to require metropolitan-wide organization in order to be performed adequately. Circulation control (the whole problem of transport within the area) probably does. Civil defense probably does. So does air-pollution control, particularly as it involves control of the automobile. (The need to control the moving automobile requires area-wide administration for each of these functions.) It is impossible to be sure about even these functions, however, since those who claim that they are metropolitan-area problems do not specify in a clear and unambiguous way what they mean by "adequate" performance.

It will be seen that definition itself can make any function one which can be "adequately" performed only on a metropolitan basis. Dogcatching, for example, could be done "adequately" only through a metropolitan-wide government if the following arguments were accepted: dogs are no respecters of municipal boundaries; the control of stray dogs is essential to the health and safety of urban populations; there must be quick and complete circulation of information regarding stray dogs throughout the metropolitan area; dogcatching services must be of the same quality throughout the area; dog pounds must be located so as to be within easy access of all population groups within the area; the need for dog control is so great and the professionalization of personnel so difficult that it would be dangerous to rely upon any cooperative dog-control arrangements among the separate local governments concerned; and "Balkanization" of local government prevents leaders in dogcatching from operating within the central cities where their services are most needed.

Other functions may be defined so as to make area-wide jurisdiction requisite for their "adequate" performance. Land-use planning, tax assessment, recreation, police (here the analogy with dogcatching is particularly close) are often so defined. Whether or not such functions are actually administered on an area-wide basis is often a matter of political persuasion rather than of technology.

Like all who think about these matters, the authors of this study must fall back upon their own notions of what is "needed" and what is "adequate" fulfillment of needs. By their standards, some aspects of circulation, civil defense, and air-pollution control are almost everywhere metropolitan-area problems in the sense that they are needs which cannot adequately be met without area-wide organization.

To the extent that circulation, civil defense, and air pollution are being dealt with today, it is by the action of many governments, including the Federal. The Federal government plays a leading part in transportation. Although sluggish about fully recognizing the fact, it undoubtedly has the leading role in civilian defense. As the experience of Los Angeles indicates, air-pollution control will sooner or later get Federal action. The Federal government's position in all these fields does not relieve the metropolitan areas of their responsibility. (This is true even with respect to civilian defense, where the national military primacy must be complete.) Nevertheless, it is clear that the relatively few essentially area-wide problems tend also to be nation-wide problems, or at least national urban ones. Their solution, therefore, demands not merely a higher degree of metropolitan integration, but also the most intimate linkage of metropolitan areas with other levels of government.

A good number of the so-called metropolitan-area organization problems turn out on examination to involve something less than the whole metropolitan area. Generally speaking, in the nonarid parts of the country there is enough water so that supplies can be organized on a less-than-metropolitan basis. (Where control is needed, it is generally on a larger-than-metropolitan basis.) If newer technologies are employed, waste disposal may be highly decentralized. With regard to most aspects of public health, recreation, police and fire protection, adequate performance (still distinguished from economical performance) does not require metropolitan-area organization. These are usually subarea problems and imply for their solution subarea governments.

What are area problems in some places are, of course, subarea ones in others. If one looks at the differences among areas, one sees at once that the number and kind of problems requiring area-wide treatment vary from place to place, and that in general the number of such matters decreases as the size of the area increases. It is possible, for example, that Nashville, a metropolitan area of 300,000 population, ought to operate its hospitals on an area-wide basis, but it is hardly likely that the same type of operation will serve the New York–New Jersey area, which contains almost one-tenth of the population of the United States. Size aside, topographical or resource limitations will bring some areas, but not others, to area-wide programs. Water supply may be important in one place as an area-wide function; sewage disposal in another. But adequacy (and economy, too) in the performance of these same functions may be readily achievable in other areas on a less-than-metropolitan-area basis.

Most of the arguments for metropolitan government turn out to be, on inspection, something less than compelling, and the total case for metropolitan integration of local governments is a shaky one.[8] This is not to say, however, that the governments of metropolitan areas as they exist today should not be altered. If they do not make a case for wholesale integration, the arguments examined in this chapter nevertheless indicate both points of weakness and perspectives for future action.

Not all functions need to be organized on a metropolitan basis to achieve economic scale; most functions, however, cannot be economically operated (leaving intangibles out of consideration for the moment) in very small jurisdictions. Ordinarily there will be waste unless jurisdictions of at least 50,000 population are achieved by cooperative arrangements or other means, including consolidation. Subarea arrangements (as distinguished from metropolitan-wide arrangements) are indicated on grounds of both economy and adequacy for some functions in almost every metropolitan area. Given the prevailing notions of "adequacy," a few functions probably need area-wide jurisdictions in most places. Finally, what constitutes a metropolitan-wide "need" is in the long run what the relevant publics decide. As they change their definitions of area-wide needs, what is appropriate governmental structure will also change.

NOTES

1. Powell B. McHaney, President, General American Life Insurance Company, speaking before the National Conference on Metropolitan Problems, East Lansing, Michigan, Apr. 30, 1956. Mr. McHaney's address appears

in the conference proceedings published by the Government Affairs Foundation, Washington, 1957.

2. *The New York Times*, Sept. 24, 1957, p. 29.

3. See William Anderson, *The Units of Government in the United States*, Public Administration Service, Chicago, 1942; also the literature cited in *State-Local Relations*, Report of the Committee on State-Local Relations, The Council of State Governments, Chicago, 1946, pp. 183 ff. But the optimum scale of governmental functions—and therefore the optimum scale of municipal organization—has never been established. It could be done only if some very important simplifying assumptions were made and then only by a major research effort.

4. An early theorist on this topic was H. G. Wells. In "A Paper on Administrative Areas Read before the Fabian Society" (reprinted as an appendix to *Mankind in the Making*, Charles Scribner's Sons, New York, 1904, pp. 389–390) he spoke of the "new urban region." "I would suggest that watersheds make excellent boundaries. Let me remind you that railways, tramways, drain-pipes, water-pipes, and high-roads have this in common—they will not climb over a watershed if they can possibly avoid doing so, and that population and schools and poor tend always to distribute themselves in accordance with these other things. You get the minimum of possible overlap—such overlap as the spreading out of the great midland city to meet London must some day cause—in this way. I would suggest that for the regulation of sanitation, education, communications, industrial control, and poor relief, and for the taxation for these purposes, this area should be one, governed by one body, elected by local constituencies that would make its activities independent of imperial politics."

5. The notion of "community" as the basis of local government jurisdiction is itself full of ambiguities. Some geographers suppose that the trade area has some claim to be taken as the "logical" basis of political and administrative jurisdictions. In his book on *Human Ecology* (Ronald Press, New York, 1950), Amos Hawley defines the community as ". . . that area, the resident population of which is interrelated and integrated with reference to its daily requirements, whether contacts be direct or indirect." On the basis of this definition, it is hard to tell whether the people of the New York metropolitan area are any more or less a community than are the people of the whole United States. But, apart from this lack of operational value, there is no special reason to believe that integration with regard to daily needs should be the basis of political and administrative jurisdictions.

For a recent discussion by a sociologist of the problem of defining the metropolitan community, see Albert J. Reiss, Jr., "The Community and the Corporate Area," *University of Pennsylvania Law Review*, vol. 105, February, 1957, pp. 443–463.

6. Herbert A. Simon, *Fiscal Aspects of Metropolitan Consolidation*, Bureau of Public Administration, University of California, Berkeley, 1943, p. 20.

7. For example, in the Chicago region, according to F. T. Aschman, at least nine major services "present problems for study on an area-wide basis." These are transportation, water distribution, drainage and sewage disposal, garbage and refuse disposal, fire protection, recreational services, health and welfare services, law enforcement, and schools. ["Chicago Metropolitan Area Problems," in Leverett S. Lyon (ed.), *Governmental Problems in*

the Chicago Metropolitan Area, University of Chicago Press, Chicago, 1957, pp. 50–51.]

In the San Francisco Bay Region, according to John C. Bollens, the important regional problems are transportation, sewage, and recreation. Others, which he says deserve "brief mention," are water supply, public health, and fire and police protection. (*The Problem of Government in the San Francisco Bay Region,* Bureau of Public Administration, University of California, Berkeley, 1948, pp. 33–53.)

Luther Gulick takes a more discriminating view of what constitutes a metropolitan problem. In the New York–New Jersey region, according to Gulick, the four important needed regional services are a unified water supply; transportation policy and structure; waste disposal and pollution control, both of water and of air; and development of the port as a world trade center. ("The Next Twenty-five Years in Government in the New York Metropolitan Region," *Metropolis in the Making,* Regional Plan Association, Inc., New York, 1955, p. 65.)

Background for Action (St. Louis Metropolitan Survey, 1957) lists six "weaknesses that stem from the complex governmental pattern of the St. Louis City–St. Louis County area." These are (1) disparity in number and extent of governmental services; (2) variation in ability of communities to finance essential services; (3) inadequacy of some services essential to the development of the area due to absence of single governmental jurisdiction (e.g., transit facilities and traffic control); (4) creation of sanitary problems in some communities by irresponsible action of others; (5) competition for tax resources that impedes land use planning; and (6) inequitable distribution of service costs.

8. A careful inspection of the arguments *against* metropolitan integration would reveal that they, too, are not always persuasive.

Can Citizens Be Represented?

EQUALITY AND POWER IN AMERICAN SOCIETY

ROBERT A. DAHL

. . . let me turn now to another interpretation of certain problems of American communities—problems created by their failure to measure up to the exacting demands of democratic ideals.

My emphasis, however, will be on *appraisal* rather than on description or explanation. What I want to evaluate are the distribution and patterns of influence over political decisions in American life. I shall lean heavily on New Haven for information on the distribution and patterns of influence, but I do so in the belief that New Haven is similar to many other communities and strikingly similar in many ways to the United States as a whole. Where there are differences, I shall try to take these into account.

To appraise, one needs standards of appraisal, criteria of performance, values. Many different criteria are relevant to the task of arriving at an appraisal of the distribution and patterns of influence. I propose, however, to concern myself with only one, the criterion of political equality. Obviously, other criteria might also be invoked. I will not attempt here to justify my choice of equal-

From Robert Dahl, "Equality and Power in American Society," in William D'Antonio and Howard J. Erlich (eds.) *Power and Democracy in America*, pp. 77–89. Copyright © 1961 by University of Notre Dame Press. Reprinted with permission of University of Notre Dame Press.

ity, except to say that it is a value that has always been a salient aspect of democratic beliefs.

When one examines a political decision—that is, a decision determining the policies enforced by governmental officials—or what persons become officials—one usually finds that for any particular sector of policy only a small number of persons ever initiate alternatives or veto the proposals of others. These individuals are leaders or policy-makers. One may say that they have the greatest *direct* influence on decisions. A larger number of persons, subleaders, generally have moderate influence. But most citizens usually have little or no *direct* influence in this sense: they never initiate or veto any alternatives.

One is also likely to find, however, that some leaders are extremely sensitive to the attitudes and preferences of individuals and groups who do not directly initiate or veto alternatives. Often this indirect influence is *anticipatory*: a leader initiates or vetoes a particular alternative because he anticipates rewards for choosing from one set of alternatives, or sanctions if he chooses from a different set. In this way, persons or groups who are not leaders may exert great indirect influence on the choice of alternatives even though they never directly initiate or veto.

In New Haven, for example, the present mayor has not until this present year ever advocated an increase in taxes, although he has done almost everything else to raise money. Why has he not tried to increase taxes? It was not, I think, because someone said, "Mayor Lee, don't you dare raise taxes!" For the mayor grew up in New Haven; he knows enough about the city to know that raising taxes is politically risky. He *anticipated* what might happen to him in the next election if he should raise taxes. If the decision to take the risk is made, at least it is a fact that the risk involved has been anticipated.

Indirect influence, which is often anticipatory in character, is very important for some kinds of leaders, particularly those who have to win elections. Yet even when indirect influence of this sort is taken into account, the distribution of influence in most sectors of policy is very far indeed from the perfect equality that some democratic theorists would regard as ideal.

One of the main reasons why the system does not very closely approximate political equality is the unequal distribution of access to political resources—that is, to inducements of all kinds. One's influence is partly a function of the political resources to which one has access—labor time, money and credit, jobs, information, popularity, wealth, social standing, legality, and the like. An examination of any one of these political resources will show that some persons have much greater access to it than others. So long as this is the case, political equality is not likely to be approximated. This is hardly a novel conclusion, for a great many writers on politics have said in one way or another that a high degree of equality in the distribution of political resources is a necessary—though by no means a sufficient—condition for a high degree of equality of control over political decisions. This was, for example, one of Tocqueville's key propositions in his analysis of democracy in America.

In appraising inequality in political resources, it is important not to make the mistake of assuming that what we are trying to judge is a ruling elite masquerading in the name of democracy. For if citizens do not rule the system as political equals neither does a unified elite control decisions, at least not in New Haven. There may be exceptions in specific communities, but I am inclined to think that most cities and states, and certainly the national government, are in this respect rather like New Haven.

To condemn our political system for inequality is one thing; to condemn it for being dominated by a ruling elite is another. In my view, appraisal is infinitely more complicated, precisely because the political system is neither a democracy in which citizens share equally in all important decisions nor an oligarchy ruled by an elite. Rather, it combines elements of both.

In the American system (insofar as New Haven is a fair prototype), though political equality is certainly not attained and political resources are unequally distributed, democracy is not wholly subverted into oligarchy because the growth of oligarchy is inhibited both by the *patterns* according to which political resources are allocated and by the ways in which resources are actually *used*.

Let me try to make my point clearer first by some abstract considerations on the nature of power and influence. Abstractly, there is no reason to assume that the relative influence different individuals or groups exert on the decisions of one another is simply and solely a function of the "size" of their resources, that is, of the inducements they have at their disposal.

In the first place, an individual need not *use* his political resources to gain direct or indirect influence over officials of government. To be sure, the extent to which one is willing to use his political resources for political ends, depends *in part* on the magnitude of his resources; for example a millionaire who contributed $100 to a political campaign gives up fewer alternative opportunities than a poor man. But the extent to which a person uses his political resources will depend on other factors as well, including his confidence in the success of his effort, the extent to which he has alternative ways of gaining his ends other than through politics, and the extent to which he expects he will be benefited or injured by government policies. In New Haven, we have found variations attributable to each of these factors.

For example, Negroes in New Haven, a minority of probably 10 or 12 per cent of the population, operate at a much higher level of political participation than any other single isolated group in the community. What is the reason for this? The political arena is one area where Negroes are not thwarted and blocked by substantial discrimination. They can get jobs, patronage, and city contracts; they have their votes; their votes are legitimate, and they are counted; and so it has been for a century. This isn't true in the other sectors of community life; so Negroes work harder in the political arena to compensate for their disadvantages.

In the second place, one individual may use his political resources more *skillfully* than another—a variation known to students of politics for several centuries. By a skillful use of limited resources, in fact, a political entrepreneur—Machiavelli's Prince— can increase his resources and thus his influence.

In the third place, the relative influence of different potential coalitions will depend in part on the extent to which individuals and groups actually *combine* their resources. The combined political resources of a very numerous group of individuals who are not very well off may easily exceed the combined political resources of a small elite, each member of which is, individually, very well off. The extent to which people in a group actually combine their resources depends, of course, on the degree of political unity among them. There is no a priori reason for supposing that the rich will display more unity than the poor; and even if they do, it does not follow that the combined resources of the well-off strata will inevitably exceed the combined resources of the badly-off strata of a society.

Now, when we turn from these abstract considerations to the way in which different kinds of inducements—political resources —are actually distributed in New Haven we discover that a most significant change seems to have taken place during the last century and a half. In 1800, the citizens of New Haven were not only very unequal in access to political resources of all kinds but their inequalities were *cumulative*. That is, the same tiny elite possessed the highest social standing, wealth, dominance in economic affairs, superior education, control over educational and religious institutions, a monopoly of public offices, evidently a large measure of legitimacy, and perhaps (though this is more doubtful) even popularity. Today, however, inequalities that exist with respect to all these resources tend to be noncumulative or *dispersed*. I can find no single elite at the top of the heap; instead there are many different varieties of political resources, with a somewhat different elite at the top of each. I am inclined to think that this pattern is not peculiar to New Haven but is common throughout the United States, though one would doubtless find exceptions to it here and there.

Moreover, I am tempted toward the hypothesis that the pattern of dispersed inequalities is a likely product of an advanced industrial society, at least if it operates with the kinds of political institutions that most of us would call democratic. The impact of Marx and Weber on habits of thought about industrial society has been very great, even among non-Marxists and non-Weberians, and both men lead us to expect that an advanced industrial society will be rather neatly and consistently stratified along lines shaped by economic class or bureaucratic position. I believe we should entertain the hypothesis that any industrial society in an advanced stage enters on a profound change that can be held back, if at all, only by a most vigorous and oppressive centralized regime. In a moderately free political system, at this stage, increasing affluence, widespread education, impersonal standards of recruitment, incredible specialization of functions and skills, the varieties of popularity, prestige, and achievement, standardization of consumer goods, social and geographical mobility, and probably many other factors, all tend to produce a pattern of dispersed rather than cumulative inequalities. The advance of industrial society may somewhat reduce inequalities in political resources; it does not, however, erase them. Nonetheless, in New Haven, and I think in American society generally, these inequalities are no longer cumulative.

To the extent that inequalities persist, tendencies toward oligarchy also exist in advanced industrial societies. But to the extent that inequalities are dispersed rather than cumulative—as I am suggesting they are in the United States—the growth of a unified oligarchy is inhibited. For the pattern of dispersed inequalities

means that an individual or a group at a disadvantage with respect to one resource may compensate for his handicap by exploit-
ing his superior access to a different resource. In New Haven, for
example, for the past half century men whose main political resources were popularity and ethnic solidarity have been able to
win elections. Very few individuals or groups in New Haven, and
I believe this to be true in the United States, are totally lacking in
political resources *of some kind.*

The possibility of turning to alternative kinds of resources
would be less significant if one kind of resource—say wealth or
social standing—dominated all the others, in the sense that a person or group superior in the one resource would invariably exert
superior influence in a conflict with persons who drew on other
political resources. Yet—and this is the second great limit on the
growth of oligarchy—this is simply not the case, despite a tradition of economic determinism that runs in a straight line from
Madison to Veblen, Beard, the Lynds, and C. Wright Mills.
Surely if the New Deal demonstrated anything, it proved that
leaders with popularity and votes can—even if they do not
always do so—carry out their policies despite the opposition of
leaders supported by men of wealth and social standing. This is a
point that was perfectly obvious to both Aristotle and Tocqueville, who considered the problem in the light of observations
made on radically different sorts of political systems.

In the third place, individuals or groups who are at a disadvantage in their access to resources can sometimes compensate by using their resources at a relatively high level. In New Haven, Negroes who, as I said before, are more active politically than any
other identifiable ethnic group in the city, have overcome some
of the disadvantages imposed by their incomes, status, and occupations.

Fourth, an individual or group at a disadvantage in resources
may compensate by developing a high level of political skill. For-
tunately the skills required in electioneering and party politics are
by no means a monopoly of any stratum in the community; one
might even conclude that leaders drawn from the well-to-do tend
to be somewhat less likely to develop these skills to a high peak
of proficiency than leaders drawn from the less-well-off strata of
the community. In fact, many sorts of politicking run more
sharply counter to the norms of the upper strata than of the lower
or lower-middle strata.

Fifth, a group of citizens each of whom is weak in political resources may compensate by combining resources so that in the aggregate these are formidable. One resource that can be most easily aggregated by the less-well-off strata is the ballot. In New Haven, historically the least well-off citizens in the community have been Negroes and members of various immigrant groups whose circumstances produce a unity at the polls that declines as assimilation progresses. This unity among the poor has enabled them—or more accurately, perhaps, their leaders—to influence nominations, elections, and policies (often, to be sure, covert rather than overt policies) despite their lowly status, their low incomes, and their poverty in many other political resources.

Sixth, competitive elections insure that elected officials attempt to shape their covert and overt policies so as to win elections, hence to maximize votes, or at any rate to gain more votes than any rival. Consequently, whenever the many are believed to hold views on government policies at odds with the views held among the few, there exists one set of persons, elected politicians, who are strongly impelled to win votes by shaping or seeming to shape governmental policies according to the views of the many.

The system would be easier to judge either if it did not fall so far short of the goal of political equality—or, ironically, if it fell much shorter than it does. In the first case one might conclude that we possess a reasonable approximation of political equality, and approve the fact; in the other, one might conclude that we have an oligarchy, and condemn it roundly. But in my view the facts do not permit either judgment.

Some of you might draw comfort from the belief that the American system, if I have described it rightly, comes close to the mixture of democracy and oligarchy that Aristotle concluded was "the best constitution and the best way of life for the *majority* of states and men," and which he called a polity. I cannot forbear quoting here a few lines from Barker's translation of *The Politics*.

> It is a good criterion of a proper mixture of democracy and oligarchy that a mixed constitution should be able to be described indifferently as either. . . . A properly mixed 'polity' should look as if it contained both democratic and oligarchical elements—and as if it contained neither. It should owe its stability to its own intrinsic strength, and not to external support; and its intrinsic strength should be derived from the fact, not that a majority are in favor of its continuance . . . , but rather that there is no single section in all the state which would favor a change to a different constitution. . . . It is clear from our argument, first, that the best

form of political society is one where power is vested in the middle class, and secondly, that good government is attainable in those states where there is a large middle class—large enough, if possible, to be stronger than both of the other classes, but at any rate large enough to be stronger than either of them singly. (*pp. 177, 178, 180*)

You will recall also Aristotle's observation that polities of this kind were in fact rather rare, because in most states the middle class was small, and both the masses and the rich sought to install the constitution most favorable to them, either democracy or oligarchy.

For those who do not want to yield up the marvelous Utopian objective that animated the Declaration of Independence and the Gettysburg address, Aristotle's words will scarcely give complete comfort. Unless we abandon the ideal of political equality, and with it the American Dream, I do not see how we can live comfortably with the inequalities of power and political resources that we find around us. Can anyone who holds democratic beliefs remain satisfied with the American political system simply because it is not an oligarchy?

Unfortunately, however, solutions to the problem of political inequality are not as simple as they may have seemed to many hopeful democrats a century or more ago. In order to eliminate large inequalities in direct influence on governmental policies we should have to make far-reaching, indeed revolutionary, alterations in the character of modern society, such as the destruction of the national state and the elimination of all forms of bureaucratic organization including the business corporation. It would also require a world at peace. Even then, so long as individuals had different motives, interests, and skills, sizable differences in direct influence undoubtedly would appear. I do not believe that enough people are interested in these changes—which would generate their own train of uncertainties and impose great costs to other values we all hold—to make it worth the effort to explore them here, even though attempts to think through these problems realistically should continue.

Nor should one be misled by glib solutions. It might be argued, for example, that if inequalities in direct influence are inevitable, at least we should insure that there is equal opportunity to *gain* influence. Many persons are handicapped in the contest for office and influence by inequalities in resources that can be reduced, such as handicaps stemming from gross differences in income and inherited wealth, handicaps arising from inadequate opportunities for education, and handicaps arising from discriminatory practices based on race, ethnic group, religion, or social class. To the extent that these are remediable, surely we should not rest on our oars until the race is won.

But we must not be beguiled into assuming that equality of opportunity to *gain* influence will produce equality of *influence*. In fact, we are reducing and probably in the future will reduce even more many old inequalities in opportunities. But this merely insures that individuals will start out more or less even in a race for unequal influence. Even a modern dictatorship can achieve that. In fact some dictatorships seem to do a tolerably good job of it. It might be thought, too, that inequalities in direct influence over government policies could be reduced solely to *legitimate* differences in the relative influence of government officials, particularly elected officials, and ordinary citizens. No one, I suppose, would quarrel with the proposition that the President or the Secretary of State should have much greater influence over foreign policies, because of official position, than any other citizen. Yet it would be misleading to suppose that we are likely to reach a state of affairs in which reality corresponds to the simple model of democratic representation whereby appointive officials are merely the agents of elected officials, and elected officials are merely the agents of the majority. For in many sectors of policy, including most of the highly critical ones, elected and appointive officials have enormous leeway; public opinion and voting often provide only the vaguest sort of guide as to what is preferred by or even acceptable to a majority of voters. Views are often highly plastic: it is not so much the elected officials who are the agents of a majority as the other way round—voters wait for their trusted leaders to indicate what lines of policy should be followed.

If we are not likely—at least in the present state of national and world organization—to reduce very greatly the enormous differences that now exist with respect to direct influences on government policies, the problem of indirect influence is somewhat more manageable. The most promising means for providing an equal though indirect influence on policies is, surely, through participation in nominations, campaigns, and elections. Here the situation strikes me as a very hopeful one, for political self-confidence and participation are so much a function of education that the wide diffusion of educational opportunities is likely to reduce to insignificance many of the differences in political participation that stem from socioeconomic position rather than differences in personality. (Perhaps it is just as well that the differences in personality still elude control.)

Even in the case of campaigns and elections, however, wide participation is no cure-all. A formidable problem arises because of the enormous differences in opportunities for influencing the voters themselves. The problem is much more serious at the national than at the local level, for it is incomparably more expensive and more difficult to obtain a national hearing than a local one. Political theory has barely been extended to cover this problem; in particular, liberal democratic theory has often started with the assumption that the preferences of individuals, whether voters or consumers, should be taken as given, as autonomous to the individual rather than socially determined. To be sure, Tocqueville, Mill, and Bryce all looked beyond the individual to the towering influence of majority opinion on the views of the individual; and critics at the right and left have looked beyond the majority to the influence on its opinions wielded by key minorities of wealth, status and skill. There have been some innovations, like equal time, and more recently the famous TV debates between the presidential candidates. But clearly we have barely begun to grapple with this problem.

There can be no doubt, then, that our political system falls far short of the high standards of performance indicated by the criterion of political equality. No one who places a high value on political equality can afford to be complacent about the achievements of the American political system.

Nonetheless, it is misleading in the extreme to interpret the inequalities of power that mark our political life as signs of oligarchy. For in our system of dispersed inequalities, almost every group, as said before, has access to some resources that it can exploit to gain influence. Consequently, any group that feels itself badly abused is likely to possess both the resources it needs to halt the abuse and the incentive to use these resources at a high enough level to bring about changes. Nearly every group has enough potential influence to mitigate harsh injustice to its members, though not necessarily enough influence to attain a full measure of justice. The system thus tends to be self-corrective, at least in a limited fashion. If equality and justice are rarely attained, harsh and persistent oppression is almost always avoided. To this extent, the system attains one of the important ends of political equality without the means.

PLURALISM, RACE, AND THE
URBAN POLITICAL SYSTEM

STEPHEN M. DAVID AND JEWEL BELLUSH

It was not until the late 1950's that political scientists began to give serious attention to the study of community power and influence. Up to that time, sociologists had held a monopoly of the field, while political scientists had been preoccupied with promoting "good government" prescriptions for city management and writing dry texts. By and large, those early sociological studies had concluded that a power elite, representing an upper class (whose definition varied from study to study), governed American communities. Party officials and civic and labor leaders were said to hold places subordinate to this upper-class elite.[1] These conclusions were arrived at by a variety of approaches. The best known placed primary reliance either on analysis of the resource bases (sources of power) of the elite or on identifying reputed influentials in the community.[2]

Political scientists, almost en bloc, attacked such findings, complaining that sociologists had failed to verify these conclusions about the role and character of a "power elite." The major thrust of this attack was that the studies had not proved elites used their power to rule local communities; instead, sociologists had relied on potential sources of power or reputed influence, rather than on actual acts of power.[3] To avoid this error, political scientists set to work to study actual decisions made by local government officials. In this way, they hoped to determine the most influential actors and to reveal what constituted the patterns of power in American cities. Concentrating on the "case study approach" (as their method of reconstructing government decisions came to be known), they hoped to uncover the loci of power in various urban centers.[4]

From Stephen David and Jewel Bellush, "Pluralism, Race, and the Urban Political System," in Jewel Bellush and Stephen David (eds.), *Race and Politics in New York City*, pp. 3–24. Copyright © 1971 by Praeger Publishers, Inc. Reprinted with the permission of Praeger Publishers, Inc. This article has been slightly revised by the authors for this publication.

Most of these studies arrived at a conclusion sharply different from that reached by the sociologists: A pluralistic, rather than hierarchical, pattern of decision-making was the real shape of urban power. Political scientists, perceiving urban political systems to be made up of a myriad of small special-interest groups having widely differing power bases and undertaking a multitude of strategies on decisions salient to them, were able to conclude that no single power elite dominated the full spectrum of decision-making; instead, there existed a relatively wide sharing of power among leaders and groups tending to specialize in one or a few issue areas. Believing these multiple centers of power to be the norm, they argued that no single group constituted an all-encompassing power elite. The various centers, or clusters, of power provided the political system with discrete, functional arenas, each public activity operating separately with a different constellation of interests. While accepting the sociological claim that the active, interested, affected groups (always a minority of citizens) dominated the policy process, the advocates of pluralism contended that what eventually evolved into public policies was the result of bargaining and compromise; participants were constrained, checked, and balanced either by other leaders or by those they led.[5]

Thus, as the 1960's began, political scientists had designed a new pattern of urban decision-making that challenged the prevailing power elite model. The pluralists, as this group of political scientists came to be called, were initially widely praised for their studies. Their reliance on the case method to test the validity of their conclusions was considered a major improvement upon the methodology used by the sociologists. Moreover, their findings fitted the optimistic mood of the country during those years, when the process of accommodation and compromise in an open system seemed to be confirmed by daily events.

The events of the 1960's, however, forced many academics to take a closer look at the works of these political scientists. The black revolution, student rebellions, the peace movement, mounting concern for the plight of such groups as the Indians, migrant laborers, and the poor whites of Appalachia—these events raised fundamental questions about the ability of our political systems to function in an open, democratic, and responsive manner. Problems such as these could not be denied or ignored, and the prevailing political theory that could not explain them came into question.

The earliest major critique came from a group of scholars disturbed by the pluralists' sole reliance upon the case study technique, which they believed to be inadequate in the determination of the distribution of power in a given locality. These critics, holding that there were limitations inherent in the very methodology of the pluralists, described three types of situations in which a would-be participant could fail to act (though affected by the policy) and hence would not be represented in a case study reconstruction of the governmental decision.

In each of these situations, groups fail either to initiate a controversy or to promote certain positions that are in their self-interest. The first occurs when a group feels it lacks sufficient influence to affect governmental policy and thus takes no action to promote its interests. In the second, a group fails to initiate or participate in political controversies because it fears the use of sanctions were it to choose to get involved; the history of America is replete with examples of actions—such as lynchings of Southern blacks or police raids on "extremist" groups—taken to discourage political involvement. The last occurs when community norms, which are supportive of the interests of particular groups, lead either to the failure of a group to initiate a controversy or to the exclusion of a whole range of alternatives during the course of a conflict. In this last type of situation, the norms are accepted by government officials and nongovernmental groups alike. In all three cases, those groups that are advantaged by the nonoccurrence of the controversy or by the failure to consider certain alternatives have exercised influence on government officials without any action on their part. Yet, such use of power never comes within the purview of the case study approach.[6]

Criticisms of the pluralist school have not been limited to attacks on their methodology. On the contrary some of their most significant conclusions concerning the nature of urban political systems have been questioned. These pluralist findings can be broadly categorized thus: (1) Urban political systems are open and responsive; (2) there exists a workable model for decision-making; and (3) functional islands of decisions can be perceived. It is to these categories that the remainder of this essay is devoted.

OPENNESS AND RESPONSIVENESS OF THE POLITICAL SYSTEM

Although the pluralists have conceded that differential influence exists within the American political system, they have also maintained that no significant groups are left out of the system.

This view has been expressed in a variety of ways: Robert Dahl has written that any active and legitimate group can usually "make itself heard at some crucial stage in the process of decision";[7] Nelson Polsby expresses the same view, when he states that, in our pluralistic systems, "the claims of small, intense minorities are usually attended to";[8] in summing up New York City's political system, Wallace Sayre and Herbert Kaufman found it to be open and responsive, available "to all the inhabitants of the city and particularly to the active participants in the contest for the stakes of politics."[9]

The pluralists, generally drawing these conclusions from their analyses of the processes and the policy outcomes of decision-making, have maintained that most citizens most of the time are politically apathetic, getting involved and organizing themselves effectively only when their "primary goals" would be affected by political activity. The classic exposition of this pluralist view appears in Dahl's description of the metal-houses controversy in *Who Governs?*[10] In that case, a working-class, poorly educated, politically apathetic Italian community in New Haven organized itself and succeeded in preventing the construction of metal houses, which were intended as residences for blacks, in the neighborhood. These otherwise apolitical people quickly formed a civic association and were able to muster large numbers to appear at meetings of the Board of Aldermen and the Board of Zoning Appeals. At the conclusion of his description of the controversy, Dahl wrote that it illustrated several durable characteristics of the political system—most especially, that involvement in political activities occurs when there is a threat to the primary goals of an individual or group; at such times, the affected citizens will quickly and effectively organize themselves. Sayre and Kaufman wrote in a similar vein about New York:

> Some inhabitants of the city have been slower than others to make use of the weapons the political system places within their grasp, but most—even immigrants from lands with altogether different traditions—have learned quickly, and there are not many who accept passively whatever the system deals out. They have learned that governmental decisions of every kind in the city are responsive to the demands upon the decision centers.[11]

Pluralists have also maintained that each participant in a political controversy almost invariably receives some satisfaction from its outcome. Thus, Sayre and Kaufman wrote that "if there is any single feature of the system of government and politics . . . that may be called ubiquitous and invariant, it would seem to be the prevalence of mutual accommodation. Every program and policy represents a compromise among the interested participants."[12]

The validity of the pluralists' views can be challenged at a number of points. To begin with, in their analysis and conclusions concerning political activation the pluralists argued that political involvement is conditioned upon a threat (be it government action or inaction) to primary goals. When such a threat does not exist, citizens are apathetic, the assumption being that their greatest desires (for example, security, sex, love, food, self-esteem) are best attained by channeling their efforts into nonpolitical activities.[13] This view of the cause of political activation led the pluralists to describe the apathetic state of the general populace in our cities as indicating satisfaction with the prevailing political system. According to pluralist reasoning, since the system was open for those groups of citizens who felt threatened, their failure to become politically involved signified their general approval of the actions of public officials.[14] Such reasoning is, however, simplistic. The pluralists failed to consider a crucial question: How does the citizen become informed of governmental action (or inaction) that would threaten his primary goals? Nor did they consider the processes involved in informing the citizen that public action could actually help in dealing with his daily problems. Put another way, the pluralists used an individual, rather than a societal, perspective to analyze the hindrances to activation; they failed to realize that changes in the *political system* could affect the chances of the citizen's being informed of potential or actual governmental action. In short, the pluralists failed to see the complexity of the political processes involved in activation.

These processes—which involve informing the citizen about political issues, interpreting these issues to him, relating the problems in his daily life (of which he is very aware) to the potential or actual activities of government—must be understood before one can begin to generalize about political activation. When one reflects upon these processes, one is struck by the role that society's institutional structure plays in communicating political issues to the citizen and in shaping his frame of reference for interpreting these issues as well as the events in his everyday life. He depends upon a number of institutional factors for these functions: the existence (or absence) of groups that share interests and concerns similar to his and are able to reach him; the activities of those participants in the political system that may threaten or use

sanctions against the activities of said groups; the role of television
and the newspapers in informing the citizen and shaping his perceptions; and the role of various institutions—such as the school
system, the police, the political party, or charitable organizations
—that seek to impose their definitions of the situation upon the
citizen. In short, when one begins to speculate on the processes
involved in activating the citizen, one becomes aware that these
processes do not resemble the simplistic model of the pluralists;
instead, they are highly complex and have biases built into them.
Without an analysis of these processes and built-in biases, one
cannot assume, as the pluralists did, a one-to-one relationship between citizen involvement and government threats, by action or
inaction, to primary goals. . . .

More, however, is at stake than activation. Even if a group of
citizens is politically activated, can we accept the pluralist assumptions about the spontaneous and inevitable emergence of group
action and leadership skilled in the selection of strategies necessary for success?[15] The pluralists were aware that political resources and skills were differentially distributed throughout the
system; yet they never seemed to have analyzed whether particular groups were *systematically* disadvantaged in their ability to
organize because they lacked the requisite resources and skills.
Pluralists seemed to feel that, if such communities as New Haven's
Italians could rouse themselves from their usual lethargic state
and organize effectively in a short period of time, any group of
urban residents were similarly capable of so performing.

It appears, nonetheless, that groups initially entering the political process are at a distinct disadvantage in this regard. Such
groups are usually short on funds, and material resources have
been known to be among the best inducements for getting people
to work for an organization, particularly if they are low income
with little leisure time.[16] The best-known example of a successful
organization among the low-income urban poor is the political
machine, and it depended upon such material resources. But, in
addition, the leaders of these organizations are often political
neophytes, and the acquisition of political skills stems, in large
part, from experience in the political process. If these groups
come from the poorer and less well-educated sectors of the population, as is often the case, their leaders will often lack the technical and professional expertise needed to engage successfully in
combat in today's urban political system.

Blacks, in particular, have encountered difficulties in their efforts
to organize on their own behalf. For example, New York City

black residents experienced considerable difficulty in becoming an organized force capable of challenging the relatively cohesive power alliance of Columbia University and the traditional voluntary health organizations in control of the Community Mental Health Board. On the other hand, the war on poverty's community-action program illustrates how a government program helped promote the organization and development of leadership skills among certain segments of the black community.[17] These two cases suggest that resources such as money, technical and professional expertise, and group cohesion and the skillful use of these resources are scarce commodities among New York blacks. The reality these case studies describe is a long way from the assumption that activated citizens can easily organize and become influential in politics at any time. Once again, findings of the pluralists, upon which they based their conclusion that our urban political systems are open, come into question.

Not only are there doubts about the validity of pluralist conclusions concerning the activation and organization of the citizenry, but also about their conclusion that public decisions almost invariably reflect an accommodation or compromise among the contending parties. Pluralists have claimed that the interests of all the contending parties will somehow be represented in the final outcome, even if only partially. Such a conclusion is open to attack on several grounds. Surprisingly, the pluralists have generally failed to analyze the outcomes of their case studies systematically in order to determine who gained from the final decision. They have limited their efforts instead to analyzing the extent to which the participants obtained what they asked for.[18] Pluralists have argued that an index that documents the extent to which a participant gains what he demanded during the course of a controversy is preferable to one that focuses on the outcome and ascertains who gained from that decision.[19] As a result of this choice, the outcomes the pluralists analyze represent an accommodation and compromise only for those groups that participated in the controversy; only their demands, made in the course of the conflict, are included. Yet, Nelson Polsby, who has made the best-known defense of this methodological approach, has readily admitted that these factors reflect the power realities of the community.[20] In other words, when the pluralists argue that accommodation is the rule, they are, in effect, saying compromise occurs if we limit our analysis to those who had been activated and organized and to the demands they made, which were shaped by their perceptions of what was politically attainable. By so narrowing

the definition of the political system we are seeking to characterize, the pluralists have provided us with a conclusion about the
distribution of rewards that is of limited value. One wonders
whether any political system, as defined by the pluralists, could not
be said to accommodate the demands of its various participants.

Before any conclusion concerning the responsiveness of a political system can be drawn, it would seem necessary to study those
conflicts that have been suppressed (whether such suppression be
due to a decision of the potential initiator that his demands stand
no chance of recognition or to threatened or actual use of sanctions against the initiator) and those conflicts that involve "significant" challenges to the values held by the politically dominant
groups in the community.[21] There is no gainsaying the methodological problems involved in studying such events (or nonevents);
yet without this kind of data, it seems premature to draw any
conclusions as to the responsiveness of a political system.

Even if the pluralist approach to ascertaining responsiveness
were to be used for the cases in this volume, the limited extent to
which the city's political system has accommodated the demands
of the black community would become apparent. Before discussing this question, it is necessary to raise a logically prior problem; namely, the value bias inherent in making any judgment
about the responsiveness of a political system. The determination
of whether a decision has accommodated the demands of a particular participant is a judgment based upon empirical fact *and*
upon one's value preferences. It is not enough to validate empiri-
cally that a participant received something he had sought from
the decision. To conclude that the participant has been accommodated by the outcome, one must make a judgment that the
benefits received were, in some sense, satisfactory. This judgment
should be made by the participants, not by the researcher; yet
the pluralists, after verifying that the actors in their controversies
achieved some measure of success, drew the conclusion that urban
political systems accommodated the varying demands and pressures put upon them.[22] That conclusion reflected the beliefs of
the pluralists as to what the participants in a controversy should
reasonably expect. These beliefs, of course, can be very different
from the expectations of the actors. Although it is always hazard-
ous to generalize about the biases of a group of scholars, it does
appear that the pluralists as a group placed a high value upon sta-
bility and upon change that comes about incrementally.[23] As a
result, a political system that rewarded all participants, both those
who supported the *status quo* and those who sought change,

was considered responsive. It was the pluralists, not necessarily the participants (or the potential claimants) in political controversies, who were satisfied with the outcomes of urban political systems. . . .

THE MODEL OF DECISION-MAKING

Throughout the pluralist writings, a certain model of political decision-making emerges. The actors are usually individuals who represent organizations, agencies, and organized groups, but not broad social classes. Almost invariably, there are coalitions representing the various contending parties. Participation is confined almost exclusively to those activists who represent organized interests. These actors communicate among themselves in a covert manner, avoiding public notice. The conflict is resolved through bargaining, and the resolution is usually an accommodation among the interests of all contending parties.[24]

Questions concerning a number of these characteristics of the pluralistic model can be raised. The pluralists expected participation to be limited to the leaders of organized groups; little consideration was given to participation by the membership. This was in accord with the pluralist belief that most citizens most of the time were not involved in political activities.[25] The activation and organization of the Italian community in Dahl's metal-houses case was considered a deviation from the normal processes of decision-making. Sayre and Kaufman, listing political participants, refer to the leaders of groups—for example, public officials, both elected and appointed; the leaders of the political parties; the organized public bureaucracies; nongovernmental groups; and officials and bureaucrats of other governments—with only a passing reference to the mass of the citizenry.[26] . . .

However, during the 1960's, we find larger communities of people becoming involved in the racial conflicts of the period. Controversies involving attempts at school or housing integration mobilized nearly all segments of the affected white community. Other issues perceived by the white community as having racial implications witnessed similar patterns. For example, the more massive style is exemplified in the well-known conflicts in New York City over the establishment of a Civilian Review Board and over the attempt to initiate community control of the schools in Ocean Hill–Brownsville.

This larger number of participants also cast doubt on the pluralist finding that conflicts almost invariably take place between small, well-organized groups. Instead, the character of race politics appears to be more and more a social-class or social-group phenomenon. In the controversy over community control of education, the Ocean Hill–Brownsville conflict was not merely a clash between an experimental school district and the United Federation of Teachers (UFT); it became a clash between large segments of the black community and large segments of the white community, particularly its Jewish grouping. The controversy over the establishment of a Civilian Review Board exhibited similar tendencies, with the Catholic, rather than the Jewish, community in the forefront of the white population group opposed to the black community.

The pluralist model also stressed a covert process of communication. This means of communication among the participants allowed for and promoted compromise among them. One effect of such a strategy of secrecy is to limit the number of participants. Groups (often promoting different ends from the ones being pressed by those already participating) that might have become involved are never informed of the decision process in time. This type of communication process also enables leaders to avoid public commitments to their constituents, thereby allowing greater latitude for maneuver and compromise in the negotiations.[27]

In the 1960's, however, racial controversies had a high, rather than a low, visibility, and it was therefore much more difficult for the city's bargaining process to proceed in the traditional manner described by the pluralists. Thus, in the decentralization case, the conflict was resolved, not through quiet bargaining between representatives of the union and the community but only through a highly publicized citywide strike. In effect, this conflict was fought out in the communications media. . . .

Another aspect of the pluralist decision-making model is the existence of coalitions representing the various sets of participants. Again, the pluralists assumed that alliances were an invariant characteristic of the process and that no significant groups would encounter any particular difficulties in obtaining allies. The importance of coalitions to the pluralists is stated by Polsby: One of his five conditions for success in influencing public officials is the "capacity to form coalitions with other participants in order to achieve one's goals."[28] Yet, throughout the decade, black groups encountered growing difficulty in obtaining white allies. White groups which sought to unite with blacks often found their membership resisting such moves. White elites who identified with black demands found that the risks to their leadership position increased.

In short, the pluralists appear to have believed that, in describing a covert process of decision-making with limited participation, they were dealing with universal tendencies that were not likely to change: Almost all urban controversies would be marked by participation limited to the leaders of organized groups, by the absence of involvement of the mass of the citizenry, and by the use of covert processes of communication.[29] Ironically, the pluralists, who criticized the sociologists for assuming that power distributions were permanently related to the social structure, appear to have made similar assumptions about the permanence of the processes involved in decision-making.

To understand this belief of the pluralists in the universal tendencies of the model, one needs to know their perception of American society and its political systems at all levels of government. Nelson Polsby nicely summarized much of what they believe when he wrote:

> Pluralists, who see American society as fractured into a congeries of hundreds of small special interest groups, with incompletely overlapping memberships, widely differing power bases, and a multitude of techniques for exercising influence on decisions salient to them, are not surprised at the low priority Americans give to their class memberships as bases of social action. In the decision-making of fragmented governments—and American national, state, and local governments are nothing if not fragmented—the claims of small, intense minorities are usually attended to. Hence it is not only inefficient but usually unnecessary for entire classes to mobilize when the preferences of class members are pressed and often satisfied in piecemeal fashion. The empirical evidence supporting this pluralist doctrine is overwhelming, however stratification theorists may have missed its significance for them; the fragmentation of American governmental decision-making and of American society makes class consciousness inefficient and, in most cases, makes the political interests of members of the same class different.[30]

The pluralists assumed that the fragmented nature of American society and its political system would continue indefinitely. The basis of this assumption was their belief that the claims of all of these significant small competing groups would continue to be accommodated. The responsiveness of the political system would make it unnecessary, in the words of Polsby, "for entire classes to mobilize when the preferences of class members are pressed and often satisfied in piecemeal fashion."[31]

Yet, within a decade of the pluralist writings, broad social classes did appear on the political scene. While this is not the place to work out the complex causal chain that accounts for the changes described in this section, the inability of urban political systems—as well as of political systems at other levels of government—to respond to the demands of black groups is probably of major importance.

The failure to respond to the integrationist demands of the civil rights organizations in the early 1960's presumably led to increased dissatisfaction within the black community.

This dissatisfaction, in turn, led to the organization of new black groups promoting different goals (for example, community control), to attempts by the older, more established groups to broaden their support, and, most importantly, to a growing sense within the black community that they shared a common fate in the political arena. The movement toward a unified black community has, in turn, led to a mobilization of its opponents and to the kind of political controversy unforeseen by the pluralists.[32]

FUNCTIONAL ISLANDS OF DECISIONS

The pluralists argued that there were different political arenas whose boundaries were determined by functional policy areas. Each of these arenas involved different public officials who were influenced by different nongovernmental interest groups. What little overlap existed among these functional areas was provided by city-wide officials and a few interest groups whose concerns spread over a number of functional areas, but the dominant characteristic of the political system was the relative autonomy of each functional area. Herbert Kaufman neatly presents the core of the argument:

> Each consists of a complex of decision-making "islands." From each such island emanates a flow of decisions and actions embodying the stakes and prizes of politics. The flow from any given island is only loosely related to the flow from all the others; all are, by the same token, relatively autonomous. Every island is composed of a cluster of participants especially concerned with the types of decision that issue from it.[33]

Based upon these findings concerning the degree of autonomy of the functional areas and the minimal overlap of the areas by city-wide officials and nongovernmental actors, these political scientists concluded that the system was pluralistic because there was no single power elite dominating decision-making. Instead, political influence was spread among the actors in the various functional areas. The pluralists, however, never made any attempt to determine the distribution of influence *within* these policy areas. By reconstructing only "important" decisions in each functional area surveyed rather than "representative" controversies, they ruled out such a possible determination.[34] Their choice made sense in light of their goal of determining whether a power elite existed in a particular community. Presumably, if such elite existed, it would more likely appear in "important" rather than in "trivial" issues. By limiting their focus to the "big," rather than the "representative," decisions, the pluralists could not obtain the data necessary to draw any conclusions concerning the patterns of influence within the functional areas.

Several consequences flow from this failure. One of the most important is that we cannot assume that the system is responsive to all groups merely because a power elite fails to exist. The pluralists, by spreading their net over the entire framework of urban decisions, felt satisfied that enough groups, enough pressures, enough interests, enough actors were absorbed by the subsystems to guarantee responsiveness. But how can the responsiveness of the system be judged without considering the possible controlling influence of particular groups over each functional area? What guarantee does one have that there is, for all participants, adequate access to those making official decisions in each functional island?

It may be suggested that, in various functional areas, there are elites who are capable of placing severe constraints on—or preventing public officials from accommodating—the demands of groups promoting antagonistic goals. The school bureaucracy and teachers were highly effective against the proponents of community control, as was the police officialdom in its conflict with groups concerned about police brutality. Although no generalized conclusions can be drawn about the patterns of influence in the various functional islands covered by the case studies, the controversies do uncover the existence of a number of potential elite groupings that are able to determine the responsiveness of the system in their area.

Finally, the existence of functional islands of decision has a built-in bias against those who desire to change the *status quo*. In the current urban political system, there is an obvious fragmentation of authority and power. This fragmentation, as many

pluralists have pointed out, provides participants, both those favoring and those opposing change, with a variety of points of
access. Because, however, any demand for change almost invariably requires the approval of a number of public officials, it is
necessary for those who wish to alter the *status quo* to achieve
access to all these officials. On the other hand, the supporters of
the *status quo* can prevent or limit the scope of change by achieving access to one or, at most, a few of the officials involved in the
controversy. In short, our fragmented urban political systems make
reform more difficult to obtain. As Sayre and Kaufman concluded
in their description of New York's political system: "One consequence of this ordering of the city's political relationships is that
every proposal for change must run a gauntlet that is often fatal.
The system is more favorable to defenders of the *status quo* than
to innovators. It is inherently conservative."[35]

In summary, while the pluralists made a significant contribution when they discovered the existence of these functional islands
of decisions, their assumption that such areas promoted the responsiveness of urban political systems is open to question. The
pluralists made little or no attempt to ascertain the patterns of
influence within the areas they surveyed. Finally, it is hard to
ignore the possibility that the very existence of this dispersion of
authority and power serves those who support the *status quo*,
thereby making the system less responsive to those promoting
change. . . .

A number of significant questions concerning some of the conclusions reached by the pluralist school have been raised by this
essay: The optimism of the pluralists in regard to the system's
openness and responsiveness; their belief in the primacy, if not
universality, of a particular decision-making process that promoted
the accommodation of conflicting interests; and their conclusions
about the pluralist nature of the system based on their findings
that a power elite fails to exist. All such aspects of pluralist
thought are subject to challenge.

This essay has stressed the inadequacies of the pluralist school;
its members can expect better treatment from those who will
look at their contributions from the perspective of intellectual
history. The role pluralists played in redirecting the orientation of
urban political scientists, away from the sterile efforts of the
"good government" prescriptionists who preceded them and toward
the direction of describing and explaining urban political systems,
will be applauded. They will also be praised for their concern for

methodology and empirical theory and for their writings on elite activity during a particular period in the history of our cities. At the same time, they can expect to be criticized for universalizing their conclusions and limiting their concern to the activities of political elites. We can only hope that future political scientists will both appreciate the contributions of the pluralists and transcend their limitations.

NOTES

1. This conclusion was reached in an excellent analysis of their literature by Nelson W. Polsby, *Community Power and Political Theory* (New Haven, Conn.: Yale University Press, 1963), pp. 8–10.
2. *Ibid., passim.*
3. *Ibid.*, particularly ch. 6.
4. Among the best known of these studies were Robert A. Dahl, *Who Governs?* (New Haven, Conn.: Yale University Press, 1961); Wallace Sayre and Herbert Kaufman, *Governing New York City* (New York: Russell Sage Foundation, 1960); Edward Banfield, *Political Influence* (Glencoe, Ill.: The Free Press, 1961)—although Banfield didn't primarily use the case study method for this purpose so much as for showing the workings of influence; and Frank J. Munger, *Decisions in Syracuse* (Bloomington: Indiana University Press, 1961).
5. Lewis Froman, Jr., *People and Politics* (Englewood Cliffs, N.J.: Prentice-Hall, 1962), pp. 49 ff. The pluralist approach has also attracted the attention of European scholars, and, in fact, several have applied it to community studies abroad. See for example, *The New Atlantis*, No. 2 (Winter, 1970), which is devoted to current work on community power in several European countries.
6. Peter Bachrach and Morton S. Baratz, "Two Faces of Power," *American Political Science Review*, LVI, 4, pp. 947–52; Shin'ya Ono, "The Limits of Bourgeois Pluralism," in Charles A. McCoy and John Playford, eds., *Apolitical Politics* (New York: Thomas Y. Crowell, 1967), pp. 99–123; Todd Gitlin, "Local Pluralism as Theory and Ideology," *ibid.*, pp. 124–45. For a critique of this school of thought, see Richard M. Merelman, "On the Neo-Elitist Critique of Community Power," *American Political Science Review*, LXII (June, 1968), pp. 451–60.
7. Robert A. Dahl, *A Preface to Democratic Theory* (Chicago: University of Chicago Press, 1956), p. 145. See also Dahl, *op. cit.* (note 4), p. 228.
8. Polsby, *op. cit.* (note 1), p. 118.
9. Sayre and Kaufman, *op. cit.* (note 4), p. 720.
10. Dahl, *op. cit.* (note 4), pp. 192–98.
11. Sayre and Kaufman, *op. cit.* (note 4), p. 721.
12. *Ibid.*, p. 714.
13. Dahl, *op. cit.* (note 4), ch. 19.
14. *Ibid.*, pp. 309–10.
15. Dahl, *op. cit.* (note 4), pp. 197–98.
16. This argument is persuasively made by Peter B. Clark and James Q. Wilson, "Incentive Systems: A Theory of Organization," *Administra-*

tive Science Quarterly, (September, 1961), pp. 129–66. This same analysis is made by Bellush and Hausknecht in their analysis of urban renewal politics. See Jewel Bellush & Murray Hausknecht, eds., *Urban Renewal: People, Politics and Planning* (Garden City, N.Y.: Doubleday, 1967), pp. 278–86.

17. Jewel Bellush and Stephen David, *Race and Politics in New York City* (New York: Praeger, 1971), chs. 2 and 6.

18. This methodology was followed by Dahl in *Who Governs?* See his description on pages 332–36 of the appendix of that volume. The rationale for this approach is found in Polsby, *op. cit.* (note 1), pp. 132–36.

19. Polsby, *op. cit.* (note 1), pp. 132–36.

20. *Ibid.*, pp. 134–35.

21. This argument is covered more extensively by Peter Bachrach and Morton S. Baratz, *Power and Poverty* (New York: Oxford University Press, 1970), part one.

22. Sayre and Kaufman, *op. cit.* (note 4), pp. 712–14.

23. Polsby, *op. cit.* (note 1), p. 134; Dahl, *op. cit.* (note 4), ch. 28; Sayre and Kaufman, *op. cit.* (note 4), pp. 736–38.

24. For a description of some of the aspects of this model, see Sayre and Kaufman, *op. cit.* (note 4), pp. 712–14. See also J. David Greenstone and Paul E. Peterson, *Race and Authority in Urban Politics* (New York: Russell Sage, 1973), ch. IX.

25. See the discussion is this chapter on the pluralist views toward citizen apathy.

26. Sayre and Kaufman, *op. cit.* (note 4), ch. 3.

27. For an illustration of this point, see the description of how secrecy aided the promoters of urban renewal, by Jewel Bellush and Murray Hausknecht, "Entrepreneurs and Urban Renewal: The New Men of Power," in Bellush and Hausknecht, *op. cit.*, p. 221.

28. Polsby, *op. cit.* (note 1), p. 137.

29. After describing this controversy, Dahl wrote that "conflict of this intensity is a rarity. Ordinarily, political decisions move along in an atmosphere of apathy, indifference, and general agreement." *Op cit.* (note 4), p. 198.

30. Polsby, *op. cit.* (note 1), p. 118.

31. *Ibid.*

32. Much of the difficulty of the pluralists on this point is perhaps explained by Jacobs and Lipsky, when they criticized the pluralists for their almost exclusive focus on elite activity rather than on other strata in local politics. Attention to this latter realm might have forewarned the pluralists of possible changes in the political system. See Herbert Jacobs and Michael Lipsky, "Outputs, Structure, and Power: An Assessment of Changes in the Study of State and Local Politics," in M. D. Irish, ed., *Political Science: Advance of the Discipline* (Englewood Cliffs, N.J.: Prentice-Hall, 1968), pp. 236–38.

33. Herbert Kaufman, *Politics and Policies in State and Local Governments* (Englewood Cliffs, N.J.: Prentice-Hall, 1963), p. 110.

34. For a discussion of the reasons the pluralists chose to reconstruct "important" decisions, see Polsby, *op. cit.* (note 1), pp. 95–96.

35. Sayre and Kaufman, *op. cit.* (note 4), p. 716.

II
Government, Citizens, and Public Policy

The Politics of Housing

INTRODUCTION

The provision of adequate living quarters for all Americans is the central problem for housing policy-makers. It is difficult to determine the number of individuals and families who live in unsatisfactory housing. The most often used criteria are those of the U.S. Bureau of Census. The Bureau, which relies on physical structural standards, defines "substandard housing units" as units that are physically dilapidated and that do not have hot water and plumbing within the unit. Based on that standard, United States housing stock has improved over the years and, by 1970, only about 10 per cent of all housing units were substandard. However, definitions of substandard housing are not fixed, but vary according to judgments as to what constitutes adequate housing. Thus, the Census Bureau does not consider deteriorating housing (as distinguished from dilapidated housing) with inadequate plumbing facilities to be "substandard" housing. Nor does it consider overcrowding as a factor in its definition. Lastly, it fails to take into account a related problem: the proportion of family income spent for rent or ownership costs. If all these factors are considered, then estimates of the proportion of the population living in inadequate housing vary from 15 per cent to 25 per cent (10 to 17 million households),[1] and a disproportionate number of these households are made up of poor nonwhites.

In the United States, governmental efforts to improve the quality of housing did not begin until the turn of the century. During the nineteenth century, slum properties were considered good investments. The continuous supply of immigrants to the cities provided sufficient demand for such housing. And, because of this heavy demand for low-rental housing, the maintenance costs on the properties were minimal. As a result, slum housing was a good business for the builder, the lender, and the owner.

The initial pressures for government action against slum housing came, not from the poor, but from middle-class groups associated with the late nineteenth-century Progressive movement. These groups were generally composed of Protestant, native Americans opposed to the activities and ethos of the immigrant and his political machine. They sought better housing for the poor out of a belief that the slum environment caused the undesirable vices they associated with the immigrant. Better housing was intended as an instrument for socializing the ethnic population into more middle-class values. This pattern, whereby groups with superior status and higher incomes purport to represent the interests of the poor in the housing arena, has continued to the present time. In the discussion to follow, these groups will be referred to as *surrogate groups*.

Around the turn of the century, these surrogate groups began to obtain the passage of building codes by municipal governments. These codes specified standards of lighting, ventilation, sanitation, and fire prevention. The effect of these codes on the private-housing sector during the following half century was to make the low-rental housing market less attractive. The additional building and maintenance costs required by the codes became one of the factors that led to significant changes within the private sector regarding this housing market. The construction of such housing solely by private enterprise all but disappeared. Large financial institutions ceased accepting such properties as securities for loans, and large property owners sold their holdings to small-scale, speculative operators. These operators, in order to keep down maintenance costs, have tried to prevent the enforcement of the building codes, and city governments, anxious to prevent the abandonment of slum properties, have succumbed to their demands. As a result, slum residents have found these codes to be of little help when they seek to improve the quality of their housing or maintenance services.[2]

The next significant intervention by government into the housing market occurred at the time of the Great Depression in the 1930's. The two most important New-Deal housing programs involved federal legislation; they were a mortgage-insurance program (the Federal Housing Administration—FHA) and a public-housing program. Unlike municipal building codes, these programs were responses to pressures for public aid to increase the supply of housing rather than attempts to prevent the construction of inferior housing.

The FHA mortgage-insurance program, enacted in 1935, insured mortgages extended by lending institutions. The FHA set regulations determining the interest charge, the amount of down-payment required, and the maximum time period for the mortgages. Over the years, these regulations have been liberalized; home buyers are now required to make both smaller down-payments and smaller monthly payments as the result of the lengthened time period permitted for the mortgages. It was not until 1967 that the FHA would guarantee loans when there seemed to be substantial risks concerning repayment.

From the time it was enacted, and to the present day, the program has served the interests of the private sector exceedingly well. Pressures from the private-housing market were primarily responsible for the passage of the legislation. The construction of homes had all but ceased; the real-estate market had collapsed; and lending institutions were holding sour mortgages and foreclosing on property which had sharply depreciated in value. The result of the FHA mortgage-insurance program, reports the National Commission on Urban Problems in the reading found in this section, has been to permit financial institutions "to make practically risk-free loans on new and old homes." Home builders and realtors, too, have profited from the expansion of the potential market for their services. In short, the FHA mortgage-insurance program, from the point of view of the financiers, real-estate brokers and contracting industry, has increased their profits and protected them against loss.

The chief consumer beneficiaries of the FHA program have been suburban middle-income home buyers rather than working-class or poor families residing in the central cities. By insuring well over 90 per cent of the appraised value of new homes, the FHA program has enabled millions of Americans to become home-owners in suburbia. The FHA, until recently, has been generally unwilling to insure mortgages to poor and working-class members (particularly blacks), because they have been regarded as bad credit risks. Related to this decision by the FHA has been its reluctance to insure homes in the central city. Not only was the FHA insurance program never intended as a program to aid the poor, but its effect has also been to increase the disparities between the haves and have-nots.

On the other hand, the public-housing program, also initiated during the New-Deal era, was intended to benefit the poor. However, the poor have only benefited from the program to a limited extent. The major enabling legislation was the Low Rent Housing Bill of 1937. The law established the United States Housing Authority (USHA), which was to regulate the activities of municipal public-housing authorities. These authorities would construct, own, and control public-housing projects. Two provisions in the legislation enabled these authorities to maintain low rents for the residents. The local authorities were eligible to obtain long-term loans from the USHA for clearing the land and constructing the project. The long-term nature of the loan meant that the local authorities would be paying a lower debt charge, thereby lowering its costs. In addition, the USHA was authorized to make grants to the local authorities to cover the difference between the rents necessary to cover the costs of the projects and the actual rental income; the rents were required to be at a level which the low-income tenants could afford. As laudatory as these features were, they were offset by a number of regulations issued by USHA that resulted in inferior housing, including limitations on the physical structure of the project (maximum size of rooms, maximum costs per room) and income limitations on tenants (both maximum and minimum). And these were not substantially altered when the continuation of the public-housing program was authorized by the Housing Act of 1949.

From the outset, private-housing interests viewed public housing as competitive to their market and damaging to the demand for older homes and apartments.[3] Moreover, they have always been concerned about the possible extension of this type of governmental intervention into other housing markets. Unlike the FHA mortgage-insurance program, in which governmental backing expands their potential market, public housing is potentially competitive to their efforts. The effectiveness of their opposition to the program increased over the years. The initial legislation contained provisions that limited the proportion of the housing market that could and would make use of public housing. These provisions included the above-mentioned maximum income limitations on residents and inferior standards for the physical structure of the project. Other triumphs of private producer interests in the post–World War II era are described in the Freedman reading. At the present time, appropriations for the program have all but ceased. Public housing currently constitutes only 1 per cent of the nation's housing stock.

As Freedman's data reveal, the surrogate groups promoting public housing encompassed a wider scope of participants than earlier housing-reform efforts. In addition to such middle-class groups as social workers, charitable organizations, and "good government" groups, support for the program came from organized labor and minority groups representing middle-class blacks (for example, the NAACP and the Urban League). However, no organizations that could be said to represent the poor—the potential tenants in the projects—were major actors in the political arena of public housing. Without the direct, personal stake in the issue that the poor themselves had, the surrogate groups were all too willing to reach an accommodation that severely limited the number of public-housing units to be constructed.

This pattern is unfortunately all too clear in the case of the urban-renewal program, which was the major urban housing legislation in the post–World War II era. Urban renewal, initiated in 1949, provided first for slum clearance by the local government and then for sale of the cleared land to a private developer who would build residential housing on the site. The federal government paid two-thirds of the cost of the city's loss in buying and preparing the land for the private developer. The legislation was amended in 1954 and subsequent years to provide that increasingly larger percentages of the cleared land could be developed for nonresidential uses. As a result, a significant portion of urban-renewal developments came to be used for more profitable commercial purposes.

The urban-renewal program is a classic example of the use of government incentives to aid the private housing market. Under the public-housing program, slums had been razed and replaced with locally-owned low-rental housing. Under urban renewal, the slum-cleared sites were turned over to private developers at a price invariably less than the costs incurred by the city. The private interests then owned the land and could retain all profits achieved from their investments. These investments generally involved commercial buildings and high-rise, upper-middle-income housing.

Aside from the private sector, the major participants in the politics of urban renewal were the mayors of central cities, businessmen with central city investments, "good government" groups, the press, and urban planners. All of these groups saw urban renewal as a means of expanding the city's tax base, improving its aesthetic appearance, and making the central city more attractive to middle- and upper-middle-income groups.

The interests of the poor, again, were not represented by their own organizations, but by other participants in the system. The poor were expected to benefit from the program by the relocation into public housing of those whose slum housing was torn down. The same 1949 legislation that authorized the urban-renewal program also authorized the construction of public housing for the families uprooted by slum clearance. However, the relocation aspects of the program have never been successful. As mentioned above, the public-housing program has been underfinanced, and a sufficient number of units have never been built. The poor have had to undergo the difficult process of relocation to make way for the more expensive housing constructed on the sites of their former homes. They have generally settled in other slum areas of the city, often in housing of the same or only slightly better quality, but with more expensive rents.

The 1960's witnessed a new approach in dealing with the housing problems of the poor. Because the public-housing program was stalled by the opposition of the private housing groups, this new direction sought to merge the interests of the private sector with those of the poor. The federal government, increasingly represented by the FHA, began providing financial subsidies in order to induce the private sector to build for this previously unrewarding market. Typical of this genre are two FHA-administered programs enacted in 1968. The first, seeking to enable the low- and moderate-income family to possess their own home, provides a mortgage subsidy that in some cases leaves the buyer with only 1-per-cent interest to pay (Section 235 of the Housing Act of 1968). The subsidy is paid to the financial institution lending the money. The other legislation is intended to lower the rents for low- and moderate-income tenants. The Rental Housing Assistance program (Section 236 of the Housing Act of 1968), which also relies on a mortgage subsidy to the lending institution, is intended to lower the amortization costs of the landlord, enabling him to charge lower rents. By 1971, 25 per cent of all new housing was financed through these two programs or other subsidy programs following this pattern.[4]

Even though these new housing programs are intended specifically for low-income groups, the major participants in the political arena involved in their enactment and administration have been the private sector and surrogate groups.[5] Most private interests viewed these programs as in the tradition of previous government intervention that enlarged the potential market for their services. The surrogate groups, which included almost the very same groups that supported public housing, saw this approach as an acceptable compromise between their concern to enlarge and improve the housing supply for these income groups and the business interests of the private sector.

The results of these programs are still not entirely known and are the subject of current conflicts over housing policy.[6] However, it appears that it has been the moderate- rather than the low-income group (families whose income is too high for public housing but too low for conventional housing) that has primarily benefited. Moreover, it was not until this date that governmental efforts first began to assist this working-class group. The FHA also, in administering these programs, has left undisturbed the present patterns of housing segregation by on the one hand limiting their aid to nonwhites solely to financing central city residences while on the other hand helping white families to obtain homes in suburbia.

Lastly, governmental efforts to end segregation in housing have been extremely limited. Prior to the 1960's, the FHA, responding to pressures generated by the private sector, refused to approve mortgages to blacks seeking to live in white neighborhoods. The enactment of a fair-housing law by Congress in 1968 has had little impact. The selection in this volume by the National Commission on Urban Problems describes how the fragmentation of suburbia has promoted segregated housing.

The limited success of governmental efforts to provide adequate housing for the poor is explained, in part, by the political system that has developed around housing. The major participants in the system have been groups representing the interests of the private-housing sector and surrogate groups claiming to represent the urban poor. The private market has been represented by associations speaking for builders of housing, financial institutions that provide credit for the construction and purchase of homes, and realtors who trade in property and housing. These groups have sought to ensure that governmental intervention would increase the number of potential customers for their services. For example, banks that deal in housing mortgages have approved of the government insuring their mortgages, but have opposed direct government loans to home buyers. Builders have supported government subsidies that enable them to construct homes for income groups that otherwise could not afford such housing, but they oppose the government itself constructing homes for these groups.

The surrogate groups that have pressed for governmental involvement in the housing field have included organized labor, social workers, church groups, professional organizations, and local governmental officials. These groups have tried to increase the quantity and quality of housing available to low- and moderate-income groups and, to achieve this, have been willing to enter into partnership with the private sector. By these accommodations, they have sought to encourage the private sector to serve as large a percentage of the market as possible, with government intervention intended to aid and expand these private efforts. However, groups whose membership is largely urban poor—the potential beneficiaries of these programs—seldom, if ever, have achieved much access and cannot be considered participants in the political system that evolves housing policy. It is ironic that the middle-class "do-good" organizations, whose surrogate activities ostensibly were on behalf of the poor, have only legitimized the latter's exclusion.

The cooperation between the private interests and the surrogate groups has prevented any serious consideration of housing proposals that might disturb the market of the private sector. There are no groups in the arena to propose alternatives such as massive federal efforts to construct housing for low-income residents, direct income grants to the poor themselves rather than subsidies to the private sector, or serious attempts to house the nonwhite poor in suburbia. Whatever the merits of these programs, they share the common characteristic of threatening the private-housing market. Federal construction of low-income housing would remove this group as potential customers for private housing. Direct grants to the poor might not be spent on housing. Programs aimed at housing integration disturb the "normal" workings of a housing market that segregates homeowners by race.

It has been argued that the private sector has been meeting the housing needs of the poor as a result of a "filtering" process in which residences become available to the poor as each successively lower-income group is able to move into better housing. Apologists for the housing policies followed since the 1930's have used this argument to maintain that public programs that aided higher-income groups eventually redounded to the benefit of the poor.[7] However, it is questionable whether the poor are indeed receiving adequate housing as a result of this filtering process. As noted at the beginning of this essay, millions of American families can be considered "ill-housed." The slums of our cities are replete with deteriorating and discarded buildings. Moreover, the racial restrictions of the housing market limit the volume and quality of housing available to blacks as a result of filtering.

The net result of the political system that has developed around housing is that we have government programs for almost all income groups except the poor. The newly enacted FHA subsidy programs, the traditional FHA-insured mortgages, and the urban-renewal program aid all but the very rich and the poor, particularly the black poor. These patterns can be expected to continue as long as the private-housing sector continues to play a dominant role in the politics of housing, and as long as groups representative of ghetto residents are denied an effective voice in the making of housing policy.

NOTES

1. Robert Lineberry and Ira Sharkansky, *Urban Politics and Public Policy* (New York: Harper and Row, 1971), p. 320; Anthony Downs, *Urban Problems and Prospects* (Chicago: Markham, 1971), pp. 115–20.
2. Harold Wolman, *Politics of Federal Housing* (New York: Dodd, Mead, 1971), p. 25.
3. Thomas R. Dye, *Politics in States and Communities* (Englewood Cliffs, New Jersey: Prentice-Hall, 1969), p. 436.
4. "DHA—From Suburb to Ghetto," *New York Times*, III, May 7, 1972, p. 1.
5. Wolman, *op. cit.*, chap. 3.
6. *New York Times*, April 18, 1972, p. 30; *New York Times*, July 24, 1972, p. 1.
7. For example, see Bernard J. Frieden, "Housing and National Urban Goals: Old Policies and New Realities," in James Q. Wilson, ed., *The Metropolitan Enigma; Inquiries into the Nature and Dimensions of America's "Urban Crisis"* (Garden City, New York: Doubleday, 1970), pp. 170–225.

BIBLIOGRAPHY

ABRAMS, CHARLES. *The City Is The Frontier*. New York: Harper and Row, 1965.

BELLUSH, JEWEL, and HAUSKNECHT, MURRAY, eds. *Urban Renewal: People, Politics and Planning*. Garden City, New York: Doubleday, 1967.

DAVIES, J. CLARENCE, III. *Neighborhood Groups and Urban Renewal*. New York: Columbia University Press, 1966.

92   *The Politics of Housing*

FREEDMAN, LEONARD. *Public Housing*. New York: Holt, Rinehart, and Winston, 1969.

GANS, HERBERT. "The Failure of Urban Renewal." *Commentary* (April, 1965), pp. 29–37.

KAPLAN, HAROLD. *Urban Renewal Politics*. New York: Columbia University Press, 1963.

MEYERSON, MARTIN, and BANFIELD, EDWARD. *Politics, Planning, and the Public Interest*. New York: Free Press, 1955.

MEYERSON, MARTIN, et al. *Housing, People, and Cities*. New York: McGraw-Hill, 1962.

WILSON, JAMES Q. "Planning and Politics: Citizen Participation in Urban Renewal." *Journal of the American Institute of Planners* XXIX (November, 1963), pp. 242–49.

WOLMAN, HAROLD. *Politics of Federal Housing*. New York: Dodd, Mead, 1971.

FINANCING OF HOUSING: FHA

NATIONAL COMMISSION ON URBAN PROBLEMS

Few Americans can afford to pay cash for a house. Most people must go into debt to buy a home. Despite a traditional conservative bias against personal indebtedness, an exception has almost always been made for home purchase.

Homeownership is not a new goal. Everyone pays for shelter in some form. The form of purchasing by borrowing enables young families to pay off their debt in lieu of rent when their earning power is steady or growing, and promises security to those who complete payments and achieve full ownership before their earning power dwindles.

To provide the necessary credit and enable a family to have its own home when the need for it is greatest, an elaborate financing system has developed. The various institutions that serve the credit needs of home buyers are:

Governmental institutions:
Federal Housing Administration (FHA).
Veterans' Administration (VA).
Federal National Mortgage Association (FNMA).
Private and conventional credit institutions:
Mutual savings banks.
Savings and loan associations.
Commercial banks.
Life insurance companies.

During the century preceding the Depression of the 1930's, home loans, or mortgages, were handled entirely by private money lenders. They charged high interest, required large downpayments, and required rapid repayment, typically in 7 to 10 years. Buyers short of cash to meet approximately 35 percent of purchase price as downpayment had to borrow further from a

From the National Commission on Urban Problems, *Building the American City* (Washington, D.C.: U.S. Government Printing Office, 1969), pp. 94–107.

second mortgage at still higher interest rates. Periodic payments often covered only the interest, with the full principal due at the expiration date. Buyers who could not meet payments because of illness or loss of jobs were in a precarious position, in danger of losing their homes and all the savings invested in them. Understandably, money lenders often were painted as villains in plays and novels, and the term "mortgage" was surrounded with an aura of fear.

The optimism of the 1920's tended to hide these risks, however. Home buying increased greatly at the same time that values became highly inflated. When the economy collapsed in 1929, millions lost their homes in foreclosures and other millions were about to lose them. One measure of the severity of the crash is that new housing units were being built at an annual rate of 900,000 a year in the years before the Depression and only one-tenth of this amount, or 90,000 housing units, were built in 1934.

This disaster brought the Federal Government into the picture. First, under the Hoover administration, the Federal Home Loan Banks were set up to supply capital advances to home loan institutions. Under the Roosevelt administration, to stem the continuing defaults, the Home Owners Loan Corporation was created to put Federal funds behind distressed mortgages; first interest, and then both interest and principal, were insured.

Also in the mid-1930's, the Government invested about $275 million in federally chartered savings and loan associations, insuring depositors against loss. The whole structure of home financing was purified. The "balloon payments" at the end of the mortgage term (which posed such an unmanageable financial burden on the poor purchaser) were eliminated by amortizing the principal in regular payments over the life of the loan. Interest rates were reduced.

Both homeowners and lenders who held the mortgages were substantially aided by these Government measures, and hence by the taxpayers. Strangely the same economic middle class which then received these benefits, and in large measure still does, often forgets its debt to society; many of its members are frequently in the forefront of opposition to housing programs designed to help less fortunate Americans.

While the Government kept a significant number of Americans from losing their homes through the policies described, the hoped-for recovery of the housing market did not occur. Financial institutions handling the mortgages were stabilized, but they were still fearful of making home loans for which they might not be repaid. In 1935, to stimulate construction and homeownership, the Federal Housing Administration was created to provide more direct support for those wishing to acquire homes by insuring their mortgages under certain circumstances.

Despite rising building costs and interest rates, the pattern of FHA mortgage financing has enabled many more families, and many with lower incomes than formerly would have been in the market, to become homeowners. They have become debt-encumbered, to be sure, but homeowners nevertheless. The chief means of achieving this end have been (1) reduced downpayment requirements, and (2) extended mortgage life.

Mortgage financing has grown to vast proportions. As table 1 shows, there was a doubling of mortgage debt in the 9 years noted.

TABLE 1.—TOTAL MORTGAGE DEBT IN NONFARM
1- TO 4-FAMILY HOUSES

	Billion
1958	$118
1964	198
1967	236

While there are still some individual lenders, the bulk of the mortgage business is institutionalized. The FHA does not make direct loans to borrowers, but rather insures the mortgages extended by institutions. The same is primarily true of mortgages insured by the Veterans' Administration. Mortgages extended by private lending institutions without recourse to either FHA or VA are called "conventional financing."

Interest Rates, Length of Term, Downpayments—
Some Relationships

The discussion of housing costs [described] how the total and monthly costs of housing vary with changes in interest rates, length of the mortgage term, etc.

Table 2 shows that while the average cost of homes rose 52 percent in the 13 years from 1952 to 1965, the downpayment to the average buyer decreased by about $1,800 because FHA was insuring a larger percentage of the mortgage.

TABLE 2.—Average Home Costs and Downpayments

Year	Average cost of home	Down payment required (percentage)	Cash outlay for down- payment (rounded)
1952	$11,300	27.0	$3,100
1965	17,200	7.4	1,300

Monthly payments were reduced by extending the life of the mortgage from 20 to 35 years.

Rising interest rates tended to offset these reductions to the home buyers. They added to the initial cash outlay, insofar as points had to be paid to the lender to compensate for his acceptance of an FHA loan at a legally set interest rate below the market rate. Rising interest rates also added, of course, to monthly charges and to total interest charges.

Successful attempts to lower downpayments and monthly charges were thus accomplished through Government programs by saddling the buyer with more future debt and higher total interest payments. The interest payments were rationalized as (1) compensation to the lender for the owner's inability to make a 100 percent cash outlay for the house at the purchase time, or as (2) the owner's charge for the privilege of using the house on credit, while he is earning and saving to pay the full cost.

Conventional, FHA and VA Financing: How They Share the Mortgage Market

Conventional financing provided for 23 million, or 65 percent, of the 30.6 million new housing units built from 1946 through 1967. Mortgages insured by the Federal Housing Administration have financed 4.4 million new units, or approximately 15 percent of the total, since World War II, while Veterans' Administration guarantees have helped to provide nearly 2.9 million new housing units for veterans, or a little more than 9 percent of the total. The two together have assisted in the building of 7.3 million new housing units, or 24 percent of the total.

Government guarantees in one form or another, therefore, helped to stimulate nearly a quarter of the new housing units during the period of 1946 through 1967. The same three methods—

FHA, VA, and conventional financing—also operated in the purchase and the improvement of existing housing.

THE FEDERAL HOUSING ADMINISTRATION

Capsule Summary

In essence, the FHA has been a mortgage guarantee program.

The guarantee does not go to the home buyer. If he fails to
meet his payments, the FHA does not bail him out. He loses his
home. The guarantee is given to the lender, assuring him of repayment even if the borrower defaults.

FHA thus bolsters the lending institutions, permitting them to
make practically risk-free loans on new and old homes, and on
home repair work.

FHA helps home buyers indirectly; first, by encouraging lenders
to make mortgage loans; second, by helping to bring about lower
downpayments; and third, by inducing lower monthly payments.
These benefits to borrowers have been accomplished over the
years as FHA has insured or guaranteed an increasing portion of
the cost of the home and has applied this guarantee to mortgages
for which payments could be stretched out over an increasing
period of years.

FHA thus, also indirectly, supports the homebuilding industry
by providing a credit instrument that greatly expands housing
production and consumption.

The FHA pattern of benefits stems from (1) the depression era
from which it emerged; (2) the various changes over the years,
such as the congressional mandates, the housing desires of the
public, the suburbanization of the metropolis; and (3) the administrative policies within FHA itself.

The chief beneficiaries of FHA have been the middle-income
home buyers, the suburban areas of the cities, the well-to-do
insofar as they are among the lenders and builders, and a sparse
number of the poor and near-poor. . . .

A GENERAL APPRAISAL OF FHA

Within its limits, FHA has performed well. By insuring a large
portion of the appraised value, it greatly diminished the amount
of down payment required. Recourse to costly second mortgages in

this field was reduced. It made first mortgages more attractive and increased the amount of capital invested in them.

As the proportion of the appraised value which is insured has risen to well over 90 percent, the amount of the down payment has, of course, been correspondingly reduced. With risks reduced and payments lower, millions of young families have enjoyed homeownership at a much earlier age, and have been able to bring their children up in what we like to think of as the conventional American manner.

An increasing proportion of home purchase money was being financed on credit. Financial institutions in effect were possessing a larger share of the value of the house. Homeownership was expanded by letting the "owner" become more of a renter.

FHA has also been a vital factor in financing and promoting the exodus from the central cities and in helping to build up the suburbs. That is where the vast majority of FHA-insured homes have been built. The suburbs could not have expanded as they have during the postwar years without FHA. Superhighways constructed at Government expense have also opened up the areas outside the cities and supported the exodus of a large proportion of the white middle class.

By prescribing minimum standards of construction, including toilet and hot water facilities, and by discouraging the use of shoddy building materials, FHA has lessened the possibility that the new suburbs would soon turn into slums. At the same time, while it did not enthusiastically embrace new methods of construction and materials, it has been more receptive to them than have most of the building code writers and officials of the central cities. For example, FHA permitted Romex and plastic pipe when these new products were effectively forbidden by most codes. FHA actions in this respect have been beneficial.

Taking all factors into consideration, it is difficult to see how any institution could have served the emerging middle class more effectively than has the FHA and its counterpart, the Federal home loan bank systems. Most important, FHA helped to end the practice of letting the big final payment of principal come due at the end of the mortgage term, supplanting this with amortization of this amount over the life of the mortgage. It has brought consumer protection into the entire mortgage field, with conventional lenders following FHA's lead. For example, interest is only computed on the amounts actually owed. Many investors and lenders have been influenced by FHA to moderate their terms as regards interest, down payments, and length of mortgages. All of these steps have brought in more purchasers among the lower and middle sections of the middle class.

The Decline in the Relative Volume of FHA Insurance

Yet, despite its constructive services, it became apparent that FHA was becoming relatively less important.

During the 20 years from 1935 to 1954, FHA insured 3.76 million homes, or almost 23 percent of the 16.57 million that were built. The proportion dropped to 14 percent in 1957, but revived to 22.5 percent in 1958. By 1963, it had fallen to 14 percent, and remained below that proportion through 1967.

No one has given a fully satisfactory reason for this decline, but it was probably due to the fact that such lending institutions as savings and loan associations, savings banks, and insurance companies were being given more money to invest by depositors and were themselves moving more aggressively into the real estate field. Savings deposits in commercial banks were also rising rapidly. All these institutions were increasingly willing to make mortgage loans without being insured against loss. In this way, the borrower saved the yearly insurance premium of one-half percent a year of the outstanding value of the mortgage.

What FHA Has Not Done

The main weakness of FHA from a social point of view has not been in what it has done, but in what it has failed to do—in its relative neglect of the inner cities and of the poor, and especially Negro poor. Believing firmly that the poor were bad credit risks and that the presence of Negroes tended to lower real estate values, FHA has generally regarded loans to such groups as "economically unsound." Until recently, therefore, FHA benefits have been confined almost exclusively to the middle class, and primarily only to the middle section of the middle class. The poor and those on the fringes of poverty have been almost completely excluded. These and the lower middle class, together constituting the 40 percent of the population whose housing needs are greatest, received only 11 percent of FHA mortgages. [See Table 3.]

Redlining

This tendency to neglect the poor has been reinforced and partially extended by the FHA tendency to shun the central cities and concentrate on the suburbs. The experience of members of

TABLE 3.—Purchasers of FHA Homes in 1965, by Income Class

Income class	Income range	Percent of FHA mortgages
Poor and near poor	$4,000 and under	0.5
	4,000 to 5,000	2.9
Total		3.4
Lower middle class	$5,000 to $6,000	7.6
Middle and upper middle	$6,000 to $8,000	30.0
	$8,000 to $10,000	26.0
	$10,000 to $15,000	27.0
Total		83.0
Well to do	$15,000 and over	6.0

the Commission and others convinced us that up until the summer of 1967, FHA almost never insured mortgages on homes in slum districts, and did so very seldom in the "gray areas" which surrounded them. Even middle class residential districts in the central cities were suspect, since there was always the prospect that they, too, might turn as Negroes and poor whites continued to pour into the cities, and as middle and upper-middle income whites continued to move out.

The result was a general, even if unwritten, agreement between lending institutions and FHA that most of the areas inside the central cities did not have a favorable economic future, and that their property values were likely to decline. Each group blamed the other for the failure to help the cities. Apologists for FHA asked how could they be expected to insure mortgages if the lending institutions would not lend. The lending institutions asked how could they be expected to lend if the FHA would not insure the mortgages. Each passed the buck to the other.

A third set of institutions, the fire insurance companies, was drawn into the circle of mutual alibis, for there were certain sections of the cities, notably the Negro slums, where insurance companies would not insure against fires. The sad experience of the last 2 years of burnings may be seen by some as proving that this refusal had a solid basis. But the years of neglect of these districts by FHA, by lenders, by insurers, and often by local governments (especially in terms of low levels of community services and facilities), must be listed among the causes for the eventual urban conflagrations. Redlining by insurers weakened still further the ability of the slums to obtain loan capital with which to improve existing housing or to construct new units.

There was evidence of a tacit agreement among all groups—lending institutions, fire insurance companies, and FHA—to block off certain areas of cities within "red lines," and not to loan or insure within them. The net result, of course, was that the slums and the areas surrounding them went downhill farther and faster than before.

Segregated Housing

For many years FHA operated with the conventional racial prejudice characteristics of many middle class real estate men. The agency's original personnel was primarily recruited from this group in the 1930's. Until 1948, when restrictive covenants or written agreements not to sell to Negroes were declared unconstitutional by the Supreme Court, FHA actually encouraged its borrowers to give such guarantees and was a powerful enforcer of the covenants. The FHA definition of a sound neighborhood was a "homogeneous" one—one that was racially segregated.

FHA's segregation position cannot be defended by any current standard of what is right for the home, the neighborhood, the city, or the Nation (although it may be understood in the context of the Nation's overall backwardness in race matters at the time FHA policies were forged).

Yet the FHA had a strong case for its economic conservatism which, in all fairness, needs to be stated and understood. Defaults by homeowners on mortgage obligations prior to 1960 were, as we have seen, originally very low. By 1950, out of 2.5 million home mortgages, 15,300 had gone into what is known as termination default, the step just prior to foreclosure, and these losses were amply covered by the insurance reserve. In the next 10 years, up to 1960, 35,600 more went to default out of an additional 3 million insured mortgages. While the cumulative defaults had increased to a total of nearly 51,000, the number of total mortgages insured had also increased to about 5.6 million. The overall default rate had risen slightly to 0.9 percent, still relatively low. Financially, FHA remained in a very sound and solid position.

Meanwhile FHA was failing to reach lower income families, central city residents and Negroes. It had not, in fact, been designed especially to help these groups. Also, the suburban trend originally had not been clearly foreseen. FHA managers could, therefore, claim that they were following both the letter and the intent of the original 1934 act. As restrictive FHA policies were subjected to the pressure of increasing public and congressional criticism, the standard for some lending was changed from economic soundness to reasonable risk. As a result, FHA did relax its policies to some extent. It did not venture into the slums and gray areas of the central cities, but it did insure the mortgages of some of the weaker suburban subdivisions and of financially dubious individual homes in the suburbs. Unfortunately, the number of terminal defaults rose more rapidly than the number of insured mortgages.

By computing defaults as a percentage of the cumulative total of insured mortgages, FHA was able to show that the total record was still not alarming. But this understated the risks inherent in the new mortgages, since it included the full volume of the past mortgages which had been made to stable income elements. Thus, the cumulative default average rose from 0.9 percent in 1960 to 3.7 percent in 1967. But on the basis of the *rate* at which additional defaults occurred from year to year as compared with the increase in the number of insured mortgages, the increase was much more startling. It went from 2.16 percent in 1960 to 8.1 in 1965. These figures, of course, overstate the risk factor in new loans since a considerable, although unknown, proportion of defaults occurred on mortgages which had been previously insured. The truth about the relative safety of the new loans, therefore, lay somewhere between the cumulative average and the incremental. But by either standard, a great increase in risk showed up at the same time that the insurance criteria were being liberalized. . . .

A group of financially conservative Members of Congress, though unaware of the full extent of the losses, was frightened by the increased number of foreclosures. This group, therefore, demanded greater caution in insuring. On the other hand, congressional liberals, seeing the deterioration of the central cities, and also unaware of FHA losses, wanted FHA to take more chances and to help rebuild at least the gray fringes of the central cities. FHA was caught between two fires. It was damned if it did and damned if it didn't. . . .

Its new losses, however, were not really in the central cities. There was little insuring going on there. It was rather in the so-called inferior subdivisions in the suburbs, where the loans were going sour. After the Watts riots and again during the widespread riots of 1967, FHA was again accused of being too conservative, and once again those who felt FHA should have a social as well as a business purpose urged it to insure in the gray and slum areas of the inner cities. In the summer of 1967, the regional directors of FHA and important local representatives were summoned to Washington and told by the head of FHA that they should be more receptive to such mortgages and should look favorably on the various special assistance programs. There has not been time enough to determine how the new program is working out, but there seems to be evidence that FHA has, on the whole, tried to meet the criticisms leveled against it and to follow the instructions of its chief. Whatever its sins in the past, there is little one can criticize about its recent national leadership. Whether this will continue in the future is an open question. It depends on public opinion and on Congress. Certainly there remain deep pockets of resistance to liberalizing policies within regional and local staffs.

PUBLIC HOUSING AND GROUP PRESSURES

LEONARD FREEDMAN

Each of the innumerable stages in the making of decisions governing the public housing program provided a "point of access" for
a wide array of private and public housing groups. These groups
used the abundant opportunities the system offered to influence
the outcome significantly.

The extent of this influence was not as great as claimed by
some critics. Public policy, after all, is rarely the simple resultant
of group pressures. Legislators respond not only to special interests, but also to presidential leadership, party loyalties, other
legislators, their own consciences, and the tides of opinion in their
constituencies. Nonetheless, in the public housing case there was
an extraordinary amount of activity by interest groups. There is
no way to calculate precisely the impact of their pressure on the
decisions that were made. Yet, it is unlikely that public housing
would have suffered such severe punishment had it not been for
the sustained and furious attack on the program by national and
local organizations.

THE OPPOSITION GROUPS

National Groups

Both nationally and locally, opposition groups included most of
the trade associations directly and indirectly engaged in the building, selling, or financing of housing. At the national level, three
of these associations carried the major part of the campaign:

The National Association of Real Estate Boards (NAREB)
is a trade association of "realtors"—real estate brokers who are
accepted into membership on local real estate boards. When the

From Leonard Freedman, *Public Housing: The Politics of Housing*, pp.
58–91. Copyright © 1969 by Holt, Rinehart and Winston, Inc. Reprinted
by permission of Holt, Rinehart and Winston, Inc.

Taft-Ellender-Wagner program was enacted in 1949, the association included approximately 44,000 realtors in over 1100 real
estate boards in communities encompassing most of the nation's
urban areas. By the time the 1965 housing act was law, the membership was approaching 75,000 individuals in nearly 1500 local
boards. The association describes itself as "a trade and professional
organization, to improve the real estate business, to exchange
information, and, incidentally, to seek to protect the commodity
in which we deal, which is real property, and to make home ownership and the ownership of property both desirable and secure."[1]
The headquarters of NAREB is in Chicago, but the association
maintains a Washington office, which houses the Realtors' Washington Committee, the organization's legislative arm. Executive
vice-president of the association for thirty-two years until his re-
tirement in 1955 was Herbert U. Nelson, a well-known figure on
Capitol Hill for most of those years.

The National Association of Home Builders (NAHB) grew
out of one of the specialized institutes of NAREB—the Home
Builders Institute—and became an autonomous organization in
1943. In 1949 there were 16,500 member home-building companies, mostly small-scale operations typically constructing about
fifteen houses a year.[2] By 1965 membership had grown to 40,000,
close to 80 percent of the total number of house builders in the
country. During the period of the struggle against public housing,
the organization's executive vice-president was Frank W. Cortwright, whose offices were in the impressive Washington headquarters of the association.

The United States Savings and Loan League (USSLL) had
close to 3700 members in 1949, including most of the savings and
loan associations in every state in the country. The number had
reached 5000 by 1965. The primary business of the league is to
make long-term loans for the purchase and construction of homes,
originally for lower-income groups, but in recent years mainly for
those of middle and upper incomes. The league's headquarters is
in Chicago, and there is a Washington office. The chairman of
the executive committee for many years, Morton Bodfish, lived in
Chicago, but he was active and influential in Washington.

These three groups and their leaders—Nelson, Cortwright, and
Bodfish—were the major spokesmen for the opposition to public
housing in the decisive years after 1949. They were closely backed

by other powerful organizations. The United States Chamber of Commerce, with 2600 local chambers in 1949 (2900 in 1965), worked against public housing through its construction division. Then there were the Mortgage Bankers Association of America, the American Bankers Association, the National Apartment Owners Association, the Producers' Council, and a number of specialized associations of building-material manufacturers and subcontractors, including the National Association of Retail Lumber Dealers, the National Association of Lumber Manufacturers, the Associated General Contractors of America, and the Building Products Institute.[3]

Each week in Washington, twenty-three of the private housing organizations met for lunch as the "National Homes Foundation," for which NAREB provided the secretariat. The foundation did not constitute a close-knit general staff, and there were many issues on which the component organizations disagreed fundamentally. But during the period of greatest controversy over public housing, they were united in their dislike of the proposed program. It was, they declared, a threat by government to the well-being and integrity of the private industry that they represented.

Their efforts to counter this threat from the late 1940s through the mid-1950s were brilliantly executed. Most of the private housing groups had able and experienced representatives in Washington, professionals at their craft of lobbying. In their campaigns against public housing, they neglected none of the techniques described in many case studies of pressure-group operations.

Working in the approved tradition, they helped to write speeches for congressmen; provided them with searching questions to fire at administration officials;[4] and drafted bills and amendments, either at the request of a legislator or for submission to any one of several legislators known to agree with their policies.[5] They advised congressmen as to which legislative procedures would best obstruct public housing proposals.[6] They stood ready, as the lobbyist always does, to "give the facts" to congressional committees. While the entertainment they offered members of Congress was rarely on the lavish scale of an earlier and cruder era, they did discuss business with them over lunch and dinner. Sometimes handsomely paid speaking engagements were arranged for friendly legislators, and the private housing leaders sought ways to be of personal service to congressmen and their families.[7]

All of these tactics have been used at one time or another by every effective lobby in Washington. The private housing groups practiced them with at least as much skill as any other congerie of lobbyists. But there was another technique deployed by the housing groups more effectively than by almost anyone else: This was the application of grass-roots pressure from all around the country at strategic times and places in the Washington legislative process. The use of this device is a natural consequence of the fact that most of the power sources of the American national legislature are back home in the states and districts. The private housing organizations were especially well equipped to take advantage of this condition. Savings and loan leagues and units of the NAHB were widely distributed throughout the country and were frequently important forces in their communities. To an even greater extent, the NAREB had its roots in the local situation, for there was a real estate board in almost every sizeable community. It is not surprising that the Buchanan Committee's investigation of lobbying in 1950 should have found that "the National Association of Real Estate Boards . . . has systematized all means of direct contact between its members and legislators more completely than any other group appearing before this committee."[8] Perhaps the American Medical Association has an even greater advantage in this respect, since every member of Congress has his own doctor, and doctors are even more widely distributed (and have much greater prestige) than realtors. Nonetheless, during the struggle over public housing, NAREB developed a machinery for the application of local pressures on the national scene which no other organization could match. . . .

The Communities

As soon as the Taft-Ellender-Wagner Bill was passed, the Washington offices of several of the national housing associations sent appeals to their local units to mount campaigns against the implementation of public housing in the communities. The response in several cities was enthusiastic. Coalitions quickly formed, usually led by organizations affiliated with the national associations. The composition of the alliances varied from place to place (the lumber industry, for example, played a more prominent role in the Northwest than elsewhere), but in most cases the real estate board was very much involved; and often the local chamber of commerce played an active part.

The fact that these groups were related to national organizations was generally helpful to the opposition campaigns. NAHB and the USSLL supplied their members with packages of material providing arguments and techniques for attacking public housing.[9] The national offices also facilitated the flow of suggestions from city to city. The best of the locally prepared materials came from the Seattle Master Builders, who commissioned and made generally available a kit of materials giving a detailed description of their successful campaign, with copies of radio and TV spots, newspaper and billboard ads, and day-by-day news stories.

These processes brought a considerable measure of uniformity to the local campaigns. The same slogans appeared all over the country. Newspapers in various cities carried accounts of identical speeches made on the same day by local organization leaders.[10] Identical editorials on "socialized housing" appeared in Hearst newspapers in four of the cities where public housing was under attack.[11] In addition, staff members from the Washington offices showed up from time to time to lobby before city councils.

These various kinds of national intervention were pointed to by defenders of public housing as proof that the battles in the communities were merely part of a carefully planned and coordinated campaign that was controlled and directed from Washington, the local units of the associations acting without volition of their own. This assessment was not accurate. . . .

A number of community groups with no national affiliations were also involved in the battles against public housing. There were the owners, for example, of small rental properties (many of them dilapidated) which might be pulled down to make way for public housing or whose tenants might move into public housing. Thus, in Los Angeles "the dirty work in the fight was done by . . . the Small Property Owners League . . . which furnished the mass base which the other organizations lacked."[12] But there was an even broader mass base to be found in the associations of property owners who lived and worked in the vicinity of proposed housing projects. In Los Angeles, three such groups, two of them created for this purpose, engaged in a fierce attack on a projected public housing site close to their own neighborhoods.[13] In Chicago, about 200 neighborhood associations provided the bulk of the opposition, supported by the State Street Council, "a powerful group of merchants who were able to act in concert."[14] National leadership in the Chicago case was discounted by Meyerson and Banfield in their study of the controversy there: "Elaborate and ramified as it undoubtedly was, the national real estate lobby and its Chicago affiliates would have little direct influence in the struggle over sites in Chicago. . . . The organizations themselves would stay somewhat aloof from the struggle."[15]

Clearly, even had there been no national opposition to public housing, the program would have had its troubles in some communities. It was an element for change in residential areas; and whenever changes in the "character of the neighborhood" are proposed, the antipathies of local communities tend to be aroused.

Still, if it is necessary to refute the charge that the local campaigns were totally controlled from Washington, it does not follow that the story in the cities would have been much the same had there been no intervention from the national associations. Without that intervention, the local opposition might have been bitter, but it would have been spontaneous and sporadic. While it certainly would have prevented the selection of a number of specific sites, it might not have been sufficient to bring about the total rejection of the program in a number of major cities.

In fact, the combination of local initiative on the one hand and national guidance, encouragement, and coordination on the other, happened to be the most effective possible combination for the conduct of the local campaigns. Without the national involvement, local rejections of individual sites would have had only isolated significance. Without the locally based organizations the intensity and fury of the opposition could never have been provoked. Moreover, the financing of the campaigns was essentially local, for the national organizations did not command the resources to underwrite battles in so many communities. . . .

THE PRO–PUBLIC HOUSING GROUPS

In public policy disputes in America, the organized group pressures are never on one side only. The public housing issue was no exception. The program would never have existed in the first place but for the initiative provided by a combination of labor unions, local housing officials, and various religious, racial, ethnic, and political groups who formed themselves into the National Public Housing Conference. In 1934 the conference issued "A Housing Program for the United States," acclaimed as "the first long-range and carefully considered program to be formulated in the United

States."[16] It was this coalition that Senator Wagner relied on to do most of the work of drafting the public housing provisions of the 1937 housing act.

The component units of the coalition had grown considerably by the time they entered into the struggle over the Taft-Ellender-Wagner proposal. By 1949 there were well over 3000 members in the National Association of Housing Officials; by 1965 the organization, now the National Association of Housing and Redevelopment Officials (NAHRO), included 5000 individual members, working for 1000 local agencies. NAHRO's excellent monthly publication, the *Journal of Housing*, contains a great deal of information that has been invaluable over the years to the groups supporting public housing. Organizations of local government officials, such as the National League of Cities and the National Institute of Law Officers, expressed support for the program. Consistently fighting for public housing during its period of greatest duress was the United States Conference of Mayors. Social workers, organizing as the American Association of Social Workers and the National Federation of Settlements, were vocal supporters, too.

Labor was a prime mover in the coalition. Until their merger in 1955, both the AFL and the CIO had housing committees, the AFL's directed by Boris Shishkin since 1935, the CIO's by Leo Goodman. In addition, an assortment of organizations usually numbered among the backers of welfare legislation were included in the pro-public housing coalition. There were church groups, Protestant, Catholic, and Jewish; women's organizations, such as the American Association of University Women and the League of Women Voters; Negro organizations, including the NAACP and the National Urban League; veterans' groups, including the American Legion and the American Veterans of World War II, both of which were at first hostile to the plan but changed their minds in time to support the 1949 act; and various others, including the National Association of Parents and Teachers, the American Council on Human Rights, and the National Association of Consumers.

Providing coordination between the pro-public housing groups was the National Public Housing Conference (later the National Housing Conference), which worked for both the Wagner-Steagall and the Taft-Ellender-Wagner Acts. During the struggles of the 1940s and 1950s, the conference had an able leader in its vice-president, Lee F. Johnson, an experienced Washington hand.

While the housing conference included all the major organizations backing public housing, its membership and leadership were principally representative of officials of local housing authorities.[17] In addition, the Housing Legislative Information Service brought together informally about forty of the national organizations actively involved in the fight for public housing.

In the communities, too, large numbers of individuals and groups rallied to the defense of public housing, organizing themselves in coalitions under such titles as the Citizens League for Better Homes in Portland, the Citizens Housing Committee in Seattle, the Citizens Housing Council in Los Angeles, and the Citizens Committee for Slum Clearance in Miami.

By and large, these local coalitions paralleled closely the combinations of groups supporting the program in Washington. Labor waged a strong fight in Los Angeles, Seattle, and other communities. Usually there was representation from veterans' groups, church, women's, civic, and minority group organizations, and sometimes Democratic clubs. Local housing officials were inevitably participants in the defense of their programs. In most places their involvement could not be overt, and the degree to which they provided behind the scenes leadership varied from place to place. In Los Angeles, however, the Citizens Housing Council was actually nothing more than a "list of prominent names which had no budget or workers," a paper organization through which the city housing authority worked.[18] Other official backing came from the commissioners of the housing authorities, lay people charged with the responsibility of establishing policy for the projects and of representing the programs to the public and the local governmental structure.

It was part of the standard argument of the pro-public housing forces that the techniques used by the opposition, nationally and locally, were essentially undemocratic and manipulative. Yet, none of the tactics utilized by the opposition was neglected in the defense of the program. Lee Johnson and Leo Goodman sent repeated appeals to their constituent units in the NPHC and the CIO for masses of communications from the grass roots. They cultivated their personal contacts with congressmen, and maintained a careful surveillance of legislative developments.

In the cities the public housing forces did all they could to match the opposition's tactics in influencing city-council decisions. Employees of the housing authorities sometimes turned out in force at the hearings.[19] Labor unions encouraged their members to attend, reminding them that public housing meant jobs for unemployed plumbers and other craftsmen. Nor were distortions and oversimplifications limited to the opposition side in the referendum campaigns. In Los Angeles, the brochures and other materials used by public housing's supporters were redolent with half-truths and high-pitched language. In California, officials of the housing authorities who spearheaded the attack on Proposition 10, quickly decided that the truth could not be left to speak for itself, and they hired a leading advertising agency. In Seattle, the Citizens Committee, which conducted the defense of the program, did so without recourse to the skills of the professional publicist but with subsequent regret: "We should have developed a counter slogan," said the secretary of the committee, "or, in the alternative, we should have concentrated much earlier on the 'real estate lobby.' "[20]

PLURALISM?

Any examination of the forces engaged on both sides of a public policy issue must lead to a test of the two rival theories concerning the group process in American politics. On the one hand, it is postulated that, by and large, there is a reasonable balance of interest groups and that no one, or combination, of them dominates the rest.[21] Against this, it has been argued that American politics reflects the fact that ours is essentially a business society, and that organizations representing business interests tend to prevail in the struggle over public policy.[22]

Both sides in this controversy can find evidence for their positions in the public housing case, as will be demonstrated here. In the view of the present writer, however, the group balance theory ultimately provides a less satisfactory interpretation of this case than the opposite thesis.

The Group-Balance Thesis

It is clear that the public housing program was by no means a helpless, motionless prey, waiting to be devoured by marauding private housing interests. Impressive coalitions, representing vast memberships, worked vigorously on behalf of the program, fighting back with all of the methods employed by the opposition. Moreover, the forces aligned on the public housing side did not consist only of private organizations. The federal bureaucracy helped them substantially. During the congressional campaigns on behalf of the Taft-Ellender-Wagner Bill, counsel for the federal housing agencies were made available as advisors to the Senate and House Banking and Currency Committees and "their knowledge of the legal problems involved and their judgments as to desirable courses of action doubtless exercised strong influence on the course of the legislation."[23] And, of course, the White House worked vigorously for the cause from the New Deal period through 1952, and again from 1961. In the local communities, the housing officials were fighting for their own programs, sometimes for their very jobs. Additional help was quietly given in a number of places by the field offices of the federal housing agencies.

Nor was there monolithic unity among private business interests on the public housing question. Nationally, it was true that the major business organizations testified against the program. But this antipathy was not always matched in the communities, especially in the older cities of the East and Midwest, where the major business concerns have often displayed a sense of civic responsibility and a willingness to support programs designed to help low-income people and minority groups.

To a considerable extent, the business hostility to public housing was a regional phenomenon, mostly evidenced in cities of the West and Southwest which were growing at a phenomenal pace.[24] Consequently, they were communities in which the real estate, home building, and home finance interests were flourishing and politically aggressive. . . .

Further support for the group-balance thesis can be found in the final outcome of the public housing controversy. The program still exists and continues to grow. While it was totally rejected in several communities, it was approved in many others. In the biggest local conflicts of all—those in Chicago and Los Angeles—the result was a compromise. The Chicago settlement provided for the construction of 12,500 units. In Los Angeles, almost half of the original program was salvaged. In large measure this happened because, while the opposition gained control of some of the decision points, it was unable to establish its hold on all of them. No sooner had the anti-public housing forces gained control of the mayor's office than their power in the city council slipped away. Of the three vacancies on the council which were in serious contention in the 1953 election, the *Los Angeles Times* endorsement bore fruit in only one, while the other two victors were backed by labor and could be relied on to support the housing authority. The public housing struggle provides yet one more illustration of the lack of a single, concentrated power structure in Los Angeles.

At the national level, both sides continued in their intractability for several years. But slowly a more conciliatory spirit began to emerge. While the private housing groups still told congressional committees that they disliked public housing, after 1954 other aspects of housing legislation commanded more of their attention. Urban renewal, for example, entailed higher stakes and bigger issues for the housing industry. Furthermore, once public housing had been reduced to minor proportions and provided shelter for people displaced by other programs favored by private housing groups, it hardly could continue to be regarded as a major threat to private housing interests. So, the home builders and the savings and loan leagues and most of the other organizations that had been so militant in the early years grew increasingly mellow in their attitude toward public housing. Only NAREB maintained the appearance, at least, of unyielding and total hostility; but even they were devoting much less time to the issue by the end of the 1950s.

By the time of the hearings on the 1965 housing legislation, group opposition to public housing had dwindled still further. The United States Savings and Loan League was now opposed only "to any public housing program beyond the rate of 35,000 units per year."[25] While the National Association of Home Builders continued to argue that private builders could do a better job than the PHA, a NAHB spokesman declared in 1965 that public housing needed "a thorough overhaul of its financing and construction requirements. New and existing projects should be revamped to provide much more effective housing relief for the poor and destitute families in our land."[26] This was hardly the unyielding language of the Taft-Ellender-Wagner days. This was a call for reform, not abolition. The United States Chamber of Commerce continued to invoke its research findings against public housing.[27] Yet, in clarifying comments on his House testimony, a chamber director was anxious to emphasize that his "wasn't a sweeping condemnation . . . at all"; that the program simply "left work undone" which might be better done by other government programs; and that a public housing program comprising, as it did, about 1 percent of the total housing inventory of the nation was no cause for alarm.[28] The National Lumber and Building Material Dealers Association argued against further authorizations, but went on to concede: "We also realize that Congress saw fit to approve this years ago and that the program will undoubtedly continue."[29] NAREB still inveighed against public housing, but its 1965 testimony on the subject was cursory and lacked the old self-confident ring.[30]

Moreover, as the provisions of the 1965 act went into effect, and as they were supplemented by new administrative rulings from the PHA, some of public housing's traditional foes saw new business opportunities for themselves in the program. Home builders, realtors, and apartment owners in several cities began to work closely with the local housing authorities in developing these opportunities. Thus, the opposition's drift, first apparent in the mid-1950s, toward acceptance of a limited public housing program was strongly in evidence by the mid-1960s.

This movement toward a more conciliatory posture was matched on the other side among the proponents of public housing. To some extent, their declining zeal was the product of sheer exhaustion. The battle to establish the program had been debilitating. The effort to keep it alive in the face of years of hostility in Washington and of a series of rejections in the communities was bound to sap the vitality of the movement sooner or later. But along with depleted energies went an emerging disappointment with the program.

Among the most disappointed was Catherine Bauer, whose credentials as a supporter of the program were unimpeachable. She had been one of the key people in the establishment of the original public housing program during the New Deal. She served as the U.S. Housing Authority's director of research and information. She had been deeply involved in the program as a leading member of housing organizations, as a government consultant, and as a writer and teacher. But in 1957 she wrote an article entitled "The Dreary Deadlock of Public Housing." She suggested that the reason the program "drags along in a kind of limbo, continuously controversial, not dead but never more than half alive" was partly the obstructionism of the real estate lobby and "the neuroses that come from chronic fright and insecurity" inflicted on housing officials by the incessant attacks on their program.[31] But there were also, she contended, certain "inner weaknesses" in the program itself that rendered it incapable of ever accomplishing its purposes.

Catherine Bauer's criticisms were echoed by a number of other people who hitherto had been among the most vigorous spokesmen for public housing, including Charles Abrams, one of the great figures of the movement. Like Miss Bauer, Abrams recognized that much of the problem was attributable to the opposition:

> By the time you get through all of this [lobbying for laws, fighting court cases, and pushing to get funds] it is too hard to start things all over again with a program that makes common sense.[32]

Yet, the essential point in Abrams' argument was that, in the light of experience, public housing in its existing form no longer seemed to make common sense.

Many housing officials resented this public airing of dissatisfaction; but privately there was a growing readiness in the housing agencies to recognize the weaknesses identified by the liberal critics.[33] These weaknesses were serious, and they grew worse as time passed. Most important, however, they compelled the emergence of a new empirical spirit among the public housing forces. Ideas that previously had been regarded as anathema (many of them notions first introduced by the opposition groups as substitutes for public housing) were now seriously considered as ways of modifying or supplementing the public housing program. It was this new resiliency that led to the changes in legislation and administration under President Kennedy and to the fresh approaches built into the 1965 act.

This willingness to accept modifications on the public housing side, combined with the granting of recognition to the program by the private housing industry, transformed the climate of relationships between the public and private housing forces. In the past there was little contact between them in Washington. Today, there are matters of mutual concern to discuss, and staff members from the various organizations are known to meet on occasion in a spirit of amicability.

So, in this perspective, the public housing case is an exemplification of pluralism triumphant. At the outset there had been rival alliances which, in the view of one group of scholars, were "evenly balanced."[34] They confronted each other intransigently, with no common ground and with no desire to establish any. But with the passage of time, continued pressures from both sides, changes in Congress and administrations, at last it was made clear that neither side could achieve total victory. Once this was recognized, the way was clear for that process of conciliation, compromise, and—ultimately—consensus which is the special genius of American politics. The result of this process was the 1965 housing act. The provisions of the act were not, of course, completely satisfactory to either of the contending parties. Nonetheless, the legislation gave all of the organized interests some part of their original demands, and the final product was at least tolerable to each of them. Indeed, the 1965 act ought to be seen not merely as a safe midpoint between competing claims. The public housing program under the new legislation was recognized on all sides to be a better, more imaginative and flexible instrument than it had been before. If it was a smaller program than had been provided for in 1949, it had gained in quality what it had lost in quantity. It was a compromise settlement but compromise at its most constructive and most creative.

The Group-Imbalance Thesis

The evidence just presented convincingly refutes allegations that the public housing conflict was completely one-sided and that the enemies of public housing had everything their own way. Yet, it does not necessarily contradict the view that there is a general bias in the American political system in favor of business groups. In fact, it would appear to this author that the public housing case provides more support for the group-imbalance thesis than it does for the group-balance, or pluralist, theory. Though there were strong coalitions on both sides, this does not mean they were evenly matched. If the private housing interests had to accept a compromise, it can still be argued that they got very much the best of the bargain.

First, then, the pro-public housing groups suffered from some important disadvantages. Unquestionably, both nationally and locally they had less money and staff at their disposal than the opposition, although few precise figures are available. Lobbying reports reveal only part of the story. Financial statements of the organizations are not very revealing, for most of the groups engaged in the struggle are not single-purpose organizations, and their statements do not make clear which of the items reported might have some relation to the public housing campaigns. Nonetheless, as the available information is pieced together, it reveals greater expenditures against the program than for it.[35] The difference is not of the proportions claimed by the public housing forces, who used traditional liberal rhetoric in insisting that they were heroic but puny defenders of the public welfare against the ravages of massively staffed and monied special interests. In fact, the funds committed to the attack in Congress on public housing were not unlimited, and the opposition staffs seem to have been remarkably effective in creating the impression of far greater numbers of men than were actually deployed. Just the same, the opposition groups obviously had substantial sums committed to the struggle and did not suffer from the chronic shortage of funds that afflicted the National Housing Conference, which lived in a perpetual state of financial crisis and periodically sent out emergency appeals for money simply to enable it to survive. In the communities, too, the sheer scale of some of the opposition campaigns, especially in the very expensive context of the referendum, was everywhere greater than the efforts to defend the program.[36]

Another factor favoring the opposition was the greater internal cohesion of the various opposition groups. None of them, of course, was single-minded. There is invariably a gap between leaders and many of the followers. It has already been noted that some of the local units of the private housing associations did not follow the lead of their national officers; and within the local organizations there were individuals who either acted against the positions taken by the organizations or did not care very much one way or the other. Still, the private housing groups were relatively homogeneous, and their primary interest was housing. On the public housing side, this could be said only of the housing officials. For social workers and mayors and veterans, housing was but one of many issues they must be concerned with. Furthermore, in the mass-membership organizations declaring their support for the program, the claims of the leadership to speak for their members were often dubious in the extreme. Church social action groups tend to be far more liberal than the general congregation; and in the local battles, clergy and prominent church laymen were often openly hostile to the official stands of their ministerial associations on behalf of public housing. Voting patterns in the local referenda made it obvious that not all members of labor unions agreed with their national leaders on this issue.[37] So, while the list of organizations declaring for public housing was always much longer than the opposition list, both nationally and locally, this was an illusory asset.

To some extent, the support of public housing by the federal and local bureaucracy redressed the balance of forces. Yet even this was not quite as solid a factor as the public housing side would have wished. During the critical years of the 1950s, the housing officials responsible for the program in Washington were so harassed that they could hardly be an effective force for their program. Moreover, after 1953, their top leadership pursued policies which, if not hostile to public housing, were cautious and austere.

In the communities, the officials responsible for the operation of the projects suffered from other liabilities. In the smaller cities, many of the housing officials had come into their jobs without prior public service experience. Some, indeed, came from the private housing industry and lacked a full commitment to the purposes of those who had created the public housing program. In the larger communities, on the other hand, the housing authority tended to be staffed by people with backgrounds in public administration, social work, community planning, law, and engineering. This helped to give them an understanding of the goals of public housing, but it did not always provide them with the political experience that was so necessary when the program was under attack. The problem was especially complicated because the local housing authorities were not part of the regular governmental framework. Partly because of the fear of municipal corruption, partly because most cities were close to or had reached the limits of their borrowing powers, the housing authorities had been established as semiautonomous agencies, financed through their own bond issues. They were not subject to the direct control of the local mayors and councils, although the housing commissioners were appointed by the mayors. This could be useful on occasion; but it meant that the program was denied a natural power base in the community. In some places—Los Angeles, for example —the housing authority staffs refused to be inhibited by the peculiarity of their situation. But in Chicago, as Meyerson and Banfield show, the housing authority's political rootlessness and the emphasis by the staff on professional and technical considerations to the neglect of political factors were damaging to the program's prospects.[38]

Of course, the housing commissioners were supposed to provide the link between the staffs of the housing authorities and the political community. Yet, preponderantly they represented the established local interests. Almost half of the national total of housing commissioners in 1948 came from business, banking, and industry, with a substantial number from the private housing field. Only 15 percent were wage earners or labor officials. A mere

6 percent were public officials and civic leaders.[39] This is not to say that in general the commissioners did not support public housing. Indeed, some worked with dedication in its behalf.[40] Yet, when the heat was on, when an ostensibly nonpolitical program became the focus of intense political controversy, the kind of people appointed to the housing commissions could not always be expected to supply the staunch defense so urgently needed. To enter the lists vigorously on behalf of public housing might not only alienate them from lifelong friends, but might also have continuing adverse political, personal, and professional effects. Thus, confronted with the ferocity of the attacks, many of the housing commissioners were, in fact, intimidated and failed to undertake the necessary counterattack.

Nor does a favorable interpretation necessarily emerge from the fact that the public housing forces managed to prevent the dismantling of the program, and that the struggle actually produced some improvements in the program between 1949 and 1965.

For one thing, the quantitative price that had to be paid was very high. The 1949 program, which was to have been completed in six years, has not been fully carried out in twenty. Second, while the process of group conflict has produced improvements in the program, the fact that this could only be accomplished by such an abrasive and prolonged confrontation does not reflect well on representative government. Conflict is an inevitable concomitant of democratic politics. But it can be questioned whether the conflict need be as harsh and unremitting as it was in this case. . . .

Finally, and most important, the terms of the conflict were biased from the outset against the interests of those who were most affected by the problem—that is to say, the poor themselves, who were the only ones who could qualify as tenants in the projects.

NOTES

1. U.S. Congress, House of Representatives, Select Committee on Lobbying Activities, *Housing Lobby, Hearings Pursuant to H.Res.* 298, 81st Cong., 2d sess., 1950, Exhibit 349, p. 11; hereinafter referred to as: House, *Hearings, Housing Lobby.*
2. House, *Hearings, Housing Lobby*, p. 234.
3. See *Congressional Quarterly Almanac*, V (1949), 286: House, *Hearings, Housing Lobby*, pp. 181–183.

4. House, *Hearings, Housing Lobby*, p. 400, and Exhibit 306, p. 868.
5. U.S. Congress, House of Representatives, Select Committee on Lobbying Activities, *United States Savings and Loan League*, H.R. *Rept.* 3139, Pursuant to H. Res. 298, 81st Cong., 2d sess., 1950, Exhibit 82, p. 92. (Hereinafter referred to as: House, *H.R. Rept. 3139, United States Savings and Loan League*.) This is an interoffice memorandum by Morton Bodfish in which he says: "I wonder if Monroney has seen the lobbying amendments that we developed in connection with Dirksen?"
6. See memorandum "To Harry" [Cain] headed: "Suggested Procedure for Action by the Senate Banking and Currency Committee on *S. 1459* and H.R. *3492*," from the Realtors' Washington Committee, in House, *Hearings, Housing Lobby*, Exhibit 305-B, pp. 864–865.
7. House, *H.R. Rept. 3139, United States Savings and Loan League*, Exhibit 255, p. 213, and Exhibit 166, p. 150; House, *Hearings, Housing Lobby*, p. 54.
8. U.S. Congress, House of Representatives, *General Interim Report of the House Select Committee on Lobbying Activities*, H.R. *Rept.* 3138, 81st Cong., 2d sess., 1950, p. 24.
9. NAHB prepared a packaged kit called "Home Builders' Information Material to Oppose Socialized Public Housing," which contained a basic manual, various pieces of mimeographed information about the program, accounts of successful opposition campaigns around the country, and reprints of articles and congressional speeches, some made available from the Realtors' Washington Committee, which was also sending out large numbers of reprints. In 1950 the USSLL too, produced a substantial kit containing sample slogans, advertisements, editorials, news stories, speeches, pamphlets, and articles, as well as a detailed manual on "How to Prevent the Spread of Government Housing."
10. On April 1, 1951, the *Cincinnati Enquirer* and the *New Orleans Item* carried identical statements attacking public housing that were attributed to the president of the home builders association in each of those cities. Reprinted in "Home Builders' Information Material to Oppose Socialized Public Housing" kit.
11. "Hearst Papers Use Canned Editorial," *Journal of Housing*, IX, no. 1, (1952), 17.
12. Richard Norman Baisden, "Labor Unions in Los Angeles Politics," unpublished Ph.D. dissertation, Department of Political Science, University of Chicago, 1958, p. 308.
13. See Monterey Woods Improvement Association, *Rose Hills Report* (Los Angeles: Monterey Woods Improvement Association, 1953).
14. Martin Meyerson and Edward C. Banfield, *Politics, Planning, and the Public Interest* (New York: The Free Press, 1955), p. 116.
15. Meyerson and Banfield, *Politics, Planning, and the Public Interest*, p. 117.
16. Timothy L. McDonnell, *The Wagner Housing Act* (Chicago: Loyola University Press, 1957), pp. 80–81.
17. Twenty-three of the fifty-two members of the conference's legislative committee in 1948 to 1949 were public officials. (See House, *Hearings, Housing Lobby*, Exhibit N-2, pp. 1338–1339.)
18. Baisden, "Labor Unions in Los Angeles Politics," p. 369.
19. Monterey Woods Improvement Association, *Rose Hills Report*, p. 9.

20. Kenneth A. MacDonald, "Report on the Seattle Referendum Campaign," Seattle 1950, p. 11 (Mimeographed).

21. See John Fischer, "Unwritten Rules of American Politics," *Harper's Magazine* (November 1948), pp. 27–36; and Earl Latham, "The Group Basis of Politics: Notes for a Theory," *The American Political Science Review*, XLVI, no. 2 (1952), 376–397. See also David B. Truman, *The Governmental Process* (New York: Alfred A. Knopf, 1951).

22. Elmer Eric Schattschneider, *The Semi-Sovereign People* (New York: Holt, Rinehart and Winston, Inc., 1960).

23. Martin Meyerson, Barbara Terrett, and William L. C. Wheaton, *Housing, People, and Cities* (New York: McGraw-Hill, Inc., 1962), p. 277.

24. The trend in the 1950s was for cities to lose population to the surrounding suburban communities. But the big public housing defeats in Los Angeles, Houston, and Seattle (and later, in Dallas and San Antonio) occurred in cities whose populations increased substantially between 1950 and 1960.

25. U.S. Congress, Senate, Banking and Currency Subcommittee, *Housing Legislation of 1964, Hearings on S. 2468*, 88th Cong., 2d sess., 1964, p. 1165; hereinafter referred to as: Senate, *Hearings, Housing Legislation of 1964.*

26. U.S. Congress, House of Representatives, Banking and Currency Subcommittee, *Housing and Urban Development Act of 1965, Hearings on H.R. 5840 and Related Bills*, 89th Cong., 1st sess., 1965, Pt. I, p. 548; hereinafter referred to as: House, *Hearings, Housing and Urban Development Act of 1965.*

27. See *The Impact of Federal Urban Renewal and Public Housing Subsidies* (Washington, D.C.: Construction and Community Development Department, Chamber of Commerce of the United States, 1964).

28. House, *Hearings, Housing and Urban Development Act of 1965*, Pt. 2, pp. 1006–1007.

29. U.S. Congress, Senate, Banking and Currency Subcommittee, *Housing Legislation of 1965, Hearings on S. 1354*, 89th Cong., 1st sess., 1965, p. 518; hereinafter referred to as: Senate, *Hearings, Housing Legislation of 1965.*

30. Senate, *Hearings, Housing Legislation of 1965*, p. 608.

31. *Architectural Forum*, CVI, no. 5 (1957), 140.

32. *The Housing Yearbook, 1952* (Washington, D.C.: The National Housing Conference, 1952), pp. 10–11.

33. The nature of these weaknesses will be developed in the chapters which follow.

34. Meyerson, Terrett, and Wheaton, *Housing, People, and Cities*, p. 278.

35. From 1947 through 1950, $40,000 a year was allocated from the general budget of NAREB to the Realtors' Washington Committee, and an additional $90,000 a year came in from special contributions of $5 a member solicited through the local boards. The lobbying reports reveal that approximately $260,000 was spent in 1949 to influence legislation by NAREB, NAHB, USSLL, the Associated General Contractors of America, the Building Products Institute, the Producers' Council, the National Apartment Owners' Association, and the U.S. Chamber of Commerce. On the other side, the CIO and AFL housing committees and the National Housing Conference registered lobbying expenses of

over $112,000. These figures do not accurately reveal the scale of activity on both sides. On the one hand, all the organizations mentioned had concerns that went beyond public housing. On the other hand, a great deal of effort and money expended by both sides did not go into the records, including activities defined as "education" or "public relations" and the kind of grass-roots involvement, paid for by individuals, which was an especially strong feature of the realtors' campaigns.

36. In Los Angeles, the AFL alone spent $73,000 in the 1952 referendum campaign, mostly from the building trades workers. (See Baisden, "Labor Unions in Los Angeles Politics," p. 369.) But the scale of their opponents' campaign required resources very much larger than this. In Portland it was estimated that the proponents raised $8500, the opposition $15,000. (See Chester Rapkin, "Rent-Income Ratio—Should Formula for Public Housing Be Changed?" *Journal of Housing*, XIV, no. 1 [1957], 8.) The Seattle Citizens' Housing Committee could only raise about $6000. (See MacDonald, "Report on the Seattle Referendum Campaign," p. 3.)

37. Nor did all local unions follow the lead of their national organizations with enthusiasm. Even in Seattle, where labor was a mainstay of the defending alliance, the unions did not contribute much money, and some locals were uninvolved.

38. Meyerson and Banfield, *Politics, Planning, and the Public Interest*, pp. 260–267.

39. *Journal of Housing*, VI, no. 1 (1949), 9.

40. Thus, in New Jersey a pamphlet defending public housing against some proposed hostile legislation carried the note: "This brochure is published by the commissioners of local housing authorities in New Jersey, acting as citizens with a responsibility for answering misrepresentations and distortions" (New Jersey Association of Housing Authorities, *What's Wrong with the Hillery Bill?* [New Jersey Association of Housing Authorities, n.d.]).

THE STRUCTURE OF LAND USE CONTROL

NATIONAL COMMISSION ON URBAN PROBLEMS

Many of the most serious problems facing the Nation's cities are metropolitan in scope. Problems of air and water pollution, transportation, open space, solid waste disposal, housing, and employment do not end at municipal borders. At the same time, land-use controls, which are important factors in the creation and solution of such problems, are lodged in local governments with virtually no supervision by metropolitan or State agencies.

The constituency served by local officials making land-use decisions is quite different from that of the metropolitan area as a whole, whose concerns are affected by those decisions. It is hardly surprising that the interests and desires of one small jursidiction do not always conform to the needs of the larger area of which it is a part. It is understandable, for example, that local officials—and their constituents—may not want a regional waste disposal plant within their own borders. Indeed, many officials would prefer to have as little development as possible of any kind—to keep the community just as it is. The inevitability of regional development may be obvious; but, to local officials and their constituents, it may be equally obvious that much of it should be located somewhere else. Similarly, there may well be a recognition that low- and moderate-income families within the metropolitan area need to be housed somewhere; that they need to be housed within any given jurisdiction in the area is far less readily accepted.

The problem takes on momentous proportions when compounded by the reliance of local governments on the property tax as their major source of revenue. How land within their borders is used becomes not merely a question of esthetic and social sensitivity, it is a matter of governmental solvency. Land-use controls have become a major weapon in the battle for ratables.

From the National Commission on Urban Problems, *Building the American City* (Washington, D.C.: U.S. Government Printing Office, 1969), pp. 211–17.

The game of "fiscal zoning" requires the players—i.e., zoning jurisdictions—to attract uses which add more in property taxes or local sales taxes than they require in expensive public services and to exclude uses which do not pay their own way. In essence, this means that jurisdictions are influenced to seek industrial and commercial uses and luxury housing and discourage or prohibit such uses as housing for low- and moderate-income persons.[1] A further refinement is the desire to exclude housing which attracts families with many children in favor of housing with no children or as few as possible—all this because children require schools, the most significant expenditure item of local governments. Low-income housing is bad from a purely fiscal perspective because it does not add to the tax rolls the same amount of assessed value as luxury housing and because it often brings large families into a community. In addition, the families occupying such housing may require welfare and, it is widely believed, more of other services from the local government than higher income families require.

Of course, there are sometimes important nonfiscal policies behind certain types of exclusionary land-use decisions. "Undesirable" uses such as junkyards are not very attractive. "Undesirable" people—minority groups and the poor—would not "fit in." Indeed, for many suburban dwellers it was just such "undesirable" aspects of the city that drove them out; and for central city dwellers who have managed to find neighborhoods which satisfy them, it may well be the absence of such "undesirables" that keeps them in.

Attracting industry and commerce in competition with neighboring jurisdictions is not new. Many localities have developed it into a fine art, using such magnetic devices as the issuance of municipal bonds to help private companies finance land acquisition and plant construction. The land-use control contribution is overzoning for such uses, which is common practice, or adoption of a permissive policy with respect to requests for rezonings and special exceptions for such uses. The exclusionary side of fiscal zoning takes a variety of forms which are considered below.

LARGE-LOT ZONING

The most widely discussed form of exclusion is large-lot zoning, by which a jurisdiction attempts to limit development in substantial portions of its territory to single-family residences on very large lots. The actual effects of this practice are not easy to isolate.

Many factors determine the price which a particular lot will command in the market. In a weak market, large-lot zoning may make little difference, with a 4-acre tract selling for little more than a 2-acre tract, and both sizes providing sites for shacks. In a strong market, a change from a 4-acre minimum to a 2-acre minimum may not lower the price per lot since potential developers are concerned primarily with the number of units that can be built on a given tract and will bid up the price of the rezoned tract. Comparisons of different properties are difficult. A 2-acre lot may be more valuable than a 4-acre lot because of factors unrelated to size—location, topography, etc. Broad comparisons thus become extremely suspect. Nevertheless, it does appear that land prices per lot do diminish as minimum lot size is reduced, though usually not commensurately with the change in size. That is to say, a half-acre lot will cost less than a 1-acre lot, but will cost more than half the price.

Even where prices per lot do not differ markedly from zone to zone, it does appear that large-lot zoning can have significant effects on the cost of housing. *First*, extensive large-lot zoning in a given area has the effect of substantially reducing the total amount of housing that can be accommodated. If demand for new housing is strong, this restriction of the supply of housing sites will increase residential land costs generally. Moreover, by limiting the amount of land for housing on smaller lots and multi-family units below that which the market demands, the prices for these sites may be increased.

Second, the increase in the total house-and-lot price may be greater than the increase in land price caused by large-lot zoning. Some builders will simply not build the same house on a large lot that they will on a smaller lot, believing that a larger house is necessary. Furthermore, many builders observe a rule of thumb that the price of a lot should be some specified percentage of the total price of house and lot, e.g., 20 percent. If such a rule is strictly observed, a $1,000 increase in lot cost will result in a $5,000 increase in the price of the finished house and lot.

Third, large-lot zoning generally results in added costs for land improvements. Depending on specific requirements in the zoning ordinance regarding lot width, the effect can be to increase significantly the required linear feet of streets, sidewalks, gutters, sewers and water lines.

In some instances the fiscal objectives behind large-lot zoning are quite clear. In St. Louis County, for example, the Parkway

School District has calculated that any home costing less than $26,274 does not pay its own way in educational costs. On this basis, district officials oppose any change in zoning to permit lots of less than a quarter-acre, below which they believe housing costing less than this amount can be built.

But the motives for large-lot zoning are generally not clear-cut. Rather they are a mixture of fiscal and non-fiscal factors. Where a community does not wish to bear the cost of extending water and sewer lines beyond present development, it may limit new development to large lots so that it can be served by septic tanks and wells. Some communities think of large-lot zoning as a means of retarding development or preserving rural character or open space. And, in some instances, it is clearly viewed as a technique for keeping out "incompatible" people—lower-income groups and minorities.

Large-lot zoning is a common and widespread practice in many major metropolitan areas. Data are scarce, however, since few metropolitan planning agencies or other regional groups have attempted to make consolidated area zoning maps or compile data on the total zoning pattern in the area. A Commission survey shows that 25 percent of metropolitan area municipalities of 5,000-plus permit *no* single-family houses on lots of less than one-half acre. Of these same governments, 11 percent have some two-acre zoning; 20 percent have some one-to-two-acre zoning; 33 percent have some one-half-to-one-acre zoning; and more than 50 percent have some one-fourth-to-one-half-acres zoning. . . .

EXCLUSION OF MULTIPLE DWELLINGS

Perhaps an even more important form of exclusionary zoning is the limitation of residential development to single-family houses. Again, motives are undoubtedly mixed. Apartments are viewed by many suburban dwellers as central city structures, having no place in the "pastoral" setting of suburbia. Apartment dwellers are sometimes stereotyped as transients who, not having the permanent ties to the community which homeownership provides, will not be sufficiently concerned about the community or their own residences. But fiscal motives are also present. There is a concern that apartments—especially those which have large units and thereby can accommodate large families—will not pay their way. Where low- or moderate-income units are involved, both fiscal and social concerns increase.

Multifamily housing units generally provide the best opportunities for housing persons of low and moderate incomes. The rental nature of such housing, and the savings produced by spreading land costs over a greater number of units, place such housing within the means of many who could not afford new single-family houses. Furthermore, many of the publicly assisted housing programs are multifamily programs and depend on the existence of zoning for multifamily structures.

Most jurisdictions have some zoning for multifamily structures, and it appears that more suburban zoning jurisdictions are permitting them than in the past. A Commission survey shows that 87 percent of municipalities and New England-type townships of 5,000-plus have at least one district in which multifamily housing can be built. But the figure fails to reveal the way in which such zoning comes about. In many suburban jurisdictions zoning for multifamily housing occurs only through a piecemeal rezoning process. There is at any one time little undeveloped land available for multifamily construction. The price of land zoned for such purposes is thus inflated because of the uncertainty about the total amount of land that may become available. Of the undeveloped land zoned for residential purposes in the New York metropolitan area, for example, 99.2 percent is restricted to single-family dwellings.

Minimum House Size Requirements

The most blatant, though not most extensive, exclusionary practice takes the form of excluding housing which fails to contain a minimum floor area as set out in the zoning ordinance.[2] Such requirements raise the lower limits of construction costs, and thus can be the most direct and effective exclusionary tool. An extreme application of the technique is found in Bloomington, Minn., an affluent suburb of the Twin Cities. Bloomington imposes a 1,700-square-foot minimum floor area. At a square foot construction cost of $15.82, the average for FHA Section 203 housing in the Minneapolis area in 1966, the smallest house permitted would require $26,894.00 in construction costs alone.

Administrative Practice

Some of the most effective devices for exclusion are not discoverable from a reading of zoning and subdivision ordinances.

Where rezoning is, in effect, necessary for many projects or where apartment development requires a special exception (as it does in some suburban communities), officials have an opportunity to determine the intentions of each developer with some precision. How many bedrooms will the units in his apartment house contain? What will be the rent levels? To whom does he plan to rent or sell? "Unfavorable" answers in terms of the fiscal and social objectives of such officials do not necessarily mean that permission will be denied outright. They may, however, mean long delays, attempts to impose requirements concerning dedications of land and provision of facilities over and above those which are properly required under the subdivision ordinance, and the like.

One witness heard by the Commission in Philadelphia stated the problem this way:

> Regulations are frequently written so that each apartment developer has to negotiate with the community in order to get in at all. He negotiates either to get a zoning amendment because there is no permitted area zoned for apartments in the community, or he negotiates in order to get a special exception because the zoning ordinance does not permit apartments outright. In both cases the negotiation process is one of trying to bid up the price or cost of the apartment structure in order to limit the number of people who can come in at lower cost.
>
> A subdivision ordinance was used as a club in Abington against a veterans' cooperative which had intended to build about 250 free-standing houses which conformed with the zoning ordinance. This was in the late 1950's. I was a member. . . . It was an outright question of refusing to give the approval, and keeping the matter in the courts until the veterans' group broke up because they couldn't wait for housing.[3]

INSTITUTIONS FOR ENDING METROPOLITAN GOAL DISTORTION

Agencies for resolving the conflicts of regional and local goals do not exist in most metropolitan areas at the present time. The rapid growth of regional planning suggests a recognition by States and metropolitan areas that many problems do not lend themselves to purely local decisions. But the agencies which do such planning rarely have any implementation powers other than persuasion. Popularly elected regional bodies, which might undertake supervision of certain types of local decisions, do not exist; and the States themselves have thus far done little to assume responsibility in this area. The courts, then, are the only existing decision-making institution which might resolve some of these goal conflicts. But such resolution requires policy decisions of a type the judiciary usually declines to make.

Questions of exclusion, as distinguished from more technical planning aspects of the problems of localism, would seem to involve basic constitutional issues of the sort that courts decide. Where public action—land-use control—is used to exclude large numbers of persons from certain areas on the basis of economic status, size of family, or race, fundamental questions arise for a democratic society. Generally, however, the courts have refused to consider such questions in the context of land-use control cases. They continue to view such cases as largely matters of police power vs. private property rights, with no consideration of broader social implications or the rights of the non-parties—those that are excluded.

The reasons for these are complex. *First*, property law is among the most venerable branches of the common law, and traditional notions about how to approach cases involving such rights have shown considerable staying power. *Second*, the nature and importance of these issues has only recently begun to emerge. *Third*, the Supreme Court has refused to hear any zoning case since *Nectow v. City of Cambridge*,[4] decided 40 years ago. Lower courts, lacking the leadership to see these cases in a broader perspective, often refuse to venture forth. *Fourth*, courts are reluctant to consider the motivations of public officials in arriving at particular decisions. This becomes especially important in the case of administrative practices aimed at exclusion. *Fifth*, the factual information needed to show significance of exclusionary practices simply does not exist in most areas, and the cost to a private litigant of obtaining it would prove prohibitive. As noted earlier, most metropolitan areas do not have consolidated zoning maps, showing the cumulative pattern of local zoning ordinances. More important, they do not have housing and site inventories showing the location, cost and types of housing which presently exist in the area and the sites (along with their zoning designations) which exist for future residential development. The litigant who seeks to challenge the zoning of a particular tract as exclusionary may encounter the argument that he has failed to show the absence of land zoned for the kind of development he wants elsewhere in the jurisdiction or the metropolitan area. The result of all these factors is that even some of the most outrageous exclusionary practices go unchecked by any institution outside the local government itself.

Directions

The problems of metropolitan goal distortion can be attacked by dealing with causes or with symptoms. In the long run, there is little doubt that the causes themselves must be faced and eliminated. Such an approach requires the restructuring of local governments within metropolitan areas to make them responsible to a broader cross section of the urban population and to make effective coordination possible. Such units of government must be made fiscally sound, with less reliance on property taxes and with a greater assumption of expenses by the States, regional governments, and the Federal Government. So long as new development means increased fiscal woes, the incentive to exclude will remain.

The treatment of symptoms must begin immediately. Local governments cannot continue to disregard their responsibilities toward the metropolitan area. It is essential that some institution, other than the courts, be established to reconcile local conflicts and to assure that attempts to solve regional problems are not thwarted by the parochialism of individual jurisdictions within a metropolitan area.

NOTES

1. The implications of this for job opportunities are obvious. In Part I [of *Building the American City*] there is a description of the growing disparity between new job locations, and especially blue-collar jobs, and the surplus labor force. Fiscal zoning would appear to contribute significantly to the problem.
2. Such provisions are to be distinguished from minimum floor area requirements in housing codes. Housing codes provisions, applying both to new and existing housing, plainly purport to deal with minimum health and safety requirements and not with maintaining neighborhood character or property values. They are stated in terms of minimum floor area per occupant, and typically they are lower than the minimum requirements in zoning ordinances. The American Public Health Association model housing code, for example, requires that a dwelling unit have a minimum floor space (limited to habitable room areas) of 150 square feet for the first occupant and 100 square feet for each additional occupant.
3. Testimony of Mr. Morton Lustig, *Hearings Before the National Commission on Urban Problems*, Volume 4, p. 343.
4. 277 U.S. 183 (1928).

The Politics of Transportation

INTRODUCTION

The coordination of transportation objectives with other goals desired by groups living in the metropolis is the major transportation-policy issue. Historically, most transportation decisions, especially those involving road construction, have been based exclusively on projected consumer demand for a particular facility, and the impact of these decisions on other sought-after goals has not been taken into account.

Yet, transportation judgments do have numerous by-products. Most importantly, they vitally influence the way land will be put to use. A metropolis that emphasizes the use of roads is promoting the dispersal of its population, thereby encouraging a suburban pattern of living. The promotion of mass-transit facilities permits a more concentrated use of land, thereby aiding the development of the central city and its central business district. Recent conflicts have also highlighted the impact of transportation decisions on other seemingly unrelated goals. For example, groups have objected to the construction of roads and mass-transit facilities because these projects imperiled homes, neighborhoods, and historic quarters and threatened to destroy open land used for recreational purposes or to blight aesthetically pleasing landscapes.

Prior to World War II, most important transportation decisions involved mass transit. The subway, elevated train, commuter rail line, streetcar, and bus were the common means of movement. Use of the automobile, particularly for getting to work, was

132

fairly limited. The tremendous growth of suburbia was yet to take place. There was no federal financial aid nor, in most states, state funding for the construction of city streets and highways.

The post–World War II era (1945–60) witnessed the emergence of the automobile as the dominant mode of transportation in urban areas. It is estimated that, in most cities during this fifteen-year period, half of those who had previously used public transit facilities to get to work switched to the car. Present national estimates (which include nonurban areas) are that 18-million people use mass transit to get to their jobs, while another 50 million drive to work. Moreover, travel during nonrush hours is overwhelmingly by automobile.

The effect on mass transit of this loss of patronage has been financial deficits and deteriorating service. While the number of passengers has severely declined, expenses have risen because of inflation, higher labor costs, and government requirements that service be provided for the few customers during nonrush hours. As a result, most cities have had to establish public-transit authorities to "bail out" private operators. Commuter rail lines, undergoing similar financial difficulties, have obtained state subsidies and cut costs by reducing and discontinuing service. The financial straits of mass-transit companies have forced them to continue to use obsolete equipment that has made their rides more uncomfortable and dangerous, further discouraging potential users.

While these changes in transportation use were occurring, decisions determining the financing, construction, and operation of all forms of transportation were taking place in an uncoordinated fashion. Highway decisions involved participants on the federal, state, and local levels. The federal Bureau of Public Roads administered the interstate highway system. Under the provisions of the Federal Aid Highway Act of 1956, these roads were 90-per-cent federally financed, with 25 per cent of the total funds to be spent in urban areas. The Bureau of Public Roads was also responsible for state highways systems for which the federal government provided a 50-per-cent matching grant. Both programs were financed by payments by highway users, such as tolls and excise taxes on gasoline. State highway departments, which typically were autonomous of elected officials, played the major role in planning the routes of these highways![1] The localities were usually represented by their public works, traffic, or streets department.

All of these agencies shared common values and a common

frame of reference in making decisions concerning the use of the roads. They were automobile-oriented in their approach. If they perceived a demand for their product (roads), and if the potential consumers were willing to pay for the product (through various user charges), then they promoted its construction and usage. They did not take into account the impact of building the road upon any other desired values.[2] During this post–World War II era, most decisions concerning urban roadways were made within this closed system.

The arena for decisions on mass transit resembled the political system involving the highways, although it encompassed a somewhat wider range of participants. Transit facilities within cities increasingly came under the control of public authorities during the 1950's. Although these transit authorities, like other special districts of the same genre, were relatively independent of control from elected officials, the growing need for public subsidies enabled local governmental officials to exercise some influence on transit policy. Decisions concerning commuter lines were generally made by the private operator and the state public service or utility commission (which had to approve all reduction in service). Only New York State provided financial aid to commuter lines.

The outlook of these transit authorities and the commuter rail lines was also primarily consumer-oriented. They, like the highway department, made judgments on transit service based on projected use of facilities and estimated revenue. As a result, no attempt was made to coordinate the decisions of the highway and mass-transit policy-making agencies. While the consequences of decisions made by highway and mass-transit interests affected each other (for example, increased use of the roads worsened the financial outlook for mass-transit facilities), there were few, if any, instances where the different transportation interests made their decisions jointly.

It was not until the 1960's that groups unfavorably affected by this mode of transportation decision-making were able to bring about some changes. As the interstate highway system entered urban areas, opposition developed to the plans drawn up by the highway and road interests. Most of the opposition came from groups located in the central city, such as the downtown business community, residents of neighborhoods affected by the proposed plans, and professional groups concerned with the quality of life within the city. These groups succeeded, in 1962, in amending the

Federal Aid Highway Act to require that the federal government not fund highway programs that had not been coordinated with mass-transit plans and that had not evaluated all aspects of their impact upon urban areas. This amendment, however, did not begin to be seriously implemented until the latter part of the decade.[3] Since that date, federal aid, at times, has been withheld when highway agencies have not given due consideration to such values as maintaining stable neighborhoods, preserving recreational areas, and conserving historical districts.

The second development in this direction was the establishment of the Department of Transportation (DOT) in 1966. The bureau responsible for the federal highway program (the Bureau of Public Roads) was removed from the Department of Commerce and placed under the Federal Highway Administration in DOT, and the Urban Mass Transportation Administration was transferred to DOT from the Department of Housing and Urban Development. This potential for greater coordination among transportation interests on the federal level has been encouraged by the growing support for the use of monies from the Highway Trust Fund (the large sums of money raised by user charges for the interstate system) for mass-transit facilities in urban areas. DOT has joined with groups promoting a "balanced" transportation system within our cities to have these funds used for aiding the financially ailing public-transit systems. Although this fund has not yet been tapped, Congress passed legislation, in 1964 and 1970, authorizing some limited monies for urban mass-transit facilities.[4]

Despite the recent trends toward greater coordination in this policy area, urban transportation systems are, and will remain, unbalanced. For the past twenty-five years, the highways have been built while mass-transit facilities have languished. The highway coalition—composed of, among others, the automobile, oil, rubber, construction, asphalt, and limestone industries; car dealers and renters; bus lines; trucking concerns; and motel owners—has dominated this policy arena. Moreover, the construction of roads has created a whole new set of interests in suburbia—gas-station owners, store owners located in suburban shopping centers, homeowners, and land developers—who have major stakes in the continued and expanded use of the road. The growing forces for change—central-city interests and environmentalists—may achieve some incremental gains, but these groups cannot be expected to exert the influence necessary to redress the imbalances that have already developed from the heavily road-oriented policies of the past.

These past policies have many defenders who have generally argued that they reflect the preferences of most Americans for the automobile as their desired mode of transportation. However, when public expenditures (at the federal level) have been nearly sixty times greater for road-building than mass transit and when private investment in mass transit facilities has been almost nil, has the American consumer been confronted with a *real* choice between these two modes of transportation? Almost invariably, he has found that the newly built highways have made it faster, pleasanter, and more economical to drive to work than to travel by public transportation. The road builders have, in effect, created their own market while the operators of mass transit facilities, for a variety of reasons, have failed to offer effective competition.

The readings that follow are intended to illustrate the ways in which our three problem areas helped promote the primacy of the highway and road interests. Frank Colcord describes the functional fragmentation within our metropolitan transportation systems, and the separate decisional arenas around highways, commuter railroads, and local mass transit that have enabled road interests usually to impose their narrow perspective in this policy area. Jameson W. Doig describes how metropolitan fragmentation in the New York City area limited the ability of commuter rail interests to obtain the funding needed for a balanced transportation system because no set of institutions with a metropolitan-wide orientation had sufficient influence to oppose effectively the unified road coalition.

NOTES

1. Robert Friedman, "State Politics and Highways," in Herbert Jacob and Kenneth Vines (eds.), *Politics in the American States* (Boston: Little, Brown, 1965), pp. 411–18.
2. Wilfred Owen, *The Metropolitan Transportation Problem* (Garden City, New York: Doubleday, 1966), ch. 8.
3. Thomas A. Morehouse, "The 1962 Highway Act: A Study in Artful Interpretation," *Journal of the American Institute of Planners* (May, 1969), pp. 160–68.
4. The Urban Mass Transportation Act of 1964 authorized $150 million annually in matching grants for urban transit. The 1970 legislation authorized an average of approximately $600 million annually for mass transit. Despite these two pieces of legislation, the monies available from the federal government for mass transit are miniscule compared to federal

funding of highways. From 1947 through 1970, the federal government spent $58 billion for highways and only $790 million for urban mass transit. See William V. Shannon, "The Untrustworthy Highway Fund," *New York Times Magazine* (October 15, 1972), p. 122.

BIBLIOGRAPHY

COLCORD, FRANK C., JR. "Decision-Making and Transportation Policy: A Comparative Analysis." *The Southwestern Social Science Quarterly* XLVIII (December, 1967), pp. 383–97.

DOIG, JAMESON W. *Metropolitan Transportation Politics in the New York Region.* New York: Columbia University Press, 1966.

FRIEDMAN, ROBERT S. "State Politics and Highways." In *Politics in the American States,* edited by HERBERT JACOB and KENNETH VINES. Boston: Little, Brown, 1965.

LUPO, ALAN, *et al. Rites of Way: The Politics of Transportation in Boston and the U.S. City.* Boston: Little, Brown, 1971.

MOREHOUSE, THOMAS A. "The 1962 Highway Act: A Study in Artful Interpretation." *Journal of the American Institute of Planners* (May, 1969), pp. 160–68.

OWEN, WILFRED. *The Metropolitan Transportation Problem.* Garden City, New York: Doubleday, 1966.

SHANNON, WILLIAM V. "The Untrustworthy Highway Fund." *New York Times Magazine* (October 15, 1972), p. 31.

TRANSPORTATION DECISIONMAKING
IN U.S. URBAN AREAS

ALAN LUPO, FRANK COLCORD,
AND EDMUND P. FOWLER

The story of Boston's problems with transportation planning dramatically illustrates several points. The first is that the planning and construction of transportation facilities are far more than an engineer's technical problems: it presents important political decisions that affect, directly and indirectly, the lives of millions of people, both users and persons impacted upon by the construction. In fact, those impacted upon by construction are often far more deeply influenced than the users. All decisions must be approved, or at least accepted, by political leaders. Almost all major transportation decisions are the direct responsibility of government, although a few still remain the prerogative of privately owned firms, such as railroads, business, and airlines.

The second key point is that although transportation decisions are unquestionably political, there is strong doubt that the political process has been working well to make them. A perfectly functioning democratic system should be open to the inputs of all significant groups and individuals in the affected communities; it should provide for open debate of all policy alternatives and reach decisions in an open and credible manner, so that those who "lose" know why and know that their views have been heard as well as considered. And, in such a perfect democracy, those responsible for making decisions should be obliged to confront their constituencies from time to time through the election process.

Transportation is not alone in failing to live up to these high ideals—our system, like all others, is imperfect—but this policy area is peculiarly vulnerable to the charge of consistently giving certain groups greater opportunity than others to influence decisionmaking. . . .

From Alan Lupo, Frank Colcord, and Edmund P. Fowler, *Rites of Way: The Politics of Transportation*, pp. 171–87. Reprinted by permission of Little, Brown and Co. Copyright © 1971 by Little, Brown and Company (Inc.).

Most of the material on which the following chapters are based comes from over five hundred interviews conducted in seven metropolitan areas as well as from secondary sources relating to these cities and others. Besides Boston, the cities are Baltimore, St. Louis, Kansas City, Houston, San Francisco, and Seattle. Additional information from Los Angeles, America's automobile city par excellence, was introduced from a separate research project. These eight cities represent a sample of over one-third of the twenty-one independent urban areas of the United States with a population over the one million mark. The one million cut-off point, although quite arbitrary, was selected because cities with smaller populations are not likely to be seriously considering rapid transit, a matter that generates ample controversy, as an alternative to freeways. . . .

To understand the policies and programs relating to urban transportation in the United States, it is necessary to know how decisions are made. This extraordinarily complex process involves all levels of government and many private institutions as well.

Urban transportation, by definition, refers to movement within the metropolitan area, not between major urban centers. It includes automobiles, trucks, taxis, buses, streetcars, subways, rapid transit lines, and commuter railroads, as well as ferry boats, hydrofoils, monorails, helicopters, and other more modern devices. Of the major kinds, buses, streetcars, and rapid transit lines (for example, subways) are all encompassed by the term "transit"; "rapid transit" is a more restricted term, meaning public transit with its own right-of-way.* While typically it is on rails (below, on, or above ground), rapid transit could include buses on exclusive highway lanes, a much talked of but still rare phenomenon, and even "air-cushion vehicles."[1] All forms of transit, plus the commuter railroads, fall within the general term "public transportation," as opposed to "private transportation," which refers primarily to the automobile.

In the United States, only six cities currently have any significant form of public transportation besides buses. New York, Chicago, Philadelphia, and Boston all have rapid transit and commuter railroads. Cleveland has rapid transit, and San Francisco

---

* "Transit" is defined as a system of urban public transportation (either publicly or privately owned) for passengers; however, the term does not ordinarily apply to commuter railroads. The distinction is arbitrary, but this is the common usage. The basis of the distinction is in the type of car used and in the closeness of stations: train cars are typically larger and more comfortable than subway cars, and subway stations are typically closer together than train stations.

has one commuter rail line in operation. And although the first
four have fairly complete rail systems, even these leave many outlying communities unserved. Both Washington, D.C., and San
Francisco have approved and are now building rapid transit
systems.

✦ Deteriorating service, steadily dropping patronage, and fiscal
crisis have been the near universals of public transportation since
World War II. Transit now primarily serves the ever decreasing
percentage of the total number of commuters who travel during
rush hour to and from the core city. Otherwise, during the rest of
the day and on the weekends the systems are severely underutilized but must operate to serve the few who need them. With few
exceptions, the larger U.S. urban areas are now served by public
transit authorities, which had to be established to "bail out" the
private carriers. As of 1967, fifteen of the principal transit organizations in the twenty-one metropolitan areas of over one million
were publicly owned. The responsibilities of these agencies, their
organizational structures, and sources of political control vary
considerably. Some, like those in Boston and St. Louis, have
regional jurisdictions, full operating responsibilities, and are basically state agencies run by a board appointed by the governors. In
New York City, Chicago, and Los Angeles, they are subregional.
Some are directed by locally appointed officials, as in Seattle, or
are county agencies, as in Pittsburgh. A few public transit agencies have only planning and regulating but not operating duties,
as in Baltimore and Seattle.[2]

With a few exceptions, these organizational differences are
not very significant. Regardless of whether transit is run by a
state, region, or city, costs ordinarily are the responsibility of the
local community. Only three states—New York, Pennsylvania, and
Massachusetts—provide significant financial support for urban
transit systems.[3] Elsewhere, subsidies—where they are authorized
at all—are provided by the municipalities served.

Only a few states have a statewide administrative agency responsible for public transit; the best developed of these are the
departments of transportation of New York and New Jersey. A
number of other states (for example, California and Wisconsin)
have established agencies with that name, but they do not have
responsibility for transit. Thus with few exceptions, governors of
urban states do not have any regular means of receiving advice
on total urban transportation problems or on transit in particular.[4]

At the local level, transit authorities have advantages and disadvantages common to other autonomous regional authorities.[5]

They are generally freed of traditional civil service, purchasing, and contracting restrictions, so they can operate more like a "private business." They are also freed of meaningful political control. At best, these transit authorities are strong, effective fighters for the transit-riding public. At worst, they become so oriented toward their own internal objectives (economy, labor relations, budget) that they tend to be unresponsive to other community objectives that may impinge on theirs. And, even more serious, they may be obliged to accept unqualified political appointees in order to achieve their objectives in the political decisionmaking bodies.

The transit authorities studied in this research covered the whole spectrum of problems. Boston's had almost all the above-mentioned ailments. Its top management in recent years has been of high quality, but competence beneath that level has been low. It is expansionist-minded but tends neither to work well with other planning bodies nor with the cities it serves.[6] Baltimore's transit authority was so lacking in vision that it was replaced after only a few years of existence, its planning powers effectively transferred to the Regional Planning Council. San Francisco's efficient regional transit agency is narrowly self-protective and has a history of difficulties in its local working relationships. The city transit agencies of San Francisco and Seattle are frequently criticized for a lack of imagination. The transit authorities of St. Louis and Kansas City are too new to have developed a clear-cut style.

The restriction on the powers of these agencies needs reemphasis. The lack of authority to raise needed funds for expansion and improvements tends to make them cautious in outlook. Politicians and the public often seem to expect them to perform the impossible, to operate cheaper and better service within an ever tightening revenue situation. The cities, which in many instances have provided some subsidies for transit, have been experiencing severe financial problems of their own and can ill afford to support public transit at adequate levels. The states view the transit problem as a local one.

The picture has been brighter since 1964, when Congress approved the Urban Mass Transportation Act.[7] Since that time, limited federal aid has been available for capital improvements by urban transit operations, with the federal government providing up to two-thirds of the cost of such projects. While this has stimulated significant local improvements in some cities, funds have been so limited that they have not altered the generally depressing picture. Under the 1964 act, $150 million was authorized to be appropriated annually for the grants program; this was increased to $190 million in fiscal year 1970. A maximum of 12.5 percent of the total was allowed to any one state, although the Secretary of Transportation was authorized discretionary funds of $12.5 million, which he could use to exceed this state limitation. Considering the enormous estimated costs of modernizing and expanding the existing rapid transit systems (for example, over $1 billion for Boston's "master plan," over $1 billion for New York City's current projects) and the vast expenditures needed to create new ones such as those proposed for Los Angeles ($2.5 billion), clearly these amounts could hardly make a dent in the problem.

It appears that in the 1970's federal financial assistance for transit will be vastly larger. On September 29, 1970, the House of Representatives passed H.R. 18185, Urban Mass Transportation Assistance Act, which had already been approved by the Senate. This act provides for long-term five-year financing commitments to a total of $3.1 billion. This is about four times the previous level and thus substantially brightens the future picture for transit.

The transit authority, with its limited powers, can be pictured as being literally "in the middle," receiving frequently unanswerable pressures and at the same time being relatively immune from political retaliation by its opponents. It can meet these demands only through the receipt of local, state, or federal financial assistance. Demands are local, (mostly from municipal politicians, the public, and downtown businessmen), but the local jurisdiction is least capable of meeting requests for subsidy. Demands for subsidies have fallen on deaf ears in most state legislatures because the bulk of the state's population would receive no visible benefits. Given these circumstances, federal assistance is clearly the most attractive answer. And, since so many transit systems are now feeling the financial pinch, support for more extensive federal aid has now been sufficient to achieve victory in the Congress.

Transit controversies generally emerge from rapid transit plans proposing large expenditures of local funds. Pressures for such plans usually come from civic, political, and business groups associated with the central city. In the past decade major political campaigns for new rapid transit systems have been waged in the San Francisco. Washington, Atlanta, Los Angeles, and Seattle areas to invest hundreds of millions in local funds in new rapid transit lines, but only in the first two areas were the campaigns successful. Greater success has marked efforts to extend and improve the five existing rapid transit systems, but in all cases only after extensive and prolonged debates over financing. And in no case has financing been sufficient to meet the needs of a modernized, full-scale system. Opposition to new transit investments comes from poorly served neighborhoods and voters who do not expect to make much use of the facilities.

The plight of the rail commuter is a familiar story. With the exception of two lines in Chicago, no commuter railroad in the United States admits to anything but loss on commuter service. The reasons are similar to those for transit: rising cost, declining patronage, continuing decentralization and dispersion of the city. The response of most railroads has been to cut costs at every opportunity and to plead with regulatory bodies to grant reduction or discontinuance of passenger service.[8] In only one case, the Long Island Railroad, which is the only rail line in the United States almost totally dependent on commuter fares, has the problem of commuter service resulted in the same policy response as in transit, namely public ownership. The Long Island was taken over in 1965 by the Mertopolitan Commuter Transportation Authority.

The states have been more responsive to the rail commuter than to the transit rider, but few visible improvements have yet resulted from their subsidy programs. In the early 1950's, New York state acted to stabilize and improve the financial condition of the Long Island Railroad.[9] New Jersey accepted a similar responsibility in 1961 with respect to lines running to Manhattan,[10] as did Pennsylvania in the late 1950's for the Philadelphia lines. In the early 1960's, Massachusetts and Connecticut began providing subsidies for commuter service on the New Haven Railroad, and Massachusetts began aiding the Boston and Maine line. Neither Illinois nor California has resorted to subsidy for commuter railroads. In Illinois most of the lines are operating profitably.

Decisions affecting rail commutation have become a combination of state and private responsibility. As with transit, few states have any real staff capability in this field. The governor, unless aided by a railroad "expert," and the legislature are largely dependent for knowledge on the state public service or utility commission. With the exception of the two Chicago lines and the Long Island, railroads have little interest in working with public officials to improve commuter services.

Controversies over commuter services are similar to rapid

transit disputes in that they usually concern public financial aid. A second and related type of dispute concerns the discontinuance or reduction of service. Major differences from transit disputes are that first, the train operators' primary objective is to phase out rather than to enlarge or improve their operations; second, most of the pressure for subsidy comes from the suburbs; and third, pressure is directed at the state rather than at local governments.

The last and largest of the urban transportation programs is the highway program, whose key decisionmaking body is the state highway agency commonly known as the highway department or department of public works, the latter usually encompassing other construction programs. In most states, the highway program is headed by a commission, the members of which have long overlapping terms to keep them immune from "politics." In two states (Michigan and Mississippi) the desire for independence of the program has led to the practice of direct election of the highway commissioner(s). In other states recent reform for "efficiency" reasons has led to giving the governor appointive and removal power of a director, thus placing the program under the governor's control. Illinois and Pennsylvania are examples of this. Of the six states included in this study, all now have commissions, but in Maryland and Massachusetts, departments of transportation with multi-modal responsibilities have been approved to replace the more limited agencies. . . .

State highway agencies have tended to be a power unto themselves. In most instances, they are clearly responsible neither to the governor nor to the communities through which they build highways. This situation is beginning to change in some states.

The power of the cities and counties to influence highway decisions varies greatly, and the means of asserting that power also differs from place to place. In a few states—for example, California—every municipality has an effective veto over highway plans. Prior to final approval of a design, the California Division of Highways must negotiate a "freeway agreement" with the local authorities on the closing of streets affected by the new facility. If the city objects to the design or to the highway itself, it may refuse to sign the agreement. The San Francisco Board of Supervisors used this power to effectuate their famous "freeway revolt," which ended all highway construction in most sections of the city in 1959. Several similar cases have occurred or are being threatened in the Los Angeles area. In addition to this veto power, California cities may introduce legislation to delete an objectionable piece of planned highway from the state system established by law in 1959 and force discontinuation of studies by the state Division of Highways.

The city of Baltimore has a different kind of veto power. Because it occupies the unique position in Maryland of being a city and a county, Baltimore was long ago granted full control over a portion of the state's gasoline and auto excise tax revenue and full authority to build its own highways. In 1966 this was modified somewhat by an agreement to have the state assume responsibility for the interstate system, but the city retains its veto power through the requirement that it approve all condemnations of property to be taken in the path of the highway. . . .

Except for unusual cases like California cities and Baltimore, which receive large allocations from the state gas tax, the cities covered by this study are not responsible for the construction of major highways. The city's role has generally been limited to working with the state highway engineers in developing the master plan and working out adjustments and traffic patterns required by new freeways.

The natural local agencies to handle these negotiations have been the cities' streets (or public works or engineer's) departments and the traffic departments, if they are separate organizations. These agencies are staffed by the same kinds of people as those in the state agency, with the same viewpoints and jargon. They understand each other. In some cities with powerful planning agencies, they also play a significant role, but this is the exception rather than the rule. An example is Kansas City, where good city planning has been a tradition since early in this century. In Houston also city planners have had an important input. In smaller satellite or suburban cities, city planning agencies are as a rule insufficiently staffed to have a significant role.

Unless a major controversy develops over a new highway, local political officials have generally stayed out of highway planning except to give perfunctory formal approval. Where controversy does erupt, a number of city agencies may become involved, as well as the mayor and city council. The controversies, almost always the result of a highway's damaging something of high value in the community, are sometimes stimulated by one or another of these agencies or political leaders. When a controversy between the local public works director and other local agencies arises, the political leadership has little choice but to intervene and resolve the issue or ignore it and let it remain unresolved. If the municipality has no formal power over the road and lacks other informal political means of influencing the decision, the politicians may prefer to pretend the problem doesn't exist, at the risk of losing the support of the opponents. When this happens, of course, the highway planners "win," and the politician must explain his lack of authority. If formal power resides in the city, failure to settle a dispute is tantamount to a defeat for the highway planners, since they cannot proceed.

Urban highway systems are by definition metropolitan programs. So one might reasonably ask what role metropolitan planning agencies play in highway planning. The 1960's was the decade for the establishment of such agencies in large American urban centers. Unquestionably, highways are a major factor, perhaps *the* major factor, in determining the specific directions of metropolitan development. Although one might assume a major decisionmaking role for these metropolitan planning agencies, this has not been the case.

The eight urban areas studied established these agencies during the 1960's. In San Francisco, Seattle, St. Louis, and Los Angeles, they were created by previously established metropolitan councils of government.[11] In Boston, Baltimore, Kansas City, and Houston they were established by state statute as planning bodies.[12] All are governed by boards of elected officials or their designees, although two (in Boston and Baltimore) have some state representation on the governing body as well. Without exception, these metropolitan planning agencies are staffed with competent personnel. None has more than thirty professionals and some have fewer than ten. The agencies of Seattle, Baltimore, Kansas City, and Houston, the four smallest of the eight areas, appear to be the strongest.

The reasons for the relatively insignificant roles played by these bodies are several. They are weak politically because they lack any direct relationship to an existing government, in contrast to the state highway departments. They are relatively new and small, seeking to find an appropriate and useful niche, and reluctant to get involved in major controversies. Their only weapon has been often ineffective "sweet reason." These agencies came onto the scene only after the plans on which most current highway programs are based were developed. They do participate with varying effectiveness in long-range transportation planning and particularly in transit planning.

The final and, in many respects, most important participant in urban highway programs is the federal government. The responsible agency is the Bureau of Public Roads, now lodged under the Federal Highway Administration, an agency of the Department of Transportation, established in 1966. Formerly a part of the Department of Commerce, the Bureau of Public Roads was moved to the new DOT as part of the national effort to place all major federal transportation programs under one roof. Also in this Department are the Urban Mass Transportation Administration (shifted from the Department of Housing and Urban Development to DOT in 1968), the Federal Aviation Administration, and a number of smaller units.

The federal government's interest in highways has a long history. As early as 1916, when the first Federal Aid Road Act was passed, there has been federal financial assistance to the states for highway construction. The original objective was to ensure that the states coordinate their highway planning, so that the roads would meet at state borders. The program was continued and enlarged through the years, but not until 1944 were urban areas specifically included in federal aid programs.[13] In most states the cities were expected to finance their own highways without benefit of state aid, and some still do. Both state and federal programs were thus completely rurally oriented.

The federal aid program for cities did not become important until after the passage of the Federal Aid Highway Act of 1956, which provided 90 percent federal financing.[14] That act specified that 25 percent of the total funds would be spent in urban areas, the places experiencing the most severe traffic problems. The Clay Report, which recommended this program, dwelt at some length on the need for vast expenditures for urban and suburban roads.[15] It also assumed the superiority of suburban versus urban living and argued that the new freeway program would encourage the decentralization of American cities. It has had that effect and is approved or deplored depending upon one's viewpoint and interest.

Federal aid highways fall into several categories, the most expensive of which are the interstate roads. Federal aid to the extent of 50 percent matching grants is also extended to states for what have become secondary highways. Both programs are financed from excise taxes on gasoline and other automobile-related purchases. The interstate funds are also available for studies of highway needs, relevant research and development, and for traffic control programs. They are not intended for maintenance and construction of city streets, although limited funds for aid to cities to improve the capacity of local streets are now provided under a new program called TOPICS (Traffic Operations to Improve Capacity and Safety). Costs incident to relocation have been increasingly recognized as appropriate charges to the higway fund, and they have become more generous over the years.

Until recently, federal control over the operations of federally aided state highway programs was minimal. The Bureau of Public Roads has maintained a district office in each state capital and generally worked rather closely with the state highway agencies. Routes and designs were ordinarily accepted without much question after approval at the state level. Controversies began to develop as early as the late 1950's, and increased in the 1960's, as the new highways began to enter built-up urban areas. By the mid-1960's, it was becoming more and more difficult for the federal highways organization to remain outside these controversies, and by the late 1960's, Lowell Bridwell, the first federal highway administrator, began to change the character of federal involvement in local decisionmaking.

Bridwell accepted the view that where controversies existed, the federal agency was obligated to examine the pros and cons before granting the federal dollars. In San Francisco Bridwell took the side of the city in the Junipero Serra freeway dispute. In Boston he agreed to the restudy of the Inner Belt route. In Baltimore he played a significant role in developing a new approach to freeway planning, the "design concept team," the result of which was not only a new design but a new route.

Bridwell was instrumental in encouraging state highway departments to take other values besides traffic movement into account in the development of highway plans. The San Francisco case related to esthetic and recreational considerations. The Boston and Baltimore cases were instances of serious social impacts not adequately considered in the original designs. Baltimore's road also seriously affected parks and historic districts. Numerous other cases occurred in cities such as Louisville, New York, Chicago, Detroit, Cleveland, and Philadelphia.

Bridwell seems to have succeeded in establishing this as a permanent policy for the Federal Highway Administration. With the advent of the Nixon administration, John Volpe, Governor of Massachusetts, was appointed Secretary of Transportation. The general view was that Volpe would "pave the country," since as a former DPW Commissioner in Massachusetts he had adamantly demanded the completion of the Inner Belt. However, Volpe made an early and important decision reversing a state-approved plan in New Orleans that would have cut off Jackson Square in the Vieux Carré from the Mississippi, thus suggesting the continuance of the policy of direct involvement of the federal government in such decisions.

Three separate institutional and decisionmaking structures handle the planning and operation of the metropolitan transportation system. Planning, construction, and operation of the urban freeway system is largely centered in state roads agencies, which have strong ties with the federal Bureau of Public Roads and city and county public works departments. The commuter railroads in a few places like New York and New Jersey are accepted as a state transportation department responsibility; elsewhere their fate lies in the hands of public service commissioners and the primary leadership of the state (the governor and the legislature). In most large metropolitan areas transit has become the responsibility of a regional transit authority, financed mostly with local funds and enjoying a semi-autonomous status.

Each mode of transportation has had its own political arena, rarely overlapping that of another except at the edges. Political controversies about highways, public transit, and commuter railroads reflect the differing political makeup of the decisionmaking structure of each mode. Controversies over highways are primarily concerned with opposition to particular roads or to overall plans for the metropolitan highway system. They reflect the absence of local participation in planning and a sense that decisions are made with a narrow transportation orientation from which other urban values are excluded. These controversies often are local-state confrontations, with the Federal Highway Administration sometimes stepping in as mediator.

Disputes over public transit are different. Pressures to preserve or improve an old system or to create a new one are always local in origin. Debates on these questions usually revolve around cost, which places the issue in competition with other demands for the local tax dollar. Plans or guidelines for new or improved rapid transit systems are frequently the responsibility of the metropolitan planning agency. Controversies over commuter railroad service are state-centered, and generally arise from suburban opposition to cutbacks, usually supported by the central city.

The contrast between the politics of transit and the politics of highways, in particular, is striking and illustrates the major problem of achieving a unified and responsive political and planning process for urban transportation. Forces are at work to achieve this unification, primarily at the federal and local levels. Both modes, as well as railroads, are brought together at the federal level in the cluster of responsibilities assigned to the Department of Transportation. Through federal intervention, they have been forced to come together in the regional transportation planning process, and they come together with increasing frequency in the governor's office and in the central city, both of which have usually had only informal powers to deal with the decisionmaking agencies.

NOTES

1. The first of the exclusive highway lanes have been approved by DOT for Milwaukee and Los Angeles. DOT is working with the L.A. Airport Authority on an experimental "air-cushion" line from the airport to the San Fernando Valley.
2. Both of these are authorized to operate but do not as yet.
3. Michigan, Washington, and Florida all have limited mass transit assistance programs as well.
4. While traditional public service agencies generally have regulatory responsibilities regarding transit, their orientation is rarely such that they can serve this purpose.
5. For a general discussion of the characteristics of such authorities, see John C. Bollens, *Special District Governments in the United States* (Berkeley: University of California Press, 1957), esp. pp. 116–44. Also see Robert C. Wood, *1400 Governments* (Cambridge: Harvard University Press, 1961).
6. See part 2 of Governor's Task Force on Transportation, *Report to Governor Sargent* (Boston, June 1970), pp. 18–20.
7. P.L. 38–365, 88th Congress, 2nd Session.
8. George M. Smerk, *Urban Transportation: The Federal Role* (Bloomington: Indiana University Press, 1966), pp. 51–52.
9. Jameson W. Doig, *Metropolitan Transportation Politics in the New York Region* (New York: Columbia University Press, 1966), p. 45.
10. *Ibid.*, pp. 215–17, 297.
11. The Association of Bay Area Governments (ABAG), Puget Sound Government Council (PSGC), and East-West Gateway Coordinating Council (EWGCC), respectively.
12. The Metropolitan Area Planning Council (MAPC, Boston), Regional Planning Council (RPC, Baltimore), Metropolitan Planning Commission–Kansas City (MPC), and Houston-Galveston Area Council (HGAC).
13. The Federal Aid Highway Act of 1944 (P.L. 78–521).
14. The Federal Aid Highway Act of 1956 (P.L. 84–627).
15. U.S., Congress, House of Representatives, *Needs of the National Highway Systems, 1955–84*, House Document No. 120, 84th Congress, 1st Session

(1955). See also Daniel P. Moynihan, "New Roads and Urban Chaos," *The Reporter*, Vol. 22 (April 14, 1960), pp. 13–20. The Clay Report, quoted in the *Reporter* article, says in part, "We have been able to disperse our factories, our stores, our people; in short, to create a revolution in living habits. Our cities have spread into suburbs dependent on the automobile for their existence. The automobile has restored a way of life in which the individual may live in a friendly neighborhood, it has brought city and country closer together, it has made us one country and united people." Moynihan comments, "To undertake a vast program of urban highway construction with no thought for other forms of transportation seemed lunatic."

TRANSPORTATION IN THE METROPOLIS: PROBLEMS, POLICY, AND POLITICAL POWER

JAMESON W. DOIG

Soon after the close of World War II, New York and other urban regions found their transportation systems under severe strain. Rapid increases in population and income levels resulted in major expansion of passenger and freight traffic. These changes were coupled with a shift of traffic from rail and bus to truck and automobile, causing heavy congestion during commuting hours and on weekends. In regions traditionally dependent on rail service for a significant share of transportation, falling revenues and rising costs brought economic difficulties for the mass transit systems and railroad companies, leading to fare increases and reductions in service.

The primary response of government agencies to these problems was to expand the network of highways serving urban regions. While curtailment of intercity rail service was slowed by regulatory agencies, almost no public funds were allocated to aid the private railroad companies. These approaches were consistent with policies developed before the war, and public preferences reinforced historical trends. Yet in the New York area—as in other regions with highly concentrated employment centers and residential developments built up in the rail era—continued and perhaps expanded rail service seemed to be required if the region were to prosper. Although the strength of the highway coalition, public apathy, and the fragmentation of regional leadership were impressive obstacles, in the New York region a small band of railroad men, commuters, and business groups argued that reassessment of current highway-oriented policies was essential.

In this essay, the historical development of the rail system and

From Jameson W. Doig, *Metropolitan Transportation Politics and the New York Region*, pp. 13–40. Copyright © 1966 by Columbia University Press. Reprinted with permission of Columbia University Press.

the impact of the motor age are first outlined. The political structure which supported the postwar transportation policy of the New York region is then analyzed, providing a backdrop for the efforts of the rail coalition to alter that policy during the 1950s.[1]

DEVELOPMENT OF THE RAIL SYSTEM

The century prior to World War I saw the construction of the rail networks which lace the New York area. The first railroad was the Camden and Amboy, later part of the Pennsylvania system, which opened a line across New Jersey in 1831. During the next four decades it was followed by the Central of New Jersey, the Lackawanna, the Lehigh Valley, the Erie, and finally, in 1870, the Susquehanna. These lines crisscrossed New Jersey and terminated at the western bank of the Hudson River. There they were halted by the wide expanse of water which cuts the metropolitan region in two, and passengers and freight bound for Manhattan and points east relied on ferries for this part of the journey.[2]

The Hudson River remained a major obstacle throughout the nineteenth century as several efforts to tunnel under the river failed.[3] In 1908–09, however, the Hudson and Manhattan (H&M) Railroad completed two trans-Hudson tunnels, connecting Newark, Hoboken, and Jersey City with Manhattan; and in 1910 the Pennsylvania Railroad completed its tunnel between New Jersey and midtown Manhattan.[4]

East of the Hudson, rail lines were constructed between New York City and outlying areas, and by 1850 both the New York Central and the New Haven railroads brought passengers directly into Manhattan. Long Island commuters were served by several lines of track laid down by the Long Island Rail Road.[5] Within New York City, a number of elevated rail lines were constructed during the late nineteenth century, and during the first years of the twentieth century the city government embarked on a major program of subway construction. The first section of the Manhattan subway system was placed in operation in 1904, and in the next few years the system was extended into Brooklyn, Queens, and the Bronx.[6]

By the beginning of World War I the major rail facilities of the New York region had been constructed. The eastern sector had a combination of privately and publicly owned facilities, including three important railroad networks and a growing complex of subway and elevated lines in New York City. In contrast to New York City's important rail contribution east of the Hudson, the New Jersey sector, with no dominant city and hundreds of separate municipalities, left the development of a regional transport network entirely to private enterprise. Six major rail systems crossed that state, and all but one terminated at the Hudson River. There, Jersey Central and West Shore passengers were required to take the ferry in order to reach Manhattan, and travelers on three other lines could either use ferry service or transfer to the H&M tubes. Of the major rail systems, only the Pennsylvania ran its trains directly into a Manhattan terminal. The inconvenience of travel from New Jersey to Manhattan, the center of the region, was clearly the main weakness in the urban transportation network.

The next two decades (1920–40) produced a number of studies aimed at improving the rail network. Among the major surveys were several by a state-sponsored North Jersey Transit Commission in the 1920s and by a joint board of private and public bodies during the years 1928–31.[7] The Port of New York Authority (PNYA) and the Regional Plan Association (RPA) also outlined plans for possible improvements. Most of these studies were primarily concerned with the problem of replacing trans-Hudson ferries with rail facilities, but proposals for adding rail lines in Westchester, Long Island, and Staten Island were also included.[8]

Although plans were prepared, citizens' committees formed, and resolutions adopted calling for action, no action was forthcoming. It seemed highly unlikely that major improvements in the passenger systems would be self-supporting, and the railroads showed no interest in underwriting such projects. Yet action by public agencies faced major obstacles. The regionwide extent and the deficit nature of the problem, further complicated by the interstate character of the region, made it difficult to find a governmental agency to take responsibility; the states, the local governments, and the PNYA all were reluctant to act. Even these obstacles might have been overcome, however, had not growing efforts toward action been twice blunted, first by the depression, then by World War II.[9]

IMPACT OF THE MOTOR AGE

Even as the New York region sought ways of improving its rail facilities, this system was being challenged by the automobile, the bus, and the truck. Part of a nationwide development and linked to the general trends of population increase and suburban growth, the expansion of motor transportation began well before World War II and accelerated rapidly in the postwar era.[10]

In 1930 about 24 million people entered New York City from New Jersey by automobile. Twenty years later this number had risen 390 percent, to 94 million; over half of this increase took place between 1945 and 1950. Similar trends, though less pronounced, occurred in automobile travel from the Westchester and Long Island sectors of the region. Bus and truck travel also increased sharply.[11]

As traffic increased, new vehicular facilities were constructed; and each additional artery seemed to stimulate still more traffic. Billions of dollars of state and federal funds were poured into highways,[12] and the activities and importance of the agencies concerned with motor traffic expanded greatly. The chief beneficiaries in the New York region were two semi-independent agencies, the Port of New York Authority and the Triborough Bridge and Tunnel Authority. By 1931 the bi-state PNYA had constructed the George Washington Bridge and three bridges linking Staten Island and New Jersey and was operating these as well as the Holland Tunnel (first opened in 1927 under another agency). All were operated as toll facilities, and the Holland Tunnel and George Washington Bridge were immediate financial successes. As a result the PNYA was soon able to undertake construction of the Lincoln Tunnel, the first tube of which was opened in 1937, the second in 1945. By the early 1950s consideration was being given to constructing additional trans-Hudson crossings.

In the eastern half of the region, authorities were established during the 1930s to construct and operate the Triborough Bridge, the Bronx-Whitestone Bridge, and other major New York facilities. Through mergers of several agencies, the Triborough Bridge and Tunnel Authority (TBTA) was formed in 1946 and given responsibility for constructing and operating toll bridges and tunnels within the five boroughs of New York City. In the postwar traffic boom, the Triborough Authority joined the Port Authority as a financially successful regional body.[13]

While vehicular traffic in the New York region was expanding, the rail lines found their traffic decreasing. The decline was most severe on the New Jersey railroads, which had carried 171 million riders across the Hudson in 1930. After a sharp drop during the depression, these railroads regained part of their traffic loss during the war and in 1945 carried about 140 million. But by 1950 traffic had fallen to a new low—slightly under 100 million a year. Among those severely affected were the West Shore and the Erie, which lost two-thirds of their traffic between 1930 and 1950. The decline in Westchester and Long Island traffic was less severe, but still substantial: between 1945 and 1950 Westchester traffic dropped from 65 to 50 million, Long Island traffic from 110 to 85 million.[14]

The causes for this postwar decline were several. The dispersion of suburban growth, abetted by highway expansion, reduced the percentage of the population which could conveniently use rail service for home-to-work and home-to-store trips. The shift in Manhattan destinations from downtown to midtown reduced the usefulness of the ferry system. The direct cost of auto and bus travel was often less than that of rail travel. Reduction from a six- to a five-day workweek cut rail usage significantly. Finally, the increased ownership of automobiles and the popularity of television reduced evening and weekend rail travel.[15]

But while rail travel diminished, expenses were not reduced proportionately. The rail companies retained most of their rush hour passengers while non-rush hour traffic declined sharply. Thus, the companies were required to keep manpower and equipment available to meet peak-hour loads, although most of the personnel and equipment were idle much of the day. In addition, wages and material costs continued to rise, and railroad taxes remained at high levels, with New Jersey and New York having the highest tax rates per rail mile in the country.[16]

Faced with declining passenger traffic and more rigid costs, the railroads sought to raise fares and curtail service. In 1946 and 1947 the New Jersey roads obtained their first postwar fare increases from state and federal regulatory commissions, and a second increase followed in 1949. The Lackawanna Railroad was given permission to abandon the 23rd Street ferry in 1946, and several lines eliminated little-used trains. Each fare rise or service reduction was followed by further declines in passenger traffic, however, leading the railroads to seek still further fare increases and train curtailments.[17]

Massive highway construction and a relatively passive public attitude toward rail deterioration characterized these first postwar years, but it was doubtful that present policies would adequately meet the region's future transportation needs. Although vast sums of public funds were poured into building roads, bridges, and tun-

nels to accommodate expanding motor transport, congestion continued to be a major problem, especially in the downtown business
areas into which most of the additional traffic poured. And in
spite of the declining use of rail transport, the rail network
was still of great importance during rush hours. During peak hours
each day in 1950, 240,000 commuters entered New York City by
rail, most of these bound for midtown and downtown Manhattan.
Only 103,000 commuted by automobile and bus. Even the highway enthusiast could foresee difficulties in absorbing increasing
numbers of rail travelers on the highway system if rail service continued to deteriorate.[18]

What should be done to meet these problems? Ideally (at
least from a planner's point of view), an immediate evaluation of
current highway-oriented policies should be carried out and
recommendations adopted to provide coordinated planning and
balanced financing of the rail and road systems. As the Regional
Plan Association argued in 1951, "The issue here is the paramount public need for a well balanced regional transportation system of highway, parkway *and* railroad development."[19]

But planning standards often conflict with political realities.
So it was in this case. Efforts to provide a more "balanced" transportation policy would challenge the freedom enjoyed by the
opulent and politically powerful road coalition, and the forces
supporting the challenge were relatively weak and divided. Such
efforts would also require guidance and leadership from political
institutions with regionwide perspectives, and in the fragmented
metropolis such leadership was difficult to locate.

TRANSPORT POLICY: THE POLITICAL SUBSTRUCTURE

"Certain characteristics of groups," writes Eckstein, "are likely
to determine decisively their effectiveness" in the political arena.
Among the most important are the cohesiveness and prestige of
the group and its size, wealth, and leadership. In addition, the
pattern of existing policies and the structure of relevant government institutions will aid some interests and retard the efforts of
others.[20]

These are the characteristics that concern us in analyzing the
political forces involved in transportation policy-making in the
New York region. We first consider the alliance pressing for
innovation during the first postwar decade, the rail coalition,
and then examine the elements supporting the *status quo*.

The Rail Coalition. As one surveys the interests actively concerned with obtaining changes in regional transport policy, their relatively low potential for politically effective action emerges clearly. Compared with the highway coalition, this alliance of railroads, central-city groups, and suburban interests rated poorly in organizational unity, general prestige and wealth, breadth of membership, and leadership skills. Its difficulties were reinforced by the nature of existing policy and of governmental structure. Even so, these active elements provided continued pressure against highway-oriented policies during the first postwar years and the nucleus for a broader and perhaps successful campaign if the crisis were to worsen.

The suburban railroads in the region were important participants in the coalition. Their most immediate concern, however, was the reduction of financial losses from passenger service, and much of their energy went into efforts to persuade regulatory commissions to permit fare increases and train service reductions.[21] These efforts inevitably brought the rail carriers into conflict with other members of the coalition, particularly suburban commuter interests and their allies in the state regulatory commissions.

Yet some rail officials were concerned with more basic causes and more positive solutions as well. Spokesmen for the rail lines criticized the pouring of "billions of dollars into new highways, tunnels, and bridges," while the mass transit problem was "ignored." Several, including officials of the H&M, the Lackawanna, and the Susquehanna, advocated the construction of new river crossings and additional Manhattan stations in order to eliminate reliance on ferries for trans-Hudson commutation. And a few, led by H&M president William Reid, called upon the states, the Port Authority, and the Triborough Authority to undertake such construction and other improvements, in order to provide a more stable and efficient transportation system for the region. Here the views of the rail companies and those of the other members of the coalition tended to coincide, although for somewhat different reasons: the rail officials were primarily interested in shifting their financial burdens to public agencies, the suburban and central-city spokesmen in improving the economic vitality of various parts of the region.[22]

Although suburbanites were basically allies of the railroads, their organized efforts were built mainly upon conflict with the rail lines. Suburban interests during these first postwar years were

most actively represented by municipal-commuter groups, organized in response to railroad attempts to reduce service to their
communities. As a consequence, their approach tended to be anti-
railroad and geographically narrow. Each of the half-dozen or
more commuter groups was organized along a specific rail line and
focused its attention primarily upon pressing state and federal regulatory bodies to deny railroad requests to increase rates and cut
service.

The most active of these groups in the region, and the organization with the longest history, was the Inter-Municipal Group
for Better Rail Service (IMGBRS). Formed in 1945 in response
to efforts of the Central Railroad of New Jersey to cut back on
service, the IMGBRS was composed of local public officials and
appointed private citizens in sixteen towns along the Central's
route. As each railroad proposal was submitted to the regulatory
commissions, IMGBRS representatives appeared with evidence
which purported to show that losses were not as large as stated
by the railroad, that improvements in service rather than reductions might increase net passenger income, and that "inefficient
management and the use of obsolete equipment"—not the provision of passenger services—caused the Jersey Central's financial
difficulties. The IMGBRS also emphasized the adverse impact
on suburban economic development that might result from continued service deterioration. The trend of fare increases and service
reductions was never halted, but the Inter-Municipal Group could
claim that its efforts often helped to persuade the regulatory commissions to grant less than the railroad had requested and that the
delays in final commission action caused by IMGBRS' objections
saved "hundreds of thousands of dollars to the commuters of
northern New Jersey."[23]

Similar organizations sprang up in various parts of the region
during the late 1940s and early 1950s: the Westchester Commuters Group, the Transit Committee of Bergen County, the
Jersey Shore Protective Committee, the Boonton Line Transportation Association, and several others. Some of these groups were
composed primarily of municipal officials, while others were run
by commuters; each was limited to a narrow geographic slice of
the region, and each fought a rearguard battle against unrelenting
railroad pressure.[24] Usually, these local groups could expect sympathetic treatment from the state commissions, which were sensitive to local economic and political pressures. But when service
across state lines was involved, the Interstate Commerce Com-

mission was normally allied with the railroads in placing primary emphasis on railroad financial needs, not on "the uneconomic costs of fare increases to the public."[25]

Suburbia agreed with the railroads, however, on the need for more positive approaches to the rail problem, and a number of possible steps were suggested. The IMGBRS and the Transit Committee of Bergen County pressed for construction of trans-Hudson tunnels in order to attract more passengers to the rails, and the Westchester County Planning Commission foresaw possible advantages from building new rail lines to serve Westchester and Connecticut commuters entering New York City. These and other groups called for immediate studies of the transit problem, leading to effective long-range improvements. Several major newspapers in the region urged that the PNYA consider taking action, and a few spokesmen suggested the possibility of regional tax support to maintain and improve rail services in the region.[26]

In terms of political effectiveness, however, the suburban interests had significant weaknesses. Potentially, the commuter element was important. There were more than 200,000 railroad commuters to Manhattan and thousands more with destinations in Newark, Jersey City, and other cities, and the economic significance to their local areas of these rail passengers was substantial. But few suburbanites were actively involved in the commuter associations, or in more positive efforts to improve transportation services. Most commuters limited their activities to following the controversies in local papers and in flyers passed out during recurrent crises. The pressure of other concerns and the nature of commuting itself raised obstacles of time and communication that few managed to overcome.[27]

The third major group in the rail coalition was composed of central-city business and civic interests. Most active here were such organizations as the New York Chamber of Commerce, the Citizens Budget Commission, and the Regional Plan Association, together with New York City newspapers, especially the New York *Times* and the New York *Herald Tribune.*[28] For some of these participants, the primary motivation was protection of Manhattan's economic dominance in the region. The Avenue of the Americas Association, for example, argued that traffic congestion was "causing large organizations and taxpayers to move from Manhattan into the surrounding areas" and advocated improvement of the rail system in order to relieve this congestion and thus reverse the "loss in taxable and other vital economic values" in the central city. But others, particularly the RPA (which had members throughout the area), emphasized the importance of an efficient rail system to the prosperity of the entire region.[29]

In contrast with the suburbanites, the central-city interests were sympathetic toward the railroads' financial difficulties and saw little long-run advantage to be gained from contesting fare increases and service reductions.[30] Instead, they emphasized the need for more positive action: studies, short-range improvements, and construction of expensive new facilities were advocated by various groups. Because of their concern for the economic health of both the region and the railroads and their familiarity with local subsidies for the city subway system, some of these groups were willing to support the use of public funds in order to improve the rail system. Action by the regional authorities was also suggested; Goodhue Livingston of the City Planning Commission, for example, criticized the "sprawling operations" of the Port and Triborough Authorities and argued for creation of a new transport authority to supervise both rail and road operations in the region.[31]

Conflicts of perspective and interest thus characterized the rail coalition. Much of the energy of the railroad and suburban groups, together with their regulatory commission allies, was focused on skirmishes over particular fare and service schedules. And while all three segments of the coalition agreed that more positive action was needed, they differed as to what kinds of action. Some were especially concerned about the impact of highway developments on rail service, and emphasized the need for coordinated planning and perhaps financing of the entire transport system; others, viewing such coordination as unnecessary or unfeasible, favored rail aid from general public funds. Some felt that the immediate effort must be regionwide; others would give first priority to a particular sector of the region. Finally, the coalition was divided as to whether short-range action or major improvements should be emphasized.[32] These differences did not represent definite cleavages within the coalition, but they suggested the need for establishing priorities before action could be taken.

Even if agreement on these issues were obtained, the coalition faced several difficulties in reversing existing policy. Although the central-city interests and the suburban groups included some members with prestige and political influence, it was doubtful that a unified and vigorous campaign for action could be based upon such a diversity of voluntary associations. The railroads themselves, though not without influence at the state capitals and in the region, lacked the political support to lead an effective campaign. Also, the strength of the highway coalition and the fragmentation of governmental power were major obstacles. What the coalition needed most, perhaps, was the threat of an immediate and major loss of rail service. Such an emergency could have expanded the small group of activists into a politically significant share of the region's voters and could have forced the political leaders at regional and state levels to take action. Ironically, the commuter organizations, in their stopgap efforts before the regulatory commissions, helped to avert such a dramatic crisis. The wearing away of rail service proceeded slowly during this first postwar decade, and most of the region's populace were unaware of any major transport crisis, present or potential.

The Road Coalition. In contrast to the rail group, the alliance marshaled behind postwar highway policy was highly effective politically. In the New York region, it was organized primarily around two regional agencies, the Port Authority and the Triborough Bridge and Tunnel Authority. Closely linked with them, especially as highway construction and the need for coordination increased, was a network of county and state highway agencies and the federal Bureau of Public Roads. Supporting these agencies, although not usually central participants in policy-making in the New York region, were the bus companies, automobile associations, and other beneficiaries of highway expansion.

The members of the road alliance were not necessarily opposed to maintaining rail services. Although they were inclined to doubt the need for major improvements, the Port Authority and other road interests favored public action to stabilize railroad commutation. Without such efforts, large numbers might transfer from rail to highways during the next few years, overtaxing the facilities available even with a massive road-building program. The road coalition objected, however, whenever it was suggested that highway expansion should be coordinated with rail planning or that highway funds should be used to aid the railroads. Modest efforts to aid the rail system, paid for by the general taxpayer, might be acceptable, but funds required to expand the highway network could not be diverted in order to save the railroads.

Because of their highly visible role in the region's highway program, the Port and Triborough Authorities were major objects of attack as criticism of the New York area's transport policy grew. The PNYA, owing to its interstate jurisdiction, financial strength, and original mandate to aid the railroads, was the primary target. Its efforts to retain its independence of action form a central part of the story that follows; the actions of the TBTA are also involved, though more peripherally. The background and behavior patterns of these two agencies are outlined here.[33]

The Port of New York Authority. Established in 1921 by interstate compact, the PNYA was charged with responsibility for developing the "terminal, transportation and other facilities of commerce" in the New York–New Jersey region. The compact gave the PNYA broad responsibility in the Port District, a bistate area extending about 20 miles in radius from the Statue of Liberty; its capacity to carry out these duties was limited, however, by its inability to levy taxes or assessments or to issue orders binding upon private or other public agencies.[34]

The Port Authority was at first expected to devote its main energies to the problem of freight distribution in the region. However, it found the railroads unwilling to cooperate in the establishment of joint yards, joint rights of way, or other plans to rationalize the harbor and rail system; and little progress was made toward carrying out the original program. In the late 1920s, the PNYA turned to vehicular facilities. Its network of toll bridges and tunnels was highly successful financially, and it was able to branch out. In 1932 a freight terminal was opened in Manhattan, in 1944 a grain terminal was acquired, in 1947 the PNYA leased Newark Airport and La Guardia and Idlewild Airports, and between 1948 and 1951 it took over administration of Port Newark and of Teterboro Airport and began operating two truck terminals and a bus terminal.[35]

Passenger rail operations were not entirely neglected during these three decades. Between 1928 and 1931, the Port Authority joined with other groups in the region in a study of the passenger problem, an effort abandoned because of traffic decline during the depression.[36] In 1937 the PNYA submitted a report recommending that a trans-Hudson rail tunnel be constructed; and in 1949, at the request of New Jersey Governor Alfred E. Driscoll, the PNYA submitted a report concerning a proposed rail line between Newark Airport and the waterfront.

Although the PNYA was willing to study the problem, it showed no interest in expanding its own responsibilities to include rail passenger service. In its 1937 report, the Authority estimated

that the proposed project might run a yearly deficit as high as
$5.3 million. The report concluded that the Authority itself could
not undertake the project, since lack of taxing power limited it
to "self-liquidating projects." The 1949 plan carried an estimated
annual deficit of $1.2 million, and again the Authority declared
its inability to take on such a deficit operation.[37]

As the vehicular projects, wealth, and diversity of operations of
the PNYA increased, criticism of its "neglect" of rail transit also
grew. Commuter associations and the railroads were joined by
the RPA, the Newark *News*, and other regional spokesmen in urging the PNYA to reconsider its opposition to undertaking a direct
role in rail transit. By 1950, as the need for some public action
to stem the rail decline seemed more apparent, the governors of
New York and New Jersey also began to show some interest in
the Port Authority's changing its position.[38]

In response to these criticisms and queries, the PNYA took a
firm stand, a position which it was able to maintain until 1959–60.
The PNYA argued, first, that it was "completely unable to purchase or otherwise assume deficit financing of rail transit operations." Any passenger rail facilities, the PNYA asserted, would
operate at substantial deficits, and an integrated transit system in
the New York–New Jersey area would probably involve annual
losses of $35 to $40 million. Since the Authority was required to
support its program entirely on the basis of its own income, such
a deficit operation would make it impossible for the PNYA to sell
revenue bonds for new facilities and would force contraction of
its entire program. In fact, "any implication that the Port Authority was even considering the financing of rail transit," its
officials maintained, would "seriously impair" its credit structure.
The Authority also opposed any plan that would provide tax resources to meet PNYA deficits, for such a step would subject it
to "political influence," thus destroying the "sound business" principles on which it was operated.

"The only long range solution" to the transit problem, the
PNYA argued, was the creation of an interstate public corporation, with power to "make up deficits out of taxes appor-
tioned equitably among the communities which depend upon rail
service."[39]

The position taken by the PNYA was in part unassailable. It
could not expand and perhaps not even survive if required to
assume a continuing rail deficit so large that other income could

not offset it. But some of its arguments were open to debate. Might it not be able to assume limited responsibilities in the rail field, either directly or via allocation of some of its surplus bridge and tunnel revenues to a separate organization? Also, was it in fact preferable as a matter of regional policy to create a separate and perhaps competing agency for rail, rather than integrating both rail and road under one authority, supported by its own revenues and taxes?

In maintaining its position, the Port Authority was not limited, however, to the logic of its arguments. As it entered into a long and intensive campaign to ward off responsibility for rail passenger service, the PNYA possessed a number of politically significant advantages—widespread public support, a relatively large degree of formal independence in policy-making, and well-developed political skills. The nature of each of these advantages deserves further comment.

The Port Authority's achievements and current plans have generally been supported enthusiastically by business groups, newspapers, public officials, and other regional spokesmen, and the admiration of state legislators and the two governors has usually been evident as well. Acclaimed during the postwar period for its "far-reaching program," for "imagination and resourcefulness, . . . vigor and initiative," and for its "great service to business and industry" while avoiding the "evils of governmental bureaucracy and governmental waste," the PNYA has been able to count upon widespread backing for its desire to maintain its financial autonomy and its preferred range of activities.[40]

The ability of the PNYA to determine its own policy preferences and to avoid transit projects has been greatly aided by several structural characteristics and related traditions. Whereas most state agencies are under the supervision of a single official, appointed by the governor and removable at will, the PNYA is guided by twelve commissioners, six appointed by each governor, for overlapping six-year terms. The chairman of the board of commissioners is chosen by the members themselves, and no commissioner may be removed by the governors except for cause, after a hearing. These legal factors have substantially modified the influence that either governor can wield over PNYA policy-making.

Still, the appointive power itself provides the governors with the means to select persons to represent their own views or a range of views which they believe should have influence upon an agency. In some public authorities the appointive power has been used in this way; the Chicago Housing Authority, for example, included in 1949 "a Jew, a Catholic, a Negro, a small businessman, a big businessman, a labor leader, and a social worker–intellectual."[41] Traditionally, commissioners of the Port Authority have been drawn from a far narrower stratum; banking and business predominate, and members of the board are frequently wealthy. In 1952, for example, two commissioners were presidents of banks in the region, six were board chairmen, presidents, or vice-presidents of business firms, and one was the publisher of a large newspaper, the Bergen *Evening Record*; the other three included a member of a major law firm, a consulting engineer, and a university professor. That year, commissioners of the PNYA sat on the boards of directors of more than sixty corporations, including such major companies as Prudential Insurance, American Can, Remington Rand, and New Jersey Bell Telephone.[42]

This is not to imply that business experience should disqualify one for service on the Port Authority. On the contrary, given the importance of financial criteria in its work and the complexity of management involved, it is perhaps desirable and inevitable that business competence would be sought for the PNYA. Nor should one infer that the commissioners are concerned only with business criteria and values. Some have had careers outside the business community, some of the businessmen have held other public posts, appointive or elective (and party service has at times been a criterion in appointment), and a few commissioners have identified themselves as much with their governors and broader regional concerns as they have with the immediate goals of the PNYA. On balance, however, the previous experience of the board has been consistent with the conservative approach taken by the PNYA—in opposition to taking action on a problem as financially uncertain as rail transit or to any actions which might reduce the financial and administrative autonomy of the Authority.

The relationship between the commissioners and the PNYA staff has further reinforced these policies and the general ability of the agency to determine its own priorities. The twelve commissioners are unpaid, each has a full-time job elsewhere, and the PNYA's complex activities have traditionally been carried out with great skill and success. As a result, many commissioners have lacked the time and inclination to master the Authority's methods and problems; the hurdle has been especially great for those who might consider pressing for a rethinking of traditional PNYA goals. Inevitably, the full-time staff has exerted substantial influence in the development of overall and instrumental policies.

Staff influence has been heightened by the high quality and long tenure of most top-level officials at the Authority. The executive director, Austin J. Tobin—"stocky, . . . vigorous and pugnacious-looking"—is one of the nation's outstanding administrators.[43] Although less well known than some of his counterparts, Tobin fits admirably the characterization used to describe J. Edgar Hoover and General Curtis E. LeMay:

> Both presided over major expansions of the organization while refusing to take on functions not closely related to its fundamental purpose. Both cultivated reputations for themselves as tough, nononsense, hard-driving administrators, and for their agencies as efficient, technically expert, hard-working organizations, employing the most up-to-date devices of technology in the singleminded pursuit of their mission.[44]

Closely allied with Tobin have been a number of highly qualified officials in such fields as aviation, port development, and public relations. The PNYA has been able to obtain officials of high competence in part because of the agency's high reputation and in part because it offers salaries unmatched in most public agencies. Tobin receives $60,000 a year, a government salary exceeded only by that of the President of the United States; seven top officials are paid $40,000 annually, and thirteen others receive between $27,000 and $33,000.[45]

Many of the Port Authority's senior career officials combine ability with long service in the agency. Tobin joined the PNYA in 1927 as a law clerk and worked his way up through the ranks during the next fifteen years. Several of his top aides in the early 1950s also counted their service from the 1920s. With extended service, staff members accept and indeed absorb the goals of the organization. When appointment to top positions comes after many years in an agency, officials are therefore less inclined to reassess past policy or in any way to "shake up" the organization. So it is with the PNYA, and the ability and commitment to the agency of its senior officials operates to reinforce its independent position.

Autonomy in policy-making is also a product of the Authority's independent financial resources (from tolls, rents, and other charges) and its independence in personnel and other administrative matters. Budgetary autonomy is especially important. As

Sayre and Kaufman have pointed out in their analysis of authorities operating in New York City, there are several advantages here:

> First, the authorities do not have to undergo the public budget hearings before the Board of Estimate, at which so many of the pressures on ordinary line agencies are brought to bear. Second, the authorities do not have to defend their plans and projected expenditures to budget and fiscal officers of the city or any other government. . . . Third, they are not exposed to deprivations of income through appropriations delays or slashes, a common means of subduing line agencies. Fourth, they are not limited by the detailed appropriation items of the regular expense budget of the city. In sum, their operating policy decisions, as these are reflected in their budgets, are made internally rather than in dealings with outside agencies and officials, in private rather than in public, and the authorities are the undisputed masters of their own operating resources.[46]

The broad impact of these structural characteristics is to give the PNYA a degree of independence more often associated with a private corporation than with a public agency. Such a conclusion has been accepted and indeed favored by PNYA officials. As Tobin asserted in 1953,

> An authority is designed to put revenue producing public facilities on their own feet and on their own responsibility; to free them from political interference, bureaucracy and red tape. . . . This test of management, the administrative standards of a well-managed private corporation, is the test that should be applied to the [Authority's] responsibilities and duties.

"The Commissioners of the Port Authority function as a Board of Directors," Tobin concluded. "My own executive office has the same normal responsibilities as those of the president of a private corporation."[47]

One can carry the emphasis on PNYA independence too far, however. There are several ways in which outside interests can affect its policies directly and effectively. The governor of either state may veto any action taken by the PNYA, or the state legislatures may refuse to enact laws needed for new projects. Certain municipal and other controls can also be cited.[48] The PNYA has found it necessary to develop strategies to neutralize potential opposition from these sources, and it has executed these strategies with great political skill during the postwar period.

The Authority's basic strategy has been to carry out a vigorous program along the lines of its preferred goals. Vehicular, airport, and other facilities are constantly being built and improved. This policy provides a basis for obtaining widespread public approbation; it has also insured that large reserves are not built up—reserves that the Authority might be asked to apply to rail transit.

Closely joined with its expansion policy has been a skillful public relations program, aimed at persuading the general public and political leaders of the region of the importance of current PNYA activities. The director of public relations participates in policy meetings, issues a constant stream of press releases (more than 600 from 1946 to 1951), and has made available to newspapers "reliable background information for use in determining editorial policies."[49] These publicity efforts have emphasized the achievements and "nonpolitical" nature of the PNYA and the intimate relationships between these two factors.[50]

The PNYA has not relied only on these indirect methods in warding off political pressures. The agency's views have been presented informally to the governors of both states and to influential members of the two legislatures. These efforts have been continuous and have been carried out by commissioners and top staff officers closely acquainted with the officials concerned. State legislators have also been given special tours of Port Authority facilities, and new projects have been presented to the legislatures and to the general public with a substantial publicity build-up.[51] These strategies have been largely effective in securing political support for PNYA goals and independence at the state capitals; the governors' veto power has been used infrequently, and the legislatures have rarely failed to authorize new projects.[52] The comments of New York Governor Thomas E. Dewey in 1952 typify the general view taken of the PNYA during the first postwar decade and suggest the success which the agency has had in maintaining public acceptance of its goals and methods:

> In its thirty-one years of service to the two States the Port Authority, without burden to the general taxpayer, has provided almost half a billion dollars' worth of terminal and transportation facilities. Through its great public works, it has set an example for the administration of public business on a sound and efficient basis.[53]

Because of these several factors, the PNYA was able to maintain a substantial degree of independence in policy-making during the early postwar period and was largely able to decide when and where to expand its facilities. Pressure from the rail coalition for action on rail transit posed no immediate threat to the politically powerful Authority. Still, the PNYA found it necessary to remain alert. Further rail-service deterioration could increase the size and importance of the rail coalition, and the rail group might expect to find allies in any concerted attack upon the PNYA from among those who criticized the agency for other reasons. There were the residents of the areas around PNYA airports, who were critical of the noise and danger involved in airport operation, and those from towns which lost land to PNYA projects. There were groups which attacked it concerning toll rates and other policies—positions especially prominent in Hudson County—and scholars and planners who criticized the public authorities for increasing the fragmentation of metropolitan areas. Although these critics were usually isolated minorities, their political strength could increase dramatically upon occasion (as it did temporarily following a series of plane crashes near Newark Airport in 1951–52).[54] Since pressure from the rail coalition could be augmented greatly by such groups, the PNYA could be expected to exert its considerable resources to divert the region from itself as a "solution," and if possible to help locate an alternative approach that would leave it unfettered by rail transit.

The Triborough Bridge and Tunnel Authority. The region's other major road agency—the Triborough Bridge and Tunnel Authority—is in some ways similar to the PNYA. But there is a basic difference: the PNYA is an organization headed by a skilled leadership group; the TBTA might more accurately be viewed as one man—Robert Moses—with an agency appended. The role of the TBTA, though secondary in this study, warrants a brief review of Moses and his works.

Robert Moses has long been an important and controversial figure in New York. Since working with Governor Alfred E. Smith in the 1920s, he has accumulated a series of titles and a reputation for success rarely matched in the field of public administration. In 1922 Moses prepared a plan for a state system of parks, and he began carrying it out in 1924 as president of the Long Island State Park Commission and chairman of the State Council of Parks. Subsequently, he was made chairman of the Jones Beach State Parkway Authority and the Bethpage Park Authority, both on Long Island. In 1934, he was appointed by Mayor Fiorello H. LaGuardia to be Park Commissioner for New

York City and chairman of both the Triborough Bridge Authority and the Henry Hudson Bridge Authority. Other city positions
followed, including membership on the City Planning Commission (1942), chairmanship of the Triborough Bridge and Tunnel
Authority (formed in 1946, consolidating several previous authorities), and appointment to the newly created position of City
Construction Coordinator (1946) and to the chairmanship of the
Committee on Slum Clearance (1948). Moses continued to hold
all these positions throughout the 1950s.

During these years, he became well known as a man who "gets
results"—impressive, easy-to-see results—among the most prominent of which are the Triborough Bridge, the Queens-Manhattan
tunnel, the Brooklyn-Battery tunnel, and the Whitestone Bridge.
As one commentator has said, Moses has built himself a "city–
state park–parkway–highway–bridge–tunnel empire."[55] And to that
must be added power dams, for on becoming chairman of the
New York State Power Authority in 1954 Moses directed his considerable energies toward the Niagara–St. Lawrence power projects
(not the least important of which is the Robert Moses Dam).

The nature of his work—combined with his proclivity for invec-
tive—has led Moses into conflicts with political leaders, administrative agencies, residents in the paths of his projects, and many
others. He has been criticized for "arrogance" and accused of
wanting to "do away with the democratic process." Yet the dominant view within the New York region and in Albany is highly
favorable. Endowed with intelligence, imagination, and tremendous amounts of aggressive energy, Moses has demonstrated a
unique capacity to overcome bureaucratic complexity and inertia
and to produce major achievements. As one legislator concluded
during a debate in Albany several years ago, "There have been
times when he has been somewhat vitriolic, to state it mildly, but
Mr. Moses has rendered a greater service to the State than any of
his contemporaries."[56]

The Triborough Bridge and Tunnel Authority has been one of
Robert Moses' major enterprises. At the time of its formation in
1946, the Triborough Authority controlled five toll bridges and
one tunnel connecting New York City boroughs. As the postwar
travel boom developed, the agency grew financially stronger year
by year, and in 1950 a second tunnel connecting Brooklyn and
Manhattan and a Manhattan garage were completed. By 1952,
with an annual net income exceeding $20 million, the Triborough
had developed a $90-million construction program and was look-

ing forward during the next few years to the building of a coliseum at Columbus Circle and a gigantic bridge across the Narrows, connecting Brooklyn and Staten Island.[57]

Financial affluence and expansionist tendencies have brought attacks upon the Triborough Authority, just as they have upon the Port Authority. Critics argued that some of the agency's income should be devoted to meeting New York City's subway deficits and that the plans of the Triborough should be closely coordinated with rail service planning in the city and the region. A few, the most tenacious being New York City Planning Commissioner Goodhue Livingston, have gone further. In public statements beginning in 1951, Livingston argued that the Triborough should be merged into a new Regional Transport Authority, which would control the subway system, the H&M Railroad, the Long Island Rail Road, and some Port Authority bridges, as well as all bridges and tunnels between the city boroughs. Such an authority, he asserted, would provide a means for more effective coordination of transportation development, and for more balanced financing.[58]

Moses has taken a different view. The railroads might properly be aided by tax reduction and by the states' assuming the cost of most grade-crossing eliminations, but he has seen little need for an expansion of railroad commuter facilities and no advantage in an "official, all-powerful regional agency" to coordinate and improve rail service. As to the suggestion that the Triborough Authority aid in solving rail problems, Moses was more critical. Triborough's "first rate reputation," he asserted, was based upon the "definite, limited and financially sound" nature of its program. To combine with it all of the "dubious projects" that could be called transportation would "wreck" the Authority:

> Putting all of the problems into a big new shiny basket is just a way of hastening their trip to the dump heap or the incinerator. . . . We no doubt need some smarter, more forceful and more independent people in the existing agencies, here and there less pride of authorship and more sacrifice for the common good, but we don't need powerful, new expensive bureaucratic regional administrations staffed by ambitious second rate planners, railroads eager to rid themselves of their less profitable business, and public officials anxious to dump their tougher problems on someone else.[59]

But the Triborough Authority has seemed in little danger of becoming involved in rail operations. In maintaining its independence, this Authority has been able to depend upon the political strength of chairman Moses and upon legal restrictions. In contrast to the PNYA, Triborough's jurisdiction is limited to New York City, and its contracts with current bondholders appear to prohibit it from using its borrowing authority to undertake rail transit responsibilities.[60]

The Port Authority and the Triborough Authority were major participants in the road coalition. Closely allied with them were a number of other public institutions and private groups. Several of these were coordinated through the person of Moses himself; his multiple positions provided the basis for insuring close cooperation among the Triborough Authority, the office of the City Construction Coordinator, the City Department of Parks, the Long Island State Park Commission, the Jones Beach State Parkway Authority, and the Bethpage Park Authority on Long Island. Other agencies directly involved in planning and constructing the region's arterial highway system included the New York State Department of Public Works, New York State Thruway Authority, New Jersey State Highway Department, New Jersey Turnpike Authority, New Jersey Highway Authority, the federal Bureau of Public Roads, and state and county park commissions. Bus companies and associations, automobile clubs, truckers, and other beneficiaries supported and applauded their efforts. Although conflict arose occasionally within the coalition—especially between Moses and the Port Authority—"close contact" and cooperation were the rule.[61] The alliance was reinforced by the service of other officials (in addition to Moses) in more than one of the agencies. Charles H. Sells, for example, had been Superintendent of Public Works for New York State and Westchester Commissioner of Public Works before becoming a Port Authority commissioner in 1949.

When any serious threat to the independence of the road coalition arose, auto groups and other members might be expected to voice strong objections. Usually, however, they left the battle to those most directly threatened and most capable of effective defense and counterattack—the Port Authority and Robert Moses.

A Multitude of Governments. In pressing for changes in regional transport policy, the rail coalition not only found itself divided on goals and priorities while facing a politically powerful alliance of road interests. In addition, the structure of general governmental institutions in the region provided significant obstacles to action. Barring a sudden conversion of highway interests to the transit cause, the rail coalition would need assistance from local and state governmental leaders if its goals were to be achieved. This support would be essential if general tax funds were to be tapped to aid the rail system or if sufficient leverage were to be applied to the highway coalition to yield funds from that source. Yet the characteristic fragmentation of government in the metropolis made it difficult to focus responsibility on any local or state leader, and thus favored the *status quo*.

The problem of divided authority was unusually great in the New York region. Here twenty-two counties and more than 500 cities and towns compete and cooperate in the making of governmental decisions affecting the metropolis. The interstate nature of the region adds officials at three state capitals as well as the federal government to this diversity.

The typically narrow perspective of local governments in a metropolis is found throughout the New York region. Each local unit is "preoccupied with its own problems," and conflicts over zoning, roads, and other issues are frequent. Cooperative agreements on some services have been made by small groups of adjoining municipalities, but most cities and towns lack the territorial breadth or inclination to exercise leadership on transportation development or other major regional issues.[62]

In some regions other factors have served to offset this fragmentation. In Miami and in a number of other areas most of the metropolitan growth is contained within one county; the county government can serve in such cases as a source of regional leadership. And in such large regions as Detroit and Pittsburgh, a central economic and social focus exists, facilitating private as well as public leadership on a regionwide basis.[63] But the New York region is favored with neither of these advantages. In addition to New York City, there are seventeen counties in the region; and twenty-one cities (as of 1960) with 50,000 or more inhabitants— cities that in other locations would themselves be nuclei for separate metropolitan areas. One of these, Newark, had a population of 405,000 in 1960, while Jersey City counted 276,000 residents.[64] Business and political leaders in the larger cities of the region have long felt a strong sense of competition with New York City. Intraregional rivalry, especially on an interstate basis between New Jersey cities and New York, has been a significant limiting factor in attempts to develop coordinated policies. The nature and extent of this problem were clearly outlined during the efforts (described below) to develop regional transport policies during the 1950s and early 1960s.[65]

In spite of these limitations, New York City provided an important potential base for coordinated regional action. In terms of geography and economic factors, the city holds a central role in the region. Its business and civic leaders and its public officials—especially the mayor—are more likely to view problems in a regional perspective than spokesmen from any other sector of the metropolis.[66] On the transportation issue, two specific factors reinforced the positive potential of the city. New York had a long tradition of providing public support for local transit services and thus might look favorably upon extending such aid to the suburban railroads. Also, by the early 1950s several influential private groups in the city had already declared their support for region-wide public action to improve rail service.[67]

Yet it was not certain that the city would be able to exert vigorous leadership on regional transportation. New York seemed unable to coordinate the planning and financing of its own transportation facilities. The Triborough Authority, the Department of Traffic, the city's transit agency, and several other city units worked semi-independently and often at cross purposes. Also, important as a new regional transport policy might be to New York City, the mayor and his aides found their energies occupied during the early 1950s with the problems of subway fares and deficits. Creation of a Transit Authority in 1954 reduced city-state conflict on the issue, but the complexities and political difficulties involved did little to encourage the mayor to venture into the broader intercity problem.[68] Finally—and related to these other difficulties—the mayor's office has not traditionally been a strong center of leadership, in part, because of weaknesses in the mayor's formal powers. As Sayre and Kaufman conclude,

His fiscal powers are few; his managerial reach is curtailed by insufficient staff inadequately organized for his own needs; his powers to supervise are reduced by the numerous islands of autonomy among the administrative agencies; his inclinations toward initiative and innovation are resisted by the inertial weight of the bureaucracies and their constituencies.

And in part it has been a matter of personality; many of the incumbents have lacked the capacity to use the strength of the office to its full potential.[69]

Fragmentation at the local level has left a leadership vacuum which state officials might fill. The governors of New York and New Jersey have had important incentives to respond to regional needs. In New York State, about 60 percent of the votes for governor during postwar elections have been cast by residents of the New York metropolitan region; the New Jersey proportion has exceeded 70 percent.[70] Also, the public has tended to look to the governor for leadership because of the state's important role in local affairs, the visibility of the gubernatorial chair, and the lack of an alternative source of action.[71]

On the rail transit issue, however, several obstacles stood in the way of gubernatorial action during the first postwar decade. First, there was no established pattern of active state leadership on rail transportation problems—of the sort that characterized education and highways, for example. Although in the early 1950s New York took more positive steps to meet the special problems of the Long Island Rail Road, traditional state policy had been concerned almost entirely with regulation of passenger service. Second, it was not clear what actions would be useful. The technical and financial complexities were considerable, especially when the question of constructing new rail lines was involved and when interstate coordination might be required. Vigorous gubernatorial action would be difficult under these circumstances. Third, no major crisis developed during the first postwar decade. Pressures upon the governor to overcome past tradition and cut through the complexities to a prompt solution were not strong.

Finally, the governors faced many other demands upon their limited resources. State programs in education, welfare, and other areas demanded the executives' attention and tended to take precedence—since the traditional role of the states was larger in these areas, the political costs of inaction were perceived to be greater, or at least more immediate, and the possible lines of productive action seemed clearer. Little time or political energy remained for the rail transit issue.[72]

During the early postwar years, gubernatorial action was tentative and exploratory, except under conditions of crisis. Between 1951 and 1954, after bankruptcy and a series of major accidents had beset the Long Island Rail Road, New York State did act to stabilize and improve that line's financial condition.[73] In the late 1940s, New Jersey's Governor Driscoll investigated several plans for improving rail service in northern New Jersey, but no action was taken because of the projected deficits involved. And sporadically during the early 1950s, Governors Dewey and Driscoll explored the possibility of Port Authority action to build a New Jersey–Manhattan rail system.[74] These were the limits of gubernatorial action on the region's rail problem during the early postwar period.

Important obstacles also stood in the way of effective legislative action on the region's transportation problems. Although representatives from the region held a majority in three of the four legislative houses of New York and New Jersey (all but the New Jersey Senate), they did not form a self-conscious, organized bloc. On the contrary, they were divided by political party and, on some problems, further subdivided by geography. Since in this period the Republicans usually controlled all four houses, Republican legislators from the region—from suburban Bergen and Westchester, for example—were especially influential in the making of policy affecting the metropolis. To some extent this Republican bias improved the outlook for legislative action on an issue as important to the suburbs as commuter rail service, but nonregional delegates were not dependable allies if the use of substantial state funds to assist one area was involved. In addition, the limited influence of the Democratic leaders of the region's major cities in the state legislatures might make it difficult to develop policies which would obtain the cities' positive cooperation.

The pattern of political forces in the New York region thus provided a firm base for continuing the highway-oriented policies of the first postwar decade and little reason for optimism on the part of those who wanted more "balanced" development of road and rail facilities. The road coalition was opposed to contributing its funds to aid rail services or to restricting its independence through a cooperative planning effort, and the fragmentation of governmental leadership mitigated against a reassessment of transport policy by local or state officials. Even so, continued deterioration of rail service could unify and extend the rail coalition and increase the possibility of direct action in the future, especially from two sources: the governors, who—though reluctant—might feel impelled to act, and the Port Authority, which in spite of its political strength was potentially the most vulnerable member of the road coalition because of its wealth and regional transportation mandate.

Meanwhile, the proponents of further aid to the rail system

sought to develop an interim strategy—a comprehensive study of the transportation problem—which might effectively serve its long-range goals.

NOTES

1. For the purpose of this study, the New York region includes twenty-two counties in three states: nine in New Jersey—Bergen, Essex, Hudson, Middlesex, Monmouth, Morris, Passaic, Somerset, and Union; five in New York City—New York (Manhattan), Bronx, Queens, Kings (Brooklyn), and Richmond (Staten Island); seven New York counties outside New York City—Nassau, Suffolk, Dutchess, Orange, Putnam, Rockland, and Westchester; and Fairfield in Connecticut. This is the region as defined by the RPA, the area's major private organization concerned with overall planning. For some purposes, one additional county in New Jersey, Mercer, may also be included.

   The U.S. Bureau of the Census includes only seventeen of the twenty-two counties in its comparable unit, now called the New York–Northeastern New Jersey Standard Consolidated Area. Excluded from the Bureau's tabulation are several of the outlying counties—Dutchess, Orange, Putnam, Monmouth, and Fairfield (which was subdivided into three separate metropolitan areas in the 1960 census tabulations).

2. See John T. Cunningham, *Railroading in New Jersey* (Newark, Associated Railroads of New Jersey, 1951), pp. 6–61, 35–55, and *passim*, also references therein, p. 107. See also Jean Gottmann, *Megalopolis: The Urbanized Northeastern Seaboard of the United States* (New York, Twentieth Century Fund, 1961), Chap. 3.

3. The first major effort was begun in the 1870s by an engineer, D. C. Haskins. The project was first halted in 1880, when part of the structure collapsed, killing twenty men; in 1882, after building 1,800 feet of tunnel, Haskins' company went into bankruptcy. The company was reorganized eight years later and carried the tunnel forward another 1,800 feet before again going into bankruptcy. See Cunningham, *Railroading in New Jersey*, pp. 62–63.

4. The Pennsylvania then continued the tunnel under the East River to provide direct access to Manhattan for passengers and freight on the Long Island Rail Road, which the Pennsylvania now controlled.

5. See New York State, Public Service Commission for the First District, *Report . . . for the Year Ending December 31, 1913*, Vol. V: *Documentary History of Railroad Companies* (New York, 1914), pp. 605–20, 768–72, 881–84, 978; Alvin F. Harlow, *The Road of the Century: The Story of the New York Central* (New York, Creative Age Press, 1947), pp. 130, 204–06.

6. The system begun in 1904 was the Interborough Rapid Transit (IRT); it was constructed and owned by the city and leased for operation to a private firm. In 1913 the Brooklyn Rapid Transit Company, later Brooklyn-Manhattan Transit (BMT), entered the subway field, and in 1925 construction of a city-owned system, the Independent (IND), was begun.

7. The joint board, known as the Suburban Transit Engineering Board,

included representatives from the Port of New York Authority, Association of Railroad Executives, New York City Board of Transportation, North Jersey Transit Commission, and the county boards of supervisors of Westchester, Nassau, and Suffolk. See Erwin W. Bard, *The Port of New York Authority* (New York, Columbia University Press, 1942), pp. 128–32.

8. In the plans of the North Jersey Transit Commission and the joint board, passengers would transfer in Hudson County from the New Jersey railroads to a new trans-Hudson rail line. This line would carry them under the Hudson River in one of two tunnels and deliver them to stations between 57th Street and the Battery in Manhattan. The Port Authority's 1937 plan was a limited version of this proposal. Another approach to the trans-Hudson problem, used in L. Alfred Jenny's 1936 plan, involved the construction of larger tunnels in order to transport the railroad trains directly into Manhattan; a terminal to receive the trains would be constructed at about 42nd Street and Sixth Avenue. In addition to the New Jersey–Manhattan plans, the North Jersey Commission included several new rail linkages in New Jersey and a new rapid transit line from Manhattan to Westchester, the joint board would have connected Long Island to Manhattan via a new subway loop, and the Port Authority plan included a linkage from the New Jersey–Manhattan system to Staten Island. See L. Alfred Jenny, "Report on the Acute Transportation Problem Existing between Northeastern New Jersey and the City of New York" (Trenton, Department of Conservation and Economic Development, State of New Jersey, 1951), pp. 7–11, 15–29; RPA, *Regional Plan Bulletin*, No. 25 (New York, June 17, 1935); Bard, *Port of New York Authority*, pp. 128–34; PNYA, *Suburban Transit for Northern New Jersey*, March 1, 1937; statements of Austin J. Tobin and Walter P. Hedden on behalf of the PNYA, before the New York Metropolitan Rapid Transit Commission, Nov. 12, 1953.

9. See especially Bard, *Port of New York Authority*, p. 132; Jenny, "Report on the Acute Transportation Problem," pp. 17–23, 27; statement of Austin J. Tobin, Nov. 12, 1953, pp. 2–6.

10. See RPA, *Regional Plan Bulletin*, No. 77 (New York, July, 1951), Wilfred Owen, *The Metropolitan Transportation Problem* (Washington, D.C., The Brookings Institution, 1956), *passim*. On this section and the rest of this chapter, see Robert C. Wood (with V. V. Almendinger), *1400 Governments: The Political Economy of the New York Metropolitan Region* (Cambridge, Mass., Harvard University Press, 1961), especially pp. 123–44.

11. NYMRTC and NJMRTC, *Joint Report* (March 3, 1954), pp. 10–11, 14, 65; RPA, *Regional Plan Bulletin*, No. 77.

12. Federal-aid highway plans for urban areas approved between 1944 and 1955, for example, involved $3 billion in state and federal funds. Owen, *Metropolitan Transportation Problem*, p. 62. The highway program was greatly expanded by the Federal-Aid Highway Act of 1956.

13. On the Port Authority, see Bard, *Port of New York Authority*, Part II, and Wallace S. Sayre and Herbert Kaufman, *Governing New York City: Politics in the Metropolis* (New York, Russell Sage Foundation, 1960; paperback edition, New York, Norton, 1965), pp. 321–22. On the Triborough Authority, see State of New York, Temporary State Commission

on Coordination of State Authorities, *Staff Report on Public Authorities under New York State*, March 21, 1956, pp. 26, 30–31, and *passim*.

14. NYMRTC and NJMRTC, *Joint Report*, pp. 12–13.

15. See Gottmann, *Megalopolis*, Chap. 4; Owen, *Metropolitan Transportation Problem*, Chap. 3. The ferry problem warrants a word of explanation. The trans-Hudson ferries carried passengers from the New Jersey railroad terminals across the river to terminals in downtown Manhattan. Because lower Manhattan was narrow, these terminals were within easy walking distance of employment centers in the area. But when the midtown area expanded rapidly, the railroad-ferry system was unable to serve the new job centers effectively. A longer, up-river ferry trip would have been required, and the greater width of mid-Manhattan would have left the commuters many blocks from their destinations.

16. See Owen, *Metropolitan Transportation Problem*, especially pp. 99–104; Interstate Commerce Commission, "Railroad Passenger Train Deficit," Docket No. 31954, decided May 18, 1959; Robert W. Purcell, "Special Report to the Governor on Problems of the Railroads and Bus Lines in New York State" (New York, March 12, 1959), pp. 51–52.

17. Passenger service problems were especially important factors in the financial difficulties of the Long Island Rail Road and the H&M, both of which went into bankruptcy during the early post-war years.

18. The 240,000 railroad commuters included 106,000 from New Jersey, 59,000 from Westchester and Fairfield, and 75,000 from Long Island. The count included those entering the city between 7:00 and 10:00 A.M. on a weekday. See RPA, *Regional Plan Bulletin*, No. 77, p. 6. According-ing to an estimate made several years later, if all the rail commuters from New Jersey were to shift to automobiles, twenty new expressway lanes in New Jersey, ten trans-Hudson tubes, and 250 acres of parking space in Manhattan would be required to handle the additional traffic. MRTS, *Report of the Project Director* (New York, May 20, 1957), p. 14.

19. RPA, *Regional Plan Bulletin*, No. 77, p. 2. Cf. Owen, *Metropolitan Transportation Problem*, Chap. 9.

20. Harry Eckstein, *Pressure Group Politics: The Case of the British Medical Association* (London, George Allen and Unwin, 1960), p. 34; see also pp. 33–38. Cf. David B. Truman, *The Governmental Process: Political Interests and Public Opinion* (New York, Knopf, 1951), pp. 506–07, 322 ff., and *passim*.

21. For the views of railroad officials on these problems, see, for example, the statement of Roland Davis, Jr., of the Lackawanna Railroad and the statement of E. C. Nickerson of the New York Central system before the NYMRTC, Nov. 13, 1953. In a broad sense, the city agency responsible for the New York City subway system is a member of the rail coalition; but the direct responsibilities of this agency (the Board of Transportation until 1953, the New York City Transit Authority subsequently) are limited to the city, and it has rarely had an important role in the development of transport policies for the broader region. Also, access to large amounts of public funds and other factors place it in a very different political milieu from that of the private railroads. On the politics of the Transit Authority, see Sayre and Kaufman, *Governing New York City*, pp. 323 ff.

22. The quotations above are found in remarks by William Reid, president

of the H&M, at the Sixth Regional Plan Conference, Oct. 9, 1951. See also his statement of Feb. 9, 1953, and his "Report on Proposed New York–New Jersey Rapid Transit System," Nov. 1, 1953; statement of Roland Davis, Jr., of the Lackawanna, and statement of Henry K. Norton, president of the Susquehanna, before the NYMRTC, Nov. 13, 1953; speech by David I. Mackie, chairman, Eastern Railroad Presidents Conference, before the American Association of Port Authorities, Sept. 24, 1953.

23. IMGBRS, "Report," Dec. 1, 1950, pp. 14, 34. This report includes a history of IMGBRS activities through 1950; see also other reports, briefs, and petitions prepared by IMGBRS during the late 1940s and early 1950s.

24. Some of the attitudes and activities of these organizations are outlined in their 1953 statements before the NYMRTC, which are summarized in NYMRTC and NJMRTC, *Joint Report*, pp. 101–02; see also IMGBRS, "Report," Dec. 1, 1950, pp. 11–12; Newark *Evening News*, Feb. 23, 1954, and Dec. 7, 1958. Compare the comments on commuter organizations in Chicago; Edward C. Banfield, *Political Influence* (New York, Free Press, 1960), especially pp. 111–12.

25. "Petition for Reconsideration" by the IMGBRS, before the Interstate Commerce Commission and Board of Public Utility Commissioners of the State of New Jersey, I&S Docket No. 5585, July 1, 1949, p. 52.

26. See IMGBRS, "Report," Dec. 1, 1950, p. 25; statement of Carleton G. MacLean, chairman of the Transit Committee of Bergen County, before the NYMRTC, Nov. 12, 1953; statement of the Westchester County Planning Commission before the NYMRTC, Nov. 13, 1953. Suggestions that the Port Authority consider taking on transit responsibilities are found, for example, in the Newark *Sunday News*, Sept. 27, 1953, and the Bergen *Evening Record*, Sept. 29, 1953. The possibility of local tax support was suggested by the New Brunswick *Daily Home News*, Nov. 6, 1951, and by the Westchester County Planning Commission, statement, Nov. 13, 1953.

27. For a contrasting view of the commuter, see Robert C. Wood, "A Division of Powers in Metropolitan Areas," in Arthur Maass, ed., *Area and Power: A Theory of Local Government* (New York, Free Press, 1959), pp. 53–69.

28. For background information on these central-city interests, see Sayre and Kaufman, *Governing New York City*, especially pp. 76–86, 481–515; Forbes B. Hayes, *Community Leadership: The Regional Plan Association of New York* (New York, Columbia University Press, 1965). An analysis of similar interests in Chicago is presented in Banfield, *Political Influence*, Chaps. 9, 10, and *passim*.

29. The views of the Avenue of the Americas Association are outlined in its memorandum submitted to the NYMRTC and the NJMRTC, Nov. 10, 1953; the quotation is on p. 12. For positions taken by other groups, see, for example, the Report of the New York Chamber of Commerce, December, 1951; RPA, *Regional Plan Bulletin*, No. 77, July, 1951; statement of the Citizens Budget Commission, Nov. 13, 1953; New York *Herald Tribune*, April 9, 1954.

30. The central-city interests took a more sympathetic view of the railroad companies' problems, partly because of the private enterprise orientation

of the city associations and partly because they were less directly affected by rail service deterioration than were the commuter groups. In addition, railroad officials were often important members of the city organizations; in the 1950s, for example, the president of the H&M was chairman of the transportation committee of the Avenue of the Americas Association, and a New York Central vice-president held a similar position with the West Side Association of Commerce.

31. Livingston's views are outlined in his statement before the NYMRTC, Nov. 12, 1953. See also Luther Gulick, "The Next Twenty-five Years in Government in the New York Metropolitan Region," Oct. 6, 1954, re-printed in *Metropolis in the Making: The Next Twenty-five Years in the New York Metropolitan Region* (New York, RPA, 1955), pp. 58–77.

32. See especially the sources cited in Notes 21, 22, 24, 26, and 29 of this chapter.

33. For an excellent analysis of the political behavior of these two agencies and other public authorities operating in New York City, see Sayre and Kaufman, *Governing New York City*, Chap. 9.

34. For a more detailed presentation of the early development of the PNYA, see Bard, *Port of New York Authority*, especially pp. 54 ff., 177 ff., 329 ff.

35. PNYA acquisition of the region's airports is described in Herbert Kaufman, "Gotham in the Air Age," in Harold Stein, ed., *Public Administration and Policy Development: A Case Book* (New York, Harcourt, Brace, 1952), pp. 143–97.

36. The PNYA decided to take part in a study of the rail passenger problem in the face of objections by New York Governor Alfred E. Smith. In defense of its actions, the Port Authority argued that "no adequate or effective transportation development could take place without taking full account of transportation of passengers as well as freight." (Resolution adopted by the Board of Commissioners, June, 1928; see Bard, *Port of New York Authority*, pp. 128–32.)

37. PNYA, *Suburban Transit for Northern New Jersey*, March 1, 1937, p. 10; this report is reprinted in U.S. House of Representatives, Committee on the Judiciary, *Port of New York Authority, Hearings before Subcommittee No. 5*, 86th Cong., 2d Sess. (1960) pp. 1965–99. The 1949 plan is described in Jenny, "Report on the Acute Transportation Problem," pp. 31–33, and in Tobin, statement before the NYMRTC, Nov. 12, 1953, p. 6–7.

38. See RPA, *Regional Plan Bulletin*, No. 77; Newark *Sunday News*, Sept. 27, 1953; and Tobin, statement before the NYMRTC, Nov. 12, 1953, pp. 6–10, where the interest of Governor Driscoll is outlined briefly.

39. See Austin J. Tobin, "The Work and Program of the Port of New York Authority," Feb. 10, 1953; PNYA, *Annual Report, 1952*, p. 1. In contrast with many public agencies, whose end-systems are complex and often reflect "compromise among essentially incompatible interests," the Port Authority had a relatively clear and consistent set of goals. Thus, it could pursue its interests in vigorous and single-minded fashion, while its less fortunate brethren followed a more hesitant path. See Edward C. Banfield, "Ends and Means in Planning," *International Social Science Journal*, XI (1959), 361–68; also, Martin Meyerson and Edward C. Banfield, *Politics, Planning, and the Public Interest: The Case of Public Housing in Chicago* (New York, Free Press, 1955), pp. 320 ff.

40. The quotations are from Newark's Mayor Leo Carlin (Newark *Evening News*, March 25, 1954); Newark *Evening News*, editorial, April 30, 1951; and Chamber of Commerce of the State of New York, "A Statement of American Economic Principles," quoted in Tobin, "The Work and Program of the Port of New York Authority," p. 21. For compilations of favorable comments on the PNYA during the early postwar period, see the booklets issued by the Port Authority on its twenty-fifth and thirtieth anniversaries (April 30, 1946 and 1951).

    Some of the praise for the Port Authority and other authorities is combined with a strong measure of dissatisfaction with the normal workings of the democratic process. As the New York *World-Telegram & Sun* editorialized, "The truth is that all too frequently men elected to office are not qualified to tangle with complicated, modern municipal management. They may be overly vote-conscious. They may be hogtied to political bosses. They may be just plain incompetent. But whatever the reason, time after time when the politicians have gotten in a jam they have had to create an authority and call on successful businessmen to bail them out" (March 12, 1952).

41. Meyerson and Banfield, *Politics, Planning, and the Public Interest*, p. 49.
42. PNYA, *Annual Report, 1952*, pp. 54–55, and "List of Port of New York Authority Commissioners and Principal Staff Members and their Corporate Affiliations," submitted to the Antitrust Subcommittee of the Committee on the Judiciary, House of Representatives, May, 1952.
43. Quoted from profile of Tobin, New York *Times*, July 14, 1959.
44. Samuel P. Huntington, *The Common Defense: Strategic Programs in National Politics* (New York, Columbia University Press, 1961), pp. 310–11. LeMay's organization was the Strategic Air Command, Hoover's the Federal Bureau of Investigation.
45. Salary figures are for 1960. See Newark *Evening News*, Feb. 26, 1960; reprinted in U.S. House of Representatives, *Port of New York Authority, Hearings before Subcommittee No. 5*, p. 181.
46. Sayre and Kaufman, *Governing New York City*, pp. 330–31.
47. Tobin, "The Work and Program of the Port of New York Authority," pp. 5–6. Tobin's business-oriented perspective is also reflected in his views on local government: "It is obvious that one of the primary subjects of citizen interest concerns the manner in which a municipality handles its finances. *Above all else*, the people expect their officials to give them prudent and conservative management of public funds." (Austin J. Tobin, "Public Relations and Financial Reporting in a Municipal Corporation," May 23, 1951, p. 11, emphasis added.) For contrasting views of the priorities in local government policy-making, see Meyerson and Banfield, *Politics, Planning, and the Public Interest*, and Sayre and Kaufman, *Governing New York City*, especially Chap. 19.
48. For example, the need to obtain approval of a municipality before connecting vehicular projects with city streets, the inability to use surplus revenues except for "such purposes as may be directed by the two states," independent audit, requirement for self-support, and removal of the commissioners for cause. The first assistant to the executive director listed these and other limitations on the Port Authority—including its annual reports and information given to the press—in concluding that the PNYA is subject to adequate democratic controls. (M. E. Lukens, "The Port of

184 The Politics of Transportation

New York Authority," address before the American Political Science Association, Sept. 12, 1953.)

49. Tobin, "Public Relations and Financial Reporting," p. 9. In Tobin's view, press releases and newspaper editorials could serve as adequate substitutes for the ballot box: "We look upon the press as the medium of exchange between our agency and the millions of people and thousands of businesses . . . for whom we are working in the Port District. During the past six years, the Port Authority has enjoyed approximately 1400 favorable editorials in the New York and New Jersey press. We feel we can interpret this as a vote of public confidence in our program" (p. 8). The effectiveness of the Port Authority's public relations program is attested to by the several awards received by the agency's director of public relations, Mrs. Lee K. Jaffe. In 1950, for example, she received the Silver Anvil of the American Public Relations Association for "the most notable public relations performance in the field of government."

50. In addition to press relations, the PNYA uses several approaches in order to insure the friendly attention of the region's publics. A community relations department maintains continuing contact with the municipalities from which the Authority had leased facilities and operates a speakers' bureau. Port Authority executives meet frequently with investment banking groups and other business associations to explain the Authority's work. And staff members are active in the affairs of several of the nongovernmental associations in the region; during the mid-1950s, for example, one PNYA official was an officer of the New York Real Estate Board, and another was a trustee of the Citizens Budget Commission.

51. The 1960 House investigation uncovered occasional examples of other relationships between the PNYA and its political environment. For several years prior to 1952, for example, the Port Authority handled part of its insurance so as to add to the income of a firm owned by an important state legislator in New York. During the period 1945–52, this assemblyman introduced twenty bills favored by the PNYA; and several resolutions calling for investigation of the Port Authority died in the Ways and Means Committee, which he chaired. See U.S. House of Representatives, *Port of New York Authority, Hearings before Subcommittee No. 5*, pp. 1173–97, 1448–57.

52. Prior to the postwar period, the minutes of the Port Authority had been vetoed only once, by Governor Herbert Lehman, and that veto had later been withdrawn. Governor Thomas E. Dewey vetoed the minutes relating to award of a bus terminal construction contract in 1949, and Alfred E. Driscoll vetoed between five and ten PNYA resolutions, most of them of little importance, during his two terms as New Jersey's governor (1947–54). The few occasions on which the veto power has been used contrast with the hundreds of actions taken by the Port Authority's Board without gubernatorial objection. In general, the governors appear to agree with the views outlined by Governor Alfred E. Smith in 1927 and quoted favorably by the Authority in subsequent years: "The reserved veto power . . . was to safeguard the states against any abuse of power by a Port Authority Commissioner. It was not intended to give the Governor of each state the power to review the acts of Commissioners and to revise their judgments."

53. Quoted in the Port Authority's *Annual Report, 1952*, frontispiece. See the similar views of Governor Driscoll on the page opposite Dewey's statement.

54. In late 1951 and early 1952, three planes crashed in the vicinity of Newark Airport, bringing the PNYA under attack and causing the airport to be closed temporarily. Hearings on the airport problem and on the Port Authority's activities generally were conducted by the New Jersey Joint Legislative Committee and by two committees of the House of Representatives. One of the House Committees, Judiciary, took testimony on a resolution introduced by Representative Alfred D. Sieminski, Democrat of Hudson County, to rescind congressional consent to the compact creating the PNYA. During this period, the agency was vigorously attacked by a number of groups; it was called a "totalitarian government" by one Newark public official and a "Mafia organization" by Sieminski. In spite of intense criticism in a few areas, the Port Authority was able to muster widespread support for its work and emerged unscathed. See Paul Tillet and Myron Weiner, *The Closing of Newark Airport* (University, University of Alabama Press, 1955); U.S. House of Representatives, Committee on the Judiciary, *Hearings before the Anti-Trust Subcommittee on a Resolution to Rescind the Consent of Congress Creating the Port of New York Authority*, 82d Cong., 2d sess. (1952), 5 vols.; New York *Herald Tribune*, May 22, 1952.

55. Herbert Kaufman, "Gotham in the Air Age" (Washington, Committee on Public Administration Cases, 1950), p. 65. On Moses, see also Sayre and Kaufman, *Governing New York City*, pp. 320 ff., 381–82; John B. Keeley, *Moses on the Green* (University, University of Alabama Press, 1959); Rexford G. Tugwell, "The Moses Effect," in Edward C. Banfield, *Urban Government: A Reader in Politics and Administration* (New York, Free Press, 1961), pp. 462–72. Later additions to the Moses empire include the Throgs Neck Bridge and the Verrazano-Narrows Bridge.

56. *New York Times*, March 24, 1959.

57. See TBTA, *Annual Report*, 1952; State of New York, Temporary State Commission on Coordination of State Activities, *Staff Report*, pp. 30–31.

58. For a detailed presentation of Livingston's views, see his statement before the NYMRTC, Nov. 12, 1953.

59. Letter to Charles H. Tuttle, chairman of the NYMRTC, Nov. 12, 1953.

60. The bond resolutions under which TBTA bonds were sold authorized it to pledge its revenues only for vehicular projects and the New York Coliseum (under the 1952 resolution). Therefore, any attempt to issue bonds for rapid transit projects would appear to subject existing bondholders to risks they could not have foreseen and thus would violate state and federal constitutional provisions against impairing the obligation of contracts. Complete refinancing, a complex procedure, would probably be required before tolls from TBTA projects could be allocated to rail transit. See the analysis in William Miller, *Metropolitan Rapid Transit Financing* (Princeton, N.J., 1957), pp. 27–29, 103–5.

61. The allusion to "close contact" among the various agencies and examples of cooperation are contained in the statement of the district engineer (New York region), New York State Department of Public Works, before the NYMRTC, Nov. 13, 1953. For the attitudes of user groups, see, for example, the praise directed toward the Port Authority by the

bus companies upon the opening of the PNYA Bus Terminal in 1949 (reprinted in U.S. House of Representatives, *Port of New York Authority, Hearings before Subcommittee No. 5,* pp. 1247–54); and Chaps. VIII-IX of this volume. Conflict between Moses and the Port Authority arose during the latter 1940s and early 1950s over the issues of construction of the PNYA bus terminal, responsibility for the region's airports, and a projected mid-Manhattan expressway. By 1954, however, the two agencies had agreed to cooperate in the expansion of arterial facilities in the region. Some of the conflicts are described by Kaufman, in Stein, ed., *Public Administration.* The fruits of cooperation between the agencies, a $570-million arterial program, are outlined in their report, *Joint Study of Arterial Facilities* (New York, January, 1955).

62. Robert C. Wood, *1400 Governments,* pp. 113, 118, and see generally Chaps. 1–3.

63. See Edward Sofen, *The Metropolitan Miami Experiment* (Bloomington, Indiana University Press, 1963); David A. Booth, *Metropolitics: The Nashville Consolidation* (East Lansing, Institute for Community Development and Services, Michigan State University, 1963); RPA, "The Handling of Metropolitan Problems in Selected Regions," 1958.

64. The twenty-one cities are Bayonne (74,000), Bloomfield (52,000), Clifton (82,000), East Orange (77,000), Elizabeth (108,000), Jersey City (276,000), Newark (405,000), Passaic (53,000), Paterson (144,000), Union (51,000), Union City (52,000), and Woodbridge (79,000) in New Jersey; Hicksville (50,000) and Levittown (65,000) on Long Island; Mount Vernon (76,000), New Rochelle (77,000), White Plains (50,000), and Yonkers (191,000) in Westchester; and Bridgeport (157,000), Norwalk (68,000), and Stamford (93,000) in Connecticut (all populations for 1960).

65. As the RPA has commented, "The region has no centralized 'business community' in the sense that some smaller regions have. . . . Leadership in the region's central cities is becoming increasingly concerned with the problems of a particular area such as Newark or downtown Manhattan, rather than with problems of a regional nature." ("The Handling of Metropolitan Problems in the Tri-State Metropolitan Region," June, 1958, p. 12). For a well-documented study of intraregional conflict in the early years of the century, see Bard, *The Port of New York Authority,* Chaps. 1 and 2.

In 1960, the U.S. Bureau of the Census renamed its seventeen-county unit the New York–Northeastern New Jersey Standard Consolidated Area. (See note 1 of this chapter.) The Bureau then subdivided the Consolidated Area into several Standard Metropolitan Statistical Areas. This change had been urged upon the Bureau by representatives of Newark and other cities in the region and was received in these cities with satisfaction. It was attacked by New York City and other regional spokesmen, however, as being in conflict with the economic interdependence of the entire region.

66. On the discussion that follows, see Sayre and Kaufman, *Governing New York City,* especially Chaps. 13, 15, 18, 19. See also Chapter VII of this volume, concerning the crucial role of the city's mayor and his aides in the establishment of the Metropolitan Regional Council.

67. See discussion of the rail coalition, pp. 21–27 of this volume.

68. On the city's divided transport responsibilities, see Sayre and Kaufman, *Governing New York City*, especially Chap. 9 and pp. 295–98. On the Transit Authority, see also footnote 21 above; State of New York, Temporary State Commission on Coordination of State Activities, *Staff Report*, pp. 35–37 and *passim*; and a study of the conflict leading to creation of the Transit Authority, William Miller, "Metropolitanism, Transit, and Politics in New York City and State, 1953," unpublished undergraduate thesis, Harvard College, 1954.

69. Sayre and Kaufman, *Governing New York City*, p. 699. See generally Chap. 18.

70. Compiled from the *Legislative Manuals* of New York and New Jersey. The incentive for gubernatorial leadership in Connecticut was considerably less, since only part of one county—comprising less than one-tenth of the statewide electorate—was significantly concerned with transportation in the New York region.

71. "By law . . . and by tradition" the Governor of New York has a commanding role in policy and political leadership in the state; see Lynton Caldwell, *The Government and Administration of New York* (New York, Crowell, 1954), pp. 80 ff. With the increased tenure and powers provided by the 1947 Constitution, New Jersey also has a "strong governor" system. On gubernatorial leadership in New Jersey, see Duane Lockard, *The New Jersey Governor: A Study in Political Power* (Princeton, N.J., Van Nostrand, 1964), especially Chapter 6.

72. On the general reluctance of political leaders to act quickly and decisively, see Banfield, *Political Influence*, p. 270 ff.

73. In 1951 the state created the Long Island Transit Authority and charged it with responsibility for developing a plan to rehabilitate the railroad, if possible under private ownership. As a result of the Authority's effort, a plan was devised and was accepted by the state in 1954, calling for tax concessions, special rate-making powers, and financial assistance from the controlling corporation (the Pennsylvania Railroad). The plan included a $60-million rehabilitation program and was to last twelve years.

74. Some of the developments are discussed in Jenny, "Report on the Acute Transportation Problem," pp. 31–37; Port Authority Memorandum to Governor Driscoll, November, 1951; Newark *Evening News*, Nov. 4, 1951; Jenny, statement before the MRTC, New York Public Hearing (New York, Sept. 17, 1957), p. 111; Tobin, statement before the NYMRTC, Nov. 12, 1953.

The Politics of Urban Education

INTRODUCTION

The American elementary and secondary educational system has
been marked by three distinctive and in many ways salutary features. First, in contrast to European school systems, which provided high-quality education to a fee-paying middle class while
offering only limited educational opportunities to the working-
class masses, Americans at an early point developed a common
school serving a broader range of children in their communities.
Secondly, rather than being administered and financed by a centralized government agency, the control of local schools was left
in the hands of locally elected school boards. Thirdly, the professionalization of American schools came early, as teachers, principals, and superintendents were expected to have specialized
training in the theory and practice of teaching and educational
administration.

THE EARLY AMERICAN SCHOOL

These characteristics of late nineteenth- and early twentieth-
century school systems were in many ways appropriate to a rural,
frontier society undergoing rapid industrial development. When
America was dotted by small towns and medium-sized cities, most
neighborhood schools were in fact "common" schools, catering
to the educational needs of a fairly wide range of social groups.

188

Rich and poor, Protestants and Catholics, sons of plumbers and doctors, able and slow, all usually attended the same school.

Of course, educational institutions far from obliterated all social distinctions. Many (but not all) Catholics preferred their own parochial schools. In larger cities, neighborhood schools in ethnic and religious enclaves reinforced these divisions in the community. Above all, the educational opportunities for Southern blacks were scandalously limited: Either they had no schooling at all or they were segregated in small, dilapidated buildings with poorly prepared teachers and inadequate supplies.

But even with these important exceptions, the common school was nonetheless a great innovation that expanded educational opportunities for young Americans far beyond what their counterparts in Europe enjoyed. As Heidenheimer reports, the proportion of adolescents in secondary schools passed the "10–12-per-cent mark about 1910" in the United States, while in Europe this was generally not reached until after 1945; "the 30-per-cent mark was passed by the U.S. in the early 1920's, in Europe not until the 1960's."[1]

Local control of this educational system was also an appropriate arrangement for nineteenth-century American conditions. Although local control had its drawbacks—particularly in the poor treatment that blacks received at the hands of Southern whites—it was clearly the most feasible system of school governance. Because towns and cities were spread out over a vast geographical landscape that could be traversed only with great time and effort, more centralized administration would have been difficult. Moreover, cities and towns at that time were social and economic as well as political units. Children born in the community expected to spend their productive years in the same area. Because the impact of the schools was thus primarily local, it was reasonable that decisions concerning the schools also be made locally. Then, too, America was so diverse a nation, with so many regional, ethnic, and religious groups, that it could forestall conflict over sensitive educational policies only by permitting each community to decide curricular matters and school religious practices in ways consistent with that community's values. All in all, only a locally controlled school board could in those days have won the taxpayer support necessary to finance the rapidly expanding educational system.

Thirdly, the effort to establish high, professional standards was important for schools in a rough, crude society only a few years past its frontier days. Although Americans approved of the practical, economic value of schooling, they lacked much appreciation for the life of the intellectual. Even though schools were felt to be necessary, schoolmen were not held in particularly high esteem. In the words of the familiar cliché, "Those who can, do; those who can't, teach." Such views expressed the American belief that anyone who could read and write should be able to teach others how to do the same. More than in most countries, the job was regarded as "women's work," rather beneath the dignity of an ambitious, forceful male. Because only modest educational accomplishments were expected, teachers were poorly paid and schools were at times staffed by the relatives and friends of board members rather than the most qualified personnel available.

Concerned educators sought to reform these defects by encouraging the professionalization of teaching and educational administration. They established teachers' colleges, programs in educational administration, and agencies of accreditation. They worked in state legislatures for laws that required of teachers a specific number and variety of educational courses and practical teaching experiences. Principals and superintendents were expected to have studied the "science of administration" that was developing in the early 1900's. And these reform efforts were rewarded by more highly educated teachers, tidier administration, gradually improved salaries, and a strict separation of the workings of political parties from the conduct of educational affairs. Indeed, for many Americans, the belief that education and politics should not mix became an unquestioned truth.

THE MODERN AMERICAN SCHOOL

The characteristic features of the nineteenth- and early twentieth-century educational system have since gathered behind them the weight of historical tradition, making their alteration difficult, if not impossible. Yet, however appropriate they once were for an agrarian, postfrontier, newly developing society, these same institutional characteristics are much less adequate for the metropolitan, mobile, highly interdependent, postindustrial society that America has, in recent decades, come to be.

The common neighborhood school no longer serves a wide range of social and intellectual groups in the community. In metropolitan areas, it has become, instead, a highly stratified institution that serves distinctive student populations. The growth of cities and suburbs, together with the class, racial, and ethnic segregation of their neighborhoods, has created neighborhood schools that serve highly selective student populations. The racial segregation in our urban schools is well known. But if blacks attend their own schools, so do working-class whites, middle-class whites, the upper middle class, and, to a lesser extent, Poles, Jews, and Italians. If big-city schools always tended to be more homogeneous than those in rural areas, the recent rapid growth of metropolitan areas, with their one-class suburbs, has only accentuated and aggravated this tendency. Today, it can hardly be said that most young Americans are being educated in a "common" school.

With the change in the composition of the neighborhood school, local control has taken on a new significance. Locally elected boards of education have traditionally depended heavily on local property taxes to finance their schools. This tax falls very unevenly on citizens within the metropolitan area. In some communities, a local industrial plant or valuable residential property provides the school board with ample resources to finance local schools at an almost luxurious level. In other, sometimes adjacent communities, the presence of only modest homes, together with a large school-age population, may require that citizens make a considerable financial sacrifice in order to provide just moderately well-financed schools. Two adjacent cities in Michigan illustrate dramatically a more general pattern described by Campbell and Meranto in their article in this section. In Dearborn, property owners paid in 1970–71 a tax rate of only 25.90 mills per $100 of the assessed value of their property, but the school system was able to spend $1,297 per pupil for current expenditures.[2] In Dearborn Heights, taxpayers in that same year paid a millage rate of 27.90, which yielded enough to allow only $684 per pupil in current expenditures. The Dearborn Heights taxpayers would have had nearly to triple their tax rate to provide the same financial support for their schools that Dearborn already enjoyed at an already *lower* tax rate. The difference between the two cities is due to the large automobile plant in Dearborn; many workers employed by that plant live in Dearborn Heights, a town without industry. Such are the modern inequities of our historical legacy of local control.

Local financing of the educational system has been supplemented by state and federal assistance. But, although state aid has partially modified the inequities caused by variations in the tax base among local communities, it has hardly equalized matters.[3] For example, the Dearborn-Dearborn Heights figures take into account the state aid received by these communities. And federal aid to education, which still accounts for less than 15 per cent of the total amount spent on elementary and secondary education, has had at best only a slight equalizing impact on school district expenditures.

The professionalization of American education has also had its adverse consequences in urban America. Although it helped to modernize the country school, the very success of this reform has bred new difficulties. Nowhere is this problem more extreme than in New York City, as Marilyn Gittell documents in her case study of that system. In order to prevent patronage in the city's schools, every promotion within that organization was based on length of time in lower-level positions and performance on written and oral examinations. As a result, individuals from outside of the New York system, who may have new orientations and approaches, cannot be attracted to high-level positions. And performance on these examinations may have little to do with one's ability to act as a good principal or district superintendent. Moreover, the desire to have uniformity in operations in all schools (so as to avoid accusations of favoritism) has stifled individual creativity in a morass of bureaucratic rules, routines, and regulations. For example, the New York City supplies office once refused to issue order forms because the request was not filled out on an order form.[4]

THE POWER OF PROFESSIONALISM

The significance of the professionalization of American education is even greater in the political sphere. Because of their successful reform efforts to eliminate patronage politics from the schools, educational professionals have established themselves as the dominant voice in shaping educational policy. Professionally trained superintendents, with large supporting administrative staffs, control access to much of the information upon which a school board must make a decision. Nor can school boards easily dismiss school superintendents and/or their assistants, for this easily leads to charges of political interference in the educational process. Indeed, in most big city school systems, all employees, save only the superintendent, hold tenured positions, from which they cannot be removed unless malpractice or extreme incompetence is proven.

In recent years, teachers, too, have become an increasingly important political force. Previously, the National Education Association (NEA) and its state affiliates had sought to raise teacher salaries indirectly by campaigning for additional state and federal aid to education. In large cities, today, however, teachers are more directly influencing school-board policies affecting their salaries and working conditions. Both the more militant American Federation of Teachers and the previously less-aggresive NEA affiliates have demanded collective-bargaining agreements and carried out successful strikes when these agreements were not satisfactory. Not only have salaries in large city school systems dramatically improved, but teacher organizations are able to influence other policy questions as well. In Chicago, the teachers' union for a long time blocked all federal efforts to integrate the teaching faculty, and, in New York City, it substantially modified plans to introduce a decentralized system of administration and control.

Community organizations active in the educational arena have generally been neither very powerful nor very critical of the professional educators. The Parent-Teacher Association has local affiliates in most communities. Since these are neighborhood-oriented organizations closely associated with specific schools, they have generally had a limited impact on over-all school policy. In big cities, there is usually a city-wide organization (in New York, it is known as the Public Education Association; in Chicago, the Citizens Schools Committee) that focuses its attention on broader issues. Its membership consists largely of upper-middle-class Protestant and Jewish liberals interested in protecting the schools from political interference. Typically it has had considerable influence over the selection of school-board members. But once selected to serve, board members seldom feel very beholden to these organizations, which have too small a membership and too few financial resources to press for alternatives to plans developed by professionals within the school system itself.

Few other influential organizations sustain an active interest in the direction of school affairs. Labor unions may be interested in maintaining contact with the vocational programs, the Taxpayers Association may periodically object to increases in the tax rate for education, and the Chamber of Commerce or some other group of prominent businessmen may offer some public expression of general support for the schools in crisis situations. But, once the educational reformers chased the political parties out of education, they secured a good deal of autonomy over policy-making for themselves.

The one exception to this pattern has to do with racial issues. Although once again the educational professionals have played a major role in settling the issues of school desegregation, compensatory education, and community participation and control, they have not been able to pursue their goals free of outside pressure. Civil-rights groups, such as the NAACP, CORE, and, more frequently, *ad hoc* collections of black community organizations, have vigorously campaigned for racial integration. School professionals have not responded to these demands with great enthusiasm, and, as a result, little in the way of school integration has taken place in northern American cities.[5] But, when civil-rights groups have seen some hope of winning support from the educators, desegregation plans have aroused such intense opposition from white parents' associations and neighborhood groups that they have failed to be realized.[6] Blacks more recently have promoted the notion of community control as an alternative mechanism for improving the educational opportunities of black children. Here, they have met strong resistance from administrators and teachers, who fear this encroachment on their position of power. But with this demand, blacks may find it easier to form alliances with white neighborhood organizations, who also are demanding more community involvement.[7]

The structure of power within the educational arena is not perfectly stable; educational professionals are coming under increasing attack. The demands for community control are only one sign. The rapidly spreading "free school" idea, where parents pay money to send their children to a school that specializes in maintaining close teacher-parent contacts, is another. The increasing prestige of and state financial support for parochial schools indicate a decline in the pre-eminent position of the public school. Both liberal and conservative economists have suggested that parents be given educational vouchers that could be used to buy their children's education wherever they please. The Office of Economic Opportunity has, in fact, tried a number of experimental "tuition voucher" plans in selected cities. Elsewhere, some urban school boards are contracting particular schools to private firms, promising them extra payment if they can demonstrate that students are performing up to the level expected of them. The power of the professionals is rooted in their monopoly of control over educational opportunities. Should one or more of these various proposals for change be adopted on a widespread scale, the professionals' dominant position in the educational arena would be seriously endangered.

The traditional system is under attack, but one should not expect it to change all that quickly. Many interests in strong political positions are well served by a locally controlled, professionally directed neighborhood school system. Educational administrators have great influence in state capitols, and teachers are better organized than ever before. Politicians are still reluctant to entrap themselves in school controversies. And as Peterson notes in his essay in this section, the federal government's attempts at educational reform have made only a minor dent in local bureaucratic behavior.[8] The professionals are not the only beneficiaries, however. Local control of the public schools means that the upper middle class can have luxurious public schools for their children without providing the same, expensive education for all. Neighborhood schools also protect working- and middle-class whites from contact with the poor blacks whom they fear and distrust. The legacy of an outdated educational past will probably continue to contribute to the urban crisis.

NOTES

1. Arnold J. Heidenheimer, "The Politics of Public Education, Health and Welfare in the U.S. and Western Europe: How Growth and Reform Potentials have Differed" (paper presented at the 1972 Annual Meeting of the American Political Science Association, Washington, D.C., September 5–9, 1972), p. 5.

2. These figures are compiled from data presented in Michigan Department of Education, *Ranking of Michigan Public High School Districts by Selected Financial Data, 1970–71*, Bulletin 1012: December, 1971. The figures were compiled by Alan Thomas, Department of Education, University of Chicago, and we are indebted to Professor Thomas for his permission to use this information.

3. John E. Coons, William H. Clune III, and Stephen D. Sugarman, *Private Wealth and Public Education* (Cambridge, Mass.: Harvard University Press, 1970).

4. The example is taken from David Rogers, *110 Livingston Street* (New York: Random House, 1968), p. 274.

5. See *Ibid.*, pp. 305–23; and Robert Crain, *The Politics of Desegregation* (Chicago: Aldine Press, 1968), pp. 115–24.

6. See Rogers, *op. cit.*, Chapter 3; Bert Swanson, *The Struggle for Equality* (New York: Hobbs, Dorman, 1966); and Paul E. Peterson, "The School

Busing Controversy: Redistributive or Pluralist Politics," *Administrator's Notebook* XX (May, 1972), pp. 1–4.
7. A good discussion of the issues involved can be found in Henry M. Levin (ed.), *Community Control of Schools* (Washington, D.C.: The Brookings Institution, 1970).
8. The federal government has had a substantial impact on integration policies in the South, however. An excellent analysis of this effort can be found in Gary Orfield, *The Reconstruction of Southern Education* (New York: John Wiley and Sons, 1964).

BIBLIOGRAPHY

CRAIN, ROBERT. *The Politics of Desegregation.* Chicago: Aldine Press, 1968.

HERRICK, MARY. *The Chicago Schools: A Social and Political History.* Beverly Hills, California: Sage Publications, 1971.

MASOTTI, LOUIS H. *Education and Politics in Suburbia.* Cleveland: The Press of Case Western Reserve, 1967.

ORFIELD, GARY. *The Reconstruction of Southern Education.* New York: John Wiley and Sons, 1964.

PETERSON, PAUL E., and WILLIAM, THOMAS R. *School Politics: Chicago Model.* Forthcoming.

ROGERS, DAVID. *110 Livingston Street.* New York: Random House, 1968.

ROSENTHAL, ALAN, ed. *Governing Education.* Garden City, New York: Doubleday, 1969.

SILBERMAN, CHARLES E. *Crisis in the Classroom.* New York: Random House, 1970.

PROFESSIONALISM AND PUBLIC PARTICIPATION IN EDUCATIONAL POLICY-MAKING: NEW YORK CITY, A CASE STUDY

MARILYN GITTELL

Decision-making studies and analyses of local power structure in cities have much to contribute to an understanding of the operation of school systems. More intensive studies of decision-making and the distribution of power in school systems can, in turn, contribute significantly to knowledge of how cities are governed. Almost every study of power in large cities points to functional specialization, dispersion of power to specialists in particular areas, and an increased role of the bureaucracy in decision-making. This study of decision-making in the New York City school system concerns itself with the distribution of power, testing the hypothesis of functional specialization and hopefully expanding on its implications.

New York City as a Case Study

The New York City school system is nominally a dependent school district (that is, the school district does not have independent taxing power), and the city schools and school policy have often been described as strongly susceptible to local political influences.[1]

Concern in New York City with the failures of the education system was brought to a head by legislation introduced in the 1964 session of the Legislature to establish a fiscally independent school system. The Mayor requested the Temporary Commission

From Marilyn Gittell, "Professionalism and Public Participation in Educational Policy Making: New York City, a Case Study," in *Public Administration Review* XXVII, No. 3 (September, 1967), pp. 237–51. Copyright © 1967 by the American Society for Public Administration. Reprinted with the permission of the author and the American Society for Public Administration.

on City Finances to explore the feasibility of such a plan and to
review the general character of the administrative structure in
education, with special attention to the role of the Board of Education. An analysis of decision-making in education in New York
City was undertaken to determine the impact of fiscal independence on the existing structure. Since no previous study had fully
explored the sources and procedures of policy, there was little to
go on as to how the school system functioned under its existing
structure.

Five *areas* of decision-making were selected for study, on the
basis of diversity in the subject dealt with, the widest possible
range of participation by those involved in education, and relevance of the policy selected to the overall education function.
Generally, exploration of a continuum of policy was considered
superior to a single policy decision. Historical data and institutional analysis were utilized in all relevant areas.

Selected for intensive study were: (1) selection of the Superintendent, (2) increases in teachers' salaries, (3) budgeting, (4)
school integration, and (5) curriculum development. Other areas
of policy were reviewed in a more cursory way, to broaden the
scope of the analysis.[2]

Within any school system the potential participants in school
policy-making are essentially the same, although actual participation may vary according to the relative power of each in given circumstances. Legal power is usually divided between a board of
education and the superintendent. As regards the bureaucracy,
distinction must be made among the central administrative bureaucracy and field administrators, top supervisory staff, and middle management. Organizations representing these groups are
common in the larger school districts, and their activities can be
significant. Teachers and teacher organizations, parents and parent
organizations, are potential participants. Specialized education
interest groups (ad hoc and permanent) have been active in
many communities, and their role can be vital. In the general
community there are other potential participants, local, state, and
federal officials, civic groups, the press, business organizations, and
individual entrepreneurs seeking the rewards of the school system.[3]

The findings of the study emphasize that, in the last two decades, education in New York City has become amazingly insulated from public controls. One could accurately describe the
situation as an abandonment of public education by key forces of
potential power within the city. Bureaucratization and profession-

alization are contributing factors. Weber's theory of the emergence of a specialized bureaucracy, monopolizing power through its control of expertise, describes the role of the education bureaucracy in New York City. The claim that only the professionals can make competent judgments has been accepted. Contributing to and perhaps an outgrowth of this attitude is the change in the Mayor's role to one of noninvolvement. Civic and interest groups (other than the specialized education groups) have responded ambivalently; on the one hand they accept the notion of the professional competence of the bureaucracy, but on the other, express a hopelessness regarding their ability to change the system. The result is narrow or closed participation in large areas of decision-making. Effective influence in these areas is restricted to an inside core of top supervisory personnel in the headquarters staff of the Board of Education. Policy alternatives are rarely discussed or offered, and the inclination to support the status quo is reinforced.[4]

The kind of participation in school policy formulation may fall into one of three categories: 1. *Closed*; only the professionals in the system participate. 2. *Limited*; the Board of Education and/or the Mayor and other special interests such as the Public Education Association, United Parents Association, and the United Federation of Teachers participate. 3. *Open*; all kinds of groups not generally involved in school policy are participants.

The greater part of school policy-making in New York City falls into categories 1 and 2.

The scope of participation has been widened in some instances because of the interests of participants. The teachers' union, for instance, widened participation on the salary issue to include the Mayor because it recognized that it would gain by his participation. The scope of participation was also widened as a result of conflict. The integration issue was not resolved internally in the system, and participation was thrown into the open. In some respects the issue itself can be said to influence participation. But when decisions are not visible, those interests which might potentially become involved do not. . . .

CITY PARTICIPATION

The most significant trend in education in New York has been the isolation of school administration from city government. In each city administration since the 1940's, complaints of undue city interference have resulted in the delegation of increased responsibility to the Board of Education.

The National Education Association condemned Mayor La-Guardia for direct interference with the school system, particularly in personnel policy; the institution of a strict merit system and internal controls over promotions and transfers prevented future Mayors from engaging in similar practices. In 1951, the Strayer-Yavner Report concluded that education policy was controlled by the Board of Estimate, the Mayor, and the Budget Director of the city because of the line-item budget;[5] subsequently the lump-sum budget was adopted, giving the professionals complete control over allocation of funds.[6] Complaints about a political Board were satisfied by the institution of the civic selection panel.[7]

But it is the increased bureaucratization and overblown professionalization of the school system that has had the greatest impact on school policy-making. The professional bureaucracy has manipulated its resource of expertise to discourage opposition and alternative policies. The acceptance of technical expertise as the most relevant, if not the only, basis for sound judgment furthered the depoliticalization of education policy.

The depoliticalization process has been a two-way street. Contributing significantly to it was the last Mayor's (Robert Wagner) stated desire to delegate complete responsibility for the city's schools to the Board of Education.

Detailed review of newspaper items over the last five years substantiates the Mayor's intention to remove himself from educational policy-making.[8] His public statements were always general, in support of more and better schools. On school integration, he repeatedly stated his desire to leave the matter to the Board of Education and the professional staff. "I subscribe without reservation to the goals of quality integrated education in our schools and of equal opportunity for every child. But the plan, the means, the how, where and what—the timetable, the specific approaches and programs—that is for the educators and for the Board to determine."[9] During the most heated periods of controversy, he met with protest groups but repeatedly refused to intervene.

Requests to the Mayor in 1964 for $45.3 million in additional funds for a More Effective Schools program drew the Mayor to the fringe of the integration issue. The proposal called for obtaining additional funds and services for ten More Effective Schools in ghetto areas. Ultimately, his decision favoring a smaller appropriation was reached after consultation with school officials and staff members of educational interest groups.

An aide to the Mayor verified that the Mayor had unquestionably shifted responsibility for education policy to the Board of Education. "The Mayor did not want to get involved with school problems," the aide stated, "particularly school integration problems." The Mayor became directly involved only in instances where the Board and some other city agency came into the type of conflict that had to be reviewed and resolved before the Board of Estimate.

The Mayor and the Board of Estimate are major instruments of financial policy, determining overall budgetary appropriation. Their review of the education budget, however, has been concerned with the total amount to be allotted. The Mayor's continued involvement in fiscal matters was due more to the fact that the Board wanted to shift responsibility to him than to his own desire to participate. Although the Board of Education is charged with the legal responsibility for determining salaries and has discretion to increase salaries within the total allotted funds, it has not been adverse to relinquishing responsibility to the Mayor for negotiating salaries.[10]

The Mayor, through his negotiators, has twice made direct settlements with the union, in 1961 and 1965.[11] Financial commitments were then met by an additional city appropriation and transfers of funds within the education budget. After the 1965 contract settlement, the Superintendent expressed dismay at the settlement, which far execeeded his planned budgetary allotment for salary increases.

The union, for its part, sees an obvious advantage in shifting salary decisions to city hall. Albert Shanker, president of the union, stated that the union is in a more viable position in negotiating with the Mayor than with the Board. In Chicago, which is a fiscally independent district, the union similarly negotiated its new contract directly with the Mayor.

The Mayor's policy of noninvolvement was reinforced by two major changes in procedure instituted during his administration, the lump-sum appropriation of school funds and the panel selection of Board members.

Under a local law first passed in 1962 and re-enacted each year since then, and by way of a memorandum of understanding with the Mayor, the Board of Education has the power to determine its own allocation of funds. Budget preparation, the allocation and transfer of funds, and post-audit control are internal operations, controlled largely by the top supervisory staff. The Board is the only city agency with such budgetary independence from the municipal government.

Prior to 1961, Board appointments were made directly by the Mayor. Under the new procedure, the nine members of the Board are appointed by the Mayor from a screened list of candidates submitted by a selection panel composed of the heads of 11 educational, civic, and professional organizations. The change, made to deter "political" appointments, followed six years of hearings, numerous scandals, and finally the removal of the Board by the State Legislature.

The Mayor is still forced to take part in school policy in two general areas. The first is on issues in which conflict between major participants cannot be compromised without his involvement. Such issues often concern site selection and provoke sharp differences between the Planning Commission and the Board. Involvement also occurs where key participants decide they have more to gain by the Mayor's participation.

One of the obvious questions which arises in connection with the Mayor's role is whether the precedents established under the Wagner administration over a 12-year period have become so integral a part of the structure that they cannot be changed. Mayor Wagner's role conforms to Banfield's portrait of the Mayor of Chicago as mediator of conflicts, rather than as an initiator of policy.[12] A reform Mayor who cannot rely on party backing is less likely to accept this role and, in fact, must use his power to initiate policy to gather necessary political support. Mayoral noninvolvement has also been based on public deference to professionalism. Mayor Lindsay in his short tenure in office has already faced the charge of "political interference" in an attempt to initiate policy in the creation of a civilian police review board and in requiring or attempting to require budgeting accountability in education. Other efforts have been similarly criticized by members of the bureaucracy. The emotional commitment to professionalism, although not inviolate, tends to challenge any suggestion of change or alternate course of action as undue "political interference." The effort of the new Mayor to reassert his policy role represents a direct threat to those who have held almost complete power in decision-making in these areas.

The control of policy by the bureaucracy has been considerably enhanced by the self-removal of other potential participants, particularly civic groups. Any Mayor who decides to become more directly involved in education policy will face serious criticism, not only from the education establishment but from other groups as well. Any movement toward an increased policy role for the Mayor will also involve structural changes. Possibly, a revitalized interest by the Mayor can reactivate civic reformers and public interest sufficiently to expand participation as a basis for reviewing the instruments of policy.

THE BOARD OF EDUCATION

The nine members of the Board of Education are the official policy-making body for the school system and are responsible for long-range educational planning. Traditionally, the Mayor's appointments had reflected careful consideration of balance of interest, as well as political favor. Catholics, Protestants, and Jews were equally represented, and there was either a Negro or Puerto Rican, or both. Geographic distribution demanded by the by-laws assured borough representation. The religious and racial balances, interestingly enough, are continued in the current selection process.[13]

COMPOSITION OF THE BOARD OF EDUCATION

Religion	Old Board		New Board	
	1947	1957	1961	1965
Catholic	2	3	3	3
Protestant	3	3	3	3
Jewish	3	3	3	3

There was little question prior to 1961 that the Mayor would exercise some measure of control over the Board, and the Board members, in turn, could use their political influence with the Mayor. Strong Board Presidents who were politically oriented served as the channel for communication with the Mayor.[14]

The screening-panel procedure strengthened the role of the civic groups and reduced the discretion of the Mayor. Members of the Board nominated by civic groups are less likely to be intimates of the Mayor and less likely to consult with him on school problems. People outside the formal school structure, interviewed during the study and asked about the new appointment procedure, expressed disatisfaction with the lack of political "know-how" of Board members. They pointed out that Board members lack personal influence and no longer can play the political role expected of them by school groups. Of the nine members, there are three lawyers, one accountant, one businessman, one labor union official, a civic activist, and two educators.

The Board's role has been largely one of balancing conflicting pressures and interests. It too has become a mediator rather than an initiator of policy. As the spokesman for official policy, the Board nominally participates in all major decisions. It spends a great deal of its time, however, on sensitive issues where the balance of power in the Board has failed to produce consensus. These are not necessarily major areas of policy. For example, site-selection controversies have recently occupied a large amount of Board time.

In the areas selected for study, the Board's role varied from superficial participation in the budget process, to formulation and promulgation of policy, to failure to achieve implementation in school integration. Selecting a Superintendent was the area in which the board has exercised most direct power. Historically, the selection of the Superindent was a Board function, greatly influenced by its President and subject to the support of high-ranking administrators and education groups. In earlier years, the Mayor had on occasion controlled the appointment. The selection is influenced by the bureaucratic pressure for appointment of an "insider." Three of the last five Superintendents were chosen from the supervisory bureaucracy; the fourth was a former Deputy Mayor and local college president.[15]

The education interest groups, particularly the Public Education Association, have always been concerned with the choice of the Superintendent. Lowi points out that the interest groups in New York City have generally concentrated their attention on appointments, which is confirmed by their involvement in the selection of the Superintendent and Board members.[16] In the past, the Public Education Association has supported, without too much success, the appointment of "outsiders" with high academic credentials. It has always requested a screening panel of educators to assist the Board in the selection process, but in the final analysis the Board President controlled the choice. The Public Education Association has become more influential in the last two appointments than it had been previously. In 1961, the Board accepted the recommendations of the professional panel, selecting a highly regarded "outsider." His failure and dismissal resulted in a return to selection of the highest-ranking person from within the system.

In budgeting, the Board has tended to rely on the budget presented by the Superintendent and his staff. Individual Board members have periodically questioned expenditures, but have also made reference to their lack of information in dealing with intricate budget detail. Generally, the Board views its role as one of assuring city financial support for the total budget, satisfying staff requests and public pressures.

In school integration policy the Board has exhibited a lack of effective follow-through. In 1957 it set a general policy favoring school integration, utilizing rotation of teachers, rezoning, and site selection as the means for achieving their goals. But the Board has failed to effect implementation by the staff. Board members, who were questioned, noted the practical problems obstructing the implementation of their policy. They also pointed to staff inaction as a cause for delay. A member of the Board stated that, were she not on the Board, she would probably be out on the picket line, but dealing with the tough problem of ironing out procedures had taken the edge off her dedication to implementation. A detailed case study of school integration in New York City cites the lack of leadership and determination of the Board and its equivocation after the integration policy was established as a key factor in the failure of that policy.[17]

On the two major salary increases in recent years, the Board has participated in early negotiation but has been satisfied to shift responsibility to the Mayor for final decision-making.

The trend in the Board's participation suggests a diminished role in policy formulation under the new Board. The Board has never fulfilled its obligation for long-range planning, and the new Board has not been any more successful in that area. The lack of a strong Board staff has greatly limited the level and character of its participation. Without staff, the Board cannot realistically challenge or review the programs of the administrative bureaucracy.

It might be more accurate to say that individual members of the Board, as it was formerly constituted, were more involved in policy-making as a result of their own political stature and their association with the Mayor. As the school system has grown larger and more complex and policies demand more specialized knowledge, the Board has had to withdraw from an effective policy role. The bureaucracy and special interest groups have gained power by means of their expertise, while the Board, lacking expertise, has lost power. . . .

THE SUPERINTENDENT AND THE BUREAUCRACY

One of the most confusing aspects of school administration in New York City is the growth in the power of the administrative staff at the same time that the Superintendent has remained a relatively weak chief executive. In part, the strength of the bureaucracy has undermined the role of the Superintendent. Several other factors have contributed significantly to this result. The short tenure in office of the last four Superintendents has undoubtedly taken its toll. In the last two decades, four Superintendents have held the office, none with enough time to enhance that office's powers.[18] Open conflict with the Board was evidenced in two of these administrations, one resulting in dismissal. The last two Board Presidents have proudly claimed that they devoted at least 45 hours a week to their jobs, indicating their day-to-day involvement in school affairs that properly could be left to the Superintendent and their general lack of reliance on the Superintendent for policy recommendations. The abandonment of education by civic groups has been another loss to the Superintendent, who might otherwise use this outside support for developing his own role.

The Superintendent lacks the most essential power of a strong executive, the power of appointment and removal. The supervisory staff is developed completely through inbreeding and promotion from the ranks. Tenured supervisors expect to move to top policy-making jobs, allowing for little flexibility in appointments. No Superintendent can rely on his own team of trusted advisors. Appointments from outside the system are almost nonexistent. Loyalties developed within this environment are strong and are based on how one has received appointment. Top-level Deputy, Associate, and Assistant Superintendents have moved up in divisions of the system, and their loyalties are based on these associations.

A review of the backgrounds of the 25 top supervisory staff members showed that they followed a pattern of having served as principals or assistant principals, were brought into the Board on special assignment, and/or had served on special committees (usually as a result of contacts already established at headquarters). Assignment to headquarters staff by a school division reinforces the loyalties of staff members to that division and the supervisory staff in that division. In all school reorganization proposals, these loyalties have repeatedly fostered preservation of the status quo.

The Superintendent must cope with these potentially competing interests of his own supervisory bureaucracy.[19] He cannot freely develop his own advisory staff and is encumbered by the appointments and promotions made by his predecessors. Any Superintendent from outside the system, not himself subject to these loyalties, would find his task all the more difficult. In a recent magazine article the author noted, "I am told Calvin Gross could have made a real dent on the New York City schools if only he had a handful of trusted special assistants."[20]

Directives and policy statements issued by the Superintendent on key policies have been attacked by his own supervisory staff, both by their professional organizations and, officially, through organized committees on which they sit.[21] In March of 1964, the Council of Supervisory Associations (the overall organization for all of the individual supervisory organizations, such as the High School Principals' Association, Superintendents' Association, Junior High School Principals' Association, *et al.*) issued one of its many reports condemning policies of the Superintendent and noting his failure to consult with his professional staff before making decisions. The Council recently openly opposed the Princeton plan, school bussing, the dropping of I.Q. examinations, and school pairing, after they were adopted as official policy by the Board and the Superintendent. Invariably, policies which require fundamental institutional change are challenged by the supervisory staff.

The inability of Superintendents to use basic administrative powers is notable. They have thoroughly neglected the budget as a management tool to shape personnel or organization policy. Several days spent in the budget office at headquarters indicated that the budget office staff did not act in an advisory or policy-making capacity. Budget estimates are based essentially on pre-established ratios of books and teachers to pupils, with slight adjustment according to the category of the school. Budget approvals come from division heads and are reviewed in hearings controlled by these same people. The last Superintendent met only once all year with *his* budget director.[22]

In all of the areas studied, the Superintendent played a secondary role as an initiator of policy. He had no direct influence on curriculum, with the exception of support by one administration for complete revision of the elementary school curriculum in the 1950's. Curriculum policy has been left largely to the Curriculum Research Bureau and the Deputy Superintendent.

The Superintendent has been most concerned with budget matters and even in that capacity has shown no strong inclination to control the preparation of the budget or to utilize it as a means of controlling his staff. On integration policy, the last two Superintendents have virtually delegated their responsibility to the staff with the result that implementation has not been forthcoming. Although Board policy on integration was established in 1957, no Superintendent has considered his role one of leadership in forcing implementation. The Superintendent, like the Mayor and the Board, became a mediator of disputes, rather than an initiator of school policy.

The Administrative Staff

The education bureaucracy in New York City consists of two distinguishable groups, the headquarters staff and the operational field staff. The latter includes some 3,000 principals and assistant principals, 31 district superintendents, and 1,300 department chairmen.

The Supervisors at Headquarters

A precise figure on the size of the headquarters staff is difficult to obtain; it is estimated to be somewhere around 3,000. Close to 800 people at headquarters do not appear on that budget. Although serving as full-time headquarters personnel, they are paid out of local school budgets. A core supervisory group which holds much of the decision-making power includes some 30 headquarters staff members—including the executive Deputy Superintendent, the Deputy Superintendent in charge of instruction and curriculum, the Board of Examiners, 20 of the 30 Assistant Superintendents, and a few of the active directors of special bureaus. With the exception of two Assistant Superintendents who had earlier experience in school systems outside of New York City, this group was bred in the system, many as principals, almost all with long experience at headquarters.

In each of the decision-making areas analyzed for the study, the supervisory staff at headquarters was a primary participant.

In curriculum planning and development, the headquarters staff, lodged in the Bureau of Curriculum Research, exercises almost complete control over curriculum. The Bureau is indirectly influenced by general changes in approach to certain disciplines, i.e., the new math, but for the most part it follows a regular routine of three- to five-year review of curriculum bulletins, revisions, and presentation of new guidelines. The actual implementation of curriculum is dependent upon the action of principals and classroom teachers, and this varies considerably from school to school. Although the Bureau has curriculum assistants attached to its staff on a part-time basis (40 per cent of their time is spent in the district superintendent's office), there is no planned program for assuring implementation. In fact, the director of the Bureau expressed his reservations about their role in implementation.

In budgeting, the distribution and allocation of funds is determined on a division, bureau, and department basis with the staff person in charge the major determinant of his own needs. School appropriations are largely allocated on the basis of pre-established ratios, providing a prescribed number of teachers, specialized personnel, textbooks, and so forth, according to the number of students and the category of school. The district superintendent exercises no discretion in budgeting or in the distribution of personnel. Headquarters personnel monopolize decisions in this area. Old programs are automatically continued, and the adoption of new ones is dependent upon the approval of the Superintendent in charge of a division or bureau. The Superintendent relies on the judgment of the supervisory bureaucracy for evaluation of programs and needs. There is no internal audit except for a rather cursory and technical review by the small budget office staff. There is no procedure for evaluation of performance or elimination of ineffective programs in conjunction with the budget. Members of the Board of Education have noted their inability to evaluate the complex budget document and make recommendations, and city review of the budget in the past has been extremely limited.

In another major area of policy, school integration, the supervisory staff has been a major participant as a vetoing group. School integration policy was the only area of school policy explored in the study in which there was wide community participation. This was an outcome of the diverse interests and goals of the participants as well as the delicacy of the problem. The supervisory staff, in its inaction and public disapproval of stated Board policy, contributed inadvertently to that broadening of participation. The Board itself demonstrated its own lack of resolve in promulgating general policy favoring rotation of teachers, school pairing, rezoning, and school reorganization, yet waiting upon the bureaucracy for implementation for eight years. The supervisory staff, for its part, has not only ignored Board policy but has publicly disagreed through statements of policy by their own supervisory organizations. Several of these organizations have opposed each of the proposed plans at one time or another. The More Effective Schools program was the only plan which they supported fully. It was the only plan which would not have interfered with the existing structure because it entailed only the expansion of funds and personnel for selected schools.

In the other two areas studied, salary increases and selection of the Superintendent, one would assume the supervisory staff would have no direct influence. Actually, they are inclined to support fully higher salaries for teachers, since their own salaries hinge on an index based on increases proportionate to those received by the teaching staff. The ability of the supervisory staff to gain statutory legislation establishing the index is a significant indication of its strength. As a group, however, they are not direct participants in salary negotiations.

In the selection of the Superintendent, members of the supervisory staff are indirectly and directly influential. First, they represent the most immediate and likely source of supply, since most Superintendents are selected from their ranks. They are consulted individually by Board members and interest groups for suggestions whenever a Superintendent is appointed.

Their own preference for an "inside" appointment has been a major contributing factor in Board decisions. The Board, of necessity, is concerned with the ability of the staff to relate to the Superintendent. The recent unhappy experience with the selection of an "outsider" will more than likely encourage even greater reliance on the supervisory staff in the selection of the Superintendent.

Board members have indicated their concern with the enormous power of the supervisory staff and the inbred system of selection, but they despair in their inability to change the system.

In other areas studied, tangential to the five decision-making areas, it was evident that the professional headquarters staff, particularly the core of the 30-odd supervisors, were major policy makers. Overcentralization has long plagued the school system, and several studies have stressed the need for thorough administrative reorganization, yet Board support and efforts by the last two Superintendents along these lines have been thwarted by the vested interests of the staff in maintaining the status quo. In school construction and planning, the Assistant Superintendent in charge has successfully ignored Planning Commission recommendations, as well as integration policy, and is relatively free of other controls. He has become the expeditor of school construction. In the assignment of administrative and teaching staffs to schools, the central headquarters staff has recently increased its prerogatives. Much of the power which has been lodged in the central staff has prevented the expansion of the role of the district superintendents, who although nominally supervisory are an anachronism in the system. . . .

LOCAL CIVIC AND INTEREST GROUPS

As has already been demonstrated, education decision-making is closely circumscribed in the functional specialization characteristic of New York City politics. The professional bureaucracy is answerable only to an organized clientele which reflects the same kind of specialization. Two interest groups in New York City share the responsibility for overseeing education policy, the United Parents Association and the Public Education Association. Board membership in both organizations overlaps, and their professional staffs work closely together. The United Parents Association is a central citywide organization made up of delegates elected by school parent asociations (who have elected membership in the coordinating agency), while the Public Education Association is a composite group, made up of other interest groups in the city. Board members of the Public Education Association represent the major civic groups in New York City.

The United Parents Association, the membership of which has been drawn largely from middle-class parents, primarily concerned with local school problems and facilities, has directed much of its attention to these ends.[23] In more recent years, site-selection controversies and school integration problems have occupied much of their time. The Association speaks for parents and maintains a direct concern with the immediate effects of policy on local school situations. It has, at times, taken general policy positions on "key issues" and, when possible, makes use of direct influence with Board members. A current member of the Board was an officer of the United Parents Association prior to her appointment and still maintains active communication with the organization. The Association's executive director was recently appointed staff advisor to the Board. The Association has supported the appointment of supervisory staff in the Board of Education and appears to have viable contacts within the bureaucracy. Although it is unlikely that the Association could stimulate broad citywide parent-group support for certain policies, the threat of its large membership has been used effectively to influence Board decisions.

The Public Education Association is a composite group representing professional education interests in the city, outside of the school system itself. Its activities have centered on the more long-range educational aspects of school policy. Its strategy has been to study special problems in the system and make public recommendations based on these reports. One of the Public Education Association's reports contributed significantly to rethinking and reshaping school policy on vocational schools.[24] In general, the views of United Parents Association and Public Education Association on any issue are never far apart.

In the decisions analyzed for this study, both organizations were participants in selected areas of policy in a most limited way. Their role as overseers of educational policy is generally supportive rather than critical. Their inclination is to work within the structure, never suggesting radical change, and focusing on particular problems. Both groups exercised little influence in the area of curriculum. On occasion, one, or both, have made general statements regarding the need for inclusion of material in the curriculum, or emphasis in a given field, but neither has indicated special concern with curriculum matters. Both have supported increased school expenditures and larger city and state appropriations. The Public Education Association has tended to support greater independence for the school system in all areas, while the United Parent Association seems to prefer continued reliance on city support. Their concern with the school board is only in terms of appropriations for particular programs to which they are committed. They also lobby for state and city support for overall increases in the school budget.

The Citizens Committee for Children, which formerly played a larger role in education affairs, has concentrated its efforts on budget review. Each year the Committee holds hearings in its own offices with the supervisory bureaucracy to review the budget for the next year. Representatives of the United Parents Association and the Public Education Association are usually in attendance. Few changes in the budget result; the exercise serves to solicit interest group support for programs and findings.

The screening-panel device for selection of the Superintendent has given the United Parents Association and the Public Education Association a more direct role in the selection of Board members. Both groups are represented on the panel and exercise a notable influence in the selection process.

The Public Education Association has sought a direct role in the selection of the last four Superintendents. A change in its influence was discernible when the new Board was instituted in 1961. Prior to that time they had not been successful in their pressure to bring in an "outsider," and their recommendations had been virtually ignored. They were, however, a direct influence in the last two appointments.

PUBLIC PARTICIPATION

Public participation in policy-making can come through two obvious channels, voting and/or organized interest groups. In New York City there are no public votes on school issues. The assumption that voting in itself automatically assures meaningful public participation has long been questioned by political scientists. Within the context of a specialized area of decision-making, such as education, the degree of pluralism must be measured in terms of the role and degree of influence of the various public interest groups and elected officials.

As has already been demonstrated, elected officials in New York City play a declining role in education policy-making. Two newspapers in the city report regularly on education matters. Criticism in both has been mild and infrequent. Ethnic and religious groups have been satisfied with adequate representation on the Board. Catholic groups intermittently become concerned with textbooks and curriculum but rely on the Catholic Teachers Association and personal contact with the Board to make their minor demands.

Public participation in school policy formulation is circumscribed by the lack of visible decision-making, the shortage of information available to the public on most issues, and a deficiency in the means for participation. Parent associations are active in individual schools, dealing with highly localized and personalized problems. The highly centralized organization of the school system is a deterrent to communication between parents' groups and policy makers. Parents and teachers, the agents closest to the child, are virtually removed from policy decisions.

The school integration issue is the only area in which public response has been vociferous and active. The integration issue has attracted the widest participation of any policy decision explored.

Local groups of every shade of opinion have organized to oppose or defend individual plans. Among the most vociferous have been the Parents and Taxpayers Association (PAT) and their opposition, Parents and Neighbors United for Integrated-Quality Education (EQUAL). Civil rights groups originally entered the school policy field with the single concern of achieving an integrated system; now they are in the forefront of the demands for decentralization. Local civic groups, chambers of commerce, councilmen, and candidates for public office have voiced strong opinions on proposals. Many of these groups and individuals have never before been involved in school affairs, and their current concern has been limited to the integration issue and its ramifications. Public involvement in the integration issue indicated that more widespread participation results when there is no consensus among those with power and decisions become more visible.

Perhaps the most significant development in school decision-making in the last five years has surrounded the integration issue. Aside from its social and human implications, it has had an important political impact. For the past two decades, superintendents, boards, and school bureaucracies have been free-wheeling, with little outside pressure. They have successfully closed off school policy formulation from elected local government officials and civic groups. The integration issue has broken open the monopoly of power vested in the small core of school officials. It has raised serious questions regarding the role of professionals, their goals and interests in school policy.

Consensus decision-making, confined to the professionals, limits policy alternatives as well as public participation. A balance between professionalism and public participation is the desired end. Conflict between competing forces and differences in interests and goals guarantee the visibility of policy-making and encourage public participation. These are the characteristics of a system which are most likely to produce change and encourage adaptability.

Lowi points out that changes in New York City have come from three sources: (1) a single unpredictable individual, (2) sources outside the city (the state or federal governments), and (3) the reform system or minority party. The last is the most frequent source of innovation.[25] This conclusion would suggest that changes in education will depend on the new Mayor's leadership and perhaps his ability to enlist greater public support and interest in education policy.

Conclusion

In any policy-making structure the role of participants and potential participants is relevant. The resources of particular groups or individuals, and the way they are used, is an essential factor in evaluating power. The usual assumption, that wealth is a primary resource, is denied in educational decision-making in New York City. The key resource appears to be professional expertise. The education bureaucracy has become virtually self-contained, sealed by special training and knowledge. They have expanded their role and limited conflict by manipulation of issues to assert that they are wholly dependent upon expert judgment, which they alone have.

In a rather concise—and, one might say, almost modest—characterization of the educational world in New York City, Sayre and Kaufman noted: "On balance, the school official enjoys an unusual capacity for self-government."[26] In fact, with the exception of the integration issue, there are only three or four areas in which any appreciable outside influence is brought to bear on matters of education policy. Such influence is most direct in regard to the religious and racial balance on the Board of Education and in the distribution of appointments to the supervisory staff. To these items should be added the Mayor's role in the determination of teachers' salaries. Some outside influence can also be seen in the negotiations for individual school locations, the bargaining for school construction contracts, and the granting of minor favors by local district superintendents (in their limited sphere of operation). Basically, however, there are no forces acting to broaden education policy and balance it with other city policy.

As a political subsystem, the New York City school system can only be described as "narrow, convergent, and dominated by a consensual elite." This description is in sharp contrast to the usual view of New York City politics as "open"—or to the somewhat typical suggestion in this instance by Sayre and Kaufman that "no part of the city's large and varied population is alienated from participation in the system."[27]

For the political scientist, such a disparity poses a basic problem in creating meaningful operational categories by which power can be analyzed. The results of this study indicate the real need to examine how power is exercised in individual areas of activity. Such examinations should explore differences in the distribution of power, the kinds and levels of participation, the degree of integration by citywide elements, and the role of nonprofessional and nonsupportive interest groups. Working from this type of analysis, the methodological concern with pluralist and power elite concepts may be shifted to the development of more quantitative measurements of the determinants of open and closed political systems. Such an approach will also provide greater insights into the sources and possibilities for change in a political system.

NOTES

1. Wallace Sayre and Herbert Kaufman, *Governing New York City* (New York: Russell Sage Foundation, 1960), p. 241.
2. An area omitted which later proved worthy of further exploration was school-site selection and construction. The study reviewed this area only as it related to the integration issue and budgeting.
3. The author analyzed all newspaper items in two daily newspapers for a five-year period, recording all public statements and reports on education policy. These items were categorized by participant and issue, providing a general picture of the public roles and concerns of all participants. A series of detailed, selective interviews with professional staff and Board members was conducted. Data were cross-checked in interviews with participants outside the school system, including staff members of the Public Education Association, United Federation of Teachers, and other civic groups. Lawyers and educators knowledgeable in school affairs were also consulted. A special survey questionnaire was developed for longer interviews with the field superintendents. The files of civic groups were researched for relevant data on specific issues. A search was made of all professional and popular literature for accounts of decision-making in other school systems for comparative purposes.
4. Theodore Lowi, *At the Pleasure of the Mayor* (New York: The Free Press, 1965), p. 199, as well as the Sayre and Kaufman study (*op. cit.*, p. 716) suggested that the system (referring to the citywide power structure) is more favorable to defenders of the status quo than to innovation.
5. George D. Strayer and Louis Yavner, *Administrative Management of the School System of New York City*, Volume I, (October 1951).
6. *Local Law No. 19* passed by the City Council on April 6, 1962.
7. *Education Law*, Section 2553, subdivision 1, 2, amended L. 1961.
8. Scanning of three years of school news stories in two prominent New York City papers reveals that the Mayor's public statements were almost always in response to public pressures.
9. *New York Times* (March 1, 1965).
10. A member of the Board disagreed with this interpretation, suggesting that the Mayor had taken the initiative. The same person, however, confirmed the author's view that the Mayor did not interfere with the Board in education policy. Officers of the United Federation of Teachers confirmed the author's interpretation.
11. In 1961, the press gave credit to the Superintendent for his successful negotiation on salaries but neglected to explain why the Mayor was involved in the final settlement.

12. Edward Banfield, *Political Influence* (Glencoe: The Free Press, 1963).

13. Expectations based on the religious formula were pointed up by an item appearing in the *World Telegram and Sun* of May 29, 1963, reporting criticism expressed by the Catholic Teachers Association of Mayor Wagner's failure to appoint a Catholic to replace a retiring member, Brendan Byrne. Months later, when a Jewish member of the Board retired, a Catholic was appointed to replace him, thereby reestablishing the 3-3-3 balance.

14. In the period from 1945 to 1961, the three Board Presidents later moved on to political office. Maxmillan Moss was elected Surrogate in Brooklyn, Arthur Levitt was elected State Controller, and Charles Silver became a personal advisor to the Mayor. This would indicate not only their closeness to the Mayor but their active participation in the Democratic party.

15. The three Superintendents chosen from the bureaucracy were John Wade, William Jansen, and Bernard Donovan; the fourth mentioned is John Theobald. Of the five, Calvin Gross was the only "outsider" appointed Superintendent. At the time of the Gross appointment, the High School Administrative Assistants Association, the Association of Assistant Superintendents, and the Junior High School Principals Association reminded the Board that "home-grown talent should not be overlooked." *New York Times* (April 25, 1962; July 2, 1962).

16. Lowi, *op. cit.*, p. 199.

17. David Rogers, Unpublished manuscript on school desegregation. (Center for Urban Education). Sheldon *et al.*, "Administrative Implications of Integration Plans for Schools," in Albert J. Reiss, Jr. (ed.), *Schools in a Changing Society* (New York: The Free Press, 1965).

18. Allan Talbott, "Needed: A New Breed of School Superintendents," *Harpers Magazine* (February 1966), pp. 81–87.

19. Personal contact with Board members by the staff is not uncommon. Two years ago the situation was so bad that the Superintendent issued a statement forbidding memos from the supervisory staff directly to Board members. *World Telegram and Sun* (November 15, 1963), p. 47.

20. Talbott, *loc. cit.*

21. Both the High School Principals Association and the Junior High School Principals Association have expressed opposition to the 5-3-4 and 4-4-4 organization plans. Several associations opposed the elimination of the I.Q. examination, school pairing proposals, and the comprehensive high school plan.

22. The new Superintendent appears to be more concerned with administrative matters.

23. The United Parents Association is a recent recipient of an N.Y.C. Anti-Poverty Operations Board grant to encourage parent participation in schools in underprivileged communities.

24. *Reorganizing Secondary Education in New York City*, Education Guidance and Work Committee of the Public Education Association (October, 1963).

25. *Ibid.*, p. 200.

26. Sayre and Kaufman, *op. cit.*, p. 285.

27. *Ibid.*, p. 720.

THE POLITICS OF
EDUCATIONAL REFORM

PAUL E. PETERSON

INTRODUCTION*

Demands for change in educational practices in American cities have been made in the past decade with increasing frequency. The massive study conducted by the Office of Education under the direction of James Coleman concluded that educational systems have not yet found ways of reaching children whose family backgrounds have not already prepared them for school life.[1] This was but one contribution to a much broader discussion condemning educational practices which under-represent Negroes in curricular materials; permit the migration of better-qualified, more experienced teachers to the fringe areas of the city; assign and advise students according to intelligence tests which are alleged to be biased in favor of the middle-class, white child; and allocate resources among schools without taking into account the greater problems involved in educating the disadvantaged child.[2] Yet the energy devoted to documenting educational deficiencies has produced little alteration in school practices, particularly those affecting class and race relations. Schools seem unwilling or unable to adapt their practices in scarcely any of the directions suggested by their critics. . . .

EXPANDING THE SCHOOL SYSTEM'S CONSTITUENCY

School systems, it has frequently been alleged, have developed such autonomous political structures and have so isolated themselves from other institutions, political elites, and community interests that they have been impervious to calls for change in their

* This article is based upon material from a paper presented at the 1967 convention of the American Orthopsychiatric Association. The research was made possible through grants from the Russell Sage and Woodrow Wilson Foundations.

operations. As Marilyn Gittell has put it, "Any effort to change the school system . . . must face the concentration of power in the professional bureaucracy and the resistance by the bureaucracy to any plan that would erode its power."[3] The difficulties that prestigious foundations and federal agencies have faced when seeking to induce educational changes exemplify the bureaucracies' powers of resistance. When the Ford Foundation initially became interested in urban problems, it sought to work through the superintendents of big city school systems. But the Foundation's educational experiments, when put into practice by the resistant bureaucracies, lacked the coherence and imagination of their original design and became, as Peter Marris and Martin Rein have said, "fragmentary and diffuse."[4] Moreover, in keeping with school systems' abhorrence for independent measures of their performance, "the value of the experiments was . . . seldom thoroughly examined."[5]

Later, the federal government sought to infiltrate school systems with reform-minded teachers and administrators through the Teacher Corps program. Bernard Watson demonstrates, however, that educationists first used their power to weaken federal authority *vis a vis* local school systems and then subdued and co-opted the program through the practice of hiring "insiders" as administrators for it.[6] Consequently, the enthusiastic, reformist thrust of the program was largely diffused.

Perhaps even more significant, the Office of Education by the end of 1967 had been unable to use the leverage provided by the Civil Rights Act of 1964 and the Elementary and Secondary Education Act of 1965 (ESEA) to increase efforts for integration within northern school systems. Even though the Office doubled and tripled the percentage of Negroes going to school with whites in the South, virtually no action was taken in the North. The only time the Office applied the procedures used in the South to northern school systems, it suffered a blistering defeat. In 1965, Office of Education officials attempted to withhold funds from the Chicago school system until charges of de facto segregation had been investigated. But the decentralization of America's political party system gave the local school system leverage to resist such federal intervention. Chicago's Mayor Richard Daley, who can depend on the loyal support of a unified Congressional delegation, forced the office to reverse its decision almost immediately.[7] The conflict dramatically revealed the limited power of the Presidency and his subordinate agencies and the obstacles that must be surmounted in order to persuade autonomous educational bureaucracies to alter their traditional patterns of operation.

A . . . strategy for educational reform was developed to reduce this school system autonomy by enticing school leaders to join coordinating committees consisting of representatives of the local political and economic elite, other institutions affecting the welfare of minority groups, and eventually even representatives of the poor. Once superintendents and their administrative staffs were sitting together with other community leaders, they would join, so it was believed, in a common endeavor to find imaginative new ways of serving the needs of the disadvantaged child. The justification for this strategy was again similar to that of the "old left," but the political reasoning for this second strategy was far more tenuous. The strategy also rested on the assumption that by enlarging an agency's constituency, by enlarging the numbers and kinds of individuals and groups with whom the agency must come into contact, it would be possible to open the agency to innovative practices. Thus, the political justification for coordinated activity was not the efficiency that accompanies such cooperation but the broader, more liberal outlook which was believed to accompany a larger constituency. The mere inclusion of representatives of school systems on citywide coordinating commitees, however, does not *by itself* change the constituency to which the school system is responsive. Coordination is likely to have only marginal effect on a system's policies unless it is accompanied by more significant changes in power relations.

Support for these observations can be found in a proliferating number of studies of the Ford Foundation's "grey areas" program, the program of the President's Committee on Juvenile Delinquency and Youth Development and the OEO's community action program. All three of these programs emphasized coordination at the local level that had been impossible to achieve at the national. None of them, however, was particularly successful at using this device as a means for generating educational reform. After examining the coordinating committees for the "grey areas" and juvenile delinquency programs in 15 major cities, Marris and Rein concluded that since such committees

> had usually little power to enforce any solution, [they] brought the conflict within [their] own organization, and often stultified in indecision, unworkable compromises and endless disputes. [They] lacked authority to integrate [such] jurisdictions [as school systems], and by pressing them to innovate and cooperate, only made each more anxiously self-protective.[8]

The ineffectiveness of the citywide coordinating committees for the juvenile delinquency and "grey areas" programs in many American cities did not prevent their national directors from recommending to the OEO that such committees be the mechanism for reform through the community action program. Representative Edith Green of Oregon, the staunch and powerful defender of public school autonomy on the House Committee on Labor and Education, succeeded in eliminating from the Economic Opportunity Act any legal requirement that such committees be formed. Her familiarity with the juvenile delinquency program had convinced her that these committees had the potential for intruding on the independence of school systems. But even though Green was able to keep the Act from requiring coordinating committees, she was not able to prevent their formation, and OEO administrators, convinced that this was a viable mechanism for reform, encouraged their establishment in virtually every major city in the country. The coordinating committees for the community action agencies became not only the entities through which OEO funds to the local community were channeled, but they were also given authority by the ESEA to cooperate with local school systems in developing educational programs funded under Title I.

In general, the local community action agencies seem to have been hardly more successful in changing traditional practices through coordination than were the committees for the "grey areas" and juvenile delinquency programs. After examining the impact of the community action program on schools in six large cities throughout the country, Nicholas Masters et al., conclude:

> Local community action agencies have not in and of themselves been the major innovators or primary agents of change in decision-making with regard to educational problems and needs of the poor within the public school systems examined.[9]

Later the authors observe that "community action agencies" have not been involved "to any meaningful extent in the formulation and execution of educational policy" as a result of ESEA legislation.[10] In another study of three smaller cities, Michael Usdan and Ray Nystrand found that the relationships between the community action agencies and the school systems were affected not by the coordinating committee but by the experts involved. In two of the three cities these experts consisted solely of school district administrators.[11] In still another study of nine cities, Kirschner Associates report that:

Initially, it was envisaged that a . . . community action program, in cooperation with concerned agencies, [would] design a community-wide educational program fully responsive to the needs of the poor. After this step . . . the program would be turned over to one or more delegate agencies [usually, the public schools] for implementation. One of the basic difficulties of this approach has been that the implementation of the program has been carried out independently by each delegate agency and . . . has required operating decisions fundamentally affecting the goals, character and operations of the component. . . . The influence of the community action program was dissipated by not being involved with actual operations.[12]

It is significant that these three studies, written from different perspectives by different observers in different cities, reach such similar conclusions. If these cases are at all representative, the dominant pattern seems to be a relatively low level of change in educational policy through attempts to broaden the constituency of school systems by including them on coordinating committees.

NOTES

1. James S. Coleman et al., *Equality of Educational Opportunity* (Washington: U.S. Government Printing Office, 1966), p. 325.
2. A critical look at Harlem schools can be found in the planning document for a New York poverty program written under the direction of Kenneth Clark, *Youth in the Ghetto* (New York: Harlem Youth Opportunities, Unlimited, 1964).
3. Marilyn Gittell, *Participants and Participation* (New York: Center for Urban Education, 1967), p. 57.
4. Peter Marris and Martin Rein, *Dilemmas of Social Reform* (New York: Atherton Press, 1967), p. 17.
5. Ibid.
6. Bernard C. Watson, "The National Teachers Corps: A Tale of Three Cities," *Administrator's Notebook*, XVI (January 1968), No. 5.
7. Gary Orfield, "The Reconstruction of Southern Education" (Ph.D. diss., Department of Political Science, University of Chicago, 1965).
8. Marris and Rein, op. cit., p. 229.
9. Nicholas A. Masters et al., "Politics, Poverty and Education: An Analysis of Decision-making Structures," Report submitted to the Office of Economic Opportunity by the Institute of Public Administration (University Park, Pa.: Pennsylvania State University, February 1968), p. 366.
10. Ibid., p. 382.
11. Michael Usdan and Raphael Nystrand, "Towards Participative Decision-making: The Impact of Community Action Programs," *Teachers College Record*, LXVIII (November 1966), 101.
12. Kirschner Associates, Inc., "A Description and Evaluation of Selected Educational Components of Community Action Programs," Report submitted to the Office of Economic Opportunity, I (Albuquerque, New Mexico, May 1967), 69–70.

THE METROPOLITAN EDUCATION DILEMMA: MATCHING RESOURCES TO NEEDS*

ALAN K. CAMPBELL AND PHILIP MERANTO

The metropolitanization of American society has gained widespread attention in recent years from a notable variety of scholars, popular writers, and public officials. Some scholars have preoccupied themselves with tracing the historical roots of metropolitanism, while others have attempted to demonstrate empirical relationships between metropolitanism and the social, economic, and political dimensions of society. Popular writers have interpreted some of these findings for the general public, and they have usually stressed the so-called "decay" of large American cities and the multitude of problems plaguing these urban centers. While journalists and scholars have been describing and analyzing the metropolitan phenomenon, public officials have been struggling with its policy implications. For these officials, the fact of metropolitanism, however dimly perceived, complicates many of the problems with which they must deal and influences many of the decisions they make.

The extent of this concern with one of the major forces of change in postwar America has been beneficial but, on occasion, misleading. On the one hand, it has stimulated popular interest and knowledge of the changing character of American culture. Further, it has prompted a wide assortment of research efforts about the causes and consequences of metropolitanism. On the other hand, there has been a tendency to see nearly all of the changes and problems which characterize contemporary America

* This article is based, in part, on a Carnegie Corporation-supported larger study of *Policies and Policy-Making in Large City Education Systems* being done at the Metropolitan Studies Center, Maxwell Graduate School, Syracuse University.

From Alan K. Campbell and Philip Meranto, "The Metropolitan Education Dilemma: Matching Resources to Needs," in Marilyn Gittell (ed.), *Educating an Urban Population* (1967), pp. 15–36. Reprinted by permission of the authors and the publisher, Sage Publications, Inc.

as consequences of the metropolitan process. Too often the inter-relationships between substantive problems and metropolitanism have been blurred rather than clarified by this kind of perception. Similarly, there has been a tendency to assume that the problems involved in the provision of any public service (education, welfare, health, transportation, and so forth) are all related to or result from metropolitanism. This is not the case. With every function there are problems that would exist even if the country had not become metropolitan. Further, the fact of metropolitanism is not a problem in itself, but the dynamics which underpin it and the patterns which accompany it may be perceived by individuals and groups within the society as creating problems, and in many instances the problems thus perceived can be solved only by public action.

The tendency to equate both social change and functional concerns with metropolitanism is evident in the field of education. Much of the literature which purports to discuss the implications of metropolitanism or urbanism for education is, instead, simply a catalog of the substantive issues which characterize the education function. The metropolitan component of the problems is often assumed to be self-evident, and no effort is made to demonstrate the relationship between metropolitanism and the substantive issues.

It is the primary purpose of this article to delineate those aspects of metropolitanism which produce important consequences for the performance of the education function in large urban centers. Such an analysis necessitates, first, an investigation of basic population trends and an examination of the distributional results of these trends on income, educational attainment, race, and the nature of school population. Second, the relationships between these population attributes and the provision of educational services are analyzed, as are the relationships between education needs and the quantity and quality of resources available in the various parts of the metropolis. And finally, the public policy alternatives are examined in terms of their ability to meet the demonstrated needs.

CHARACTERISTICS OF METROPOLITAN AMERICA

The most often cited statistic about metropolitanism is the growing proportion of the American population which lives in metropolitan areas.[1] By 1964 this proportion had reached 65 percent, and projections indicate that it will approach 70 percent by 1970. A simultaneous phenomenon, perhaps of even greater significance for the education function, is the redistribution of people between the central city and its suburbs. There has been a gradual but consistent decrease in the proportion of total metropolitan population which lives within central cities. In 1900 over 60 percent of the metropolitan population lived within central cities; by 1965 this share had declined to under 50 percent. . . .

The significance of these shifts for the education function would be substantial even if the population redistribution between central city and suburbs was random relative to the socioeconomic characteristics of the people involved. But this is not the case. The shifting is not only a matter of numbers of people; it also involves a sorting-out process. In general, it is the poor, less educated, nonwhite Americans who are staying in the central city and the higher income, better educated, whites who are moving out, although this description must be qualified somewhat in terms of the size of the metropolitan area and region of the country in which it is located. The larger the metropolitan area, however, the more accurate is this description.[2]

This sorting-out process has resulted in a median family income for central city residents in 1959 which was 88.5 percent of outside central city income; $5,940 for central cities, compared to $6,707 for the suburbs. Although median family income for both central city and outside central city residents has grown since 1959, the gap is widening, with central city median family income in 1964 at $6,697, while for outside central city areas it was $7,772, a proportionate relationship of 86.2 percent.[3] . . .

The explanation for the income and education differences between central city and suburb rests in part on differences in the distribution of nonwhite population within metropolitan areas.[4] Although the nonwhite component of the American population has now distributed itself between metropolitan and nonmetropolitan areas in approximately the same proportion as the white population, the distribution within metropolitan areas follows a quite different pattern. It is well known that the proportion of nonwhites in central cities has been increasing, while the proportion in the suburban areas has been declining. This larger proportion of Negro population in central cities helps to account in part for the differences in educational achievement and income between central cities and suburbs. Due to a history of discrim-

TABLE 1.—Nonwhite Population Contrasted with Nonwhite School Enrollment for 15 Largest Cities: 1960

City	Percent Nonwhite of Total Population	Percent Nonwhite of School Population	Difference in Proportions of Nonwhite School Enrollment and Nonwhite Population
New York	14.0	22.0	8.0
Chicago	22.9	39.8	16.9
Los Angeles	12.2	20.5	8.3
Philadelphia	26.4	46.7	20.3
Detroit	28.9	42.9	14.0
Baltimore	34.7	50.1	15.4
Houston	22.9	30.2	8.7
Cleveland	28.6	46.1	17.5
Washington	53.9	77.5	23.6
St. Louis	28.6	48.8	20.2
Milwaukee	8.4	16.2	7.8
San Francisco	14.3	30.5	16.2
Boston	9.1	16.4	7.3
Dallas	19.0	26.0	7.0
New Orleans	37.2	55.4	18.2

SOURCE: U.S. Bureau of the Census, U.S. Census of Population: 1960, Selected Area Reports, Standard Metropolitan Statistical Areas and General Social and Economic Characteristics, 1960.

ination in all aspects of life, the Negro has a lower income and less education than does his white neighbor. In central cities, for example, the 1964 median family income for Negroes was $4,463, while for whites it was $7,212. In 1964 the percentage of all Negroes twenty-five years old and over having completed four years of high school was 17.1; the comparable percentage for whites was 31.3.

The impact of the growing proportion of nonwhite population in central cities is intensified for the schools by the even higher proportion of public school enrollment which is nonwhite. This difference in population and enrollment proportions is a result of age distribution, family composition, and the greater tendency of white parents to send their children to private and parochial schools. Table [1] shows, for 1960, the proportion of the total population of the largest cities which was nonwhite and the proportion of public school enrollment which was nonwhite. The ratio of nonwhites to whites is considerably higher in the school population than in the total population, and indications are that this is becoming increasingly the case.

The sorting-out process which produces significant differences in socioeconomic characteristics between central city and suburban populations is the chief background factor against which the educational implications of metropolitanism must be examined. To the extent that these differences in characteristics produce different kinds of educational problems, the fact of metropolitanism is important to the provision of educational services.

POPULATION COMPOSITION AND EDUCATIONAL PROBLEMS

The redistribution process described in the preceding section has left the central city school system with a disproportionate segment of pupils who are referred to as "disadvantaged," and this appears to be a trend that is continually increasing. These students are disadvantaged in terms of the income level and educational background of their parents, their family composition, and their general home environment. To the extent that education of the disadvantaged is a more complex phenomenon than the education of middle-income pupils, the central city school systems face a different and more serious set of problems than do suburban education systems.[5]

In the immediate postwar period, the most striking phenomenon in education related to the metropolitanization of the country was the impact on suburban areas of a rapidly increasing population. The suburbs, however, responded well to the challenge and rapidly met the new requirements in building the necessary physical facilities and the provisions of a teaching staff. The significance of the suburban expansion for the central city schools, however, was only dimly, if at all, perceived. It is now clear that the suburbanization of the country, by draining the higher income families and much economic activity from the central cities, produced greater problems for education in central cities than it did for the suburbs.

As the proportion of disadvantaged students in the central cities has increased, there has been a simultaneous increase in what are known in the community as "undesirable" schools, schools to which parents would prefer not to send their children. Many of these schools are so characterized because of the large proportion (in many cases, nearly 100 percent) of the students who are Negro. Because of population trends and the residential pattern of most of our cities, it is increasingly difficult to rearrange district lines to achieve what is referred to as "racial balance" among schools. As a result, more and more central city schools are being designated as "undesirable."

The underlying cause for the undesirable label in educational terms, however, is low income, not race. Several studies have now substantiated that the single most important determinant of educational achievement is family income.[6] In the high correlation between income and test scores, income undoubtedly is a proxy, and a fairly accurate one, for a combination of factors—family characteristics, educational attainment of parents, home environment. When white parents resist sending their children to undesirable schools, this is not necessarily a racial issue, although it is often difficult to separate the racial and educational questions which currently surround controversies over central city schools.

The undesirable schools are unattractive not only to parents but also to first-rate teachers. Teachers seek to be assigned to the "better" schools within the city system, and many abandon central city districts entirely for more attractive suburban districts. Furthermore, central city systems find it increasingly difficult to attract choice graduates of the universities as new teachers.

The resource needs for central cities relate not only to teachers but to other educational needs as well. Cities have much older school plants than do suburbs, and the site costs for building new schools within central cities are substantially higher than those for the suburbs. In addition, there is greater competition within the cities for resources for such noneducation functions as police protection, street maintenance, and welfare than is true in the suburban areas. These noneducation needs compete for the same resources which the central city schools need to meet their pressing educational problems.

This set of central city education problems exists in a society which is in need of a continuous improvement in its educational output. The very fact of metropolitanization implies extended specialization in a society which is increasingly complex. The need, therefore, is for a better and better educated work force. To some extent, the suburban areas have responded to this need through the gradual improvement and sophistication of its curricula and teaching. Curriculum improvement in central cities, however, is much less discernible and is particularly lacking in the education of the disadvantaged.[7]

The answer to this problem does not rest with providing education with a different purpose for disadvantaged pupils. A suggestion by James Conant that disadvantaged pupils should be concentrated in vocational education hardly seems appropriate.[8] Improvement in the quality of vocational education is needed, but it should not be made especially for the disadvantaged. Among the disadvantaged, there are those who are capable of achieving high educational accomplishment in a great variety of fields and options, and in terms of equity the opportunities should be the same for them as for other pupils. Further, it is apparent that the greatest employment growth of the future will be in the white-collar occupations, not in vocational fields offered by most of today's vocational schools.

One of the central issues confronting large city schools, therefore, becomes the allocation of sufficiently massive resources to the field of education for the disadvantaged to help them overcome their present handicaps. To what extent are large central cities capable of providing the resources needed to meet these problems and where are these resources to come from if the central cities cannot provide them from local assets?

THE AVAILABILITY OF RESOURCES

The educational problems confronting large cities would not be nearly as critical if cities had at their disposal an ample supply of resources to deal with these difficulties. But this is not the case. The metropolitan process has not only redistributed the population in a way that presents the central cities with a population having special educational difficulties; the process has simultaneously operated to weaken the local resource base which must be used to meet their needs.

It has already been noted that the central city component of the metropolitan area population has lower income levels than the population outside the central city. This pattern is particularly significant because it has become increasingly apparent that income is the single most important variable in explaining the expenditure levels of a community for both educational and noneducational services.[9] To a large extent, it is the income available which influences the ability of a governmental unit to meet the service requirements of its population. Central cities are simply losing ground in this respect, while their functional needs are simultaneously increasing.

Metropolitanism is characterized by the decentralization of economic activities from the core city to the surrounding areas, as well as by decentralization of population. Evidence of this trend can be found by examining the distribution of economic activity within specific metropolitan areas over time. For example, an investigation of the proportion of manufacturing carried on in the central city portion of twelve large metropolitan areas demonstrates that the central city percentage has clearly declined over the past three decades, particularly in the post–World War II period. Whereas the twelve cities accounted, on the average, for 66.1 percent of manufacturing employment in 1929, this proportion decreased to 60.8 percent by 1947 and then declined to less than half (48.9 percent) by 1958.[10]

A similar decentralizing trend for retail activity can be demonstrated by examining the growth of retail store sales in the metropolitan area as a whole, in the central city, and in the central business district of the core city for the period 1948 to 1958. Such a comparison was made for a sample of twenty-two large cities. It was found that with the exception of one (Birmingham, Alabama), the entire metropolitan area had increased its retail sales more than had the central city and far more than the central business district. This evidence illustrates that the historical dominance of the central city and its business district over regional retail activity is on the decline.[11] The patterns for manufacturing employment and retail sales reflect the fact that economic activity, like population, has migrated from the central city outward. This push for dispersal is related to a number of factors, including the need for physical space, the introduction of new industrial processes, the ascendance of the automobile and truck as means of transportation and shipping, the building of vast highway systems, and the spreading of the population throughout the metropolis.[12]

The consequences of this economic migration for the tax base of the central city have been widely discussed. As industries continue to move outward, taxable assessed valuation, the source of local property taxes, has barely held its own in many cities and has actually declined in several large cities. For example, in a recent five-year period, the percent changes in taxable assessed valuation for seven cities were as follows: Baltimore, −10.5 percent; Boston, −1.2 percent; Buffalo, −1.0 percent; Detroit, −2.0 percent; St. Louis, + 1.1 percent; Philadelphia, +2.8 percent; and Cleveland −3.4 percent.[13] These changes in taxable valuation do not yield the necessary resources to deal with the problems facing these urban centers.

Translated into educational terms, the recent performance of the tax base in large cities has not kept pace with the growth or nature of the school population in these cities. Indeed, an examination of the per pupil taxable valuation over a five-year period shows that ten large cities out of fourteen experienced a decrease in this source of revenue. Since local property taxes are the most important source of local educational revenues, large city schools can barely meet ordinary education needs let alone resolve the problems resulting from the shifting population distribution.

There is an additional factor which weighs against the capacity of central cities to meet their pressing educational needs. The postwar intensification of urbanization and metropolitanization has resulted in a demand for a wider range and higher quality of public services than at any other time in the nation's history. These demands are particularly great in the largest cities, where the necessity for providing a wide variety of welfare, public safety, sanitation, traffic control, and street maintenance services has been most pressing. An investigation of the fiscal patterns in

TABLE 2.—FIVE-YEAR CHANGES IN PER PUPIL TAXABLE ASSESSED VALUATION

| | Percent of Change over a Five-Year Period* | |
	City	State (minus cities listed)
Baltimore	−19.3	10.2
Boston	− 5.3	not available
Buffalo	− 8.6	26.1
Chicago	− 6.0	− 0.2
Cleveland	− 9.9	4.2
Detroit	− 5.7	3.4
Houston	− 2.8	18.9
Los Angeles	5.1	5.6
Milwaukee	− 9.6	− 1.1
New York City	32.4	26.1
Philadelphia	− 0.6	13.6
Pittsburgh	2.2	13.6
St. Louis	−10.6	3.1
San Francisco	5.9	5.6

* Change is for the most recent five-year period for which data are available.
SOURCE: Research Council of the Great Cities Program for School Improvement, The Challenge of Financing Public Schools in Great Cities, Chicago, 1964.

thirty-six Standard Metropolitan Statistical Areas revealed that for the year 1957, the central cities in these areas were spending $25.66 more per capita in total expenditures than the communities in the outlying areas. Unfortunately for education systems, this difference was not due to higher educational expenditures in the central cities. In fact, their education expenditures were $27.82 per capita less than what was spent on education in the corresponding suburban areas. It was in the noneducational category that the central city exceeded the outside central city area in expenditures. In this sample, central cities spent about $53.00 more per capita on noneducation services than their surrounding communities. Further, this difference is largely due to the "all other" classification, which includes the traditional municipal services that cities, unlike suburban communities, must provide. The cost and number of noneducational governmental services tend to increase with the size and density of a district and to consume a larger proportion of the budget in major cities where many services are provided for nonresidents as well as for residents. It is reasonable to suggest that this "municipal overburden" is supported at the expense of the education function.[14]

The central cities were supporting these expenditure levels by taxes that were $23.39 per capita higher than in areas outside the cities. In contrast, the cities received about $5.00 per capita less in total intergovernmental aid and, most importantly, $12.31 less per capita in education aid than did suburban areas, where income was higher. In other words, not only are central cities pressed to support a large array of services by a relatively shrinking tax base, but they tax themselves more heavily to do so and they receive less intergovernmental aid than the more wealthy communities in their metropolitan area. This fiscal pattern borders on the ironic when it is realized that central city education systems must compete for educational resources with suburban school districts which have higher income levels and receive a greater amount of state aid. In fact, the state aid system actually works to intensify rather than to resolve the educational crises facing large city school systems.

The multitude of fiscal difficulties faced by the central cities results in a lower per student expenditure in the cities than in surrounding suburbs. Specifically, an examination of the thirty-seven largest metropolitan areas in the country indicated that the central city school districts in 1962 were spending an average of $144.96 less per pupil than their suburban counterparts.[15] This considerable difference in expenditures per student between central city and suburb would be serious even if the educational problems were the same for the two type areas; but, as has already been demonstrated, such is not the case.

It is not known what amount of additional resources per student would be necessary to provide an adequate education for the culturally disadvantaged. On the basis of studies yet to be published, it is clear that the present small amounts of additional resources being used in some cities for what is generally referred to as "compensatory education" are accomplishing very little.[16] The additional resources currently being allocated to these programs are simply not sufficient. . . .

This analysis of the resources available for central city education demonstrates the disparity between needs and resources. There is little indication that present trends will substantially alter these circumstances; in fact, there is good reason to believe that the situation is becoming more serious. If these trends are to be modified, imaginative public policy decisions must be identified and pursued. What public policy alternatives exist and to what extent are they politically feasible?

Public Policy Implications

A variety of means exists for attacking the lack of fit between educational needs and resources. Some of these are politically more feasible than others.

Perhaps the most obvious solution would be to redistribute the population so as to reduce the concentration of disadvantaged pupils in cities. The demand for racial integration within public education points in this direction. There are, however, both physical and political obstacles to this course of action which, at the moment, appear to be insurmountable. First, the disadvantaged are concentrated in wide geographic areas within many cities. To redistribute these pupils throughout the city and throughout the metropolitan area, which would be necessary to achieve integration in the future, would require a transportation network so extensive and costly that it is both physically and politically impractical.

Obviously, there are neighborhood school districts where the redrawing of attendance areas within cities and perhaps the redrawing of district lines between cities and suburbs would substantially alter the present student balance in the schools. Where this is the case, however, political resistance is likely to be stiff. The recently discovered attachment of many people to the neighborhood school has produced powerful political support for present district lines and attendance areas. To assume that such changes could be accomplished on a metropolitan-wide basis is unrealistic.

There is, in fact, an inverse relationship between the intensity of political opposition to accomplishing some redistribution of pupils and the size of the area and proportion of the population involved. In cities where the proportion of disadvantaged students, particularly the proportion of Negro students, is relatively low (thereby making the redrawing of attendance area lines a meaningful alternative), the political resistance seems capable of preventing any substantial changes. Boston is a good example of this situation: On the other hand, where the political strength of the disadvantaged is great enough to initiate some change, the high proportion of students and large areas involved present a practical limitation on how much can be accomplished in this manner.

An alternative to the decentralization of disadvantaged students is the much-discussed creation of education parks or campuses which would contain many more pupils than the present single-building schools. By drawing on a larger enrollment area, school campuses would be able to concentrate services and would contain a more heterogeneous population, thereby, presumably, providing a higher quality of education for all students.

The concentration of disadvantaged students also would be lessened by the return of middle-income families to cities from the suburbs. It had been anticipated by some students of urban affairs that urban renewal would contribute to such a return. This reversal of the outward flow of people would have been beneficial in two ways: The mix of students in the schools would be improved and the tax base for supporting education would be strengthened. However, the contribution of urban renewal to revitalizing the central city has not been great. Much of the current disappointment over urban renewal has resulted from the lack of recognition of the importance of low-quality education as one of the primary factors motivating the move out of the city. It seems apparent that physical redevelopment, unless it is accompanied and closely interrelated with a variety of social improvements, particularly improvements in public education, will not attract the suburbanite back to the city.

Whatever the possibility of pupil redistribution, the central need is and will remain additional resources for the education of the disadvantaged. Whether educated where they are presently located or elsewhere, the disadvantaged have special education needs. To meet these needs, which is the only way of guaranteeing equality of educational opportunity, additional resources are required.

The present allocation pattern of state aid does little to accomplish this. In fact, the aid pattern runs exactly counter to the need pattern. It is possible that as reapportionment is accomplished and as the nature of the problem becomes more evident, state aid formulas will be revised to correspond more closely with needs. It is important to note, however, that reapportionment will result in a much greater gain in representation for the suburbs than it will for central cities.[17] It may be that the suburban representatives will recognize their stake in an improved central city education system; but if they do not, the present pattern of higher aid to the suburbs may well be accentuated rather than reversed by reapportionment.

Perhaps the single most significant policy response to the set of problems described here has been the response of the Federal government as reflected in the Elementary and Secondary Education Act of 1965.[18] This program, combined with the antipoverty program, has given recognition for the first time to the problem of allocating more resources to education for the disadvantaged. However, although the concept underpinning the legislation is sound, the amount of aid provided for large cities is relatively small in relation to the need. In the case of New York City, for instance, the new Federal aid amounts to only 6.2 percent of total 1962 education expenditures. For Chicago, the figure is 2.9 percent, for Los Angeles 2.6 percent, with the highest figure among the fifteen largest cities being for New Orleans, where the new aid will amount to 17.5 percent of 1962 school expenditures. This program is clearly moving in the right direction; the task is to fortify it with enough money so that it can have a substantial impact.

Whatever means are used to provide the resources for the provision of adequate education services, they will have to come, in large part, from the middle- and higher-income suburbanites. If, therefore, the suburbanites resist a redistribution of population or a redrawing of school district lines to create a more equitable balance in the present pupil ability distribution, the alternative— if the problem is to be met—is greater Federal and state taxes paid by persons of middle and high income.

The fundamental issue, therefore, really revolves around the ability and willingness of Federal and state governments to raise revenue and redistribute the resources according to need. If this is not done, no major improvement in the situation confronting central city school systems can be expected.

There remains, of course, the issue of the ability of school systems to make good use of additional resources. This question, which is discussed elsewhere in this issue, relates to the kinds of changes needed in both curriculum and teaching techniques if the educational disadvantages of many young people are to be overcome.

However that question is answered, the fact remains that quality education for all will not be accomplished until the resources are found to do the job.

NOTES

1. The Census Bureau definition of the metropolitan area and of its component parts is followed throughout this article. That definition is as follows: "Except in New England, a standard metropolitan statistical area (an SMAS) is a county or group of contiguous counties which contain at least one city of 50,000. In addition to the county, or counties, containing such a city or cities, contiguous counties are included in an SMAS if, according to certain criteria, they are essentially metropolitan in character and are socially and economically integrated with the central city." In New England, towns are used instead of counties.

2. For a complete discussion of these differences relative to size and region, see Advisory Commission on Intergovernmental Relations. *Metropolitan Social and Economic Disparities: Implications for Intergovernmental Relations in Central Cities and Suburbs*, Washington D.C.: U.S. Government Printing Office, 1965.

3. U.S. Bureau of the Census, *Consumer Income*, Series P-60, No. 48, April 25, 1966.

4. The terms nonwhite and Negro are used interchangeably in this article since Negroes constitute 92 percent of the nonwhite classification as defined by the Census Bureau.

5. For a sampling of the literature which deals with this topic see Frank Riessman, *The Culturally Deprived Child*, New York: Harper and Row Publishers, Incorporated, 1962; Judith R. Kramer and Seymour Leventman, *Children of the Gilded Ghetto*, New Haven, Yale University Press, 1961; A. Harry Passow (Ed.), *Education in Depressed Areas*, New York: Teachers College, Columbia University, 1963; and C. W. Hunnicutt (Ed.), *Urban Education and Cultural Deprivation*, Syracuse, N.Y.: Syracuse University Press, 1964.

6. Patricia Sexton, *Education and Income: Inequalities in Our Public Schools*, New York: The Viking Press, 1962; H. Thomas James, J. Alan Thomas, and Harold J. Dyck, *Wealth, Expenditures and Decision-Making for Education*, Stanford, Calif.: Stanford University Press, 1963; Fels

Institute of Local and States Government, University of Pennsylvania, *Special Education and Fiscal Requirements of Urban School Districts in Pensylvania*, 1964; and Jesse Burkhead, *Cost and Performance in Large City School Systems*, publication of Metropolitan Studies Center, Syracuse University, as part of the Carnegie supported study of Large City Education Systems, 1967.

7. William W. Wayson, *Curriculum Development in Large City Schools*, publication of Metropolitan Studies Center, Syracuse University, as part of the Carnegie supported study of Large City Education System, 1967.

8. James B. Conant, *Slums and Suburbs*, New York: The New American Library, 1964, pp. 33–49.

9. Alan K. Campbell and Seymour Sacks, *Metropolitan America: Fiscal Patterns and Governmental Systems*, Metropolitan Studies Center, Syracuse University, 1966.

10. See Raymond Vernon, *The Changing Economic Function of the Central City*, New York: Committee for Economic Development, 1960; and U.S. Bureau of the Census, *Census of Manufacturing, 1958*. The cities include: Baltimore, Boston, Chicago, Cincinnati, Cleveland, Detroit, Los Angeles-Long Beach, New York, Philadelphia, Pittsburgh, St. Louis, and San Francisco-Oakland.

11. See U.S. Bureau of the Census, *Census of Business, 1958* for the twenty-two cities which reported all three figures.

12. Edger M. Hoover and Raymond Vernon, *Anatomy of a Metropolis*, Garden City, N.Y.: Doubleday and Company, Inc., 1962.

13. The Research Council of the Great Cities Program for School Improvement, *The Challenge of Financing Public Schools in Great Cities*, Chicago, 1964.

14. David C. Ranney, *School Government and the Determinants of the Fiscal Support for Large City Education Systems*, unpublished doctoral dissertation, Syracuse University, 1966.

15. For a breakdown by individual city, see Seymour Sacks and David C. Ranney, "Suburban Education: A Fiscal Analysis," in Marilyn Gittell (Ed.), *Education and Urban Population* (New York: Sage, 1967), pp. 60–76.

16. Jesse Burkhead, *op. cit.*

17. Robert S. Friedman, "The Reapportionment Myth," *National Civic Review*, April, 1960, pp. 184–188.

18. Title I of this law, which accounts for about $1.06 billion of the approximately $1.3 billion authorized, provides for grants to be made to local school districts on the basis of 50 percent of the average per pupil expenditures made in their state for the school year 1963–1964 multiplied by the number of five- to seventeen-year-old children in the local school district from families with an annual income below $2,000, or with a higher income resulting from aid to dependent children relief payments. Local districts receive their proportion of the funds under this formula only after plans they have submitted indicating how they will meet the special educational needs of disadvantaged students are approved by their state education department. The politics surrounding the enactment of this legislation are analyzed in Philip Meranto, *The Politics of Federal Aid to Education in 1965: A Study in Political Innovation*, unpublished doctoral dissertation, Syracuse University, 1966.

Urban Politics and the Police

INTRODUCTION

The police power is the most awsome of state powers. Indeed, police activities are *the* distinctive activities of governments in modern societies, for only the state can *legitimately* use force and violence to achieve its purposes.[1] Without such a coercive power, government as we know it could hardly exist. The very potency of this power, however, requires that its exercise be carefully circumscribed in order to safeguard the rights and liberties of the citizenry. For this reason, the framers of the U.S. Constitution denied police power to the newly created federal government. Although Congress was given the power to declare war and raise an army to attack a foreign invader, it was not granted authority to establish a police force that could regulate and control the behavior of American citizens. This power was reserved to the states and localities, which, being more familiar to the people, were considered more trustworthy governmental institutions.

Even at the local level, the formation of a special cadre to "police" the activities of the community was not a step taken lightly. As James Wilson points out in one of the following essays, in the early nineteenth century, apprehension of criminals was left to private agencies hired by the victims of crimes. Only gradually did the problems of maintaining public order in the city become so significant that a public police force was established. Even then, police were regarded more as night watchmen expected to keep order than as law enforcers who would apprehend criminals whenever infractions of the law occurred.

Although today we can hardly imagine maintaining order in a complex, urban society without a professional cadre hired by the

238

community to enforce the law, establishing a police force brings with it several potential dangers that have surfaced at one time or another in American cities. Aside from the potential threat of armed patrolmen to the liberties of the community, a police force can exacerbate value conflicts in the community, can itself become a corrupt arm of criminal forces, and can use its great powers for the benefit of one or another political faction in the community. Various police reforms have been proposed to remedy these difficulties, but each reform seems to have only aggravated another separate but closely related problem.

THE NIGHT WATCHMAN

The police in the nineteenth century (and in some communities even today) seemed to be particularly sensitive to the first of these potential dangers, for they were quite adept at mediating among the value conflicts that divided various social and ethnic groups in the population. The need to do so was particularly obvious in those cases where government had legislated on matters affecting the personal moral conduct of individuals. These laws gave rise to what have become known as "victimless" crimes, illegal actions that do no direct harm to anyone, except perhaps to the perpetrators of the crimes themselves. Public drunkenness, pauperism, vagrancy, and loitering are misdemeanors in most American communities. Gambling, prostitution, homosexuality, use of both marijuana and hard drugs, and, at one time, the sale of alcoholic beverages have been regarded as more serious crimes. Far from being minor matters, these crimes are a major police preoccupation; the offense of public drunkenness alone accounts for one of every three arrests.[2]

When large groups of people engage in behaviors legally declared to be deviant, the police may find themselves in conflict with a significant segment of the community. In order to mitigate this possibility, police traditionally arrested individuals for committing victimless crimes only when the illegal actions threatened the peace and order of the community. Acting as night watchmen concerned about the public peace rather than as guardians of private morality, they tolerated, in certain parts of the community, practices that, if detected elsewhere, might be harshly punished.[3] Prostitution was permitted along the "strip"; public drunkenness in "skid row"; gambling in private clubs and in certain ethnic communities; and vagrancy in underutilized portions of public parks. During the Prohibition era, whole cities were "wet," and their police openly tolerated bootlegging, speakeasies, and rumrunners. More recently, police have become increasingly tolerant of homosexual behavior in "gay bars" and "pot smoking" in university communities.

By defining their responsibilities as maintaining public order rather than rigorously enforcing all laws, night-watchmanlike police departments eased their relationships with minority groups, the poor, and other factions of the community whose values differed from those of its lawmakers. The recruitment of policemen from low-income and immigrant families further softened conflicts between police and those "dangerous classes" in the community that the more affluent expected police to control. Policemen developed close ties to the communities in which their beats were located; after some years of patrolling the streets, they became local figures of some importance. Indeed, ties between police and community could become so close that bribery and corruption often pervaded the operations of police departments.

The potential for corruption is, after all, inherent in certain activities expected of law-enforcement agencies. Because the police are supposed to apprehend criminals and secure the evidence necessary for their conviction, policemen are brought into regular, perhaps daily, contact with individuals operating on the edges of the law. These individuals are often the best "informants" about the whereabouts of stolen goods, the sources of supply for a "dope ring," or an important clue in a "big case." Such information comes at a price, and police usually have limited budgets to spend on such confidential purposes. They thus find it convenient to create informants by arresting (or threatening to arrest) prostitutes, drug users, and other petty criminals on minor charges, offering to drop or reduce the charges if the criminals assist in the solution of bigger cases.[4] This kind of bargaining is routine in detective work, and few police officials regard it as an unacceptable practice.

The line between maintaining contacts among criminals and outright corruption is a slim one, however. If minor, especially victimless, crimes are overlooked in order to create "informants," they also can be ignored for a fee. More generally, just as other governmental agencies are frequently co-opted by the better organized of their clientele (for example, the tendency of highway departments to come under the influence of the trucking industry), so police departments have to guard themselves against too close an association with the better organized of forces outside the law, who are among the "clients" of the police.

This basic susceptibility of police departments to corrupting influences, especially in cases involving victimless crimes, was hardly discouraged by the political machines that at one time dominated American cities. Indeed, the night-watchmanlike department, which concentrated on maintaining public order rather than enforcing all laws, was well suited to nineteenth-century machine-style politics.[5] Party organizations that maintained their strength in low-income, immigrant neighborhoods by doing favors for particular individuals found it helpful to have policemen who did not take the letter of the law too seriously. Poor immigrants valued their precinct captain's ability to drop charges being brought against their son (placing him instead in the hands of the parish priest), to protect numbers and crap games, and to bail them out of jail, if necessary. More organized racketeers provided some of the "boodle" that helped "oil" the machine, in return for which the party insured police protection for their illegal, but usually "victimless," activities. Moreover, selective enforcement of laws could be of service in more directly political activities. Police could harass political opponents and ignore abuses of election laws by party workers. Not surprisingly, the police and the courts generally were among the last bastions of power that party machines conceded to reform pressures.[6]

POLICE REFORMS

The night-watchmanlike police department may have established a tolerable, even friendly relationship with the poor as it tried to maintain order in the inner city. But, the attendant corruption and undue partisan influences over police behavior that were typically a concomitant of this type of law enforcement aroused the ire of middle-class reformers at the turn of the century. Consequently, most cities witnessed persistent and increasingly successful efforts to change the character of police departments.

Before examining the actual reforms implemented, it might be instructive to consider one sweeping proposal for change that the reformers themselves never considered: revision of the law so that "victimless" crimes were no longer illegal. Norval Morris and Gordon Hawkins have argued that victimless crimes are not properly a subject for legal action.[7] However immoral, improper, or indecent public drunkenness, gambling, drug abuse, prostitution, or homosexuality may be, these actions do not disturb the public order or directly injure an innocent party. The state should consequently absolve itself of the responsibility of trying to regulate private morality. They stress that the police resources now used to detect such crimes could then be freed to combat crimes against persons and property. Equally important, we might add, the abolishment of such laws would remove many of the incentives that maintain the debilitating system of informers, bribery, and corruption that are so particularly a part of the world of victimless crimes.

Reformers did not consider this approach to resolving the problems of selective law enforcement and police corruption. Very likely, such proposals would have been too controversial to win much public support but, significantly, the reformers themselves made no effort to repeal laws regulating personal conduct. They were too interested in creating better citizens in a better community, too oriented toward creating the good "City on a Hill," and too concerned with the moral improvement of others to encourage permissive legislation.[8] In a sense, the reformers' very strength was their weakness. They were appropriately concerned about dishonesty in government, unfair police practices, and the close association between politicians and special interests. Morally outraged, they campaigned for reform when most people were only apathetic about public affairs. Yet, their very moral fervor made it difficult for them to tolerate differences in values that were so much a part of the pluralistic life of American cities.

The police reforms that they proposed were far different. Rather than changing the law, reform concentrated on a variety of normative and structural changes that together were intended to bring police practice into conformity with the existing law. According to reformers, police officers should be paid more, have more education, and have more extensive pre-service and in-service training. In this way, reformers hoped to recruit a better class of policemen, who would be carefully trained in the norms of behavior that reformers felt properly governed police activities. Reformers also sought more centralized direction of the police force in order to insure more uniform enforcement of the law and less opportunity for corruption by low-ranking patrolmen. Accordingly, they sought to eliminate neighborhood offices and establish a system of rotation whereby no officer would remain in one neighborhood for too long a period. Centralization could also be furthered by requiring detailed reports concerning all incidents that patrolmen encountered. A more extensive division of labor was proposed in order to permit specialization within the police force, closer supervision of sensitive tasks, and the recruitment of especially qualified men for high-level positions. As a result, more "advanced" departments established vice squads, traffic details, and aggressive patrolling task forces. Over the years, new technological innovations, including police cars with elaborate communications equipment, were introduced not only to speed police reaction time to reported incidents but also to bring police under still more centralized direction. All these and other changes reduced the opportunities for low-ranking patrolmen to develop, in their communities, the personal contacts that might lead to corruption.[9]

Early reformers also sought to separate the police force from partisan influences. Recruitments to and promotions within the force came to be governed by performance on examinations. Civil-service coverage was extended to policemen, which precluded removal of officers from the force unless corruption or extreme incompetence could be clearly established. Eventually, all appointments to high-ranking positions, save perhaps only that of police commissioner, had to be made from within the existing ranks of the organization—a rule designed to eliminate the appointment of party favorites to key positions.

With the decline of the political machine, many of these reform measures have been widely adopted. The old connections between police officers and party precinct captains have all but disappeared. The improved training of police officers has very likely reduced police brutality and differential enforcement of the law among various social and racial groups. Police interference with balloting on election day, once quite prevalent in inner-city areas, now rarely occurs. It also seems that police relationships with organized crime are less extensive than they were during the Prohibition era. (On the other hand, the recent widespread use of illegal drugs is creating an atmosphere that encourages police collaboration with "pushers" quite comparable to their collaboration with "bootleggers" in the 1930's).

Yet these police reforms have not come without costs. Although law enforcement is more uniform, it thereby loses sensitivity to variations in the cultures and life-styles of differing groups in the community. Teen-age rowdyism, which policemen once brought under control with a bit of manhandling on the spot, now leads to arrests and juvenile court proceedings. Family squabbles, once ended by the mere presence of policemen, now more frequently lead to indictments based on the reports officers are expected to file. Rigid, universalistic enforcement of the law has increased tensions between police and those relatively powerless groups (such as blacks and young people) whose moral code differs from that dominant in the larger society. The extensive, almost exclusive use of patrol cars in big cities has sharply limited informal contacts between police and community. Rotation of police officers among beats and districts has further made the police officer more of a soldier in an army of occupation and less of a neighborhood leader. Civil-service examinations have made it difficult to recruit and promote blacks, Puerto Ricans, and Chicanos in numbers proportionate to their share of the urban population, and efforts of politicians to achieve increased minority recruitment have been attacked as undue political interference.

Nor have the elaborate technological innovations, complex administrative structures, and specialized departments typical of big-city police departments markedly improved the levels of law enforcement. In a careful comparative study of two black suburbs with three inner-city black neighborhoods in Chicago, Ostrom and Whitaker found little difference in the quality of police services, as reported by a random sample of citizens in these five communities.[10] What differences they did find indicated somewhat higher levels of satisfaction in the suburban communities, even though the Chicago police were better paid, had more extensive training, and were assisted by a more elaborate set of supporting services. Although Chicago was spending fourteen times as much on a per-capita basis as were the suburban communities, the quality of service was much the same.

Finally, the reform of the police has not taken police out of politics. If most departments no longer have close ties with a political machine, they have become more active as an independent force in city affairs.[11] In recent years, police have used such tactics as "blue" sickness, excessive ticket-writing for minor infractions, and even outright strikes in order to secure salary increases and other desired changes. Through their patrolmen's associations, they have openly campaigned against civilian review boards, "lenient" judges, and mayoral candidates thought to be insufficiently strong supporters of "law and order." In Philadelphia, in fact, police enthusiastically helped elect their own commissioner, Frank Rizzo, as mayor.

POLICE AND THE BLACK COMMUNITY

These developments are not unrelated to the changing racial composition of the central cities of the North. The estrangement between police and urban blacks has made law enforcement a major issue in the contemporary urban crisis. White citizens are afraid to walk the streets at night, flee to suburban "fortresses"

that guard against black penetration, and support overt, even pro-
vocative political activities by law-enforcement officials that previously would have been strongly condemned. At the same time,
blacks have become increasingly hostile to the officers in charge of
maintaining order in their communities. Nearly all the major riots
in the late 1960's were sparked by an incident between police and
a black suspect. Black leaders have demanded civilian review
boards that would have the power to investigate allegations of
police brutality. And, out of concern for their own safety, officers
have insisted that they patrol black communities (both in cars
and on foot) in pairs rather than singly. For many blacks, police
have become an army of occupation within their territory, a grim
realization of the possibility that opponents of any police force
feared over a century ago.

There is little solid evidence that black suspicion of the police
is due to discriminatory behavior by white policemen against
blacks in particular. It is true that policemen make racial slurs
when referring to blacks behind their backs and, sometimes, to
their faces.[12] But if police call blacks "niggers" and "coons," that
seems little different than their references to Italians as "wops"
and to people of Polish descent as "Polacks." Street language is
not invariably polite; it hardly seems the root of the problem.
More significantly, it is difficult to find conclusive evidence in
modern departments that policemen treat blacks in a discriminatory fashion. For example, Skolnick found little evidence that
policemen collecting fines for cumulative traffic and parking
violations called the paddy wagon any more frequently for blacks
than for whites (once social class and permanence of residence
had been taken into account).[13] Reiss found a high incidence of
police brutality directed especially against those who question
the officer's authority, but he found no higher incidence of brutal
treatment of black than white suspects.[14] And Wilson found that
modernized, reformed departments arrested far fewer blacks on
the vague charge of public drunkenness than did more traditional,
night-watchmanlike departments.[15] Police are far from color-blind,
but there is some evidence that they find characteristics other
than race more useful in making routine decisions on patrol.

The tensions between police and the black community are
nonetheless very real. A variety of interpretations of this fact exist,
and the evidence for any one is skimpy at best. Still, the changes
in the structure of urban police departments seem to be at least
one important factor. The reforms that have modernized the
police have perhaps made them more honest, efficient (in a

narrow sense of the word), and equitable. Yet the centralization of control has so divorced the patrolmen from the communities for which they have responsibility that it has made vastly more difficult the development of a sense of trust between police and community. Ironically, the very steps taken to improve the police have added to the mutual distrust that has typically characterized relations between police and a city's poorer minority groups. If reform is to succeed in the future, it must focus not so much on increasing police efficiency as on creating the conditions of trust between police and the law-abiding community, upon which effective law enforcement ultimately depends.

In this context, proposals for community control of the police have some merit. Although the unforeseen consequences of previous reforms caution against suggesting that any panacea is available, community-controlled police would offset many of the tendencies of today's modernized, reformed police departments. Officers would be more likely to live in the neighborhoods they patrolled and to share the communities' racial, ethnic, and class characteristics. If directed by representatives of their local community, they would enforce the laws selectively whenever such was necessary for maintaining peace and trust with community residents.

Some have argued that community control of police would mean conflict among armed racial groups within the central city. Others seem to fear that in black areas law and order would totally break down. Such criticisms ignore the fact that community control of police is prevalent in the mostly white suburban areas; it is not easy to see the justification for accepting such a governing structure there but opposing it for the central city. The claim that blacks could not or would not enforce order in their own community, aside from bordering on the most blatant racism, ignores the fact that blacks, more often victims than any other group, are concerned about "crime in the streets." Admittedly, coordinating police work among competing jurisdictions would require cooperative mechanisms among community-controlled departments, but establishing once again a respect for law officers, as well as for the law, seems to be a higher priority.

Notes

1. Providing a widely accepted definition, Max Weber is willing to refer to an organization as the "state" only if "its administrative staff successfully upholds a claim to the *monopoly* of the *legitimate use* of physical force in the enforcement of its order." Max Weber, *The Theory of So-*

cial and Economic Organization, ed. by Talcott Parsons (New York: Free Press, 1947), p. 154.

2. Norval Morris and Gordon Hawkins, *The Honest Politician's Guide to Crime Control* (Chicago: University of Chicago Press, 1970), p. 6.

3. James Q. Wilson, *Varieties of Police Behavior* (Cambridge, Mass.: Harvard University Press, 1968), Ch. 5. Wilson argues that police traditionally used these laws more to maintain public order than to regulate personal conduct. On the other hand, these laws do permit police abuse of "drunks," vagrants, and other outcasts of society. See Albert J. Reiss, "How Much 'Police Brutality' Is There?" *TRANS-action*, IV, 8 (July/August, 1967), pp. 10–19.

4. Jerome Skolnick, *Justice Without Trial* (New York: John Wiley and Sons, 1967), Ch. 6.

5. John Gardiner, "The Politics of Corruption," in Task Force on Organized Crime, The President's Commission on Law Enforcement and Administration of Justice, *Task Force Report: Organized Crime* (Washington: U.S. Printing Office, 1963), pp. 61–79.

6. Wallace Sayre and Herbert Kaufman, *Governing New York City* (New York: W. W. Norton, 1965), pp. 538–48.

7. Morris and Hawkins, *op. cit.*, Ch. 1.

8. On the moralistic flavor of the reform movement, see Richard Hofstadter, *The Age of Reform* (New York: Random House, 1955); see also Daniel Elazar, *Cities of the Prairie* (New York: Basic Books, 1968).

9. Together, these reforms have been the basis for the "legalistic" style of law enforcement, which Wilson contrasts with the "Nightwatchman" style of an early period. See Wilson, *Varieties of Police Behavior*, Ch. 6.

10. Elinor Ostrom and Gordon Whitaker, "Black Citizens and the Police: Some Effects of Community Control." Paper presented before the Annual Meeting of the American Political Science Association, Chicago, Illinois, September, 1971.

11. This problem is discussed in some detail in Jerome Skolnick, *The Politics of Protest* (New York: Ballantine, 1969), pp. 286–89.

12. Skolnick, *Justice Without Trial*, pp. 80–83.

13. *Ibid.*, pp. 83–90.

14. Reiss, *op. cit.*, pp. 15–17.

15. Wilson, *op. cit.*, pp. 188–99.

BIBLIOGRAPHY

MORRIS, NORVAL, and HAWKINS, GORDON. *The Honest Politician's Guide to Crime Control*. Chicago: University of Chicago: Press, 1970.

NIEDERHOFER, ARTHUR. *Behind the Shield: The Police in Urban Society*. Garden City, New York: Doubleday, 1967, p. 60.

REISS, ALBERT J., JR. "How Much 'Police Brutality' Is There?" *TRANS-action*, IV, 8 (July/August 1967), pp. 10–19.

———. *The Police and the Public*. New Haven: Yale University Press, 1971.

SKOLNICK, JEROME H. *Justice Without Trial: Law Enforcement In Democratic Society*. New York: John Wiley and Sons, 1967.

———. *The Politics of Protest*. New York: Ballantine, 1969.

WILSON, JAMES Q. *Varieties of Police Behavior: The Management of Law and Order in Eight Communities*. Cambridge, Mass.: Harvard University Press, 1970.

THE POLICE DEPARTMENT

WALLACE SAYRE AND HERBERT KAUFMAN

The Police Commissioner [of New York City] heads the most visible, the most publicized, the most dramatic and controversial of the city's line agencies. His Department is also one of the city's largest, its staff numbering over 26,000 at the end of 1957, of which more than 25,000 were members of the uniformed force. Representing one of the oldest of the city government's functions, but confronted with constantly changing problems and pressures in its assignments, the Department presents to the Police Commissioner and his deputies complexities and dilemmas not often matched in difficulty in the city's other line agencies.

The Police Department has the broadest regulatory assignment among all the regulatory activities of the city government. From the charter alone, the Department derives a sweeping obligation and power to "preserve the public peace, prevent crime, detect and arrest offenders, . . . preserve order . . . , enforce and prevent the violation of all laws and ordinances . . . ," accompanied by a series of more specific assignments. But the greater body of the Department's assignments comes from state laws and local ordinances and codes containing extensive regulatory and law enforcement provisions which the Department is expected to apply to all violators. Still other provisions of charter and statute make the Police Commissioner the licensing, inspecting, or supervising authority over certain trades (for example, public dance halls, cabarets, taxicabs and taxi drivers, pawnbrokers, cartmen, and others). To all these regulatory assignments of the Department there must also be added the traditional and widespread expectations that the police force is a service agency, obliged to attend to the countless necessities and conveniences of an urban population for whom the police are a visible and available resource. The Commissioner can find few boundaries to his respon-sibilities; he has less difficulty in discovering the limits of his opportunities and resources.

The Police Commissioner's hopes for the exercise of personal leadership and initiative as the responsible head of his Department revolve around his capacity to secure internal control over his agency, his relations with the Mayor, with other city officials and the party leaders, and with the Department's complex consti-tuency. These basic conditions of his leadership and initiative are rarely fully mastered by the Police Commissioner. Resolute out-siders and insiders, in their turn as Commissioners, have each ex-pended great energies and varied strategies upon this dilemma without triumphant results. Other Commissioners have accepted the prevailing arrangements, expressing satisfaction in quite mar-ginal increments of change; still others have moved quickly on to more responsible or less taxing environments.

Securing internal control of the Department is the insurmount-able barrier to leadership, initiative, and innovation by Police Commissioners. The Commissioner is not lacking in formal power for this purpose. The charter declares that he "shall have cognizance and control of the government, administration, dis-position and discipline of the department, and control of the police force of the department" and, further, that he "shall be the chief executive officer of the police force." But these formal powers must in reality be exercised in the context of a personnel system which blunts their use, in the face of the close-knit orga-nized police bureaucracies determined to limit the Commis-sioner's initiative and discretion, and through an organization structure designed to preserve the traditions of the force and its settled patterns of operation. The Commissioner has few "civil-ian" helpers; they are mainly clerical and custodial. The person-nel system dictates that every member of the uniformed police force must be first recruited and inducted as a patrolman, a "rookie" without special skills or knowledge who enters upon a long apprenticeship in the tradition-centered doctrines and prac-tices of the force, rising slowly rank by rank through examinations which also emphasize seniority and mastery of the Department's established codes of police practice.

The police captains who emerge from this process of advance-ment by apprenticeship, indoctrination, and seniority constitute the pool of talent from which the Commissioner must select his officers for the command posts and the managerial tasks of the

Department—the deputy inspectors, the inspectors, the deputy chief inspectors, the assistant chief inspectors, and the Chief Inspector who is the head of the uniformed force. In recent decades, Police Commissioners have increasingly chosen, or have been persuaded, to select their deputy commissioners from this group also. Thus the Commissioner is enclosed within (or ostracized by, if he does not conform) a personnel system which limits his choices of key personnel and provides him but rarely with fellow champions of innovation, or with experts and specialists in fields of knowledge (technological and sociological) which might transform police administration under his leadership, or even with that modicum of competition in ideas among different segments of his staff which might give him limited opportunities for catalytic action as Commissioner.

If the personnel system confronts the Commissioner with a tradition-centered top command—"the top brass," composed of approximately 100 inspectors at various grades and of not quite 200 captains—the organized police bureaucracies (lieutenants, sergeants, patrolmen) bring additional restrictive pressures to bear upon him. Mayor McClellan observed long ago that the Police Department was "run by the inspectors," not by the Commissioner; for the past several decades, he would have needed to add "and by the police bureaucracies." They have power inside the Department to mold the behavior of their members in such ways as will reduce the impact of any change in policy or procedure sponsored by the Commissioner. They have secured special protections for their members in both state statutes and city rules, which preserve their capacity to resist without much risk of reprisal or severe discipline. They have power in the more general political arena, where officials and party leaders have learned to listen to them and to act sympathetically. Police Commissioners may bristle at bureaucratic boldness and evoke the symbols of command and discipline, but the organized police groups are confident and persistent; they are on familiar ground and have often waited out these storms before. Their goal is self-direction in their accustomed ways, not an eager responsiveness to either the "top brass" or the current Commissioner.

The twin forces of the Department's closed personnel system and the organized police bureaucracies help to preserve a third barrier to leadership by the Commissioner—an organization structure awkwardly suited to the Commissioner's purposes of leadership and innovation. The basic structure is traditional and does not yield much to the requirements of changes in policies and in assignments, or of advances in police technology developed elsewhere. Organizationally, the Department is wedded to performing its work through geographical units—precincts, districts and divisions, borough commands—at the expense of greater specialization and mobility of its resources. The major concessions to specialization which have been made (the detective, traffic, and emergency service patrol groups) are themselves each organized geographically. In this and other ways specialized personnel is almost invariably squeezed into the geographical chains-of-command. Methods and procedures must also conform to the mold of geography, affecting adversely the attraction and feasibility of almost every proposed change in technology or police. Police Commissioners are only occasionally aware of this tyranny of geography as an organizational vise; they have no managerial staff to develop for them the alternatives in police organization and procedures which might give them unsuspected opportunities for breaking the crust of custom and habits in police administration. For example, the Police Commissioner was forced in 1949 to yield the traffic planning assignment to a new city agency because his personnel system and his organizational arrangements could produce neither the specialized personnel (the traffic planners, traffic engineers, and statistical analysts) nor the specialized methods necessary to handle the traffic problem at a high level of experiment and innovation.

The closed personnel system, the power of the police bureaucracies, and the inflexible organization structure of the Department have an additional by-product for the Commissioner: he must expend a great part of his energies in attempts at "policing the police." His problems are concentrated in two phenomena: police corruption and police violence. However aggressively the Commissioner pursues the goal of police integrity by the use of special squads to investigate the force, by shake-ups and transfers of command, by swift suspensions and other forms of discipline, he accepts ultimately that police corruption is endemic to his organization, and that he is fortunate if he can prevent its reaching epidemic proportions. He lacks the resources to do more. On the score of police violence, he is compelled to yield in a different fashion: he must almost invariably take a tough line in justification of the use of force by the police, whether it be rationalizing the promiscuous use of the club, the gun, or the "third degree." His organization (and his own training, if he is a career Commissioner) does not permit him to depart from this doctrine.

Police Commissioners thus exercise formal but essential peripheral control over the Police Department. They can dramatize the role of the Department in the life of the city; they can urge forcefully and often successfully the expansion of the Department in numbers and budget and thus win some internal support; they can lead crusades against selected targets ("round-ups" of alleged vagrants; raids on gamblers, narcotic "rings," houses of prostitution; arrests of alleged subversives); and they can be stern disciplinarians in dealing with individual members of the force who violate overtly the regulations of the Department. But these are the outer boundaries of their control. The more positive measures of leadership are beyond their reach.

Police Commissioners in New York City have long sought an autonomous status for their Department with freedom from supervision by the Mayor, from interventions by party leaders, and from jurisdictional invasions by other governmental agencies. "No outside interference" has been their uniform motto for several decades, and all external influences have usually been condemned as "politics." In seeking to maximize the self-directing capacity of the Department, Commissioners have presumably sought also to maximize their own opportunities for leadership and direction of the police agency. But autonomy for the Department has also meant isolation for the Commissioner from sources which might help him in his difficult task of securing internal control. The police bureaucracy seems to be the main beneficiary of the autonomy which the Police Commissioners have secured.

Freedom from supervision by the Mayor has been a special target of the drive for police autonomy. Mayoral interest in police policy and police administration has been consistently rebuffed by equating it with the interests of party leaders or, more ambiguously, with politics. In their acceptance of this formula for ostracizing Mayors from any opportunities to assume general responsibility for leadership in law enforcement, the Police Commissioners have had the support of the police bureaucracy, the civic groups, the communication media, and others. There is a general consensus that Mayors merit only the blame for police failures. The assistance which Mayors might give Police Commissioners in their efforts to acquire leadership within the Department has been forfeited in preference for the ambiguous formula of autonomy.

Removal of the influence of party leaders from police administration has also been a goal of most Police Commissioners, supported by the police bureaucracy and by almost all the articulate
voices in the city. Several Commissioners have given this problem high priority, and the long-term trend in the Department
has been to reduce steadily the opportunities of party leaders to
intervene overtly either in the personnel system or in police policy.
The most striking example is the neutralization of the police role
in election administration. The upper limits of the trend are to be
found, however, in the disposition of individual members of the
force to build mutually useful relationships with party leaders.
It party leaders have been largely excluded at headquarters, they
are not yet ignored in the precincts or other local commands. One
consequence of this development may be that the Commissioner
is isolated from the party leaders in a way in which his lieutenants,
detectives, captains, and inspectors are not.

Other governmental agencies give Police Commissioners less
difficulty. The Police Commissioners are especially able to escape
some of the tight controls of the overhead agencies—Budget,
Personnel, Law, Investigation, and others—which so often burden
the discretion of other department heads. With other line agencies, the relations are often more complex and sometimes characterized by jurisdictional friction, for example, with District
Attorneys, and the Departments of Education, Fire, Health, Sanitation, Traffic, Welfare, the Youth Board, and the special authorities. In the main, however, the Police Department tends more
often to have its own way, the other agencies yielding to its
power, its autonomy, and its cohesiveness. The other side of the
medal is the Police Commissioner's limited opportunities to offer
firm cooperation with other agencies even when he wishes to do
so. His control over his own Department is not sufficient for him
to pledge its affirmative participation in programs involving important innovations in police attitudes or methods.

The Police Department has one of the most complex constituencies among the city's line agencies. It is the object of relatively
constant attention from a wider range of nongovernmental groups
than any other single agency. With such extensive attention directed at them, Police Commissioners have great difficulty in deciding to which voices they must listen most receptively, and on
what subjects. The most relevant constituency elements are difficult to identify. Fragmentation in organization and ambivalence
in attitudes toward the Department are their most distinctive

characteristics. Police Commissioners never quite succeed in identifying the hard core either of their supporting groups or of the
opposition groups with whom they must come to terms. The for-
mations and their attitudes tend to be fluid and unpredictable.

There are a few certainties upon which the Police Commissioner can reasonably depend in his dealings with the Department's constituency, but the sum total of these several certainties
is likely to confront him with as many inconsistencies as clarifica-
tions. He can usually expect more support than opposition for
proposals to expand the size of the police force; the economy
groups have a traditional tolerance for police budgets, and most
other groups are regularly demanding more police services. He can
count upon the groups licensed or inspected by the Department
to attempt to capture the licensing and inspection units of his
organization, thus threatening his control over policy and exposing
him to the risks of unfavorable exposés. He can reasonably anticipate that the communication media, especially the press, will be
ambivalent in their attitudes toward him and his agency, publiciz-
ing with equal zeal and emphasis the dramatic accomplishments
of the police and the sordid chapters of police corruption and violence. He will note, too, that the merchant and automobile associations urging more effective traffic control are also inclined to
condemn "arbitrary" or "rigid" enforcement techniques. Each
religious group presses for its doctrines of law enforcement. Em-
ployer groups urge strict supervision of picketing; labor unions
emphasize their hard-won standards of strict neutrality by the
police in labor disputes. Some groups demand a hard line by police toward juvenile delinquents; others insist upon a subordinate
role for the police in such matters. Some voices advocate wide use
of the nightstick and the dragnet against gangsters, punks, and
gamblers; others, such as bar associations, civil liberties groups,
and some communication media, remind the Police Commissioner of the due process of law. There are no "peak associations"
tying these groups together, either as support or opposition. The
prime difficulty for the Police Commissioner is that, while his
highly fragmented constituency can cause him much trouble, he
cannot expect much help from it; he cannot, in fact, find even a
stable and significant center of opposition with which he might
reach long-term accommodations. Nor does his constituency
furnish him with a lever which he might use to move the police
bureaucracy toward greater responsiveness to his leadership.

The Police Commissioner—isolated from the Mayor and other

elected officials, from the party leaders, and from other agencies, and confronted by an unstructured, fragmented constituency—is thus cut off from effective external alliances and thrust back upon his own limited resources in attempting to lead and direct the police bureaucracy. Autonomy for the Department spells isolation for the Commissioner. With energy and resolution, and some public relations skill, he may create a favorable public image of himself as an omnipresent, incorruptible, and determined administrator. He may exploit the competitive relation between the 300 members of "the brass" and the 24,000 members of the rank and file, in ways that may increase somewhat his influence with both; he may emphatically invoke the semimilitary command structure and vocabulary of the Department to make his purposes unambiguous. He may find tangible and intangible rewards to bestow as incentives for innovation and for responsiveness to his leadership, and he may exhort his officers and men to aspire to the status of a profession, to embrace the trends toward modernization, to take the lead among police systems. All these efforts will help him in his leadership, but their combined long-range increment is not strikingly large. In the end, whatever the dash and determination at the beginning, the Commissioners yield to the necessity of being more the spokesman and the advocate than the leader and the innovator.

WHAT MAKES A BETTER POLICEMAN?

JAMES Q. WILSON

Current discussions of the problems of the American police seem fraught with paradox. While everyone seems to agree about remedies, criticisms of the police arise out of radically different conceptions of the police function. Some people see the police as the chief means of ending or reducing "crime in the streets"; others see them as an agency by which white society confines and suppresses black ghettos; still others view them as an organization caught on the grinding edge of a class conflict among competing standards of order and propriety. Yet despite these utterly disparate diagnoses, the prescribed treatment tends to be quite conventional and generally endorsed—higher salaries, better training, clearer policies, more modern equipment. And a further paradox: despite this apparent agreement on what should be done, little, in fact, happens. In some places, voters and politicians appear to be universally sympathetic to the needs of the police, but they are unwilling to appropriate more money to meet those needs. In other places, the extra funds have been spent but the criticisms remain—little, apparently, has changed.

One reason for this confusion or inaction lies, I believe, in the fact that the police perform a number of quite different functions. The controversies in which the police are embroiled reveal this as various disputants emphasize crime prevention, or law enforcement, or the maintenance of order, or political power. Liberty, order, legitimacy—important and fundamental values are in conflict. The adherents of various points of view take refuge in a common (and perhaps peculiarly American) set of proposals: spend money, hire better men, buy more things. I suspect that spending more money and hiring better men *are* essential to police improvement, but I also suspect that one reason so little extra money is spent and so few men are hired is that beneath our

From James Q. Wilson, "What Makes a Better Policeman?" in *The Atlantic Monthly* (March, 1969), pp. 129–34. Copyright © 1969 by the Atlantic Monthly Company, Boston, Massachusetts. Reprinted with permission.

agreement on means, we remain in deep disagreement on ends. Spend the money on *what*, and *why*? What *is* a "better" policeman, anyway?

This is not a new issue. The history of the American municipal police is in great part a history of struggles to define their role in our society. What makes the controversy so intense today is only partly that it is linked to the question of race; indeed, in the past the police have repeatedly been in conflict with new urban migrants of whatever color. The reason for the heat generated by the police question is probably the same as the reason for the emotions aroused by the crime issue: we compare present circumstances with an earlier period when we thought we had solved the problem. Police behavior, like crime, was not a major issue in the 1940s and 1950s. When the police did become an issue, it was usually because a department was found to be corrupt, and that discovery produced a standard response—bring in a reform chief, reorganize the force, and get back to work.

CROOK CATCHERS

That work was law enforcement, or so it was thought. The job of the police was to prevent crime and catch crooks. Corruption was a serious problem because it seemed to mean that crime was not being prevented and crooks were not being caught. Organized criminals were buying protection, or petty thieves were putting in a "fix," or the police themselves were stealing on the side. Reforming a department not only meant ending corruption and alliances with criminals; it also meant improving training and developing new methods—more courses on crime detection, tighter departmental discipline to prevent misconduct, better equipment to facilitate getting to the scene of a crime and analyzing clues. When the public was invited to inspect a refurbished department, it was shown the new patrol cars, the new crime laboratory, the new communications center, and perhaps the new pistol range. The policeman was portrayed as a "crime fighter," and to an important degree, of course, he was.

But that was not all or even the most important thing he was. Given the nature of the crime problem, it was impossible for him to be simply a crime fighter. Most crime is not prevented and most criminals are not caught, even in the best-run, best-manned departments. Murder, for example, is a "private" crime, occurring chiefly off the streets and among "friends" or relatives. No police methods can prevent it, and only general domestic disarmament, an unlikely event, might reduce it. Many, if not most, assaults are similarly immune from police deterrence. Most crimes against property—burglary, auto theft, larceny—are also crimes of stealth, and though the police might, by various means, cut the rate somewhat, they cannot cut it greatly because they cannot be everywhere at once. Street crimes—robberies, muggings, purse snatches —are more susceptible to police deterrence than any other kind, though so far few, if any, departments have had the resources or the community support to carry out a really significant strategy to prevent street crime.

The result of this state of affairs is that though some police departments are regarded as "backward" and others as "modern" and "professional," neither kind seems able to bring about a substantial, enduring reduction of the crime rate. If this is true, then the characterization of the police as primarily crime fighters places them in a potentially embarrassing position, that of *being judged by a goal they cannot attain.* In the 1950s, when crime rates were either stabilized or ignored, this awkward situation and the police response to it were not apparent.

What most policemen were doing even when they were being thought of as crime fighters was not so much enforcing the law as maintaining order. In a recent study, I have tried to show what makes up the routine work-load of patrolmen, the police rank which has the largest number of men. The vast majority of police actions taken in response to citizen calls involve either providing a service (getting a cat out of a tree or taking a person to a hospital) or managing real or alleged conditions of disorder (quarreling families, public drunks, bothersome teen-agers, noisy cars, and tavern fights). Only a small fraction of these calls involve matters of law enforcement, such as checking on a prowler, catching a burglar in the act, or preventing a street robbery. The disorders to which the police routinely respond are not large-scale. Riots and civil commotions are, in any given city, rare occurrences and when they happen, the police act en masse, under central leadership. Rather, the maintenance of order involves handling disputes in which only two or three people participate and which arise out of personal misconduct, not racial or class grievances.

The difference between order maintenance and law enforcement is not simply the difference between "little stuff" and "real crime" or between misdemeanors and felonies. The distinction is fundamental to the police role, for the two functions involve quite dissimilar police actions and judgments. Order maintenance arises out of a dispute among citizens who accuse each other of being at fault; law enforcement arises out of the victimization of an innocent party by a person whose guilt must be proved. Handling a disorderly situation requires the officer to make a judgment about what constitutes an appropriate standard of behavior; law enforcement requires him only to compare a person's behavior with a clear legal standard. Murder or theft is defined, unambiguously, by statutes; public peace is not. Order maintenance rarely leads to an arrest; law enforcement (if the suspect can be found) typically does. Citizens quarreling usually want the officer to "do something," but they rarely want him to make an arrest (after all, the disputants are usually known or related to each other). Furthermore, whatever law is broken in a quarrel is usually a misdemeanor, and in most states, an officer cannot make a misdemeanor arrest unless he saw the infraction (which is rare) or unless one party or the other will swear out a formal complaint (which is even rarer).

Because an arrest cannot be made in most disorderly cases, the officer is expected to handle the situation by other means and on the spot, but the law gives him almost no guidance on how he is to do this; indeed, the law often denies him the right to do anything at all *other* than make an arrest. No judge will ever see the case, and thus no judge can decide the case for the officer. Alone, unsupervised, with no policies to guide him and little sympathy from onlookers to support him, the officer must "administer justice" on the curbstone.

Early Patterns

In the nineteenth century, it was widely recognized that the maintenance of order was the chief function of the police. Roger Lane's informative history, *Policing the City: Boston, 1822–1885* (Cambridge: Harvard University Press, 1967), recounts how that department, the oldest in the United States, was first organized as a night watch to keep the peace in the streets. Beginning in 1834, men drafted from the citizenry were required to take their turns in seeing (as the governing statute required) "that all disturbances and disorders in the night shall be prevented and suppressed." Wild creatures, human and animal alike, were to be kept off the street, and a hue and cry was to be set up should fire or riot threaten.

The job of law enforcement—that is, of apprehending criminals who had robbed or burgled the citizenry—was not among the duties of the watchmen; indeed, it was not even among the duties of the government. A victim was obliged to find the guilty party himself. Once a suspect was found, the citizen could, for a fee, hire a constable who, acting on a warrant, would take the suspect into custody. Even after detectives—that is, men charged with law enforcement rather than the maintenance of order—were added to the force in the nineteenth century, they continued to serve essentially private interests. The chief concern of the victim was restitution, and to that end, the detectives would seek to recover loot in exchange for a percentage of the take. Detectives functioned then as personal-injury lawyers operate today, on a contingency basis, hoping to get a large part, perhaps half, of the proceeds.

Since in those days there was no law against compounding a felony, the detectives were free to employ any methods they wanted to recover stolen property. And with this as their mission, it is not surprising, as Lane notes, that the best detectives were those who by background and experience were most familiar with the haunts and methods of thieves.

The emergence of a municipal police force out of its watchmen antecedents was not so much the result of mounting crime rates as of growing levels of civil disorder. In time, and with the growth of the cities to a size and heterogeneity too great to permit the operation of informal social controls, the problem of order maintenance became too severe to make reliance on part-time or volunteer watchmen feasible. The Boston Police Department was created to deal with riots, as was the Department in Philadelphia. The Boston police first acquired firearms in the aftermath of the Draft Riot of 1863, though they were not fully armed at public expense until 1884.

The Philadelphia case is illustrative of many. Like Boston, that city relied on watchmen rather than an organized, quasimilitary constabulary. But a series of riots among youthful gangs (the Rats, the Bouncers, the Schuylkill Rangers, and the Blood Tubs, among several) persuaded the city fathers that stronger measures were necessary. To a degree, the riots were under semiofficial auspices, thus magnifying the embarrassment the politicians faced. It seems that volunteer fire companies were organized to handle conflagrations. The young toughs who sat about waiting for fires to happen found this boring and, worse, unrewarding, whereupon some hit upon the idea of starting a fire and racing other companies to the scene to see who could put the blaze out more quickly, and just as important, who could pick up the most loot from the building. Though this competitive zeal may have been a commendable aid to training, it led to frequent collisions between companies speeding to the same fire, with the encounter often leading to a riot. It is only a slight exaggeration to say that the Philadelphia policemen were created in part to control the Philadelphia firemen.

Sometimes on Sunday

The growth and formal organization of the police department did not, in themselves, lead to changes in function. The maintenance of order was still the principal objective. What did lead to a change was twofold: the bureaucratization of the detectives (putting them on salary and ending the fee system), and the use of the police to enforce unpopular laws governing the sale and use of liquor. The former change led to the beginning of the popular confusion as to what the police do. The detective became the hero of the dime novel and the cynosure of the public's romantic imagination; he, and not his patrolman colleague, was the "real" police officer doing "real" police work. Enforcing liquor laws caused the police to initiate prosecutions on their own authority rather than on citizen complaint, particularly in cases where the public was deeply divided regarding the wisdom of the law. In Philadelphia, enforcing the Sunday closing laws, especially with regard to saloons, was widely resented, and when the mayor ordered the police to do it, he was, according to a contemporary account, "caricatured, ridiculed, and denounced." In Boston Mayor Jonathan Chapman was led to remark that police enforcement of temperance laws had created a situation in which "the passions of men are aroused and the community is kept in a constant state of ferment."

What kept the police from being utterly destroyed by the liquor controversy was their determination to do no more than was absolutely necessary, given whatever regime was in power. Edward Savage, the able chief of the Boston force in the 1870s and 1880s, was a man of modest but much exercised literary talents, and in one of his better-known essays, entitled "Advice to a Young Policeman," he set forth the essential role of good police work: "In ordinary cases, if you find yourself in a position of not knowing exactly what to do, better to do too little than too much; it is easier to excuse a moderate course than an overt act."

In addition, the police provided on a large scale a number of services to citizens, especially to those who, because of drink, indolence, or circumstance, were likely to become sources of public disorder. Roger Lane calculates that in 1856 the Boston police provided "lodgings" to over nine thousand persons, not including those who had been arrested for drunkenness. By 1860 the total exceeded seventeen thousand. Perhaps because the police were the principal city agency to witness the lot of the poor, perhaps because one of the original collateral duties of the police chief was superintendent of public health, the officers provided a wide range of services in addition to lodgings—coal for needy families, soup kitchens for the hungry, and jobs as domestics for girls they thought could be lured away from a life of prostitution.

In time, this service policy, which probably did much to mitigate the hostility between police and public occasioned by the enforcement of liquor laws, was curtailed on the complaint of the leaders of the organized charities who objected, apparently, to unfair competition. The advocates of "scientific charity," it seems, did not believe the police were competent to distinguish between the deserving and the undeserving poor.

The relations between police and public even during the period of free soup were not consistently amicable. One issue was the appointment of Irish police officers. For political purposes, the Boston Whigs demanded that, as we would say today, "representatives of indigenous and culturally-deprived groups" be added to the force. Then as now, the "culturally deprived" were responsible for a disproportionate share of those arrested for crimes. Then as now, the police objected to the appointment of an Irishman on the grounds that the man selected by the politicians was not qualified and had himself been arrested for a crime a few years earlier—it seems he had participated in a riot. The police, of course, denied that they were prejudiced but claimed that appointing a person on grounds of ethnicity would be destructive of morale on the force. The mayor insisted that the appointment take place. On November 3, 1851, the new man reported for work, announcing himself loudly and proudly as "Barney McGinniskin, fresh from the bogs of Ireland!"

THE CHIEF EVIL

By the end of the nineteenth century, the groundwork had been laid for the modern municipal police force, and for the modern problems of the police. The bureaucratization of the detectives and the police enforcement of liquor laws had not as yet overshadowed the order-maintenance function of the police, but two events of the twentieth century ensured that they would— Prohibition and the Depression. The former required the police everywhere to choose between being corrupted and making a nuisance of themselves; the latter focused public attention on the escapades of bank robbers and other desperadoes such as John Dillinger, Baby Face Nelson, and Bonnie and Clyde. Police venality and rising crime rates coincided in the public mind, though in fact they had somewhat different causes. The watchman function of the police was lost sight of; their law enforcement function, and their apparent failure to exercise it, were emphasized.

President Herbert Hoover did what most Presidents do when faced with a major political issue for which the solution is neither obvious nor popular—he appointed a commission. In 1931 the National Commission on Law Observance and Law Enforcement —generally known, after its chairman, as the Wickersham Commission—made its report in a series of volumes prepared by some of the ablest academic and police experts of the day. Though many subjects were covered (especially the question of whether immigrants were more criminal than native-born Americans), the volume on the police was of special importance. On page one, the first paragraph stated a twentieth-century conception of the police function and a new standard by which policemen were to be judged:

> The general failure of the police to detect and arrest criminals guilty of the many murders, spectacular bank, payroll, and other hold-ups, and sensational robberies with guns, frequently resulting in the death of the robbed victim, has caused a loss of public confidence in the police of our country. For a condition so general there must be some universal underlying causes to account for it.

Now, of course there may have been some "universal underlying causes," but the ones that come readily to mind—Prohibition, post-war readjustment, and the economic cycle—were not ones about which a presidential commission could at that time speak very candidly. Besides, it was far from clear what could be done about at least the second and third of these causes. What was necessary was to find a "universal cause" about which something could be done. Needless to say, two groups on whom we have long felt free to cast blame for everything from slums to hoof-and-mouth disease—the police and the politicians—seemed appropriate targets. Accordingly, the Commission wrote:

> The chief evil, in our opinion, lies in the insecure, short term of service of the chief or executive head of the police force and in his being subject while in office to the control of politicians in the discharge of his duties.

Some Proposals

Following on this analysis, the Commission detailed a number of specific proposals—putting the police on civil service, buying modern equipment ("the wireless"), and of course, hiring better men and giving them better training. In truth, there probably was a need for some police reforms; many departments had become dumping grounds for the fat relatives of second-rate politicians, and modern bank robbers were in many cases more mobile and efficient than the police chasing them. But the "professional" view of the police went further than merely proposing changes in equipment and manpower; it argued in addition that since the police *can* prevent crime, if the crime rate gets out of hand, it is in good measure because the police are incompetent as a result of political influence.

Now, some members of the Commission were no doubt perfectly aware that the police do not cause crime, but, like many commissions anxious to make a strong public impression and generate support for desirable changes, they inevitably overstated the case in their report. A report that said that many improvements in police practice were necessary but that these improvements, if adopted, would have only a slight effect on the crime rate would not generate many headlines. (Thirty-seven years later, the Kerner Commission had not forgotten this lesson; what made the newspapers was not its proposals for action but its charge of "white racism.")

The consequences of assigning to the police a law-enforcement, crime-prevention function to the exclusion of anything else were profound. If the job of the police is to catch crooks, then the police have a technical, ministerial responsibility in which discretion plays little part. Since no one is likely to disagree on the value of the objective, then there is little reason to expose the police to the decision-making processes of city government. *Ergo,* take the police "out of politics." So powerful (or so useful) did this slogan become that within a few decades whenever a big-city mayor tried to pick his own police chief or take charge of his department for the purpose of giving it a new direction, *the police themselves* objected on the grounds that this was an effort to exercise "political influence" over the force.

Furthermore, if the technical objective of law enforcement was primary, then non-law-enforcement duties should be taken away from the police: no more soup kitchens; no more giving lodging to drunks; no more ambulance driving. These things are not "real police work." Let the police see the public only in their role as law enforcers. Let the public, alas, see the police only as adversaries. Of course, these changes were more in the public's mind than in everyday reality. If politics was taken out of the police, the police were not taken out of politics. They continued—in fact, with the decline of party machines, they increased—their involvement in electoral politics, city hall intrigue, and legislative lobbying. And whatever professional police leadership may have said, the patrolman on the beat knew that his job was not primarily law enforcement—he was still handling as many family fights and rowdy teen-agers as ever. But lacking support in the performance of these duties, he came also to believe that his job "wasn't real police work," and accordingly that it was peripheral, if not demeaning.

But perhaps the most important consequence was the police response to the public expectation that they could prevent crime. Their response was perfectly rational and to be encountered in any organization that is judged by a standard it cannot meet— they lied. If police activity (given the level of resources and public support available) could not produce a significant decline in crime rates, police record-keeping would be "adjusted" to keep the rates in line. Departments judged by professional standards but not controlled by professional leaders were at pains to show progress by either understating the number of crimes or overstating the number of crimes "cleared" by arrest. Often this was not the policy of the chief, but the result of judging officers by crime and arrest records.

In the public's eye, the "hero cop" was the man who made the "good pinch." For a while (until the mass media abandoned the standards of the middle-aged and the conservative in favor of the standards of the young and the radical), the ideal cop was the "G Man." FBI agents, of course, are different from municipal police forces precisely because their task *is* law enforcement, and often enforcing important laws against quite serious criminals. Few special agents need to wade into a skid-row brawl. But within city departments, the emphasis on the "good pinch" grew. This was only partly because the newspapers, and thus the public, rewarded such accomplishments; it was also because the departments rewarded it. The patrolman could look forward, in the typical case, to remaining a patrolman all his life *unless* he could get promoted or be made a detective. Promotion increasingly came to require the passing of a written examination in which college men would usually do better than less articulate but perhaps more competent "street men." Appointment as a detective, however, was in many departments available to men with a good arrest record (or a strategically placed friend in headquarters). If you want to get away from drunks, kids, and shrews, then make a pinch that will put you in line for becoming a dick. Though there is in principle nothing wrong with rewarding men for having a good arrest record, one frequent result of this system has been to take the best patrolmen off the street and put them into a headquarters unit.

POLICE REFORM: THE CHOICES AHEAD

Today, the conception of the police role underlying the foregoing arrangements is being questioned. Perhaps the landmark event was the 1967 report of the President's Commission on Law Enforcement and Administration of Justice, the executive director of which was James Vorenberg of the Harvard Law School. Unlike the Wickersham or Kerner Commission reports, this document made relatively few headlines, and the reason, I think, was that it did not provide the reporters with a catchy slogan. The nine volumes of the Vorenberg report insisted that the problems of crime and police work are complicated matters for which few, if any, easy solutions are available. There were no dramatic scandals to uncover; the police "third degree" (on which the Wickersham Commission, in the report drafted by Zechariah Chafee, lavished much attention) had declined in occurrence and significance. Most police departments had been taken out of the control of party machines (in some cases, it would appear, only to be placed under the influence of organized crime). Instead, the Commission devoted considerable attention to the order-maintenance function of the police:

A great majority of the situations in which policemen intervene are not, or are not interpreted by the police to be, criminal situations in the sense that they call for arrest. . . . A common kind of situation . . . is the matrimonial dispute, which police experts estimate consumes as much time as any other single kind of situation.

The riots in Watts and elsewhere had, by the time the report appeared, already called the attention of the public to the importance (and fragility) of public order. The rise of demands for "community control" of various public services, including the police and the schools, has placed the problem of order on the political agenda. Whether the problems of managing disorder can best be handled by turning city government over to neighborhood groups is a complicated question. (Provisionally, I would argue that war becomes more, not less, likely when a political system is balkanized.) In any case, we have come full circle in our thinking about the function of the police.

Or almost full circle. The current anxiety about crime in the streets continues to lead some to define the police task as wholly or chiefly one of crime deterrence, and thus any discussion of redefining the police role or reorganizing police departments to facilitate performing their other functions tends to get lost in the din of charges and countercharges about whether or not the police have been "handcuffed." This is unfortunate, not because crime in the streets is a false issue (the rates of street crime, I am convinced, *are* increasing in an alarming manner), but because handling this problem cannot be left solely or even primarily to the police; acting as if it could raises false hopes among the citizens and places unfair and distorting demands on the police. At least as much attention to the courts and correctional systems will be necessary if much progress is to be shown in reducing street crime.

The simultaneous emergence of a popular concern for both crime and order does put in focus the choices that will have to be made in the next generation of police reforms. In effect, municipal police departments are two organizations in one serving two related but not identical functions. The strategy appropriate for strengthening their ability to serve one role tends to weaken their ability to serve the other. Crime deterrence and law enforcement require, or are facilitated by, specialization, strong hierarchical authority, improved mobility and communications, clarity in legal codes and arrest procedures, close surveillance of the community, high standards of integrity, and the avoidance of entangling alliances with politicians. The maintenance of order, on the other hand, is aided by departmental procedures that include decentralization, neighborhood involvement, foot patrol, wide discretion, the provision of services, an absence of arrest quotas, and some tolerance for minor forms of favoritism and even corruption.

There is no magic formula—no prepackaged "reform"—that can tell a community or a police chief how to organize a force to serve, with appropriate balance, these competing objectives. Just as slogans demanding "taking the police out of politics" or "putting the police in cars" have proved inadequate guides to action in the past, so also slogans demanding "foot patrolmen" or "community control" are likely to prove inadequate in the future. One would like to think that since both points of view now have ardent advocates, the debate has at last been joined. But I suspect that the two sides are talking at, or past, each other, and not *to* each other, and thus the issue, far from being joined, is still lost in rhetoric.

HOW MUCH "POLICE BRUTALITY" IS THERE?

ALBERT J. REISS

"For three years, there has been through the courts and the streets a dreary procession of citizens with broken heads and bruised bodies against few of whom was violence needed to effect an arrest. Many of them had done nothing to deserve an arrest. In a majority of such cases, no complaint was made. If the victim complains, his charge is generally dismissed. The police are practically above the law."

This statement was published in 1903, and its author was the Hon. Frank Moss, a former police commissioner of New York City. Clearly, today's charges of police brutality and mistreatment of citizens have a precedent in American history—but never before has the issue of police brutality assumed the public urgency it has today. In Newark, in Detroit, in Watts, in Harlem, and, in fact, in practically every city that has had a civil disturbance, "deep hostility between police and ghetto" was, reports the Kerner Commission, "a primary cause of the riots."

Whether or not the police accept the words "police brutality," the public now wants some plain answers to some plain questions. How widespread is police mistreatment of citizens? Is it on the increase? Why do policemen mistreat citizens? Do the police mistreat Negroes more than whites?

To find some answers, 36 people working for the Center of Research on Social Organization observed police-citizen encounters in the cities of Boston, Chicago, and Washington, D.C. For seven days a week, for seven weeks during the summer of 1966, these observers, with police permission, sat in patrol cars and monitored booking and lockup procedures in high-crime precincts.

Obtaining information about police mistreatment of citizens is no simple matter. National and state civil-rights commissions receive hundreds of complaints charging mistreatment—but proving these allegations is difficult. The few local civilian-review boards,

Published by permission of Transaction Inc. from *TRANS-action*, Vol. 4 No. 8 (July/August 1967). © 1967 by Transaction Inc.

such as the one in Philadelphia, have not produced any significant volume of complaints leading to the dismissal or disciplining of policemen for alleged brutality. Generally, police chiefs are silent on the matter, or answer charges of brutality with vague statements that they will investigate any complaints brought to their attention. Rank-and-file policemen are usually more outspoken: They often insinuate that charges of brutality are part of a conspiracy against them, and against law and order.

THE MEANING OF BRUTALITY

What citizens mean by police brutality covers the full range of police practices. These practices, contrary to the impression of many civil-rights activists, are not newly devised to deal with Negroes in our urban ghettos. They are ways in which the police have traditionally behaved in dealing with certain citizens, particularly those in the lower classes. The most common of these practices are:

the use of profane and abusive language,
commands to move on or get home,
stopping and questioning people on the street or searching them
    and their cars,
threats to use force if not obeyed,
prodding with a nightstick or approaching with a pistol, and
the actual use of physical force or violence itself.

Citizens and the police do not always agree on what constitutes proper police practice. What is "'proper," or what is "brutal," it need hardly be pointed out, is more a matter of judgment about what someone did than a description of what police do. What is important is not the practice itself but what it means to the citizen. What citizens object to and call "police brutality" is really the judgment that they have not been treated with the full rights and dignity owing citizens in a democratic society. Any practice that degrades their status, that restricts their freedom, that annoys or harasses them, or that uses physical force is frequently seen as unnecessary and unwarranted. More often than not, they are probably right.

Many police practices serve only to degrade the citizen's sense of himself and his status. This is particularly true with regard to the way the police use language. Most citizens who have contact with the police object less to their use of four-letter words than to *how* the policeman talks to them. Particularly objectionable is the habit policemen have of "talking down" to citizens, of calling them names that deprecate them in their own eyes and those of others. More than one Negro citizen has complained: "They talk down to me as if I had no name—like 'boy' or 'man' or whatever, or they call me 'Jack' or by my first name. They don't show me no respect."

Members of minority groups and those seen as nonconformists, for whatever reason, are the most likely targets of status degradation. Someone who has been drinking may be told he is a "bum" or a "shitty wino." A woman walking alone may be called a "whore." And a man who doesn't happen to meet a policeman's standard of how one should look or dress may be met with the remark, "What's the matter, you a queer?" A white migrant from the South may be called a "hillbilly" or "shitkicker"; a Puerto Rican, a "pork chop"; a young boy, a "punk kid." When the policeman does not use words of status degradation, his manner may be degrading. Citizens want to be treated as people, not as "nonpersons" who are talked about as if they were not present.

That many Negroes believe that the police have degraded their status is clear from surveys in Watts, Newark, and Detroit. One out of every five Negroes in our center's post-riot survey in Detroit reports that the police have "talked down to him." More than one in ten says a policeman has "called me a bad name."

To be treated as "suspicious" is not only degrading, but is also a form of harassment and a restriction on the right to move freely. The harassing tactics of the police—dispersing social street-gatherings, the indiscriminate stopping of Negroes on foot or in cars, and commands to move on or go home—are particularly common in ghetto areas.

Young people are the most likely targets of harassing orders to disperse or move on. Particularly in summer, ghetto youths are likely to spend lots of time in public places. Given the inadequacy of their housing and the absence of community facilities, the street corner is often their social center. As the police cruise the busy streets of the ghetto, they frequently shout at groups of teenagers to "get going" or "get home." Our observations of police practices show that *whites as well as Negro youths* are often harassed in this way.

Frequently the policeman may leave the car and threaten or force youths to move on. For example, one summer evening as the scout car cruised a busy street of a white slum, the patrolmen observed three white boys and a girl on a corner. When told to move on, they mumbled and grumbled in undertones, angering the police by their failure to comply. As they slowly moved off, the officers pushed them along the street. Suddenly one of the white patrolmen took a lighted cigarette from a 15-year-old boy and stuck it in his face, pushing him forward as he did so. When the youngsters did move on, one policeman remarked to the observer that the girl was "nothing but a whore." Such tactics can only intensify resentment toward the police.

Police harassment is not confined to youth. One in every four adult Negroes in Detroit claims he has been stopped and questioned by the police without good reason. The same proportion claim they have been stopped in their cars. One in five says he has been searched unnecessarily; and one in six says that his car was searched for no good reason. The members of an interracial couple, particularly a Negro man accompanying a white woman, are perhaps the most vulnerable to harassment.

What citizens regard as police brutality many policemen consider necessary for law enforcement. While degrading epithets and abusive language may no longer be considered proper by either police commanders or citizens, they often disagree about other practices related to law enforcement. For example, although many citizens see "stop and question" or "stop and frisk" procedures as harassment, police commanders usually regard them merely as "aggressive prevention" to curb crime.

PHYSICAL FORCE—OR SELF-DEFENSE

The nub of the police-brutality issue seems to lie in police use of physical force. By law, the police have the right to use such force if necessary to make an arrest, to keep the peace, or to maintain public order. But just how much force is necessary or proper?

This was the crucial problem we attempted to answer by placing observers in the patrol cars and in the precincts. Our 36 observers, divided equally between Chicago, Boston, and Washington, were responsible for reporting the details of all situations where police used physical force against a citizen. To ensure the observation of a large number of encounters, two high-crime police precincts were monitored in Boston and Chicago; four in Washington. At least one precinct was composed of primarily Negro residents, another primarily of whites. Where possible, we also tried to select precincts with considerable variation in social-class composition. Given the criterion of a high-crime rate, however, people of low socio-economic status predominated in most of the areas surveyed.

The law fails to provide simple rules about what—and how much—force that policemen can properly use. The American Bar Foundation's study *Arrest,* by Wayne La Fave, put the matter rather well, stating that the courts of all states would undoubtedly agree that in making an arrest a policeman should use only that amount of force he reasonably believes necessary. But La Fave also pointed out that there is no agreement on the question of when it is better to let the suspect escape than to employ "deadly" force.

Even in those states where the use of deadly force is limited by law, the kinds of physical force a policeman may use are not clearly defined. No kind of force is categorically denied a policeman, since he is always permitted to use deadly force in self-defense.

This right to protect himself often leads the policeman to argue self-defense whenever he uses force. We found that many policemen, whether or not the facts justify it, regularly follow their use of force with the charge that the citizen was assaulting a policeman or resisting arrest. Our observers also found that some policemen even carry pistols and knives that they have confiscated while searching citizens; they carry them so they may be placed at a scene should it be necessary to establish a case of self-defense.

Of course, not all cases of force involve the use of *unnecessary* force. Each instance of force reported by our observers was examined and judged to be either necessary or unnecessary. Cases involving simple restraint—holding a man by the arm—were deliberately excluded from consideration, even though a policeman's right to do so can, in many instances, be challenged. In judging when police force is "unwarranted," "unreasonable," or "undue," we rather deliberately selected only those cases in which a policeman struck the citizen with his hands, fist, feet, or body, or where he used a weapon of some kind—such as a nightstick or a pistol. In these cases, had the policeman been found to have used physical force improperly, he could have been arrested on complaint and, like any other citizen, charged with a simple or aggravated assault. A physical assault on a citizen was judged to be "improper" or "unnecessary" only if force was used in one or more of the following ways:

If a policeman physically assaulted a citizen and then failed to make an arrest; proper use involves an arrest.

If the citizen being arrested did not, by word or deed, resist the

policeman; force should be used only if it is necessary to make
the arrest.

If the policeman, even though there was resistance to the arrest,
could easily have restrained the citizen in other ways.

If a large number of policemen were present and could have assisted in subduing the citizen in the station, in lockup, and in
the interrogation rooms.

If an offender was handcuffed and made no attempt to flee or
offer violent resistance.

If the citizen resisted arrest, but the use of force continued even
after the citizen was subdued.

In the seven-week period, we found 37 cases in which force was
used improperly. In all, 44 citizens had been assaulted. In 15 of
these cases, no one was arrested. Of these, 8 had offered no verbal
or physical resistance whatsoever, while 7 had.

An arrest was made in 22 of the cases. In 13, force was exercised
in the station house when at least four other policemen were present. In two cases, there was no verbal or physical resistance to the
arrest, but force was still applied. In two other cases, the police
applied force to a handcuffed offender in a field setting. And in
five situations, the offender did resist arrest, but the policeman
continued to use force even after he had been subdued.

Just how serious was the improper use of force in these 44 cases?
Naturally there were differences in degree of injury. In about one-
half of the cases, the citizen appeared little more than physically
bruised; in three cases, the amount of force was so great that the
citizen had to be hospitalized. Despite the fact that cases can
easily be selected for their dramatic rather than their representative quality, I want to present a few to give a sense of what the
observers saw and reported as undue use of force.

OBSERVING ON PATROL

In the following two cases, the citizens offered no physical or
verbal resistance, and the two white policemen made no arrest.
It is the only instance in which the observers saw the same two
policemen using force improperly more than once.

The police precinct in which these incidents occurred is typical
of those found in some of our larger cities, where the patrolmen
move routinely from gold coast to slum. There are little islands
of the rich and poor, of old Americans and new, of recent migrants and old settlers. One moves from high-rise areas of middle-

and upper-income whites through an area of the really old Americans—Indians—to an enclave of the recently arrived. The recently arrived are primarily those the policemen call "hillbillies" (migrants from Kentucky and Tennessee) and "porkchops" (Puerto Ricans). There are ethnic islands of Germans and Swedes. Although there is a small area where Negroes live, it is principally a precinct of whites. The police in the district are, with one exception, white.

On a Friday in the middle of July, the observer arrived for the 4 to 12 midnight watch. The beat car that had been randomly chosen carried two white patrolmen—one with 14 years of experience in the precinct, the other with three.

The watch began rather routinely as the policemen cruised the district. Their first radio dispatch came at about 5:30 P.M. They were told to investigate two drunks in a cemetery. On arriving they found two white men "sleeping one off." Without questioning the men, the older policeman began to search one of them, ripping his shirt and hitting him in the groin with a nightstick. The younger policeman, as he searched the second, ripped away the seat of his trousers, exposing his buttocks. The policemen then prodded the men toward the cemetery fence and forced them to climb it, laughing at the plight of the drunk with the exposed buttocks. As the drunks went over the fence, one policeman shouted, "I ought to run you fuckers in!" The other remarked to the observer, "Those assholes won't be back; a bunch of shitty winos."

Not long after they returned to their car, the policemen stopped a woman who had made a left turn improperly. She was treated very politely, and the younger policeman, who wrote the ticket, later commented to the observer, "Nice lady." At 7:30 they were dispatched to check a suspicious auto. After a quick check, the car was marked abandoned.

Shortly after a 30-minute break for a 7:30 "lunch," the two policemen received a dispatch to take a burglary report. Arriving at a slum walkup, the police entered a room where an obviously drunk white man in his late 40s insisted that someone had entered and stolen his food and liquor. He kept insisting that it had been taken and that he had been forced to borrow money to buy beer. The younger policeman, who took the report, kept harassing the man, alternating between mocking and badgering him with rhetorical questions. "You say your name is Half-A-Wit [for Hathaway]? Do you sleep with niggers? How did you vote on the bond issue? Are you sure that's all that's missing? Are you a virgin yet?"

The man responded to all of this with the seeming vagueness and joviality of the intoxicated, expressing gratitude for the policemen's help as they left. The older policeman remarked to the observer as they left, "Ain't drunks funny?"

For the next hour little happened, but as the two were moving across the precinct shortly after 10 P.M., a white man and a woman in their 50s flagged them down. Since they were obviously "substantial" middle-class citizens of the district, the policemen listened to their complaints that a Negro man was causing trouble inside the public-transport station from which they had just emerged. The woman said that he had sworn at her. The older policeman remarked, "What's a nigger doing up here? He should be down on Franklin Road!"

With that, they ran into the station and grabbed the Negro man who was inside. Without questioning him, they shoved him into a phone booth and began beating him with their fists and a flashlight. They also hit him in the groin. Then they dragged him out and kept him on his knees. He pleaded that he had just been released from a mental hospital that day and, begging not to be hit again, asked them to let him return to the hospital. One policeman said: "Don't you like us, nigger? I like to beat niggers and rip out their eyes." They took him outside to their patrol car. Then they decided to put him on a bus, telling him that he was returning to the hospital; they deliberately put him on a bus going in the opposite direction. Just before the Negro boarded the bus, he said, "You police just like to shoot and beat people." The first policeman replied, "Get moving, nigger, or I'll shoot you." The man was crying and bleeding as he was put on the bus. Leaving the scene, the younger policeman commented, "He won't be back."

For the rest of the evening, the two policemen kept looking for drunks and harassing any they found. They concluded the evening by being dispatched to an address where, they were told, a man was being held for the police. No one answered their knock. They left.

The station house has long been suspected of harboring questionable police practices. Interrogation-room procedures have been attacked, particularly because of the methods the police have used to get confessions. The drama of the confession in the interrogation room has been complete with bright lights and physical torture. Whether or not such practices have ever existed on the scale suggested by popular accounts, confessions in recent years, even by accounts of offenders, have rarely been accompanied by such high drama. But recently the interrogation room has come under fire again for its failure to protect the constitutional rights of the suspect to remain silent and to have legal counsel.

Backstage at the Station

The police station, however, is more than just a series of cubicles called interrogation rooms. There are other rooms and usually a lockup as well. Many of these are also hidden from public view. It is not surprising, then, that one-third of all the observations of the undue use of force occurred within the station.

In any station there normally are several policemen present who should be able to deal with almost any situation requiring force that arises. In many of the situations that were observed, as many as seven and eight policemen were present, most of whom simply stood by and watched force being used. The custom among policemen, it appeared, is that you intervene only if a fellow policeman needs help, or if you have been personally offended or affronted by those involved.

Force is used unnecessarily at many different points and places in the station. The citizen who is not cooperative during the booking process may be pushed or shoved, have his handcuffs twisted with a nightstick, have his foot stomped, or be pulled by the hair. All of these practices were reported by policemen as ways of obtaining "cooperation." But it was clear that the booking could have been completed without any of this harassment.

The lockup was the scene of some of the most severe applications of force. Two of the three cases requiring hospitalization came about when an offender was "worked over" in the lockup. To be sure, the arrested are not always cooperative when they get in the lockup, and force may be necessary to place them in a cell. But the amount of force observed hardly seemed necessary.

One evening an observer was present in the lockup when two white policemen came in with a white man. The suspect had been handcuffed and brought to the station because he had proved obstreperous after being arrested for a traffic violation. Apparently he had been drinking. While waiting in the lockup, the man began to urinate on the floor. In response, the policemen began to beat the man. They jumped him, knocked him down, and beat his head against the concrete floor. He required emergency treatment at a nearby hospital.

At times a policeman may be involved in a kind of escalation of force. Using force appropriately for an arrest in the field seemingly sets the stage for its later use, improperly, in the station. The following case illustrates how such a situation may develop.

Within a large city's high-crime rate precinct, occupied mostly by Negroes, the police responded to an "officer in trouble" call. It is difficult to imagine a call that brings a more immediate response, so a large number of police cars immediately converged at an intersection of a busy public street where a bus had been stopped. Near the bus, a white policeman was holding two young Negroes at gun point. The policeman reported that he had responded to a summons from the white bus-driver complaining that the boys had refused to pay their fares and had used obscene language. The policeman also reported that the boys swore at him, and one swung at him while the other drew a screwdriver and started toward him. At that point, he said, he drew his pistol.

The policemen placed one of the offenders in handcuffs and began to transport both of them to the station. While driving to the station, the driver of one car noted that the other policeman, transporting the other boy, was struggling with him. The first policeman stopped and entered the other patrol car. The observer reported that he kept hitting the boy who was handcuffed until the boy appeared completely subdued. The boy kept saying, "You don't have any right to beat me. I don't care if you kill me."

After the policemen got the offenders to the station, although the boys no longer resisted them, the police began to beat them while they were handcuffed in an interrogation room. One of the boys hollered: "You can't beat me like this! I'm only a kid, and my hands are tied." Later one of the policemen commented to the observer: "On the street you can't beat them. But when you get to the station, you can instill some respect in them."

Cases where the offender resists an arrest provide perhaps the most difficulty in judging the legitimacy of the force applied. An encounter that began as a dispatch to a disturbance at a private residence was one case about which there could be honest difference in judgment. On arrival, the policemen—one white, the other Negro—met a white woman who claimed that her husband, who was in the back yard and drunk, had beaten her. She asked the policemen to "take him in." The observer reported that the police found the man in the house. When they attempted to take him, he resisted by placing his hands between the door jamb. Both policemen then grabbed him. The Negro policeman said, "We're going to have trouble, so let's finish it right here." He grabbed the offender and knocked him down. Both policemen then wrestled with the man, handcuffed him, and took him to the station. As they did so, one of the policemen remarked, "These sons of bitches want to fight, so you have to break them quick."

A MINIMAL PICTURE?

The reader, as well as most police administrators, may be skeptical about reports that policemen used force in the presence of observers. Indeed, one police administrator, indignant over reports of undue use of force in his department, seemed more concerned that the policemen had permitted themselves to be observed behaving improperly than he was about their improper behavior. When demanding to know the names of the policemen who had used force improperly so he could discharge them—a demand we could not meet, since we were bound to protect our sources of information—he remarked, "Any officer who is stupid enough to behave that way in the presence of outsiders deserves to be fired."

There were and are a number of reasons why our observers were able to see policemen behaving improperly. We entered each department with the full cooperation of the top administrators. So far as the men in the line were concerned, our chief interest was in how citizens behave toward the police, a main object of our study. Many policemen, given their strong feelings against citizens, fail to see that their own behavior is equally open to observation. Furthermore, our observers are trained to fit into a role of trust—one that is genuine, since most observers are actually sympathetic to the plight of the policeman, if not to his behavior.

Finally, and this is a fact all too easily forgotten, people cannot change their behavior in the presence of others as easily as many think. This is particularly true when people become deeply involved in certain situations. The policeman not only comes to "trust" the observer in the law-enforcement situation—regarding him as a source of additional help if necessary—but, when he becomes involved in a dispute with a citizen, he easily forgets that an observer is present. Partly because he does not know what else to do, in such situations the policeman behaves "normally." But should one cling to the notion that most policemen modify their behavior in the presence of outsiders, one is left with the uncomfortable conclusion that our cases represent a minimal picture of actual misbehavior.

Superficially it might seem that the use of an excessive amount of force against citizens is low. In only 37 of 3826 encounters observed did the police use undue force. Of the 4604 white citizens in these encounters, 27 experienced an excessive amount of force —a rate of 5.9 for every 1000 citizens involved. The comparable rate for 5960 Negroes, of whom 17 experienced an excessive amount of force, is 2.8. Thus, whether one considers these rates high or low, the fact is that the *rate of excessive force for all white citizens in encounters with the police is twice that for Negro citizens.*

A rate depends, however, upon selecting a population that is logically the target of force. What we have just given is a rate for *all* citizens involved in encounters with the police. But many of these citizens are not logical targets of force. Many, for example, simply call the police to complain about crimes against themselves or their property. And others are merely witnesses to crimes.

The more logical target population consists of citizens whom the police allege to be offenders—a population of suspects. In our study, there were 643 white suspects, 27 of whom experienced undue use of force. This yields an abuse rate of 41.9 per 1000 white suspects. The comparable rate for 751 Negro suspects, of whom 17 experienced undue use of force, is 22.6 per 1000. If one accepts these rates as reasonably reliable estimates of the undue force against suspects, then there should be little doubt that in major metropolitan areas the sort of behavior commonly called "police brutality" is far from rare.

Popular impression casts police brutality as a racial matter— white police mistreating Negro citizens. The fact is that white suspects are more liable to being treated improperly by the police than Negro suspects are. This, however, should not be confused with the chances a citizen takes of being mistreated. In two of the cities we studied, Negroes are a minority. The chances, then, that any Negro has of being treated improperly are, perhaps, more nearly comparable to that for whites. If the rates are comparable, then one might say that the application of force unnecessarily by the police operates without respect to the race of an offender.

Many people believe that the race of the policeman must affect his use of force, particularly since many white policemen express prejudice against Negroes. Our own work shows that in the police precincts made up largely of Negro citizens, over three-fourths of the policemen express prejudice against Negroes. Only 1 percent express sympathetic attitudes. But as sociologists and social psychologists have often shown, prejudice and attitudes do not necessarily carry over into discriminatory actions.

Our findings show that there is little difference between the rate of force used by white and by Negro policemen. Of the 54 policemen observed using too much force, 45 were white and 9 were Negro. For every 100 white policemen, 8.7 will use force; for every 100 Negro policemen, 9.8 will. What this really means, though, is that about one in every 10 policemen in high-crime rate areas of cities sometimes uses force unnecessarily.

Yet, one may ask, doesn't prejudice enter into the use of force? Didn't some of the policemen who were observed utter prejudiced statements toward Negroes and other minority-group members? Of course they did. But the question of whether it was their prejudice or some other factor that motivated them to mistreat Negroes is not so easily answered.

Still, even though our figures show that a white suspect is more liable to encounter violence, one may ask whether white policemen victimize Negroes more than whites. We found, for the most part, that they do not. Policemen, both Negro and white, are most likely to exercise force against members of their *own* race:

67 percent of the citizens victimized by white policemen were white.

71 percent of the citizens victimized by Negro policemen were Negro.

To interpret these statistics correctly, however, one should take into account the differences in opportunity policemen have to use force against members of their own and other races. Negro policemen, in the three cities we studied, were far *less* likely to police white citizens than white policemen were to police Negroes. Negro policemen usually policed other Negroes, while white policemen policed both whites and Negroes about equally. In total numbers, then, more white policemen than Negro policemen used force against Negroes. But this is explained by the fact that whites make up 85 percent of the police force, and more than 50 percent of all policemen policing Negroes.

Though no precise estimates are possible, the facts just given suggest that white policemen, even though they are prejudiced toward Negroes, do not discriminate against Negroes in the excessive use of force. The use of force by the police is more readily explained by police culture than it is by the policeman's race. Indeed, in the few cases where we observed a Negro policeman using unnecessary force against white citizens, there was no evidence that he did so because of his race.

The disparity between our findings and the public's sense that Negroes are the main victims of police brutality can easily be resolved if one asks how the public becomes aware of the police misusing force.

The Victims and the Turf

Fifty years ago, the immigrants to our cities—Eastern and Southern Europeans such as the Poles and the Italians—complained about police brutality. Today the new immigrants to our cities—mostly Negroes from the rural South—raise their voices through the civil-rights movement, through black-nationalist and other race-conscious organizations. There is no comparable voice for white citizens since, except for the Puerto Ricans, they now lack the nationality organizations that were once formed to promote and protect the interests of their immigrant forbears.

Although policemen do not seem to select their victims according to race, two facts stand out. All victims were offenders, and all were from the lower class. Concentrating as we did on high-crime rate areas of cities, we do not have a representative sample of residents in any city. Nonetheless, we observed a sizable minority of middle- and upper-status citizens, some of whom were offenders. But since no middle- or upper-class offender, white or Negro, was the victim of an excessive amount of force, it appears that the lower class bears the brunt of victimization by the police.

The most likely victim of excessive force is a lower-class man of either race. No white woman and only two Negro women were victimized. The difference between the risk assumed by white and by Negro women can be accounted for by the fact that far more Negro women are processed as suspects or offenders.

Whether or not a policeman uses force unnecessarily depends upon the social setting in which the encounter takes place. Of the 37 instances of excessive force, 37 percent took place in police-controlled settings, such as the patrol car or the precinct station. Public places, usually streets, accounted for 41 percent, and 16 percent took place in a private residence. The remaining 6 percent occurred in commercial settings. This is not, of course, a random sample of settings where the police encounter suspects.

What is most obvious, and most disturbing, is that the police are very likely to use force in settings that they control. Although only 18 percent of all situations involving suspects ever ended up at the station house, 32 percent of all situations where an excessive amount of force was used took place in the police station.

No one who accepts the fact that the police sometimes use an excessive amount of force should be surprised by our finding that they often select their own turf. What should be apparent to the nation's police administrators, however, is that these settings are under their command and control. Controlling the police in the field, where the policeman is away from direct supervision, is understandably difficult. But the station house is the police administrator's domain. The fact that one in three instances of excessive force took place in settings that can be directly controlled should cause concern among police officials.

The presence of citizens who might serve as witnesses against a policeman should deter him from undue use of force. Indeed, procedures for the review of police conduct are based on the presumption that one can get this kind of testimony. Otherwise, one is left simply with a citizen complaint and contrary testimony by the policeman—a situation in which it is very difficult to prove the citizen's allegation.

In most situations involving the use of excessive force, there were witnesses. In our 37 cases, there were bystanders present three-fourths of the time. But in only one situation did the group present sympathize with the citizen and threaten to report the policeman. A complaint was filed on that incident—the only one of the 37 observed instances of undue force in which a formal complaint was filed.

All in all, the situations where excessive force was used were devoid of bystanders who did not have a stake in being "against" the offender. Generally, they were fellow policemen, or fellow offenders whose truthfulness could be easily challenged. When a policeman uses undue force, then, he usually does not risk a complaint against himself or testimony from witnesses who favor the complainant against the policeman. This, as much as anything, probably accounts for the low rate of formal complaints against policemen who use force unnecessarily.

A striking fact is that in more than one-half of all instances of undue coercion, at least one other policeman was present who did not participate in the use of force. This shows that, for the most part, the police do not restrain their fellow policemen. On the contrary, there were times when their very presence encouraged the use of force. One man brought into the lockup for threatening a policeman with a pistol was so severely beaten by this policeman that he required hospitalization. During the beating, some fellow policemen propped the man up, while others shouted encouragement. Though the official police code does not legitimate this practice, police culture does.

VICTIMS—DEFIANT OR DEVIANT

Now, are there characteristics of the offender or his behavior that precipitate the use of excessive force by the police? Superficially, yes. Almost one-half of the cases involved open defiance of police authority (39 percent) or resisting arrest (9 percent). Open defiance of police authority, however, is what the policeman defines as *his* authority, not necessarily "official" authority. Indeed in 40 percent of the cases that the police considered open defiance, the policeman never executed an arrest—a somewhat surprising fact for those who assume that policemen generally "cover" improper use of force with a "bona-fide" arrest and a charge of resisting arrest.

But it is still of interest to know what a policeman *sees* as defiance. Often he seems threatened by a simple refusal to acquiesce to his own authority. A policeman beat a handcuffed offender because, when told to sit, the offender did not sit down. One Negro woman was soundly slapped for her refusal to approach the police car and identify herself.

Important as a threat to his authority may appear to the policeman, there were many more of these instances in which the policeman did *not* respond with the use of force. The important issue seems to be whether the policeman manages to assert his authority despite the threat to it. I suspect that policemen are more likely to respond with excessive force when they define the situation as one in which there remains a question as to who is "in charge."

Similarly, some evidence indicates that harassment of deviants plays a role in the undue use of force. Incidents involving drunks made up 27 percent of all incidents of improper use of force; an additional 5 percent involved homosexuals or narcotics users. Since deviants generally remain silent victims to avoid public exposure of their deviance, they are particularly susceptible to the use of excessive force.

It is clear, though, that the police encounter many situations involving deviants where no force is used. Generally they respond to them routinely. What is surprising, then, is that the police do not mistreat deviants more than they do. The explanation may lie in the kind of relationships the police have with deviants. Many are valuable to the police because they serve as informers. To mistreat them severely would be to cut off a major source of police intelligence. At the same time, deviants are easily controlled by harassment.

Clearly, we have seen that police mistreatment of citizens exist. Is it, however, on the increase?

Citizen complaints against the police are common and allegations that the police use force improperly are frequent. There is evidence that physical brutality exists today. But there is also evidence, from the history of our cities, that the police have long engaged in the use of unnecessary physical force. No one can say with confidence whether there is more or less of it today than there was at the turn of the century.

What we lack is evidence that would permit us to calculate comparative rates of police misuse of force for different periods of American history. Only recently have we begun to count and report the volume of complaints against the police. And the research reported in this article represents the only attempt to estimate the amount of police mistreatment by actual observation of what the police do to citizens.

LACK OF INFORMATION

Police chiefs are notoriously reluctant to disclose information that would allow us to assess the nature and volume of complaints against the police. Only a few departments have begun to report something about citizen complaints. And these give us very little information.

Consider, for example, the 1966 Annual Report released by the New Orleans Police Department. It tells us that there were 208 cases of "alleged police misconduct on which action was taken." It fails to tell us whether there were any allegations that are *not* included among these cases. Are these all the allegations that came to the attention of the department? Or are they only those the department chose to review as "police disciplinary matters"? Of the 208 cases the department considered "disciplinary matters," the report tells us that no disciplinary action was taken in 106 cases. There were 11 cases that resulted in 14 dismissals; 56 cases that resulted in 72 suspensions, fines, or loss of days; and 35 cases involving 52 written or verbal "reprimands" or "cautionings."

The failure of the report to tell us the charge against the policeman is a significant omission. We cannot tell how many of these allegations involved improper use of force, how many involved verbal abuse or harassment, how many involved police felonies or misdemeanors, and so on. In such reports, the defensive posture of the nation's police departments is all too apparent. Although the 1966 report of the New Orleans Police Department tells us much about what the police allege were the felonies and misdemeanors by citizens of New Orleans, it tells us nothing about what citizens allege was misconduct by the police!

Many responsible people believe that the use of physical brutality by the police is on the wane. They point to the fact that, at least outside the South, there are more reports of other forms of police mistreatment of citizens than reports of undue physical coercion. They also suggest that third-degree interrogations and curbstone justice with the nightstick are less common. It does not seem unreasonable, then, to assume that police practices that degrade a citizen's status or that harass him and restrict his freedom are more common than police misuse of force. But that may have always been so.

Whether or not the policeman's "sense of justice" and his use of unnecessary force have changed remains an open question. Forms may change while practices go on. To move misuse from the street to the station house, or from the interrogation room to the lockup, changes the place but not the practice itself.

Our ignorance of just what goes on between police and citizens poses one of the central issues in policing today: How can we make the police accountable to the citizenry in a democratic society and yet not hamstring them in their legitimate pursuit of law and order? There are no simple answers.

Police departments are organizations that process people. All people-processing organizations face certain common problems. But the police administrator faces a problem in controlling practice with clients that is not found in most other organizations. The problem is that police contact with citizens occurs in the community, where direct supervision is not possible. Assuming our unwillingness to spend resources for almost one-to-one supervision, the problem for the police commander is to make policemen behave properly when they are not under direct supervision. He also faces the problem of making them behave properly in the station house as well.

Historically, we have found but one way—apart from supervision—that deals with this problem. That solution is professionalization of workers. Perhaps only through the professionalization of the police can we hope to solve the problem of police malpractice.

But lest anyone optimistically assume that professionalization will eliminate police malpractice altogether, we should keep in mind that problems of malpractice also occur regularly in both law and medicine.

III
Can the Political Systems
of Cities Be Changed?

INTRODUCTION

Our analysis of four public policy areas suggests that two broad classes of interests appear to be underrepresented in urban political systems.[1] The most obvious of these are lower-class and minority-group interests. In housing, for example, most government programs, such as urban renewal, FHA mortgage insurance, and FHA subsidy programs, have directly benefited every income group but the poor; only the nation's severely restricted public housing program and the questionable workings of the "filtering process" have improved the housing stock available to poor ghetto residents. The schools in our country are not successfully educating the children of lower-class and minority-group families; groups representing these families have failed to persuade the system to adopt such reforms as school integration, community control, or the use of educational vouchers. The conflicts between the police and ghetto groups are well known, with the latter finding the system unresponsive to their claims concerning police brutality, police corruption, and discriminatory law-enforcement practices. Even in the transportation area, the substantially greater expenditures for roads have worked to the disadvantage of the poor; the nonwhite seeking transportation to work and the aged or infirm unable to afford or operate an automobile suffer the greatest from the lack of mass transit.

The second category of underrepresented interests consists of those that may be termed "diffuse interests"—those societal objectives shared by most citizens but of central concern to few of them. Environmental quality is a current example of a diffuse interest. While producer groups involved in the transportation arena have been able to shape governmental behavior for their own benefit, environmental groups concerned about the quality of our city air until recently found themselves generally ignored. Other "public interest" concerns, as we have seen, have been no match for organized special interests. In education, for example, the teachers and school-system administrators have been able to protect their interests, while city-wide organizations representing upper-middle-class liberals have all but been ignored in their attempts to combat the deleterious consequences of the traditional neighborhood school system. Upper-middle-class "do-gooders" have unsuccessfully sought adequate housing for all Americans, regardless of income, while producer groups have benefited extensively from governmental housing efforts shaped by producer demands. Reforms of police departments have provided policemen with higher salaries and better working conditions, but the efforts of patrolmen's associations have thwarted attempts to improve significantly police effectiveness in deterring and coping with street crime.

Because the policy objectives of these two broad interests often entail increased public expenditures, it is important to note that they have been underrepresented not only at the local level but also at the federal and state levels of government. The superior competitive position of the federal and state levels in obtaining tax revenues has resulted in their providing a larger and larger proportion of municipal budgets[2] through both the grant-in-aid programs of recent years and the just begun revenue-sharing program. Without support from these primary sources of funding for major expansions of governmental responsibility, many policy and programmatic changes sought by proponents of these interests are not likely to be realized.

On the local level, black or lower-class interests and diffuse interests have been thwarted by the three major political problems described in Part I: the multiplicity of governments within metropolitan areas, the functional fragmentation of local political systems, and the limited citizen participation in urban affairs.

What then are the possibilities for change at the local level? Are there any trends that portend a change in the distribution of power in urban political systems that will make the systems more responsive to these two broad classes of interests? An examination of demographic patterns and the strategy of coalition-formation will aid in answering this question.

During the past half century, there has been a steady increase in the number of minority-group members residing in central cities. At the turn of the century, 90 per cent of the black population lived in the South, mostly residing in rural areas. By the

1960's, 60 per cent of black Americans were living in the central cities of metropolitan areas. According to the 1970 census, in the twelve cities with more than 2 million people, 28 per cent of the population is black (this figure does not include other nonwhite groups). During the last two decades, there has been a massive migration from Southern farms and cities to Northern central cities. Moreover, there is every reason to assume that the increase in the nonwhite population of our cities will continue. The mechanization of agriculture in the South, the refusal of the federal government to enact a nationwide public assistance program, and the continued successful resistance on the part of suburbia to any large influx of nonwhites (according to the census, nonwhites comprised 4.5 per cent of the population of suburban areas in 1960 and 4.7. per cent in 1970) portends no change.

This demographic pattern has both short-term and long-term effects on the political systems of our cities. In the immediate future, nonwhite groups will continue to be, in most major cities, a large and growing minority among the city's electorate. At such time, divisions along racial lines will be heightened, and whites will support candidates and policies perceived as antagonistic to the minority community (witness recent mayoralty elections in Philadelphia, Cleveland, and Detroit). Over the long run, however, most large cities seem to be moving in the direction of Washington, D.C., Newark, and Gary, Indiana, where nonwhite majorities are able to determine the outcomes of local elections. The question then will be not whether minority groups command effective access in the city's political system, but what the policy and programatic consequences of their power will be. One can guess that this redistribution of power at the local level will have a much greater impact on those issues in which the availability of financial resources is not of central concern. For example, minority groups can be expected to significantly influence the policies of local public-school systems, but will have little impact in determining the amount of monies available to such systems. It may be that minority groups will be forced to relinquish some of their potential control over the workings of urban bureaucracies in order to obtain the funds necessary to support such bureaucracies from the larger, wealthier white community (via state and federal grants).

In the immediate future, however, which is to say, for the next ten to twenty years, more and more large cities will find themselves with a large nonwhite minority. Can these cities avoid the polarization that has generally plagued those cities already faced with this situation? From the perspective of groups representing the two classes of interests underrepresented in urban political systems, is there any course of action that will enable them to wield effective influence?

To answer that question, we must first determine whether these two groups of "have-nots" in urban political systems—the proponents of diffuse interests and minority-group interests—could form an effective and stable alliance to achieve their aims jointly. The experience of the late-nineteenth-century reform movement is instructive on that score. This movement, whose base of support was upper-middle-class professionals, academics, and businessmen, sought greater recognition for what we have labeled diffuse interests. The essence of reform, its unifying element, was its opposition to the influence wielded by narrow, private interests in the politics of the cities—interests associated with the immigrant and his political machine. However, although they were often successful in altering the structure of city government, the reformers were unable to gain acceptance of their policy preferences. Urban governments continued to follow policies favorable to special interests.

The reform movement failed to achieve its objective for two reasons. The first related to the different priorities of the reformer and the immigrant. Support for the diffuse interests promoted by the reformers came primarily from their own ranks, the professionally oriented upper middle class. These people, either self-employed or employed by private, profit-making businesses, usually availed themselves of private-sector social services and housing. They had personal resources to fall back on in dealing with all but the most serious disturbances in their lives. In short, the satisfaction of what today would be termed their "basic needs" was taken care of; they could afford the "luxury" of involving themselves with issues of broader scope and less immediate personal importance.

The immigrants and the poor, on the other hand, had little time to concern themselves with "good government" or "clean streets" or any such "frills." The strength of the urban machine came from its ability to provide for the immediate personal needs of these people, whether with a city job, or a friend in court, or some other specific want of a distressed individual. Naturally enough these voters preferred institutions—for example, the machine—that dealt on a one-to-one basis with their needs for protection against the vicissitudes of life rather than alternatives such as the reform movement, which promised an improvement in municipal services that were of little direct relevance to their lives.

Despite the limited base of support that the reformers could expect to win through their promotion of diffuse interests, they still could have furthered their cause by forming alliances with other groups having different goals. It is a common phenomenon in politics for groups with different interests to trade support so that each may achieve its objectives. Yet the reformers apparently never attempted to form alliances with any major institutions—such as labor unions, the Catholic Church, or the machine—associated with the immigrant population. From the reformers' perspective, these institutions were examples of the special, partial interests that were already too influential in the political arena. Indeed, these institutions were particular targets of the upper-middle-class reformers. The attitude of the reformers toward organized labor has been described as "blind (when it was not hostile)."[3] Strong nativist tendencies among significant numbers of reformers precluded a working relationship with the Catholic Church; many reformers were active in promoting the enactment of the Immigration Act of 1921, which established quotas biased in favor of Northern-European Protestant immigrants and against Southern- and Eastern-European Catholic immigrants.[4] The machine, of course, was *the* urban institution that the reform movement sought to extinguish. In short, without some support from immigrant groups, the reform movement doomed itself to minority status.

Today's proponents of diffuse interests and minority-group interests can be expected to encounter the same difficulties as the reformers and immigrants in past years. The supporters of diffuse interests come from the same professional upper-middle-class sector of the population as did the reformers. Generally labeled as liberals, they and minority-group leaders can be expected to concern themselves with different goals and to have a different set of priorities. The liberal will be more likely to focus on broader, "public" concerns; minority-group spokesmen will probably promote class and racial-group interests. While the liberal concerns himself with the problems of air pollution and educational opportunity, minority elites will be seeking specific material benefits, such as jobs or status rewards for their constituents.

Moreover, these different goals will often be in conflict, thus inhibiting the formation of an alliance, based on complementary interests, between the two groups. For example, while the liberal seeks to keep cars out of the central city because of the air pollution problem, most members of minority groups, forced to live in the central city, desire ownership of a car for the status it entails and as a means of temporarily escaping from the ghetto.

To give an example from yet another area: To the liberal, reform of the educational system often means greater concern for the development of children's creativity, individuality, and self-expression; to most blacks, educational reform means teaching black children the basic skills necessary for obtaining jobs and promoting racial identity. It is not surprising that local party reformers, again in such cities as New York, Chicago, and Los Angeles, have had limited success in obtaining black support for their candidates.[5]

Lastly: Even if the liberal and minority groups would be able to form an alliance on some issues on the local level, would it be sufficiently effective to change the decisions emanating from local political systems? The problem is that the liberals comprise a very small group within our cities today. Most potential members of this group now live in suburbia; there are only very small enclaves of such groups in our large cities (for example, certain lake shore areas in Chicago and mid-Manhattan in New York City). In short, it is doubtful that these two groups, even in the unlikely event that they formed a stable coalition, could exercise effective influence. It would appear that additional support will be needed before minority-group and diffuse interests receive sufficient recognition in the political arena.

Most proponents of these interests look toward organized labor to fill this gap—to be the force that will alter the distribution of power on the local level. The white majorities in our major cities are largely made up of white ethnic homeowners; a group which has generally opposed local governmental efforts intended to benefit these interests.[6] However, a significant number of the members of the various ethnic groups are also working class union members, and proponents of change have hoped that the leaders of organized labor would persuade their members to support a more expansive governmental role. Bayard Rustin is typical of those who expect union leadership to successfully follow this course of action. In the reading that follows, he argues that liberals, the organized-labor movement, and the minority community can be brought into an effective coalition around economic and social issues.

Whatever the possibilities of these groups joining together on the national level over some issues, an alliance on the local level seems highly unlikely. One must first note that the unions that get involved in local politics are not representative of the labor movement nationwide.[7] Instead, they are those unions whose jobs and job-related benefits depend on decisions of the city government. They fall into two categories: those unions that represent municipal employees and those unions of skilled craftsmen, such as the building-trades unions, that work on municipal construction projects and are regulated by local governments. In general, because these unions necessarily represent their members' interests as producers, they have usually found themselves in conflict with the proponents of minority-group consumers of public services. Whether the issue be one of community control of school personnel, civil-service requirements, boards to review police behavior, or entrance into the craft unions, these groups have been pitted against each other. There would seem little reason, on the local level, to expect organized labor and minority-group organizations to ally.

The Lipsky reading addresses the issue of black Americans obtaining political allies. It begins by noting that minority groups are among the power-poor groups in our political system, and that alliances are essential if such groups are to obtain sufficient bargaining resources. However, based upon the experience of Jessee Gray's Harlem-based rent-strike group, Lipsky does not believe that lower-class and minority groups can exercise significant influence.

Lipsky's pessimism appears to be well founded; not only with respect to the proponents of minority and lower-class interests, but also with respect to those central-city liberals seeking support for diffuse interests. In most of our large cities, each group alone has too small a base of support, while the possibilities of their forming a stable coalition are limited by their different goals, which goals are often conflicting rather than complementary. Moreover, even if such an alliance were to be formed, it still would not command sufficient support to significantly alter the decisions made on the local level. Support is yet needed from another quarter. Most proponents of these interests look toward organized labor as the most likely potential ally that would make the difference. However, the experience of recent years has witnessed sharp and bitter conflicts between the minority groups and those unions with major stakes in city politics. There is little reason to believe that major changes in urban politics and public policy will occur in the foreseeable future.

NOTES

1. This is not to say that these classes of interests are the only ones underrepresented. This reader has only examined four of the policy arenas within the cities and was intended to suggest that, by focusing on the many functional areas, we can learn much about the distribution of power within urban political systems.
2. Charles R. Adrian and Charles Press, *Governing Urban America*, 4th edition (New York: McGraw-Hill, 1972), pp. 324–25, 330–35.
3. Grant McConnell, *Private Power and American Democracy* (New York: Knopf, 1966), pp. 31–32.
4. Thomas R. Dye, *Politics in States and Communities* (Englewood Cliffs, New Jersey: Prentice-Hall, 1969), p. 266.
5. James Q. Wilson, *The Amateur Democrat* (Chicago: The University of Chicago Press, 1962), pp. 273–77.
6. James Q. Wilson and Edward Banfield, "Public Regardingness as a Value Premise in Voting Behavior," *American Political Science Review*, 58 (December, 1964), pp. 876–87; Robert Lineberry and Ira Sharkansky, *Urban Politics and Public Policy* (New York: Harper & Row, 1971), pp. 70–71.
7. Charles R. Adrian and Charles Press, *Governing Urban America*, 4th. ed. (New York: McGraw-Hill, 1972), pp. 129–30.

"BLACK POWER"
AND COALITION POLITICS

BAYARD RUSTIN

There are two Americas—black and white—and nothing has more clearly revealed the divisions between them than the debate currently raging around the slogan of "black power." Despite—or perhaps because of—the fact that this slogan lacks any clear definition, it has succeeded in galvanizing emotions on all sides, with many whites seeing it as the expression of a new racism and many Negroes taking it as a warning to white people that Negroes will no longer tolerate brutality and violence. But even within the Negro community itself, "black power" has touched off a major debate—the most bitter the community has experienced since the days of Booker T. Washington and W. E. B. Du Bois, and one which threatens to ravage the entire civil-rights movement. Indeed, a serious split has already developed between advocates of "black power" like Floyd McKissick of CORE and Stokely Carmichael of SNCC on the one hand, and Dr. Martin Luther King of SCLC, Roy Wilkins of the NAACP, and Whitney Young of the Urban League on the other.

There is no question, then, that great passions are involved in the debate over the idea of "black power"; nor, as we shall see, is there any question that these passions have their roots in the psychological and political frustrations of the Negro community. Nevertheless, I would contend that "black power" not only lacks any real value for the civil-rights movement, but that its propagation is positively harmful. It diverts the movement from a meaningful debate over strategy and tactics, it isolates the Negro community, and it encourages the growth of anti-Negro forces.

In its simplest and most innocent guise, "black power" merely means the effort to elect Negroes to office in proportion to Negro

From Bayard Rustin, " ' Black Power' and Coalition Politics," *Commentary* XLII, No. 3 (September, 1966), pp. 35–40. Reprinted from *Commentary*, by permission; Copyright © 1966 by the American Jewish Committee.

strength within the population. There is, of course, nothing wrong with such an objective in itself, and nothing inherently radical in the idea of pursuing it. But in Stokely Carmichael's extravagant rhetoric about "taking over" in districts of the South where Negroes are in the majority, it is important to recognize that Southern Negroes are only in a position to win a maximum of two congressional seats and control of eighty local counties. (Carmichael, incidentally, is in the paradoxical position of screaming at liberals—wanting only to "get whitey off my back"—and simultaneously needing their support: after all, he can talk about Negroes taking over Lowndes County only because there is a fairly liberal federal government to protect him should Governor Wallace decide to eliminate this pocket of black power.) Now there might be a certain value in having two Negro congressmen from the South, but obviously they could do nothing by themselves to reconstruct the face of America. Eighty sheriffs, eighty tax assessors, and eighty school-board members might ease the tension for a while in their communities, but they alone could not create jobs and build low-cost housing; they alone could not supply quality integrated education.

The relevant question, moreover, is not whether a politician is black or white, but what forces he represents. Manhattan has had a succession of Negro borough presidents, and yet the schools are increasingly segregated. Adam Clayton Powell and William Dawson have both been in Congress for many years; the former is responsible for a rider on school integration that never gets passed, and the latter is responsible for keeping the Negroes of Chicago tied to a mayor who had to see riots and death before he would put eight-dollar sprinklers on water hydrants in the summer. I am not for one minute arguing that Powell, Dawson, and Mrs. Motley should be impeached. What I am saying is that if a politician is elected because he is black and is deemed to be entitled to a "slice of the pie," he will behave in one way; if he is elected by a constituency pressing for social reform, he will, whether he is white or black, behave in another way.

Southern Negroes, despite exhortations from SNCC to organize themselves into a Black Panther party, are going to stay in the Democratic party—to them it is the party of progress, the New Deal, the New Frontier, and the Great Society—and they are right to stay. For SNCC's Black Panther perspective is simultaneously utopian and reactionary—the former for the by now obvious reason that one-tenth of the population cannot accomplish much by itself, the latter because such a party would remove Negroes from the main area of political struggle in this country (particularly in the one-party South, where the decisive battles are fought out in Democratic primaries), and would give priority to the issue of race precisely at a time when the fundamental questions facing the Negro and American society alike are economic and social. It is no accident that the two main proponents of "black power," Carmichael and McKissick, should now be co-sponsoring a conference with Adam Clayton Powell and Elijah Muhammad, and that the leaders of New York CORE should recently have supported the machine candidate for Surrogate—because he was the choice of a Negro boss—rather than the candidate of the reform movement. By contrast, Martin Luther King is working in Chicago with the Industrial Union Department of the AFL-CIO and with religious groups in a coalition which, if successful, will mean the end or at least the weakening of the Daley-Dawson machine.

The winning of the right of Negroes to vote in the South insures the eventual transformation of the Democratic party, now controlled primarily by Northern machine politicians and Southern Dixiecrats. The Negro vote will eliminate the Dixiecrats from the party and from Congress, which means that the crucial question facing us today is who will replace them in the South. Unless civil-rights leaders (in such towns as Jackson, Mississippi; Birmingham, Alabama; and even to a certain extent Atlanta) can organize grass-roots clubs whose members will have a genuine political voice, the Dixiecrats might well be succeeded by black moderates and black Southern-style machine politicians, who would do little to push for needed legislation in Congress and little to improve local conditions in the South. While I myself would prefer Negro machines to a situation in which Negroes have no power at all, it seems to me that there is a better alternative today—a liberal-labor-civil rights coalition which would work to make the Democratic party truly responsive to the aspirations of the poor, and which would develop support for programs (specifically those outlined in A. Philip Randolph's $100 billion Freedom Budget) aimed at the reconstruction of American society in the interests of greater social justice. The advocates of "black power" have no such programs in mind; what they are in fact arguing for (perhaps unconsciously) is the creation of a *new black establishment.*

Nor, it might be added, are they leading the Negro people

along the same road which they imagine immigrant groups traveled so successfully in the past. Proponents of "black power"—accepting a historical myth perpetrated by moderates—like to say that the Irish and the Jews and the Italians, by sticking together and demanding their share, finally won enough power to overcome their initial disabilities. But the truth is that it was through alliances with other groups (in political machines or as part of the trade-union movement) that the Irish and the Jews and the Italians acquired the power to win their rightful place in American society. They did not "pull themselves up by their own bootstraps"—no group in American society has ever done so; and they most certainly did not make isolation their primary tactic.

In some quarters, "black power" connotes not an effort to increase the number of Negroes in elective office but rather a repudiation of nonviolence in favor of Negro "self-defense." Actually this is a false issue, since no one has ever argued that Negroes should not defend themselves as individuals from attack. Non-violence has been advocated as a *tactic* for organized demonstrations in a society where Negroes are a minority and where the majority controls the police. Proponents of non-violence do not, for example, deny that James Meredith has the right to carry a gun for protection when he visits his mother in Mississippi; what they question is the wisdom of his carrying a gun while participating in a demonstration.

There is, as well, a tactical side to the new emphasis on "self-defense" and the suggestion that non-violence be abandoned. The reasoning here is that turning the other cheek is not the way to win respect, and that only if the Negro succeeds in frightening the white man will the white man begin taking him seriously. The trouble with this reasoning is that it fails to recognize that fear is more likely to bring hostility to the surface than respect; and far from prodding the "white power structure" into action, the new militant leadership, by raising the slogan of black power and lowering the banner of non-violence, has obscured the moral issue facing this nation, and permitted the President and Vice President to lecture us about "racism in reverse" instead of proposing more meaningful programs for dealing with the problems of unemployment, housing, and education.

"Black power" is, of course, a somewhat nationalistic slogan and its sudden rise to popularity among Negroes signifies a concomitant rise in nationalist sentiment (Malcolm X's autobiography is quoted nowadays in Grenada, Mississippi as well as in Harlem). We have seen such nationalistic turns and withdrawals back into the ghetto before, and when we look at the conditions which brought them about, we find that they have much in common with the conditions of Negro life at the present moment: conditions which lead to despair over the goal of integration and to the belief that the ghetto will last forever.

It may, in the light of the many juridical and legislative victories which have been achieved in the past few years, seem strange that despair should be so widespread among Negroes today. But anyone to whom it seems strange should reflect on the fact that despite these victories *Negroes today are in worse economic shape, live in worse slums, and attend more highly segregated schools than in 1954.* Thus—to recite the appalling, and appallingly familiar, statistical litany once again—more Negroes are unemployed today than in 1954; the gap between the wages of the Negro worker and the white worker is wider; while the unemployment rate among white youths is decreasing, the rate among Negro youths has increased to 32 *per cent* (and among Negro girls the rise is even more startling). Even the one gain which has been registered, a decrease in the unemployment rate among Negro adults, is deceptive, for it represents men who have been called back to work after a period of being laid off. In any event, unemployment among Negro men is still twice that of whites, and no new jobs have been created.

So too with housing, which is deteriorating in the North (and yet the housing provisions of the 1966 civil-rights bill are weaker than the anti-discrimination laws in several states which contain the worst ghettos even with these laws on their books). And so too with schools: according to figures issued recently by the Department of Health, Education and Welfare, 65 per cent of first-grade Negro students in this country attend schools that are from 90 to 100 per cent black. (If in 1954, when the Supreme Court handed down the desegregation decision, you had been the Negro parent of a first-grade child, the chances are that this past June you would have attended that child's graduation from a segregated high school.)

To put all this in the simplest and most concrete terms: the day-to-day lot of the ghetto Negro has not been improved by the various judicial and legislative measures of the past decade.

Negroes are thus in a situation similar to that of the turn of the century, when Booker T. Washington advised them to "cast down their buckets" (that is to say, accommodate to segregation and disenfranchisement) and when even his leading opponent, W. E. B. Du Bois, was forced to advocate the development of a group economy in place of the direct-action boycotts, general strikes, and protest techniques which had been used in the 1880's, before the enactment of the Jim-Crow laws. For all their differences, both Washington and Du Bois then found it impossible to believe that Negroes could ever be integrated into American society, and each in his own way therefore counseled withdrawal into the ghetto, self-help, and economic self-determination.

World War I aroused new hope in Negroes that the rights removed at the turn of the century would be restored. More than 360,000 Negroes entered military service and went overseas; many left the South seeking the good life in the North and hoping to share in the temporary prosperity created by the war. But all these hopes were quickly smashed at the end of the fighting. In the first year following the war, more than seventy Negroes were lynched, and during the last six months of that year, there were some twenty-four riots throughout America. White mobs took over whole cities, flogging, burning, shooting, and torturing at will, and when Negroes tried to defend themselves, the violence only increased. Along with this, Negroes were excluded from unions and pushed out of jobs they had won during the war, including federal jobs.

In the course of this period of dashed hope and spreading segregation—the same period, incidentally, when a reorganized Ku Klux Klan was achieving a membership which was to reach into the millions—the largest mass movement ever to take root among working-class Negroes, Marcus Garvey's "Back to Africa" movement, was born. "Buy Black" became a slogan in the ghettos; faith in integration was virtually snuffed out in the Negro community until the 1930's when the CIO reawakened the old dream of a Negro-labor alliance by announcing a policy of non-discrimination and when the New Deal admitted Negroes into relief programs, WPA jobs, and public housing. No sooner did jobs begin to open up and Negroes begin to be welcomed into mainstream organizations than "Buy Black" campaigns gave way to "Don't Buy Where You Can't Work" movements. A. Philip Randolph was able to organize a massive March on Washington demanding a wartime FEPC; CORE was born and with it the non-violent sit-in technique; the NAACP succeeded in putting an end to the white primaries in 1944. Altogether, World War II was a period of hope for Negroes, and the economic progress they made through wartime industry continued steadily until about 1948 and remained stable for a time. Meanwhile, the non-violent movement of the 1950's and 60's achieved the desegregation of public accommodations and established the right to vote.

Yet at the end of this long fight, the Southern Negro is too poor to use those integrated facilities and too intimidated and disorganized to use the vote to maximum advantage, while the economic position of the Northern Negro deteriorates rapidly.

The promise of meaningful work and decent wages once held out by the anti-poverty programs has not been fulfilled. Because there has been a lack of the necessary funds, the program has in many cases been reduced to wrangling for positions on boards or for lucrative staff jobs. Negro professionals working for the program have earned handsome salaries—ranging from $14- to $25,000—while young boys have been asked to plant trees at $1.25 an hour. Nor have the Job Corps camps made a significant dent in unemployment among Negro youths; indeed, the main beneficiaries of this program seem to be the private companies who are contracted to set up the camps.

Then there is the war in Vietnam, which poses many ironies for the Negro community. On the one hand, Negroes are bitterly aware of the fact that more and more money is being spent on the war, while the anti-poverty program is being cut; on the other hand, Negro youths are enlisting in great numbers, as though to say that it is worth the risk of being killed to learn a trade, to leave a dead-end situation, and to join the only institution in this society which seems really to be integrated.

The youths who rioted in Watts, Cleveland, Omaha, Chicago, and Portland are the members of a truly hopeless and lost generation. They can see the alien world of affluence unfold before them on the TV screen. But they have already failed in their inferior segregated schools. Their grandfathers were sharecroppers, their grandmothers were domestics, and their mothers are domestics too. Many have never met their fathers. Mistreated by the local storekeeper, suspected by the policeman on the beat, disliked by their teachers, they cannot stand more failures and would rather retreat into the world of heroin than risk looking for a job downtown or having their friends see them push a rack in the garment district. Floyd McKissick and Stokely Carmichael may accuse Roy Wilkins of being out of touch with the Negro ghetto, but nothing more clearly demonstrates their own alienation from ghetto youth than their repeated exhortations to these young men to oppose the Vietnam war when so many of them tragically see it as their only way out. Yet there is no need to labor the significance of the fact that the rice fields of Vietnam and the Green Berets have more to offer a Negro boy than the streets of Mississippi or the towns of Alabama or 125th Street in New York.

The Vietnam war is also partly responsible for the growing disillusion with non-violence among Negroes. The ghetto Negro does not in general ask whether the United States is right or wrong to be in Southeast Asia. He does, however, wonder why he is exhorted to non-violence when the United States has been waging a fantastically brutal war, and it puzzles him to be told that he must turn the other cheek in our own South while we must fight for freedom in South Vietnam.

Thus, as in roughly similar circumstances in the past—circumstances, I repeat, which in the aggregate foster the belief that the ghetto is destined to last forever—Negroes are once again turning to nationalistic slogans, with "black power" affording the same emotional release as "Back to Africa" and "Buy Black" did in earlier periods of frustration and hopelessness. This is not only the case with the ordinary Negro in the ghetto; it is also the case with leaders like McKissick and Carmichael, neither of whom began as a nationalist or was at first cynical about the possibilities of integration. It took countless beatings and 24 jailings—that, and the absence of strong and continual support from the liberal community—to persuade Carmichael that his earlier faith in coalition politics was mistaken, that nothing was to be gained from working with whites, and that an alliance with the black nationalists was desirable. In the areas of the South where SNCC has been working so nobly, implementation of the Civil Rights Acts of 1964 and 1965 has been slow and ineffective. Negroes in many rural areas cannot walk into the courthouse and register to vote. Despite the voting-rights bill, they must file complaints and the Justice Department must be called to send federal registrars. Nor do children attend integrated schools as a matter of course. There, too, complaints must be filed and the Department of Health, Education and Welfare must be notified. Neither department has been doing an effective job of enforcing the bills. The feeling of isolation increases among SNCC workers as each legislative victory turns out to be only a token victory—significant on the national level, but not affecting the day-to-day lives of Negroes. Carmichael and his colleagues are wrong in refusing to support the 1966 bill, but one can understand why they feel as they do.

It is, in short, the growing conviction that the Negroes cannot win—a conviction with much grounding in experience—which accounts for the new popularity of "black power." So far as the ghetto Negro is concerned, this conviction expresses itself in hostility first toward the people closest to him who have held out the most promise and failed to deliver (Martin Luther King, Roy Wilkins, etc.), then toward those who have proclaimed themselves his friends (the liberals and the labor movement), and finally toward the only oppressors he can see (the local storekeeper and the policeman on the corner). On the leadership level, the conviction that the Negroes cannot win takes other forms, principally the adoption of what I have called a "no-win" policy. Why bother with programs when their enactment results only in "sham?" Why concern ourselves with the image of the movement when nothing significant has been gained for all the sacrifices made by SNCC and CORE? Why compromise with reluctant white allies when nothing of consequence can be achieved anyway? Why indeed have anything to do with whites at all?

On this last point, it is extremely important for white liberals to understand—as, one gathers from their references to "racism in reverse," the President and the Vice President of the United States do not—that there is all the difference in the world between saying, "If you don't want me, I don't want you" (which is what some proponents of "black power" have in effect been saying) and the statement, "Whatever you do, I don't want you" (which is what racism declares). It is, in other words, both absurd and immoral to equate the despairing response of the victim with the contemptuous assertion of the oppressor. It would, moreover, be tragic if white liberals allowed verbal hostility on the part of Negroes to drive them out of the movement or to curtail their support for civil rights. The issue was injustice before "black power" became popular, and the issue is still injustice.

In any event, even if "black power" had not emerged as a slogan, problems would have arisen in the relation between whites and Negroes in the civil-rights movement. In the North, it was inevitable that Negroes would eventually wish to run their own movement and would rebel against the presence of whites in positions of leadership as yet another sign of white supremacy. In the South, the well-intentioned white volunteer had the cards stacked against him from the beginning. Not only could he leave the struggle any time he chose to do so, but a higher value was set on his safety by the press and the government—apparent in the differing degrees of excitement generated by the imprisonment or murder of whites and Negroes. The white person's importance to the movement in the South was thus an ironic outgrowth of racism and was therefore bound to create resentment.

But again: however understandable all this may be as a response to objective conditions and to the seeming irrelevance of so many hard-won victories to the day-to-day life of the mass of Negroes, the fact remains that the quasi-nationalist sentiments and "no-win" policy lying behind the slogan of "black power" do no service to the Negro. Some nationalist emotion is, of course, inevitable, and "black power" must be seen as part of the psychological rejection of white supremacy, part of the rebellion against the stereotypes which have been ascribed to Negroes for three hundred years. Nevertheless, pride, confidence, and a new identity cannot be won by glorifying blackness or attacking whites; they can only come from meaningful action, from good jobs, and from real victories such as were achieved on the streets of Montgomery, Birmingham, and Selma. When SNCC and CORE went into the South, they awakened the country, but now they emerge isolated and demoralized, shouting a slogan that may afford a momentary satisfaction but that is calculated to destroy them and their movement. Already their frustrated call is being answered with counter-demands for law and order and with opposition to police-review boards. Already they have diverted the entire civil-rights movement from the hard task of developing strategies to realign the major parties of this country, and embroiled it in a debate that can only lead more and more to politics by frustration.

On the other side, however—the more important side, let it be said—it is the business of those who reject the negative aspects of "black power" not to preach but to act. Some weeks ago President Johnson, speaking at Fort Campbell, Kentucky, asserted that riots impeded reform, created fear, and antagonized the Negro's traditional friends. Mr. Johnson, according to the New York *Times*, expressed sympathy for the plight of the poor, the jobless, and the ill-housed. The government, he noted, has been working to relieve their circumstances, but "all this takes time."

One cannot argue with the President's position that riots are destructive or that they frighten away allies. Nor can one find fault with his sympathy for the plight of the poor; surely the poor need sympathy. But one can question whether the government has been working seriously enough to eliminate the conditions which lead to frustration-politics and riots. The President's very words, "all this takes time," will be understood by the poor for precisely what they are—an excuse instead of a real program, a cover-up for the failure to establish real priorities, and an indication that the administration has no real commitment to create new jobs, better housing, and integrated schools.

For the truth is that it need only take ten years to eliminate poverty—ten years and the $100 billion Freedom Budget recently proposed by A. Philip Randolph. In his introduction to the budget (which was drawn up in consultation with the nation's leading economists, and which will be published later this month), Mr. Randolph points out: "The programs urged in the Freedom Budget attack all of the major causes of poverty—unemployment and underemployment, substandard pay, inadequate social insurance and welfare payments to those who cannot or should not be employed; bad housing; deficiencies in health services, education, and training; and fiscal and monetary policies which tend to redistribute income regressively rather than progressively. The Freedom Budget leaves no room for discrimination in any form because its programs are addressed to all who need more opportunity and improved incomes and living standards, not to just some of them."

The legislative precedent Mr. Randolph has in mind is the 1945 Full Employment bill. This bill—conceived in its original form by Roosevelt to prevent a postwar depression—would have made it public policy for the government to step in if the private economy could not provide enough employment. As passed finally by Congress in 1946, with many of its teeth removed, the bill had the result of preventing the Negro worker, who had finally reached a pay level about 55 per cent that of the white wage, from making any further progress in closing that discriminatory gap; and instead, he was pushed back by the chronically high unemployment rates of the 50's. Had the original bill been passed, the public sector of our economy would have been able to insure fair and full employment. Today, with the spiralling thrust of automation, it is even more imperative that we have a legally binding commitment to this goal.

Let me interject a word here to those who say that Negroes are asking for another handout and are refusing to help themselves. From the end of the 19th century up to the last generation, the United States absorbed and provided economic opportunity for tens of millions of immigrants. These people were usually uneducated and a good many could not speak English. They had nothing but their hard work to offer and they labored long hours, often in miserable sweatshops and unsafe mines. Yet in a burgeoning economy with a need for unskilled labor, they were able to find jobs, and as industrialization proceeded, they were gradually able to move up the ladder to greater skills. Negroes who have been driven off the farm into a city life for which they are not prepared and who have entered an economy in which there is less and less need for unskilled labor, cannot be compared with these immigrants of old. The tenements which were jammed by newcomers were way-stations of hope; the ghettos of today have become dead-ends of despair. Yet just as the older generation of immigrants—in its most decisive act of self-help—organized the trade-union movement and then in alliance with many middle-class elements went on to improve its own lot and the condition of American society generally, so the Negro of today is struggling to go beyond the gains of the past and, in alliance with liberals and labor, to guarantee full and fair employment to all Americans.

Mr. Randolph's Freedom Budget not only rests on the Employment Act of 1946, but on a precedent set by Harry Truman when he believed freedom was threatened in Europe. In 1947, the Marshall Plan was put into effect and 3 per cent of the gross national product was spent in foreign aid. If we were to allocate a similar proportion of our GNP to destroy the economic and social consequences of racism and poverty at home today, it might mean spending more than 20 billion dollars a year, although I think it quite possible that we can fulfill these goals with a much smaller sum. It would be intolerable, however, if our plan for domestic social reform were less audacious and less far-reaching than our international programs of a generation ago.

We must see, therefore, in the current debate over "black power," a fantastic challenge to American society to live up to its proclaimed principles in the area of race by transforming itself so that all men may live equally and under justice. We must see to it that in rejecting "black power," we do not also reject the principle of Negro equality. Those people who would use the current debate and/or the riots to abandon the civil-rights movement leave us no choice but to question their original motivation.

If anything, the next period will be more serious and difficult than the preceding ones. It is much easier to establish the Negro's right to sit at a Wollworth's counter than to fight for an integrated community. It takes very little imagination to understand that the Negro should have the right to vote, but it demands much creativity, patience, and political stamina to plan, develop, and implement programs and priorities. It is one thing to organize sentiment behind laws that do not disturb consensus politics, and quite another to win battles for the redistribution of wealth. Many people who marched in Selma are not prepared to support a bill for a $2.00 minimum wage, to say nothing of supporting a redefinition of work or a guaranteed annual income.

It is here that we who advocate coalitions and integration and who object to the "black-power" concept have a massive job to do. We must see to it that the liberal-labor-civil rights coalition is maintained and, indeed, strengthened so that it can fight effectively for a Freedom Budget. We are responsible for the growth of the "black-power" concept because we have not used our own power to insure the full implementation of the bills whose passage we were strong enough to win, and we have not mounted the necessary campaign for winning a decent minimum wage and extended benefits. "Black power" is a slogan directed primarily against liberals by those who once counted liberals among their closest friends. It is up to the liberal movement to prove that coalition and integration are better alternatives.

PROTEST AS A POLITICAL RESOURCE*

MICHAEL LIPSKY

The frequent resort to protest activity by relatively powerless groups in recent American politics suggests that protest represents an important aspect of minority group and low income group politics.[1] At the same time that Negro civil rights strategists have recognized the problem of using protest as a meaningful political instrument,[2] groups associated with the "war on poverty" have increasingly received publicity for protest activity. Saul Alinsky's Industrial Areas Foundation, for example, continues to receive invitations to help organize low income communities because of its ability to mobilize poor people around the tactic of protest.[3] The riots which dominated urban affairs in the summer of 1967 appear not to have diminished the dependence of some groups on protest as a mode of political activity.

This article provides a theoretical perspective on protest activity as a political resource. The discussion is concentrated on the limitations inherent in protest which occur because of the need of protest leaders to appeal to four constituencies at the same time. As the concept of protest is developed here, it will be argued that protest leaders must nurture and sustain an organization comprised of people with whom they may or may not share common

* This article is an attempt to develop and explore the implications of a conceptual scheme for analyzing protest activity. It is based upon my studies of protest organizations in New York City, Washington, D.C., Chicago, San Francisco, and Mississippi, as well as extensive examination of written accounts of protest among low-income and Negro civil rights groups. I am grateful to Kenneth Dolbeare, Murray Edelman, and Rodney Stiefbold for their insightful comments on an earlier draft. This paper was developed while the author was a Staff Associate of the Institute for Research on Poverty at the University of Wisconsin. I appreciate the assistance obtained during various phases of my research from the Rabinowitz Foundation, the New York State Legislative Internship Program, and the Brookings Institution.

values. They must articulate goals and choose strategies so as to maximize their public exposure through communications media. They must maximize the impact of third parties in the political conflict. Finally, they must try to maximize chances of success among those capable of granting goals. The tensions inherent in manipulating these four constituencies at the same time form the basis of this discussion of protest as a political process. It is intended to place aspects of the civil rights movement in a framework which suggests links between protest organizations and the general political processes in which such organizations operate.

I. "PROTEST" CONCEPTUALIZED

Protest activity as it has been adopted by elements of the civil rights movement and others has not been studied extensively by social scientists. Some of the most suggestive writings have been done as case studies of protest movements in single southern cities.[4] These works generally lack a framework or theoretical focus which would encourage generalization from the cases. More systematic efforts have been attempted in approaching the dynamics of biracial committees in the South,[5] and comprehensively assessing the efficacy of Negro political involvement in Durham, N.C. and Philadelphia, Pa.[6] In their excellent assessment of Negro politics in the South, Matthews and Prothro have presented a thorough profile of Southern Negro students and their participation in civil rights activities.[7] Protest is also discussed in passing in recent explorations of the social-psychological dimensions of Negro ghetto politics[8] and the still highly suggestive, although pre-1960's, work on Negro political leadership by James Q. Wilson.[9] These and other less systematic works on contemporary Negro politics,[10] for all of their intuitive insights and valuable documentation, offer no theoretical formulations which encourage conceptualization about the interaction between recent Negro political activity and the political process.

Heretofore the best attempt to place Negro protest activity in a framework which would generate additional insights has been that of James Q. Wilson.[11] Wilson has suggested that protest activity be conceived as a problem of bargaining in which the basic problem is that Negro groups lack political resources to exchange. Wilson called this "the problem of the powerless."[12]

While many of Wilson's insights remain valid, his approach is limited in applicability because it defines protest in terms of mass

action or response and as utilizing exclusively negative inducements in the bargaining process. Negative inducements are defined
as inducements which are not absolutely preferred but are preferred over alternative possibilities.[13] Yet it might be argued that
protest designed to appeal to groups which oppose suffering and
exploitation, for example, might be offering positive inducements
in bargaining. A few Negro students sitting at a lunch counter
might be engaged in what would be called protest, and by their
actions might be trying to appeal to other groups in the system
with positive inducements. Additionally, Wilson's concentration
on Negro civic action, and his exclusive interest in exploring the
protest process to explain Negro civic action, tend to obscure comparison with protest activity which does not necessarily arise
within the Negro community.

Assuming a somewhat different focus, protest activity is defined
as a mode of political action oriented toward objection to one or
more policies or conditions, characterized by showmanship or display of an unconventional nature, and undertaken to obtain rewards from political or economic systems while working within the
systems. The "problem of the powerless" in protest activity is to
activate "third parties" to enter the implicit or explicit bargaining arena in ways favorable to the protesters. This is one of the
few ways in which they can "create" bargaining resources. It is
intuitively unconvincing to suggest that fifteen people sitting un-
invited in the Mayor's office have the power to move City Hall.
A better formulation would suggest that the people sitting in may
be able to appeal to a wider public to which the city administration is sensitive. Thus in successful protest activity the *reference
publics* of protest *targets* may be concevied as explicitly or implicitly reacting to protest in such a way that target groups or individuals respond in ways favorable to the protesters.[14]

It should be emphasized that the focus here is on protest
by relatively powerless groups. Illustrations can be summoned, for
example, of activity designated as "protest" involving high status
pressure groups or hundreds of thousands of people. While such
instances may share some of the characteristics of protest activity,
they may not represent examples of developing political resources
by relatively powerless groups because the protesting groups may
already command political resources by virtue of status, numbers
or cohesion.

It is appropriate also to distinguish between the relatively restricted use of the concept of protest adopted here and closely related political strategies which are often designated as "protest" in popular usage. Where groups already possess sufficient resources with which to bargain, as in the case of some economic boycotts and labor strikes, they may be said to engage in "direct confrontation."[15] Similarly, protest which represents efforts to "activate reference publics" should be distinguished from "alliance formation," where third parties are induced to join the conflict, but where the value orientations of third parties are sufficiently similar to those of the protesting group that concerted or coordinated action is possible. Alliance formation is particularly desirable for relatively powerless groups if they seek to join the decision-making process as participants.

The distinction between activating reference publics and alliance formation is made on the assumption that where goal orientations among protest groups and the reference publics of target groups are similar, the political dynamics of petitioning target groups are different than when such goal orientations are relatively divergent. Clearly the more similar the goal orientations, the greater the likelihood of protest success, other things being equal. This discussion is intended to highlight, however, those instances where goal orientations of reference publics depart significantly, in direction or intensity, from the goals of protest groups.

Say that to protest some situation, A would like to enter a bargaining situation with B. But A has nothing B wants, and thus cannot bargain. A then attempts to create political resources by activating other groups to enter the conflict. A then organizes to take action against B with respect to certain goals. *Information concerning these goals must be conveyed through communications media* (C, D, and E) *to* F, G, and H, *which are B's reference publics.* In response to the reactions of F, G, and H, or in anticipation of their reactions, B responds, *in some way*, to the protesters' demands. This formulation requires the conceptualization of protest activity when undertaken to create bargaining resources as a political process which requires communication and is characterized by a multiplicity of constituencies for protest leadership.

A schematic representation of the process of protest as utilized by relatively powerless groups is presented in Figure 1. In contrast to a simplistic pressure group model which would posit a direct relationship between pressure group and pressured, the following discussion is guided by the assumption (derived from observation) that protest is a highly indirect process in which communications media and the reference publics of protest targets play critical roles. It is also a process characterized by reciprocal relations, in which protest leaders frame strategies according to their perception of the need of (many) other actors.

In this view protest constituents limit the options of protest leaders at the same time that the protest leader influences their perception of the strategies and rhetoric which they will support. Protest activity is filtered through the communications media in influencing the perceptions of the reference publics of protest targets. To the extent that the influence of reference publics is supportive of protest goals, target groups will dispense symbolic or material rewards. Material rewards are communicated directly to protest constituents. Symbolic rewards are communicated in part

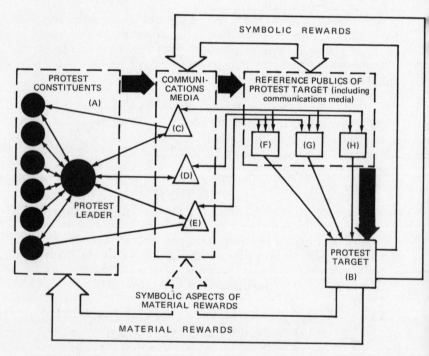

FIG. 1. Schematic representation of the process of protest by relatively powerless groups.

to protest constituents, but primarily are communicated to the reference publics of target groups, who provide the major stimuli for public policy pronouncements.

The study of protest as adopted by relatively powerless groups should provide insights into the structure and behavior of groups involved in civil rights politics and associated with the "war on poverty." It should direct attention toward the ways in which administrative agencies respond to "crises." Additionally, the study of protest as a political resource should influence some general conceptualizations of American political pluralism. Robert Dahl, for example, describes the "normal American political process" as one in which there is a high probability that an active and legitimate group in the population can make itself heard effectively at some crucial stage in the process of decision.[16]

Although he agrees that control over decisions is unevenly divided in the population, Dahl writes:

> When I say that a group is heard "effectively" I mean more than the simple fact that it makes a noise; I mean that one or more officials are not only ready to listen to the noise, but expect to suffer in some significant way if they do not placate the group, its leaders, or its most vociferous members. To satisfy the group may require one or more of a great variety of actions by the responsive leader: pressure for substantive policies, appointments, graft, respect, expression of the appropriate emotions, or the right combination of reciprocal noises.[17]

These statements, which in some ways resemble David Truman's dicussion of the power of "potential groups,"[18] can be illuminated by the study of protest activity in three ways. First, what are the probabilities that relatively powerless groups can make themselves heard effectively? In what ways will such groups be heard or "steadily appeased"?[19] Concentration on the process of protest activity may reveal the extent to which, and the conditions under which, relatively powerless groups are likely to prove effective. Protest undertaken to obstruct policy decisions, for example, may enjoy greater success probabilities than protest undertaken in an effort to evoke constructive policy innovations.[20]

Second, does it make sense to suggest that all groups which make noises will receive responses from public officials? Perhaps the groups which make noises do not have to be satisfied at all, but it is other groups which receive assurances or recognition. Third, what are the probabilities that groups which make noises will receive tangible rewards, rather than symbolic assurances?[21] Dahl lumps these rewards together in the same paragraph, but dispensation of tangible rewards clearly has a different impact upon groups than the dispensation of symbolic rewards. Dahl is undoubtedly correct when he suggests that the relative fluidity of American politics is a critical characteristic of the American political system.[22] But he is less precise and less convincing when it comes to analyzing the extent to which the system is indeed responsive to the relatively powerless groups of the "average citizen."[23]

The following sections are an attempt to demonstrate the utility of the conceptualization of the protest process presented above. This will be done by exploring the problems encountered and the strains generated by protest leaders in interacting with four constituencies. It will be useful to concentrate attention on the maintenance and enhancement needs not only of the large formal organizations which dominate city politics,[24] but also of the ad hoc protest groups which engage them in civic controversy. It will also prove rewarding to examine the role requirements of individuals in leadership positions as they perceive the problems of constituency manipulation. In concluding remarks some implications of the study of protest for the pluralist description of American politics will be suggested.[25]

II. PROTEST LEADERSHIP AND ORGANIZATIONAL BASE

The organizational maintenance needs of relatively powerless, low income, ad hoc protest groups center around the tension generated by the need for leadership to offer symbolic and intangible inducements to protest participation when immediate, material rewards cannot be anticipated, and the need to provide at least the promise of material rewards. Protest leaders must try to evoke responses from other actors in the political process, at the same time that they pay attention to participant organizational needs. Thus relatively deprived groups in the political system not only receive symbolic reassurance while material rewards from the system are withheld,[26] but protest leaders have a stake in perpetuating the notion that relatively powerless groups retain political efficacy despite what in many cases is obvious evidence to the contrary.

The tension embraced by protest leaders over the nature of inducements toward protest participation accounts in part for the style adopted and goals selected by protest leaders. Groups which seek psychological gratification from politics, but cannot or do not anticipate material political rewards, may be attracted to militant protest leaders. To these groups, angry rhetoric may prove a desirable quality in the short run. Where groups depend upon the political system for tangible benefits, or where participation in the system provides intangible benefits, moderate leadership is likely to prevail. Wilson has observed similar tendencies among Negro leaders of large, formal organizations.[27] It is no less true for leadership of protest groups. Groups whose members derive tangible satisfactions from political participation will not condone leaders who are stubborn in compromise or appear to question the foundations of the system. This coincides with Truman's observation: "Violation of the rules of the game normally will weaken a group's cohesion, reduce its status in the community, and expose it to the claims of other groups."[28] On the other hand, the cohesion of relatively powerless groups may be strengthened by militant, ideological leadership which questions the rules of the game and challenges their legitimacy.

Cohesion is particularly important when protest leaders bargain directly with target groups. In that situation, leaders' ability to control protest constituents and guarantee their behavior represents a bargaining strength.[29] For this reason Wilson stressed the bargaining difficulties of Negro leaders who cannot guarantee constituent behavior, and pointed out the significance of the strategy of projecting the image of group solidarity when the reality of cohesion is a fiction.[30] Cohesion is less significant at other times. Divided leadership may prove productive by bargaining in tandem,[31] or by minimizing strain among groups in the protest process. Further, community divisions may prove less detrimental to protest aims when strong third parties have entered the dispute originally generated by protest organizations.

The intangible rewards of assuming certain postures toward the political system may not be sufficient to sustain an organizational base. It may be necessary to renew constantly the intangible rewards of participation. And to the extent that people participate in order to achieve tangible benefits, their interest in a protest organization may depend upon the organization's relative material success. Protest leaders may have to tailor their style to present participants with tangible successes, or with the appearance of success. Leaders may have to define the issues with concern for increasing their ability to sustain organization. The potential for protest among protest group members may have to be manipulated by leadership if the group is to be sustained.[32]

The participants in protest organizations limit the flexibility of protest leadership. This obtains for two reasons. They restrict public actions by leaders who must continue to solicit active participant support, and they place restraints on the kinds of activities which can be considered appropriate for protest purposes. Poor participants cannot commonly be asked to engage in protest requiring air transportation. Participants may have anxieties related to their environment or historical situation which discourages engagement in some activities. They may be afraid of job losses, beatings by the police, or summary evictions. Negro protest in the Deep South has been inhibited by realistic expectations of retribution.[33] Protests over slum housing conditions are undermined by tenants who expect landlord retaliation for engaging in tenant organizing activity.[34] Political or ethical mores may conflict with a proposed course of action, diminishing participation.[35]

On the other hand, to the extent that fears are real, or that the larger community perceives protest participants as subject to these fears, protest may actually be strengthened. Communications media and potential allies will consider more soberly the complaints of people who are understood to be placing themselves in jeopardy. When young children and their parents made the arduous bus trip from Mississippi to Washington, D.C. to protest the jeopardizing of Head Start funds, the courage and expense represented by their effort created a respect and visibility for their position which might not have been achieved by local protest efforts.[36]

Protest activity may be undertaken by organizations with established relationship patterns, behavior norms, and role expectations. These organizations are likely to have greater access to other groups in the political system, and a demonstrated capacity to maintain themselves. Other protest groups, however, may be ad hoc arrangements without demonstrated internal or external relationship patterns. These groups will have different organizational problems, in response to which it is necessary to engage in different kinds of protest activity.

The scarcity of organizational resources also places limits upon the ability of relatively powerless groups to maintain the foundations upon which protest organizations develop. Relatively powerless groups, to engage in political activity of any kind, must command at least some resources. This is not tautological. Referring again to a continuum on which political groups are placed according to their relative command of resources, one may draw a line somewhere along the continuum representing a "threshold of civic group political participation." Clearly some groups along the continuum will possess some political resources (enough, say, to emerge for inspection) but not enough to exercise influence in civic affairs. Relatively powerless groups, to be influential, must cross the "threshold" to engage in politics. Although the availability of group resources is a critical consideration at all stages of the protest process, it is particularly important in explaining why some groups seem to "surface" with sufficient strength to command attention. The following discussion of some critical organizational resources should illuminate this point.

Skilled professionals frequently must be available to protest organizations. Lawyers, for example, play extremely important roles in enabling protest groups to utilize the judicial process and avail themselves of adequate preparation of court cases. Organizational reputation may depend upon a combination of ability to threaten the conventional political system and of exercising statutory rights in court. Availability of lawyers depends upon ability to pay fees and/or the attractiveness to lawyers of participation in protest group activity. Volunteer professional assistance may not prove adequate. One night a week volunteered by an aspiring politician in a housing clinic cannot satisfy the needs of a chaotic political movement.[37] The need for skilled professionals is not restricted to lawyers. For example, a group seeking to protest an urban renewal policy might require the services of architects and city planners in order to present a viable alternative to a city proposal.

Financial resources not only purchase legal assistance, but enable relatively powerless groups to conduct minimum programs of political activities. To the extent that constituents are unable or unwilling to pay even small membership dues, then financing the cost of mimeographing flyers, purchasing supplies, maintaining telephone service, paying rent, and meeting a modest payroll become major organizational problems. And to the extent that group finances are supplied by outside individual contributions or government or foundation grants, the long-term options of the group are sharply constrained by the necessity of orienting group goals and tactics to anticipate the potential objections of financial supporters.

Some dependence upon even minimal financial resources can

be waived if organizations evoke passionate support from constituents. Secretarial help and block organizers will come forward to work without compensation if they support the cause of neighborhood organizations or gain intangible benefits based upon association with the group. Protest organizations may also depend upon skilled non-professionals, such as college students, whose access to people and political and economic institutions often assist protest groups in cutting across income lines to seek support. Experience with ad hoc political groups, however, suggests that this assistance is sporadic and undependable. Transient assistance is particularly typical of skilled, educated, and employable volunteers whose abilities can be applied widely. The die-hards of ad hoc political groups are often those people who have no place else to go, nothing else to do.

Constituent support will be affected by the nature of the protest target and whether protest activity is directed toward defensive or assertive goals. Obstructing specific public policies may be easier than successfully recommending constructive policy changes. Orientations toward defensive goals may require less constituent energy, and less command over resources of money, expertise and status.[38]

III. Protest Leadership and Communications Media

The communications media are extremely powerful in city politics. In granting or withholding publicity, in determining what information most people will have on most issues, and what alternatives they will consider in response to issues, the media truly, as Norton Long has put it, "set . . . the civic agenda."[39] To the extent that successful protest activity depends upon appealing to, and/or threatening, other groups in the community, the communications media set the limits of protest action. If protest tactics are not considered significant by the media, or if newspapers and television reporters or editors decide to overlook protest tactics, protest organizations will not succeed. Like the tree falling unheard in the forest, there is no protest unless protest is perceived and projected.

A number of writers have noticed that the success of protest activity seems directly related to the amount of publicity it receives outside the immediate arena in which protest takes place. This view has not been stated systematically, but hints can be found in many sources. In the literature on civil rights politics, the relevance of publicity represents one of the few hypotheses available concerning the dynamics of successful protest activity.[40]

When protest tactics do receive coverage in the communications media, the way in which they are presented will influence all other actors in the system, including the protesters themselves. Conformity to standards of newsworthiness in political style, and knowledge of the prejudices and desires of the individuals who determine media coverage in political skills, represent crucial determinants of leadership effectiveness.

The organizational behavior of newspapers can partly be understood by examining the maintenance and enhancement needs which direct them toward projects of civic betterment and impressions of accomplishment.[41] But insight may also be gained by analyzing the role requirements of reporters, editors, and others who determine newspaper policy. Reporters, for example, are frequently motivated by the desire to contribute to civic affairs by their "objective" reporting of significant events; by the premium they place on accuracy; and by the credit which they receive for sensationalism and "scoops."

These requirements may be difficult to accommodate at the same time. Reporters demand newsworthiness of their subjects in the short run, but also require reliability and verifiability in the longer run. Factual accuracy may dampen newsworthiness. Sensationalism, attractive to some newspaper editors, may be inconsistent with reliable, verifiable narration of events. Newspapers at first may be attracted to sensationalism, and later demand verifiability in the interests of community harmony (and adherence to professional journalistic standards).

Most big city newspapers have reporters whose assignments permit them to cover aspects of city politics with some regularity. These reporters, whose "beats" may consist of "civil rights" or "poverty," sometimes develop close relationships with their news subjects. These relationships may develop symbiotic overtones because of the mutuality of interest between the reporter and the news subject. Reporters require fresh information on protest developments, while protest leaders have a vital interest in obtaining as much press coverage as possible.

Inflated reports of protest success may be understood in part by examining this relationship between reporter and protest leader. Both have role-oriented interests in projecting images of protest strength and threat. In circumstances of great excitement, when competition from other news media representatives is high, a reporter may find that he is less governed by the role requirement of verification and reliability than he is by his editor's demand for "scoops" and news with high audience appeal.[42]

On the other hand, the demands of the media may conflict with the needs of protest group maintenance. Consider the leader whose constituents are attracted solely by pragmatic statements not exceeding what they consider political "good taste." He is constrained from making militant demands which would isolate him from constituents. This constraint may cost him appeal in the press.[43] However, the leader whose organizing appeal requires militant rhetoric may obtain eager press coverage only to find that his inflammatory statements lead to alienation of potential allies and exclusion from the explicit bargaining process.[44]

News media do not report events in the same way. Television may select for broadcast only thirty seconds of a half-hour news conference. This coverage will probably focus on immediate events, without background or explanatory material. Newspapers may give more complete accounts of the same event. The most complete account may appear in the weekly edition of a neighborhood or ethnic newspaper. Differential coverage by news media, and differential news media habits in the general population,[45] are significant factors in permitting protest leaders to juggle conflicting demands of groups in the protest process.

Similar tensions exist in the leader''s relationships with protest targets. Ideological postures may gain press coverage and constituency approval, but may alienate target groups with whom it would be desirable to bargain explicitly. Exclusion from the councils of decision-making may have important consequences, since the results of target group deliberations may satisfy activated reference publics without responding to protest goals. If activated reference public are required to increase the bargaining position of the protest group, protest efforts thereafter will have diminished chances of success.

IV. PROTEST LEADERSHIP AND "THIRD PARTIES"

I have argued that the essence of political protest consists of activating third parties to participate in controversy in ways favorable to protest goals. In previous sections I have attempted to analyze some of the tensions which result from protest leaders' attempts to activate reference publics of protest targets at the same time that they must retain the interest and support of protest organization participants. This phenomenon is in evidence when Negro leaders, recognized as such by public officials, find their support eroded in the Negro community because they have engaged in explicit bargaining situations with politicians. Negro leaders are thus faced with the dilemma that when they behave like other ethnic group representatives they are faced with loss of support from those whose intense activism has been aroused in the Negro community, yet whose support is vital if they are to remain credible as leaders to public officials.

The tensions resulting from conflicting maintenance needs of protest organizations and activated third parties present difficulties for protest leaders. One way in which these tensions can be minimized is by dividing leadership responsibilities. If more than one group is engaged in protest activity, protest leaders can, in effect, divide up public roles so as to reduce as much as possible the gap between the implicit demands of different groups for appropriate rhetoric, and what in fact is said. Thus divided leadership may perform the latent function of minimizing tensions among elements in the protest process by permitting different groups to listen selectively to protest spokesmen.[46]

Another way in which strain among different groups can be minimized is through successful public relations. Minimization of strain may depend upon ambiguity of action or statement, deception, or upon effective inter-group communication. Failure to clarify meaning, or falsification, may increase protest effectiveness. Effective intragroup communication may increase the likelihood that protest constituents will "understand" that ambiguous or false public statements have "special meaning" and need not be taken seriously. The Machiavellian circle is complete when we observe that although lying may be prudent, the appearance of integrity and forthrightness is desirable for public relations, since these values are widely shared.

It has been observed that "[t]he militant displays an unwillingness to perform those administrative tasks which are necessary to operate an organization. Probably the skills of the agitator and the skills of the administrator . . . are not incompatible, but few men can do both well."[47] These skills may or may not be incompatible as personality traits, but they indeed represent conflicting role demands on protest leadership. When a protest leader exhausts time and energy conducting frequent press conferences, arranging for politicians and celebrities to appear at rallies, delivering speeches to sympathetic local groups, college symposia and other forums, constantly picketing for publicity and generally making "contacts," he is unable to pursue the direction of office routine, clerical tasks, research and analysis, and other chores.

The difficulties of delegating routine tasks are probably directly related to the skill levels and previous administrative experiences of group members. In addition, to the extent that involvement in protest organizations is a function of rewards received or expected by individuals because of the excitement or entertainment value of participation, then the difficulties of delegating routine, relatively uninteresting chores to group members will be increased. Yet attention to such details affects the perception of protest groups by organizations whose support or assistance may be desired in the future. These considerations add to the protest leader's problem of risking alienation of protest participants because of potentially unpopular cooperation with the "power structure."

In the protest paradigm developed here, "third parties" refers both to the reference publics of target groups and, more narrowly, to the interest groups whose regular interaction with protest targets tends to develop into patterns of influence.[48] We have already discussed some of the problems associated with activating the reference publics of target groups. In discussing the constraints placed upon protest, attention may be focused upon the likelihood that groups seeking to create political resources through protest will be included in the explicit bargaining process with other pressure groups. For protest groups, these constraints are those which occur because of class and political style, status, and organizational resources.

The established civic groups most likely to be concerned with the problems raised by relatively powerless groups are those devoted to service in the public welfare and those "liberally" oriented groups whose potential constituents are either drawn from the same class as the protest groups (such as some trade unions), or whose potential constituents are attracted to policies which appear to serve the interest of the lower class or minority groups (such as some reform political clubs).[49] These civic groups have frequently cultivated clientele relationships with city agencies over long periods. Their efforts have been reciprocated by agency officials anxious to develop constituencies to support and defend agency administrative and budgetary policies. In addition, clientele groups are expected to endorse and legitimize agency aggrandizement. These relationships have been developed by agency officials and civic groups for mutual benefit, and cannot be destroyed, abridged or avoided without cost.

Protest groups may well be able to raise the saliency of issues on the civic agenda through utilization of communications media and successful appeals or threats to wider publics, but admission to policy-making councils is frequently barred because of the angry, militant rhetorical style adopted by protest leaders. People in power do not like to sit down with rogues. Protest leaders are likely to have phrased demands in ways unacceptable to lawyers and other civic activists whose cautious attitude toward public policy may reflect not only their good intentions but their concern for property rights, due process, pragmatic legislating or judicial precedent.

Relatively powerless groups lack participation of individuals with high status whose endorsement of specific proposals lend them increased legitimacy. Good causes may always attract the support of high status individuals. But such individuals' willingness to devote time to the promotion of specific proposals is less likely than the one-shot endorsements which these people distribute more readily.

Similarly, protest organizations often lack the resources on which entry into the policy-making process depends. These resources include maintenance of a staff with expertise and experience in the policy area. This expertise may be in the areas of the law, planning and architecture, proposal writing, accounting, educational policy, federal grantsmanship or publicity. Combining experience with expertise is one way to create status in issue areas. The dispensing of information by interest groups has been widely noted as a major source of influence. Over time the experts develop status in their areas of competence somewhat independent of the influence which adheres to them as information-providers. Groups which cannot or do not engage lawyers to assist in proposing legislation, and do not engage in collecting reliable data, cannot participate in policy deliberations or consult in these matters. Protest oriented groups, whose primary talents are in dramatizing issues, cannot credibly attempt to present data considered "objective" or suggestions considered "responsible" by public officials. Few can be convincing as both advocate and arbiter at the same time.

V. Protest Leadership and Target Groups

The probability of protest success may be approached by examining the maintenance needs of organizations likely to be designated as target groups.[50] For the sake of clarity, and because protest activity increasingly is directed toward government, I shall refer in the following paragraphs exclusively to government agencies at the municipal level. The assumption is retained, however, that the following generalizations are applicable to other potential target groups.

Some of the constraints placed on protest leadership in influencing target groups have already been mentioned in preceding sections. The lack of status and resources that inhibit protest groups from participating in policy-making conferences, for example, also helps prevent explicit bargaining between protest leaders and city officials. The strain between rhetoric which appeals to protest participants and public statements to which communications media and "third parties" respond favorably also exists with reference to target groups.

Yet there is a distinguishable feature of the maintenance needs and strategies of city agencies which specifically constrains protest organizations. This is the agency director's need to protect "the jurisdiction and income of his organization [by] . . . [m]anipulation of the external environment."[51] In so doing he may satisfy his reference groups without responding to protest group demands. At least six tactics are available to protest targets who are motivated to respond in some way to protest activity but seek primarily to satisfy their reference publics. These tactics may be employed whether or not target groups are "sincere" in responding to protest demands.

1. Target groups may dispense symbolic satisfactions. Appearances of activity and commitment to problems substitute for, or supplement, resource allocation and policy innovations which would constitute tangible responses to protest activity. If symbolic responses supplement tangible pay-offs, they are frequently coincidental, rather than intimately linked, to projection of response by protest targets. Typical in city politics of the symbolic response is the ribbon cutting, street corner ceremony or the walking tour press conference. These occasions are utilized not only to build agency constituencies,[52] but to satisfy agency reference publics that attention is being directed to problems of civic concern. In

this sense publicist tactics may be seen as defensive maneuvers. Symbolic aspects of the actions of public officials can also be recognized in the commissioning of expensive studies and the rhetorical flourishes with which "massive attacks," "comprehensive programs," and "coordinated planning" are frequently promoted.

City agencies establish distinct apparatus and procedures for dealing with crises which may be provoked by protest groups. Housing-related departments in New York City may be cited for illustrations. It is usually the case in these agencies that the Commissioner or a chief deputy, a press secretary and one or two other officials devote whatever time is necessary to collect information, determine policy and respond quickly to reports of "crises." This is functional for tenants, who, if they can generate enough concern, may be able to obtain shortcuts through lengthy agency procedures. It is also functional for officials who want to project images of action rather than merely receiving complaints. Concentrating attention on the maintenance needs of city politicians during protest crises suggests that pronouncements of public officials serve purposes independent of their dedication to alleviation of slum conditions.[53]

Independent of dispensation of tangible benefits to protest groups, public officials continue to respond primarily to their own reference publics. Murray Edelman has suggested that: "Tangible resources and benefits are frequently not distributed to unorganized political group interests as promised in regulatory statutes and the propaganda attending their enactment."[54] His analysis may be supplemented by suggesting that symbolic dispensations may not only serve to reassure unorganized political group interests, but may also contribute to reducing the anxiety level of organized interests and wider publics which are only tangentially involved in the issues.

2. Target groups may dispense token material satisfactions. When city agencies respond, with much publicity, to cases brought to their attention representing examples of the needs dramatized by protest organizations, they may appear to respond to protest demands while in fact only responding on a case basis, instead of a general basis. For the protesters served by agencies in this fashion it is of considerable advantage that agencies can be influenced by protest action. Yet it should not be ignored that in handling the "crisis" cases, public officials give the appearance of response to their reference publics, while mitigating demands for an expensive, complex *general* assault on problems represented by

the cases to which responses are given. Token responses, whether or not accompanied by more general responses, are particularly attractive to reporters and television news directors, who are able to dramatize individual cases convincingly, but who may be unable to "capture" the essence of general deprivation or of general efforts to alleviate conditions of deprivation.

3. Target groups may organize and innovate internally in order to blunt the impetus of protest efforts. This tactic is closely related to No. 2 (above). If target groups can act constructively in the worst cases, they will then be able to pre-empt protest efforts by responding to the cases which best dramatize protest demands. Alternatively, they may designate all efforts which jeopardize agency reputations as "worst" cases, and devote extensive resources to these cases. In some ways extraordinary city efforts are precisely consistent with protest goals. At the same time extraordinary efforts in the most heavily dramatized cases or the most extreme cases effectively wear down the "cutting-edges" of protest efforts.

Many New York City agencies develop informal "crisis" arrangements not only to project publicity, as previously indicated, but to mobilize energies toward solving "crisis" cases. They may also develop policy innovations which allow them to respond more quickly to "crisis" situations. These innovations may be important to some city residents, for whom the problems of dealing with city bureaucracies can prove insurmountable. It might be said, indeed, that the goals of protest are to influence city agencies to handle every case with the same resources that characterize their dispatch of "crisis" cases.[55]

But such policies would demand major revenue inputs. This kind of qualitative policy change is difficult to achieve. Meanwhile, internal reallocation of resources only means that routine services must be neglected so that the "crisis" programs can be enhanced. If all cases are expedited, as in a typical "crisis" response, then none can be. Thus for purposes of general solutions, "crisis" resolving can be self-defeating unless accompanied by significantly greater resource allocation. It is not self-defeating, however, to the extent that the organizational goals of city agencies are to serve a clientele while minimizing negative publicity concerning agency vigilance and responsiveness.

4. Target groups may appear to be constrained in their ability to grant protest goals.[56] This may be directed toward making the protesters appear to be unreasonable in their demands, or to be

well-meaning individuals who "just don't understand how complex running a city really is." Target groups may extend sympathy but claim that they lack resources, a mandate from constituents, and/or authority to respond to protest demands. Target groups may also evade protest demands by arguing that "If-I-give-it-to-you-I-have-to-give-it-to-everyone."

The tactic of appearing constrained is particularly effective with established civic groups because there is an undeniable element of truth to it. Everyone knows that cities are financially undernourished. Established civic groups expend great energies lobbying for higher levels of funding for their pet city agencies. Thus they recognize the validity of this constraint when posed by city officials. But it is not inconsistent to point out that funds for specific, relatively inexpensive programs, or for the expansion of existing programs, can often be found if pressure is increased. While constraints on city government flexibility may be extensive, they are not absolute. Protest targets nonetheless attempt to diminish the impact of protest demands by claiming relative impotence.

5. Target groups may use their extensive resources to discredit protest leaders and organizations. Utilizing their excellent access to the press, public officials may state or imply that leaders are unreliable, ineffective as leaders ("they don't really have the people behind them"), guilty of criminal behavior, potentially guilty of such behavior, or are some shade of "left-wing." Any of these allegations may serve to diminish the appeal of protest groups to potentially sympathetic third parties. City officials, in their frequent social and informal business interaction with leaders of established civic groups, may also communicate derogatory information concerning protest groups. Discrediting of protest groups may be undertaken by some city officials while others appear (perhaps authentically) to remain sympathetic to protest demands. These tactics may be engaged in by public officials whether or not there is any validity to the allegations.

6. Target groups may postpone action. The effect of postponement, if accompanied by symbolic assurances, is to remove immediate pressure and delay specific commitments to a future date. This familiar tactic is particularly effective in dealing with protest groups because of their inherent instability. Protest groups are usually comprised of individuals whose intense political activity cannot be sustained except in rare circumstances. Further, to the extent that protest depends upon activating reference publics

through strategies which have some "shock" value, it becomes increasingly difficult to activate these groups. Additionally, protest activity is inherently unstable becaues of the strains placed upon protest leaders who must attempt to manage four constituencies (as described herein).

The most frequent method of postponing action is to commit a subject to "study." For the many reasons elaborated in these paragraphs, it is not likely that ad hoc protest groups will be around to review the recommendations which emerge from study. The greater the expertise and the greater the status of the group making the study, the less will protest groups be able to influence whatever policy emerges. Protest groups lack the skills and re-source personnel to challenge expert recommendations effectively.

Sometimes surveys and special research are undertaken in part to evade immediate pressures. Sometimes not. Research efforts are particularly necessary to secure the support of established civic groups, which place high priority on orderly procedure and policy emerging from independent analysis. Yet it must be recognized that postponing policy commitments has a distinct impact on the nature of the pressures focused on policy-makers.

VI. CONCLUSION

In this analysis I have agreed with James Q. Wilson that pro-test is correctly conceived as a strategy utilized by relatively pow-erless groups in order to increase their bargaining ability. As such, I have argued, it is successful to the extent that the reference publics of protest targets can be activated to enter the conflict in ways favorable to protest goals. I have suggested a model of the protest process which may assist in ordering data and indicating the salience for research of a number of aspects of protest. These include the critical role of communications media, the differential impact of material and symbolic rewards on "feedback" in protest activity, and the reciprocal relationships of actors in the protest process.

An estimation of the limits to protest efficacy, I have argued further, can be gained by recognizing the problems encountered by protest leaders who somehow must balance the conflicting maintenance needs of four groups in the protest process. This approach transcends a focus devoted primarily to characterization of group goals and targets, by suggesting that even in an environment which is relatively favorable to specific protest goals, the tensions which must be embraced by protest leadership may ultimately overwhelm protest activity.

At the outset of this essay, it was held that conceptualizing the American political system as "slack" or "fluid," in the manner of Robert Dahl, appears inadequate because of (1) a vagueness centering on the likelihood that any group can make itself heard; (2) a possible confusion as to which groups tend to receive satisfaction from the rewards dispensed by public officials; and (3) a lumping together as equally relevant rewards which are tangible and those which are symbolic. To the extent that protest is engaged in by relatively powerless groups which must create resources with which to bargain, the analysis here suggests a number of reservations concerning the pluralist conceptualization of the "fluidity" of the American political system.

Relatively powerless groups cannot use protest with a high probability of success. They lack organizational resources, by definition. But even to create bargaining resources through activating third parties, some resources are necessary to sustain organization. More importantly, relatively powerless protest groups are constrained by the unresolvable conflicts which are forced upon protest leaders who must appeal simultaneously to four constituencies which place upon them antithetical demands.

When public officials recognize the legitimacy of protest activity, they may not direct public policy toward protest groups at all. Rather, public officials are likely to aim responses at the reference publics from which they originally take their cues. Edelman has suggested that regulatory policy in practice often consists of reassuring mass publics while at the same time dispensing specific, tangible values to narrow interest groups. It is suggested here that symbolic reassurances are dispensed as much to wide, potentially concerned publics which are not directly affected by regulatory policy, as they are to wide publics comprised of the downtrodden and the deprived, in whose name policy is often written.

Complementing Edelman, it is proposed here that in the process of protest symbolic reassurances are dispensed in large measure because these are the public policy outcomes and actions desired by the constituencies to which public officials are most responsive. Satisfying these wider publics, city officials can avoid pressures toward other policies placed upon them by protest organizations.

Not only should there be some doubt as to which groups receive the symbolic recognitions which Dahl describes, but in failing to distinguish between the kinds of rewards dispensed to groups in the political system, Dahl avoids a fundamental question. It is literally fundamental because the kinds of rewards which can be obtained from politics, one might hypothesize, will have an impact upon the realistic appraisal of the efficacy of political activity. If among the groups least capable of organizing for political activity there is a history of organizing for protest, and if that activity, once engaged in, is rewarded primarily by the dispensation of symbolic gestures without perceptible changes in material conditions, then rational behavior might lead to expressions of apathy and lack of interest in politics or a rejection of conventional political channels as a meaningful arena of activity. In this sense this discussion of protest politics is consistent with Kenneth Clark's observations that the image of power, unaccompanied by material and observable rewards, leads to impressions of helplessness and reinforces political apathy in the ghetto.[57]

Recent commentary by political scientists and others regarding riots in American cities seems to focus in part on the extent to which relatively deprived groups may seek redress of legitimate grievances. Future research should continue assessment of the relationship between riots and the conditions under which access to the political system has been limited. In such research assessment of the ways in which access to public officials is obtained by relatively powerless groups through the protest process might be one important research focus.

The instability of protest activity outlined in this article also should inform contemporary political strategies. If the arguments presented here are persuasive, civil rights leaders who insist that protest activity is a shallow foundation on which to seek long-term, concrete gains may be judged essentially correct. But the arguments concerning the fickleness of the white liberal, or the ease of changing discriminatory laws relative to changing discriminatory institutions, only in part explain the instability of protest movements. An explanation which derives its strength from analysis of the political process suggests concentration on the problems of managing protest constituencies. Accordingly, Alinsky is probably on the soundest ground when he prescribes protest for the purpose of building organization. Ultimately, relatively powerless groups in most instances cannot depend upon activating other actors in the political process. Long-run success will depend upon the acquisition of stable political resources which do not rely for their use on third parties.

NOTES

1. "Relatively powerless groups" may be defined as those groups which, relatively speaking, are lacking in conventional political resources. For the purpose of community studies, Robert Dahl has compiled a useful comprehensive list. See Dahl, "The Analysis of Influence in Local Communities," *Social Science and Community Action*, Charles R. Adrian, ed. (East Lansing, Michigan, 1960), p. 32. The difficulty in studying such groups is that relative powerlessness only becomes apparent under certain conditions. Extremely powerless groups not only lack political resources, but are also characterized by a minimal sense of political efficacy, upon which in part successful political organization depends. For reviews of the literature linking orientations of political efficacy to socioeconomic status, see Robert Lane, *Political Life* (New York, 1959), ch. 16; and Lester Milbrath, *Political Participation* (Chicago, 1965), ch. 5. Further, to the extent that group cohesion is recognized as a necessary requisite for organized political action, then extremely powerless groups, lacking cohesion, will not even appear for observation. Hence the necessity of selecting for intensive study a protest movement where there can be some confidence that observable processes and results can be analyzed. Thus, if one conceives of a continuum on which political groups are placed according to their relative command of resources, the focus of this essay is on those groups which are near, but not at, the pole of powerlessness.
2. See, e.g., Bayard Rustin, "From Protest to Politics: The Future of the Civil Rights Movement," *Commentary* (February, 1965), 25–31; and Stokely Carmichael, "Toward Black Liberation," *The Massachusetts Review* (Autumn, 1966).
3. On Alinsky's philosophy of community organization, see his *Reveille for Radicals* (Chicago, 1945); and Charles Silberman, *Crisis in Black and White* (New York, 1964), ch. 10.
4. See, e.g., Jack L. Walker, "Protest and Negotiation: A Case Study of Negro Leadership in Atlanta, Georgia," *Midwest Journal of Political Science*, 7 (May, 1963), 99–124; Jack L. Walker, *Sit-Ins in Atlanta: A Study in the Negro Protest*, Eagleton Institute Case Studies, No. 34 (New York, 1964); John Ehle, *The Free Men* (New York, 1965) [Chapel Hill]; Daniel C. Thompson, *The Negro Leadership Class* (Englewood Cliffs, N.J., 1963) [New Orleans]; M. Elaine Burgess, *Negro Leadership in a Southern City* (Chapel Hill, N.C., 1962) [Durham].
5. Lewis Killian and Charles Grigg, *Racial Crisis in America: Leadership in Conflict* (Englewood Cliffs, N.J., 1964).
6. William Keech, "The Negro Vote as a Political Resource: The Case of Durham," (unpublished Ph.D. Dissertation, University of Wisconsin, 1966); John H. Strange, "The Negro in Philadelphia Politics 1963–65," (unpublished Ph.D. Dissertation, Princeton University, 1966).
7. Donald Matthews and James Prothro, *Negroes and the New Southern Politics* (New York, 1966). Considerable insight on these data is provided in John Orbell, "Protest Participation among Southern Negro College Students," this REVIEW, 61 (June, 1967), 446–456.

8. Kenneth Clark, *Dark Ghetto* (New York, 1965).

9. *Negro Politics* (New York, 1960).

10. A complete list would be voluminous. See, e.g., Nat Hentoff, *The New Equality* (New York, 1964); Arthur Waskow, *From Race Riot to Sit-in* (New York, 1966).

11. "The Strategy of Protest: Problems of Negro Civic Action," *Journal of Conflict Resolution*, 3 (September, 1961), 291–303. The reader will recognize the author's debt to this highly suggestive article, not least Wilson's recognition of the utility of the bargaining framework for examining protest activity.

12. *Ibid.*, p. 291.

13. *Ibid.*, pp. 291–292.

14. See E. E. Schattschneider's discussion of expanding the scope of the conflict, *The Semisovereign People* (New York, 1960). Another way in which bargaining resources may be "created" is to increase the relative cohesion of groups, or to increase the perception of group solidarity as a precondition to greater cohesion. This appears to be the primary goal of political activity which is generally designated "community organization." Negro activists appear to recognize the utility of this strategy in their advocacy of "black power." In some instances protest activity may be designed in part to accomplish this goal in addition to activating reference publics.

15. For an example of "direct confrontation," one might study the three-month Negro boycott of white merchants in Natchez, Miss., which resulted in capitulation to boycott demands by city government leaders. See *The New York Times*, December 4, 1965, p. 1.

16. *A Preface to Democratic Theory* (Chicago, 1956), pp. 145–46.

17. *Ibid.*

18. *The Governmental Process* (New York, 1951), p. 104.

19. See Dahl, *A Preface to Democratic Theory*, p. 146.

20. Observations that all groups can influence public policy at some stage of the political process are frequently made about the role of "veto groups" in American politics. See *Ibid.*, pp. 104 ff. See also David Reisman, *The Lonely Crowd* (New Haven, 1950), pp. 211 ff., for an earlier discussion of veto-group politics. Yet protest should be evaluated when it is adopted to obtain assertive as well as defensive goals.

21. See Murray Edelman, *The Symbolic Uses of Politics* (Urbana, Ill., 1964), ch. 2.

22. See Dahl, *Who Governs?* (New Haven, 1961). pp. 305 ff.

23. In a recent formulation, Dahl reiterates the theme of wide dispersion of influence. "More than other systems, [democracies] . . . try to disperse influence widely to their citizens by means of the suffrage, elections, freedom of speech, press, and assembly, the right of opponents to criticize the conduct of government, the right to organize political parties, and in other ways." *Pluralist Democracy in the United States* (Chicago, 1967), p. 373. Here, however, he concentrates more on the availability of options to all groups in the system, rather than on the relative probabilities that all groups in fact have access to the political process. See pp. 372 ff.

24. See Edward Banfield, *Political Influence* (New York, 1961), p. 263. The analysis of organizational incentive structure which heavily influences

Banfield's formulation is Chester Barnard, *The Functions of the Executive* (Cambridge, Mass., 1938).

25. In the following attempt to develop the implications of this conceptualization of protest activity, I have drawn upon extensive field observations and bibliographical research. Undoubtedly, however, individual assertions, while representing my best judgment concerning the available evidence, in the future may require modification as the result of further empirical research.

26. As Edelman suggests, cited previously.

27. *Negro Politics*, p. 290.

28. *The Governmental Process*, p. 513.

29. But cf. Thomas Schelling's discussion of "binding oneself," *The Strategy of Conflict* (Cambridge, Mass., 1960), pp. 22 ff.

30. "The Strategy of Protests," p. 297.

31. This is suggested by Wilson, "The Strategy of Protest," p. 298; St. Clair Drake and Horace Cayton, *Black Metropolis* (New York, 1962, rev. ed.), p. 731; Walker, "Protest and Negotiation," p. 122. Authors who argue that divided leadership is dysfunctional have been Clark, p. 156; and Tilman Cothran, "The Negro Protest Against Segregation in the South," *The Annals*, 357 (January, 1965), p. 72.

32. This observation is confirmed by a student of the Southern civil rights movement:

    Negroes demand of protest leaders constant progress. The combination of long-standing discontent and a new-found belief in the possibility of change produces a constant state of tension and aggressiveness in the Negro community. But this discontent is vague and diffuse, not specific; the masses do not define the issues around which action shall revolve. This the leader must do.

    Lewis Killian, "Leadership in the Desegregation Crises: An Institutional Analysis," in Muzafer Sherif (ed.), *Intergroup Relations and Leadership* (New York; 1962), p. 159.

33. Significantly, southern Negro students who actively participated in the early phases of the sit-in movement "tended to be unusually optimistic about race relations and tolerant of whites [when compared with inactive Negro students]. They not only *were* better off, objectively speaking, than other Negroes but *felt* better off." Matthews and Prothro, *op. cit.*, p. 424.

34. This is particularly the case in cities such as Washington, D. C., where landlord-tenant laws offer little protection against retaliatory eviction. See, e.g., Robert Schoshinski, "Remedies of the Indigent Tenant: Proposal for Change," *Georgetown Law Journal*, 54 (Winter, 1966), 541 ff.

35. Wilson regarded this as a chief reason for lack of protest activity in 1961. He wrote: ". . . some of the goals now being sought by Negroes are least applicable to those groups of Negroes most suited to protest action. Protest action involving such tactics as mass meetings, picketing, boycotts, and strikes rarely find enthusiastic participants among upper-income and higher status individuals": "The Strategy of Protest," p. 296.

36. See *The New York Times*, February 12, 1966, p. 56.

37. On housing clinic services provided by political clubs, see James Q. Wilson, *The Amateur Democrat: Club Politics in Three Cities* (Chicago, 1962), pp. 63–64, 176. On the need for lawyers among low income people, see e.g., *The Extension of Legal Services to the Poor*, Conference

Proceedings (Washington, D.C., n.d.), esp. pp. 51–60; and "Neighborhood Law Offices: The New Wave in Legal Services for the Poor," *Harvard Law Review*, 80 (February, 1967), 805–850.

38. An illustration of low income group protest organization mobilized for veto purposes is provided by Dahl in "The Case of the Metal Houses." See *Who Governs?*, pp. 192 ff.

39. Norton Long, "The Local Community as an Ecology of Games," in Long, *The Polity*, Charles Press, ed. (Chicago, 1962), p. 153. See pp. 152–154. See also Roscoe C. Martin, Frank J. Munger, *et al.*, *Decisions in Syracuse: A Metropolitan Action Study* (Garden City, N.Y., 1965) (originally published: 1961), pp. 326–327.

40. See, e.g., Thompson, *op. cit.*, p. 134, and *passim*; Martin Oppenheimer, "The Southern Student Movement: Year I," *Journal of Negro Education*, 33 (Fall, 1964), p. 397; Cothran, *op. cit.*, p. 72; Pauli Murray, "Protest Against the Legal Status of the Negro," *The Annals*, 357 (January, 1965), p. 63; Allan P. Sindler, "Protest Against the Political Status of the Negroes," *The Annals*, 357 (January, 1965), p. 50.

41. See Banfield, *op. cit.*, p. 275.

42. For a case study of the interaction between protest leaders and newspaper reporters, see Michael Lipsky, "Rent Strikes in New York City: Protest Politics and the Power of the Poor" (unpublished Ph.D. dissertation, Princeton University, 1967), pp. 139–49. Bernard Cohen has analyzed the impact of the press on foreign policy from the perspective of reporters' role requirements: see his *The Press and Foreign Policy* (Princeton, N.J., 1963), esp. chs. 2–3.

43. An example of a protest conducted by middle-class women engaged in pragmatic protest over salvaging park space is provided in John B. Keeley, *Moses on the Green*, Inter-University Case Program, No. 45 (University, Ala., 1959).

44. This was the complaint of Floyd McKissick, National Director of the Congress of Racial Equality, when he charged that ". . . there are only two kinds of statements a black man can make and expect that the white press will report. . . . First . . . is an attack on another black man. . . . The second is a statement that sounds radical, violent, extreme—the verbal equivalent of a riot. . . . [T]he Negro is being rewarded by the public media only if he turns on another Negro and uses his tongue as a switchblade, or only if he sounds outlandish, extremist or psychotic." Statement at the Convention of the American Society of Newspaper Editors, April 20, 1967, Washington, D.C., as reported in *The New York Times*, April 21, 1967, p. 22. See also the remarks of journalist Ted Poston, *ibid.*, April 26, 1965, p. 26.

45. Matthews and Prothro found, for example, that in their south-wide Negro population sample, 38 percent read Negro-oriented magazines and 17 percent read newspapers written for Negroes. These media treat news of interest to Negroes more completely and sympathetically than do the general media. See pp. 248 ff.

46. See footnote 31 above.

47. Wilson, *Negro Politics*, p. 225.

48. See Wallace Sayre and Herbert Kaufman, *Governing New York City* (New York, 1960), pp. 257 ff. Also see Banfield, *op. cit.*, p. 267.

49. See Wilson, *The Amateur Democrats*, previously cited. These groups are

most likely to be characterized by broad scope of political interest and frequent intervention in politics. See Sayre and Kaufman, *op. cit.*, p. 79.

50. Another approach, persuasively presented by Wilson, concentrates on protest success as a function of the relative unity and vulnerability of targets. See "The Strategy of Protest," pp. 293 ff. This insight helps explain, for example, why protest against housing segregation commonly takes the form of action directed against government (a unified target) rather than against individual homeowners (who present a dispersed target). One problem with this approach is that it tends to obscure the possibility that targets, as collections of individuals, may be divided in evaluation of and sympathy for protest demands. Indeed, city agency administrators under some circumstances act as partisans in protest conflicts. As such, they frequently appear ambivalent toward protest goals: sympathetic to the ends while concerned that the means employed in protest reflect negatively on their agencies.

51. Sayre and Kaufman, *op. cit.*, p. 253.

52. See *ibid.*, pp. 253 ff.

53. See Lipsky, *op. cit.*, chs. 5–6. The appearance of responsiveness may be given by city officials *in anticipation* of protest activity. This seems to have been the strategy of Mayor Richard Daley in his reaction to the announcement of Martin Luther King's plans to focus civil rights efforts on Chicago. See *The New York Times*, February 1, 1966, p. 11.

54. See Edelman, *op. cit.*, p. 23.

55. See Lipsky, *op. cit.*, pp. 156, 249 ff.

56. On the strategy of appearing constrained, see Schelling, *op. cit.*, pp. 22 ff.

57. Clark, *op. cit.*, pp. 154 ff.